WINE READS

A LITERARY ANTHOLOGY OF WINE WRITING

WINE READS

EDITED BY

JAY McINERNEY

Grove Press
New York

Published simultaneously in Canada
Printed in Canada

First Grove Atlantic hardcover edition: November 2018
First Grove Atlantic paperback edition: November 2019

This book was set in 12 point Goudy Old Style by
Alpha Design & Composition of Pittsfield, NH

Library of Congress Cataloging-in-Publication data is available for this title.

ISBN 978-0-8021-4779-0
eISBN 978-0-8021-4671-7

Grove Press
an imprint of Grove Atlantic
154 West 14th Street
New York, NY 10011

Distributed by Publishers Group West

groveatlantic.com

19 20 21 22   10 9 8 7 6 5 4 3 2 1

CONTENTS

INTRODUCTION

Jay McInerney

The late Giuseppe Quintarelli once told me that Amarone was "a wine of contemplation." I was visiting him at his home and winery outside of Verona, and I'd asked him what kind of foods might be paired with this complex, autumnal wine made from late harvested grapes that spend several months drying out, essentially becoming raisins before they are pressed and fermented. His answer suggested that Amarone should be enjoyed without food, with nothing to interfere with its appreciation. And while at the time I found his description apt, it subsequently occurred to me that it fits all wines of quality. Not that fine wine should be enjoyed without food—but that it inevitably inspires contemplation. And, since before the time of Homer, it has inspired commentary ranging in tone from the ecstatic to the analytic. The ancients overwhelmingly favored the former, creating a cult of wine worship centered on Dionysus, whom the Romans adopted as Bacchus. The Greek symposium was inevitably lubricated with wine, and Socrates was clearly a fierce devotee of Bacchus, if not a lush. Writing two millennia later, philosopher Roger Scruton makes the case that wine is conducive to a life of reflection and intellectual adventure in his memoir *I Drink Therefore I Am*. Socrates's crabby disciple Plato was a neo-prohibitionist, but the Greek and Roman poets and playwrights penned innumerable paeans to the stimulating and salutary properties of wine, as did their literary successors from Shakespeare and Keats to Baudelaire and Verlaine. These writers inevitably dwelt more on the effects of wine than on description. Modern commentary has tended more and more toward the analytical, toward an attempt to anatomize and quantify the properties of wine, as opposed to celebrating its effects—although Bill Buford, in his short essay included here about La Pauleé de New York, reminds us of the intoxicating side of oenophilia.

The kind of detailed tasting notes that fill so many contemporary publications were unknown until very recently—you won't find lists of flavor descriptors or technical details in George Saintsbury's *Notes on a Cellar-Book* (1920), long regarded as the landmark work of wine commentary in English, though in fact it hasn't aged very well, despite some pithy observations that still ring true. More recently, no one has been more influential in shaping modern wine commentary—and some would say winemaking—than Robert Parker, whose rise to become the preeminent wine critic in the world is documented in Elin McCoy's essay on the seminal 1982 Bordeaux vintage, from her biography *The Emperor of Wine*. Wine critics like Parker perform a valuable service for the consumer, but the writing collected in this volume has been chosen for its narrative and literary qualities; in selecting these readings I undoubtedly favored entertainment and felicity of expression over instruction. Parker's English counterpart, Jancis Robinson, has penned thousands of detailed tasting notes, which I find terribly useful, but she has also written discursively about her adventures in wine, notably an elegant memoir, *Tasting Pleasure*, which includes a funny and self-deprecating chapter about blind tasting.

Tasting notes, with their laundry lists of flavor analogies, may be a necessary evil, but I wish all wine critics, before penning them, would heed the advice of Auberon Waugh in his essay "Perils of Being a Wine-Writer:"

> My own feeling is that wine writing should be camped up: the writer should never like a wine, he should be in love with it; never find a wine disappointing but identify it as a mortal enemy, an attempt to poison him; sulfuric acid should be discovered where there is the faintest hint of sharpness. Bizarre and

improbable side tastes should be proclaimed: mushrooms, rotting wood, black treacle, burned pencils, condensed milk, sewage, the smell of French railway stations or ladies underwear—anything to get away from the accepted list of fruit and flowers.

When I first started writing about wine I was pretty ignorant of the details of winemaking and insecure about my knowledge of the field in general; I favored metaphors and analogies over flavor descriptors and technical specifications. I decided that comparing a California Chardonnay to Pamela Anderson, or a Chablis to Kate Moss, was at least as effective, and certainly more entertaining, than talking about new oak, minerality, and PH levels. I also discovered that the wine world is full of colorful and improbable characters; as a novelist I felt fairly confident of my ability to write about them, and as a reader I'm fascinated by stories of the eccentrics, the fanatics and the criminals of the wine world. Benjamin Wallace's bestseller *The Billionaire's Vinegar* is bursting with all of the above, as is Maximillian Potter's *The Assassin in the Vineyard*, a true crime story about the poisoning of the world's greatest vineyard. Edward Steinberg gives us a compelling portrait of one of the world's great wine personalities, Angelo Gaja. Tilar J. Mazzeo, in *The Widow Clicquot*, tells the story of one of the great figures of French winemaking, the brilliant and indefatigable woman who created an enduring empire in Champagne in the wake of Napoleon's defeat.

The first wine writing I encountered was in novels. My ambition to be a novelist and my interest in wine were both partly inspired by Ernest Hemingway's *The Sun Also Rises*. Everyone in the book was drinking wine all the time, and they were all young and jaded and good looking. I wanted to write like Hemingway and drink like Jake Barnes, who at one point downs a bottle of Château Margaux all by himself. As an aspiring novelist I also fell under the influence of *Brideshead Revisited*, and the semi delirious wine commentary of its protagonists Charles Ryder and Sebastian Flyte who spend an idyllic summer trying to drain the wine cellar at Sebastian's ancestral castle and inventing ways to describe it. ("It's a little shy wine like a gazelle," "Like a leprechaun," "and this is a wise old wine," "A prophet in a cave.")

Included here are passages from several contemporary novels including Rex Pickett's poignant and hilarious *Sideways*, which was famously translated to the screen by Alexander Payne, but stands alone as a contemporary picaresque; along with Stephanie Danler's coming-of-age novel *Sweetbitter*, with its sensuously vivid behind-the-scenes portrait of the New York restaurant world. Michael Dibdin was an English novelist who took up residence in Italy and wrote a series of literate mysteries, starring a wine-loving detective named Aurelio Zen, including *A Long Finish*, set in Piedmont, the home of truffles and Barolo. Also included, in its terse entirety, is one of the most memorable, and diabolical works of wine-inspired fiction—Roald Dahl's short story "Taste."

Food and wine are twin pleasures but too often they are divorced on the page. For years it amazed me that successive *New York Times* restaurant critics barely mentioned the wine list in their reviews (are you listening, Pete Wells?) and wine writing too often situates wine in a vacuum, as an independent pleasure rather than as a component of a meal. Happily that was not true of Eric Asimov, who handled the under $25 restaurant column for many years and now serves as the *Times* wine critic, writing about his apprenticeship to Bacchus in his memoir *How to Love Wine*. Some of my favorite wine commentary comes from gourmands like Richard Olney, M.F.K. Fisher, Joseph Wechsberg, and A.J. Liebling, the latter three of which are represented here. Wechsberg's great collection *Blue Trout and Black Truffles*, first recommended to me by none other than Robert Parker, is an episodic memoir that traces the education of the author's palate and his quest for Europe's finest food and wine. Liebling's *Between Meals* is one of the best books about Paris ever written, belonging on the shelf alongside Hemingway's *A Moveable Feast*. Despite the title, much of the book is composed of a description of meals and his discovery of French food and wine during a student year spent in Paris, allegedly studying at the Sorbonne. He spent far more time in restaurants than in classrooms, and few eaters have written as lovingly about long-digested meals, or the wines that washed them down. Liebling was a self-professed glutton, and there's undeniably a vicarious thrill in being privy to his excesses, like reading about Hunter Thompson's drug intake. I've always imagined that Liebling would have found a kindred spirit in novelist Jim Harrison, another legendary eater and drinker who heroically pursued his culinary and oenophilic passion in spite of suffering from gout. I regret that I never broke bread or killed a bottle with Liebling, but I shared several meals, and several bottles of wine with Harrison in Paris, where we would sometimes intersect on book tours; he was passionate about both, but militantly unpretentious, and scornful of those who got too precious about their pleasures; wine geeks won't fail to notice that he sometimes fails to note the domain and/or the vintage of some of his favorite wines.

It's not often that someone is a good writer and a good wine importer, to paraphrase *Charlotte's Web*, but two of my favorite wine books have been written by men who have made it their mission to scour Europe for artisanal wines to sell to the American drinking public. Thirty years after its publication, it's safe to say that Kermit Lynch's *Adventures on the Wine Route* is a classic. Its enduring appeal is in part a testament to the vivacity of the writing—it's a great travel book, a chronicle of Lynch's peregrinations through rural France, packed with vivid anecdotes and tart observations. On the one hand it conveys a sense of delighted discovery as Lynch educates his own palate and discovers buried vinous treasure in the chilly cellars of Burgundy and the Rhône and the Loire. But there is also an undertone that might be described as fiercely elegiac, as Lynch documents and laments disappearing traditions of la vieille France and deplores the onslaughts of modernity. Terry Theise's beat is Germany and Austria, his muse the somewhat underloved Riesling grape, which he is tireless and rapturous in promoting. Theise writes better prose than most poets, and he is brilliant at evoking the way in which wine inspires the imagination. Although there is a plenty of ancillary instruction in his book *Reading Between the Vines*, he is scornful of the idea of over-simplifying wine appreciation. His essay "Remystifying Wine" makes a powerful case against quantifying and dumbing down what is essentially an aesthetic experience.

I like to think of this as the kind of volume to be savored while drinking a glass of Amarone, or almost any other wine that suits the reader—a book that will pair well with anything from a young Muscadet to an old Burgundy. Ideally it will inspire new thirsts.

TASTE

Roald Dahl

There were six of us to dinner that night at Mike Schofield's house in London: Mike and his wife and daughter, my wife and I, and a man called Richard Pratt.

Richard Pratt was a famous gourmet. He was president of a small society known as the Epicures, and each month he circulated privately to its members a pamphlet on food and wines. He organized dinners where sumptuous dishes and rare wines were served. He refused to smoke for fear of harming his palate, and when discussing a wine, he had a curious, rather droll habit of referring to it as though it were a living being. "A prudent wine," he would say, "rather diffident and evasive, but quite prudent." Or, "a good-humoured wine, benevolent and cheerful—slightly obscene, perhaps, but nonetheless good-humoured."

I had been to dinner at Mike's twice before when Richard Pratt was there, and on each occasion Mike and his wife had gone out of their way to produce a special meal for the famous gourmet. And this one, clearly, was to be no exception. The moment we entered the dining room, I could see that the table was laid for a feast. The tall candles, the yellow roses, the quantity of shining silver, the three wineglasses to each person, and above all, the faint scent of roasting meat from the kitchen brought the first warm oozings of saliva to my mouth.

As we sat down, I remembered that on both Richard Pratt's previous visits Mike had played a little betting game with him over the claret, challenging him to name its breed and its vintage. Pratt had replied that that should not be too difficult provided it was one of the great years. Mike had then bet him a case of the wine in question that he could not do it. Pratt had accepted, and had won both times. Tonight I felt sure that the little game would be played over again, for Mike was quite willing to lose the bet in order to prove that his wine was good enough to be recognized, and Pratt, for his part, seemed to take a grave, restrained pleasure in displaying his knowledge.

The meal began with a plate of whitebait, fried very crisp in butter, and to go with it there was a Moselle. Mike got up and poured the wine himself, and when he sat down again, I could see that he was watching Richard Pratt. He had set the bottle in front of me so that I could read the label. It said, "Geierslay Ohligsberg, 1945." He leaned over and whispered to me that Geierslay was a tiny village in the Moselle, almost unknown outside Germany. He said that this wine we were drinking was something unusual, that the output of the vineyard was so small that it was almost impossible for a stranger to get any of it. He had visited Geierslay personally the previous summer in order to obtain the few dozen bottles that they had finally allowed him to have.

"I doubt anyone else in the country has any of it at the moment," he said. I saw him glance again at Richard Pratt. "Great thing about Moselle," he continued, raising his voice, "it's the perfect wine to serve before a claret. A lot of people serve a Rhine wine instead, but that's because they don't know any better. A Rhine wine will kill a delicate claret, you know that? It's barbaric to serve a Rhine before a claret. But a Moselle—ah!—a Moselle is exactly right."

Mike Schofield was an amiable, middle-aged man. But he was a stock-broker. To be precise, he was a jobber in the stock market, and like a number of his kind, he seemed to be somewhat embarrassed, almost ashamed to find that he had made so much money with so slight a talent. In his heart he knew that he was not really much more than a bookmaker—an unctuous, infinitely respectable, secretly unscrupulous bookmaker—and he knew that his friends knew it, too. So he was seeking now to become a man of culture, to cultivate a literary and aesthetic taste, to collect paintings, music, books, and all the rest of it. His little sermon about Rhine wine and Moselle was a part of this thing, this culture that he sought.

"A charming little wine, don't you think?" he said. He was still watching Richard Pratt. I could see him give a rapid furtive glance down the table each time he dropped his head to take a mouthful of whitebait. I could almost *feel* him waiting for the moment when Pratt would take his first sip, and look up from his glass with a smile of pleasure, of astonishment, perhaps even of wonder, and then there would be a discussion and Mike would tell him about the village of Geierslay.

But Richard Pratt did not taste his wine. He was completely engrossed in conversation with Mike's eighteen-year-old daughter, Louise. He was half turned toward her, smiling at her, telling her, so far as I could gather, some story about a chef in a Paris restaurant. As he spoke, he leaned closer and closer to her, seeming in his eagerness almost to impinge upon her, and the poor girl leaned as far as she could away from him, nodding politely, rather desperately, and looking not at his face but at the topmost button of his dinner jacket.

We finished our fish, and the maid came around removing the plates. When she came to Pratt, she saw that he had not yet touched his food, so she hesitated, and Pratt noticed her. Her waved her away, broke off his conversation, and quickly began to eat, popping the little crisp brown fish quickly into his mouth with rapid jabbing movements of his fork. Then, when he had finished, he reached for his glass, and in two short swallows he tipped the wine down his throat and turned immediately to resume his conversation with Louise Schofield.

Mike saw it all. I was conscious of him sitting there, very still, containing himself, looking at his guest. His round jovial face seemed to loosen slightly and to sag, but he contained himself and was still and said nothing.

Soon the maid came forward with the second course. This was a large roast of beef. She placed it on the table in front of Mike who stood up and carved it, cutting the slices very thin, laying them gently on the plates for the maid to take around. When he had served everyone, including himself, he put down the carving knife and leaned forward with both hands on the edge of the table.

"Now," he said, speaking to all of us but looking at Richard Pratt. "Now for the claret. I must go and fetch the claret, if you'll excuse me."

"You go and fetch it, Mike?" I said. "Where is it?"

"In my study, with the cork out—breathing."

"Why the study?"

"Acquiring room temperature, of course. It's been there twenty-four hours."

"But why the study?"

"It's the best place in the house. Richard helped me choose it last time he was here."

At the sound of his name, Pratt looked around.

"That's right, isn't it?" Mike said.

"Yes," Pratt answered, nodding gravely. "That's right."

"On top of the green filing cabinet in my study," Mike said. "That's the place we chose. A good draft-free spot in a room with an even temperature. Excuse me now, will you, while I fetch it."

The thought of another wine to play with had restored his humor, and he hurried out the door, to return a minute later more slowly, walking softly, holding in both hands a wine basket in which a dark bottle lay. The label was out of sight, facing downward. "Now!" he cried as he came toward the table. "What about this one, Richard? You'll never name this one!"

Richard Pratt turned slowly and looked up at Mike; then his eyes travelled down to the bottle nestling in its small wicker basket, and he raised his eyebrows, a slight, supercilious arching of the brows, and with it a pushing outward of the wet lower lip, suddenly imperious and ugly.

"You'll never get it," Mike said. "Not in a hundred years."

"A claret?" Richard Pratt asked, condescending.

"Of course."

"I assume, then, that it's from one of the smaller vineyards?"

"Maybe it is, Richard. And then again, maybe it isn't."

"But it's a good year? One of the great years?"

"Yes, I guarantee that."

"Then it shouldn't be too difficult," Richard Pratt said, drawling his words, looking exceedingly bored. Except that, to me, there was something strange about his drawling and his boredom: between the eyes a shadow of something evil, and in his bearing an intentness that gave me a faint sense of uneasiness as I watched him.

"This one is really rather difficult," Mike said, "I won't force you to bet on this one."

"Indeed. And why not?" Again the slow arching of the brows, the cool, intent look.

"Because it's difficult."

"That's not very complimentary to me, you know."

"My dear man," Mike said, "I'll bet you with pleasure, if that's what you wish."

"It shouldn't be too hard to name it."

"You mean you want to bet?"

"I'm perfectly willing to bet," Richard Pratt said.

"All right, then, we'll have the usual. A case of the wine itself."

"You don't think I'll be able to name it, do you?"

"As a matter of fact, and with all due respect, I don't," Mike said. He was making some effort to remain polite, but Pratt was not bothering overmuch to conceal his contempt for the whole proceeding. And yet, curiously, his next question seemed to betray a certain interest.

"You like to increase the bet?"

"No, Richard. A case is plenty."

"Would you like to bet fifty cases?"

"That would be silly."

Mike stood very still behind his chair at the head of the table, carefully holding the bottle in its ridiculous wicker basket. There was a trace of whiteness around his nostrils now, and his mouth was shut very tight.

Pratt was lolling back in his chair, looking up at him, the eyebrows raised, the eyes half closed, a little smile touching the corners of his lips. And again I saw, or thought I saw, something distinctly disturbing about the man's face, that shadow of intentness between the eyes, and in the eyes themselves, right in their centers where it was black, a small slow spark of shrewdness, hiding.

"So you don't want to increase the bet?"

"As far as I'm concerned, old man, I don't give a damn," Mike said. "I'll bet you anything you like."

The three women and I sat quietly, watching the two men. Mike's wife was becoming annoyed; her mouth had gone sour and I felt that at any moment she was going to interrupt. Our roast beef lay before us on our plates, slowly steaming.

"So you'll bet me anything I like?"

"That's what I told you. I'll bet you anything you damn well please, if you want to make an issue out of it."

"Even ten thousand pounds?"

"Certainly I will, if that's the way you want it." Mike was more confident now. He knew quite well that he could call any sum Pratt cared to mention.

"So you say I can name the bet?" Pratt asked again.

"That's what I said."

There was a pause while Pratt looked slowly around the table, first at me, then at the three women, each in turn. He appeared to be reminding us that we were witness to the offer.

"Mike!" Mrs. Schofield said. "Mike, why don't we stop this nonsense and eat our food. It's getting cold."

"But it isn't nonsense," Pratt told her evenly. "We're making a little bet."

I noticed the maid standing in the background holding a dish of vegetables, wondering whether to come forward with them or not.

"All right, then," Pratt said. "I'll tell you what I want you to bet."

"Come on, then," Mike said, rather reckless. "I don't give a damn what it is—you're on."

Pratt nodded, and again the little smile moved the corners of his lips, and then, quite slowly, looking at Mike all the time, he said, "I want you to bet me the hand of your daughter in marriage."

Louise Schofield gave a jump. "Hey!" she cried. "No! That's not funny! Look here, Daddy, that's not funny at all."

"No, dear," her mother said. "They're only joking."

"I'm not joking," Richard Pratt said.

"It's ridiculous," Mike said. He was off balance again now.

"You said you'd bet anything I liked."

"I meant money."

"You didn't *say* money."

"That's what I meant."

"Then it's a pity you didn't say it. But anyway, if you wish to go back on your offer, that's quite all right with me."

"It's not a question of going back on my offer, old man. It's a no-bet anyway, because you can't match the stake. You yourself don't happen to have a daughter to put up against mine in case you lose. And if you had, I wouldn't want to marry her."

"I'm glad of that, dear," his wife said.

"I'll put up anything you like," Pratt announced. "My house, for example. How about my house?"

"Which one?" Mike asked, joking now.

"The country one."

"Why not the other one as well?"

"All right then, if you wish it. Both my houses."

At that point I saw Mike pause. He took a step forward and placed the bottle in its basket gently down on the table. He moved the saltcellar to one side, then the pepper, and then he picked up his knife, studied the blade thoughtfully for a moment, and put it down again. His daughter, too, had seen him pause.

"Now, Daddy!" she cried. "Don't be *absurd!* It's *too* silly for words. I refuse to be betted on like this."

"Quite right, dear," her mother said. "Stop it at once, Mike, and sit down and eat your food."

Mike ignored her. He looked over at his daughter and he smiled, a slow, fatherly, protective smile. But in his eyes, suddenly, there glimmered a little triumph. "You know," he said, smiling as he spoke. "You know, Louise, we ought to think about this a bit."

"Now, stop it, Daddy! I refuse even to listen to you! Why, I've never heard anything so ridiculous in my life!"

"No, seriously, my dear. Just wait a moment and hear what I have to say."

"But I don't *want* to hear it."

"Louise! Please! It's like this. Richard here, has offered us a serious bet. He is the one who wants to make it, not me. And if he loses, he will have to hand over a considerable amount of property. Now, wait a minute, my dear, don't interrupt. The point is this. *He cannot possibly win.*"

"He seems to think he can."

"Now listen to me, because I know what I'm talking about. The expert, when tasting a claret—so long as it is not one of the famous great wines like Lafite or Latour—can only get a certain way toward naming the vineyard. He can, of course, tell you the Bordeaux district from which the wine comes, whether it is from St. Emilion, Pomerol, Graves, or Médoc. But then each district has several communes, little counties, and each county has many, many small vineyards. It is impossible for a man to differentiate between them all by taste and smell alone. I don't mind telling you that this one I've got here is a wine from a small vineyard that is surrounded by many other small vineyards, and he'll never get it. It's impossible."

"You can't be sure of that," his daughter said.

"I'm telling you I can. Though I say it myself, I understand quite a bit about this wine business, you know. And anyway, heavens alive, girl, I'm your father and you don't think I'd let you in for—for something you didn't want, do you? I'm trying to make you some money."

"Mike!" his wife said sharply. "'Stop it now, Mike, please!"

Again he ignored her. "'If you will take this bet," he said to his daughter, "in ten minutes you will be the owner of two large houses."

"'But I don't want two large houses, Daddy."

"Then sell them. Sell them back to him on the spot. I'll arrange all that for you. And then, just think of it, my dear, you'll be rich! You'll be independent for the rest of your life!"

"Oh, Daddy, I don't like it. I think it's silly."

"So do I," the mother said. She jerked her head briskly up and down as she spoke, like a hen. "You ought to be ashamed of yourself, Michael, ever suggesting such a thing! Your own daughter, too!"

Mike didn't even look at her. "Take it!" he said eagerly, staring hard at the girl. "Take it, quick! I'll guarantee you won't lose."

"But I don't like it, Daddy."

"Come on, girl. Take it!"

Mike was pushing her hard. He was leaning toward her, fixing her with two hard bright eyes, and it was not easy for the daughter to resist him.

"But what if I lose?"

"I keep telling you, you can't lose. I'll guarantee it."

"Oh, Daddy, must I?"

"I'm making you a fortune. So come on now. What do you say, Louise? All right?"

For the last time, she hesitated. Then she gave a helpless little shrug of the shoulders and said, "Oh, all right, then. Just so long as you swear there's no danger of losing."

"Good!" Mike cried. "That's fine! Then it's a bet!"

"Yes," Richard Pratt said, looking at the girl. "It's a bet."

Immediately, Mike picked up the wine, tipped the first thimbleful into his own glass, then skipped excitedly around the table filling up the others. Now everyone was watching Richard Pratt, watching his face as he reached slowly for his glass with his right hand and lifted it to his nose. The man was about fifty years old and he did not have a pleasant face. Somehow, it was all mouth—mouth and lips—the full, wet lips of the professional gourmet, the lower lip hanging downward in the center, a pendulous, permanently open taster's lip, shaped open to receive the rim of a glass or a morsel of food. Like a keyhole, I thought, watching it; his mouth is like a large wet keyhole.

Slowly he lifted the glass to his nose. The point of the nose entered the glass and moved over the surface of the wine, delicately sniffing. He swirled the wine gently around in the glass to receive the bouquet. His concentration was intense. He had closed his eyes, and now the whole top half of his body, the head and neck and chest, seemed to become a kind of huge sensitive smelling-machine, receiving, filtering, analysing the message from the sniffing nose.

Mike, I noticed, was lounging in his chair, apparently unconcerned, but he was watching every move. Mrs. Schofield, the wife, sat prim and upright at the other end of the table, looking straight ahead, her face tight with disapproval. The daughter, Louise, had shifted her chair away a little, and sidewise, facing the gourmet, and she, like her father, was watching closely.

For at least a minute, the smelling process continued; then, without opening his eyes or moving his head, Pratt lowered the glass to his mouth and tipped in almost half the contents. He paused, his mouth full of wine, getting the first taste; then he permitted some of it to trickle down his throat and I saw his Adam's apple move as it passed by. But most of it he retained in his mouth. And now, without swallowing again, he drew in through his lips a thin breath of air which mingled with the fumes of the wine in the mouth and passed on down into his lungs. He held the breath, blew it out through his nose, and finally began to roll the wine around under the tongue, and chewed it, actually chewed it with his teeth as though it were bread.

It was a solemn, impressive performance, and I must say he did it well.

"Um," he said, putting down the glass, running a pink tongue over his lips. "Um—yes. A very interesting little wine—gentle and gracious, almost feminine in the aftertaste."

There was an excess of saliva in his mouth, and as he spoke he spat an occasional bright speck of it onto the table.

"Now we can start to eliminate," he said. "You will pardon me for doing this carefully, but there is much at stake. Normally I would perhaps take a bit of a chance, leaping forward quickly and landing right in the middle of the vineyard of my choice. But this time—I must move cautiously this time, must I not?" He looked up at Mike and he smiled, a thick-lipped, wet-lipped smile. Mike did not smile back.

"First, then, which district in Bordeaux does this wine come from? That is not too difficult to guess. It is far too light in the body to be from either St. Emilion or Graves. It is obviously a Médoc. There's no doubt about *that*.

"Now—from which commune in Médoc does it come? That also, by elimination, should not be too difficult to decide. Margaux? No. It cannot be Margaux. It has not the violent bouquet of a Margaux. Pauillac? It cannot be Pauillac, either. It is too tender, too gentle and wistful for a Pauillac. The wine of Pauillac has a character that is almost imperious in its taste. And also, to me, a Pauillac contains just a little pith, a curious, dusty, pithy flavor that the grape acquires from the soil of the district. No, no. This—this is a very gentle wine, demure and bashful in the first taste, emerging shyly but quite graciously in the second. A little arch, perhaps, in the second taste, and a little naughty also, teasing the tongue with a trace, just a trace, of tannin. Then, in the aftertaste, delightful—consoling and feminine, with a certain blithely generous quality that one associates only with the wines of the commune of St. Julien. Unmistakably this is a St. Julien."

He leaned back in his chair, held his hands up level with his chest, and placed the fingertips carefully together. He was becoming ridiculously pompous, but I thought that some of it was deliberate, simply to mock his host. I found myself waiting rather tensely for him to go on. The girl Louise was lighting a cigarette. Pratt heard the match strike and he turned on her, flaring suddenly with real anger. "Please!" he said. "Please don't do that! It's a disgusting habit, to smoke at table!"

She looked up at him, still holding the burning match in one hand, the big slow eyes settling on his face, resting there a moment, moving away again, slow and contemptuous. She bent her head and blew out the match, but continued to hold the unlighted cigarette in her fingers.

"I'm sorry, my dear," Pratt said, "but I simply cannot have smoking at table."

She didn't look at him again.

"Now, let me see—where were we?" he said. "Ah, yes. This wine is from Bordeaux, from the commune of St. Julien, in the district of Médoc. So far, so good. But now we come to the more difficult part—the name of the vineyard itself. For in St. Julien there are many vineyards, and as our host so rightly remarked earlier on, there is often not much difference between the wine of one and the wine of another. But we shall see."

He paused again, closing his eyes. "I am trying to establish the 'growth,'" he said. "If I can do that, it will be half the battle. Now, let me see. This wine is obviously not from a first-growth vineyard—nor even a second. It is not a great wine. The quality, the—the—what do you call it?—the radiance, the power, is lacking. But a third growth—that it could be. And yet I doubt it. We know it is a good year—our host has said so—and this is probably flattering it a little bit. I must be careful. I must be very careful here."

He picked up his glass and took another small sip.

"Yes," he said, sucking his lips, "I was right. It is a fourth growth. Now I am sure of it. A fourth growth from a very good year—from a great year, in fact. And that's what made it taste for a moment like a third—or even a second-growth wine. Good! That's better! Now we are closing in! What are the fourth-growth vineyards in the commune of St. Julien?"

Again he paused, took up his glass, and held the rim against that sagging, pendulous lower lip of his. Then I saw the tongue shoot out, pink and narrow, the tip of it dipping into the wine, withdrawing swiftly again—a repulsive sight. When he lowered the glass, his eyes remained closed, the face concentrated, only the lips moving, sliding over each other like two pieces of wet, spongy rubber.

"There it is again!" he cried. "Tannin in the middle taste, and the quick astringent squeeze upon the tongue. Yes, yes, of course! Now I have it! This wine comes from one of those small vineyards around Beychevelle. I remember now. The Beychevelle district, and the river and the little harbor that has silted up so the wine ships can no longer use it. Beychevelle . . . could it actually be a Beychevelle itself? No, I don't think so. Not quite. But it is somewhere very close. Château Talbot? Could it be Talbot? Yes, it could. Wait one moment."

He sipped the wine again, and out of the side of my eye I noticed Mike Schofield and how he was leaning farther and farther forward over the table, his mouth slightly open, his small eyes fixed upon Richard Pratt.

"No. I was wrong. It was not a Talbot. A Talbot comes forward to you just a little quicker than this one; the fruit is nearer to the surface. If it is a '34, which I believe it is, then it couldn't be Talbot. Well, well. Let me think. It is not a Beychevelle and it is not a Talbot, and yet—yet it is so close to both of them, so close, that the vineyard must be almost in between. Now, which could that be?"

He hesitated, and we waited, watching his face. Everyone, even Mike's wife, was watching him now. I heard the maid put down the dish of vegetables on the sideboard behind me, gently, so as not to disturb the silence.

"Ah!" he cried. "I have it! Yes, I think I have it!"

For the last time, he sipped the wine. Then, still holding the glass up near his mouth, he turned to Mike and he smiled, a slow, silky smile, and he said, "'You know what this is? This is the little Château Branaire-Ducru."

Mike sat tight, not moving.

"And the year, 1934."

We all looked at Mike, waiting for him to turn the bottle around in its basket and show the label.

"Is that your final answer?" Mike said.

"Yes, I think so."

"Well, is it or isn't it?"

"Yes, it is."

"What was the name again?"

"Château Branaire-Ducru. Pretty little vineyard. Lovely old château. Know it quite well. Can't think why I didn't recognize it at once."

"Come on, Daddy," the girl said. "Turn it round and let's have a peek. I want my two houses."

"Just a minute," Mike said. "Wait just a minute." He was sitting very quiet, bewildered-looking, and his face was becoming puffy and pale, as though all the force was draining slowly out of him.

"Michael!" his wife called sharply from the other end of the table. "What's the matter?"

"Keep out of this, Margaret, will you please."

Richard Pratt was looking at Mike, smiling with his mouth, his eyes small and bright. Mike was not looking at anyone.

"Daddy!" the daughter cried, agonized. "But, Daddy, you don't mean to say he's guessed it right!"

"Now, stop worrying, my dear," Mike said. "There's nothing to worry about."

I think it was more to get away from his family than anything else that Mike then turned to Richard Pratt and said, "I'll tell you what, Richard. I think you and I better slip off into the next room and have a little chat?"

"I don't want a little chat," Pratt said. "All I want is to see the label on that bottle." He knew he was a winner now; he had the bearing, the quiet arrogance of a winner, and I could see that he was prepared to become thoroughly nasty if there was any trouble. "What are you waiting for?" he said to Mike. "Go on and turn it round."

Then this happened: The maid, the tiny, erect figure of the maid in her white-and-black uniform, was standing beside Richard Pratt, holding something out in her hand. "I believe these are yours, sir," she said.

Pratt glanced around, saw the pair of thin horn-rimmed spectacles that she held out to him, and for a moment he hesitated. "Are they? Perhaps they are. I don't know."

"Yes sir, they're yours." The maid was an elderly woman—nearer seventy than sixty—a faithful family retainer of many years' standing. She put the spectacles down on the table beside him.

Without thanking her, Pratt took them up and slipped them into his top pocket, behind the white handkerchief.

But the maid didn't go away. She remained standing beside and slightly behind Richard Pratt, and there was something so unusual in her manner and in the way she stood there, small, motionless, and erect, that I for one found myself watching her with a sudden apprehension. Her old gray face had a frosty, determined look, the lips were compressed, the little chin was out, and the hands were clasped together tight before her. The curious cap on her head and the flash of white down the front of her uniform made her seem like some tiny, ruffled, white-breasted bird.

"You left them in Mr. Scofield's study," she said. Her voice was unnaturally, deliberately polite. "On top of the green filing cabinet in his study, sir, when you happened to go in there by yourself before dinner."

It took a few moments for the full meaning of her words to penetrate, and in the silence that followed I became aware of Mike and how he was slowly drawing himself up in his chair, and the color coming to his face, and the eyes opening wide, and the curl of the mouth, and the dangerous little patch of whiteness beginning to spread around the area of the nostrils.

"Now, Michael!" his wife said. "Keep calm now, Michael, dear! Keep calm!"

A STUNNING UPSET

George Taber

A bottle of good wine, like a good act, shines ever in the retrospect.
—Robert Louis Stevenson

May 24, 1976, was a beautiful, sunny day in Paris, and Patricia Gallagher was in good spirits as she packed up the French and California wines for the tasting at the InterContinental Hotel. Organizing the event had been good fun and easy compared with other events she and Steven had dreamed up. The good thing about working for Spurrier, she told friends, was that he was so supportive of her ideas. Many of their conversations began with her saying, "Wouldn't it be fun . . ." To which he always replied, "Great. Let's do it." The two weren't looking for fame or money. They were young people doing things strictly for the love of wine and to have fun.

Gallagher packed the wine and all the paperwork into the back of the Caves de la Madeleine's van and headed off with an American summer intern to the hotel. After the California wines had arrived on May 7 with members of the Tchelistcheff tour, they were stored in the shop's cellar at a constant 54 degrees alongside the French wines for the event and the rest of Spurrier's stock.

Gallagher and the intern arrived at the hotel about an hour and a half before the 3:00 p.m. tasting was due to start. The event was to be held in a well-appointed room just off a patio bar in the central courtyard. Long, plush velvet curtains decorated the corners of the room. Glass doors opened onto the patio, and a gathering crowd watched the event from the patio. People sitting at small tables under umbrellas became increasingly curious about what was transpiring in the room, and some of them walked over to gaze through the windows much like visitors looking at monkeys in a zoo. The waiters set up a series of plain tables covered with simple white tablecloths, aligning the tables in a long row.

Spurrier and Gallagher had previously decided that this would be a blind tasting, which meant that the judges would not see the labels on the bottles, a common practice in such events. They felt that not allowing the judges to know the nationality or brand of the wines would force them to be more objective. The two did not perceive the tasting as a Franco-American showdown, but it would have been too easy, they believed, for the judges to find fault with the California wines while praising only the French wines, if they were presented with labels.

The hotel staff first opened all the red wines and then poured them into neutral bottles at Gallagher's instructions. California wine bottles are shaped slightly differently from French ones, and this group of knowledgeable judges would have quickly recognized the difference. Gallagher was also giving the wines a chance to breathe a little by opening and decanting them, since the reds, in particular, were still relatively recent vintages. This practice helps young wines, which can sometimes be too aggressive, become more mellow and agreeable.

An hour before the event, the hotel staff opened all the white wines, poured them also into neutral bottles and put them in the hotel's wine cooler. Aeration was less important for the whites than it had been for the reds, but it would do no harm to have them opened in advance. Then a few minutes before the tasting, the waiters put the whites in buckets on ice, just as they would have done for guests in the dining room. The wine would now be at the perfect temperature for the judges.

Only a half-hour before the event was to begin, Spurrier arrived. He wrote the names of the wines on small pieces of paper and asked the summer intern to pull the names out of a hat to determine the order in which the wines would be served. Then Spurrier and the others put small white labels on the bottles that read in French, for example, Chardonnay Neuf (Chardonnay Nine) or Cabernet Trois (Cabernet Three). With that done, everything was ready.

The judges began appearing shortly before 3:00 p.m. and chatted amiably until all had arrived. Most of them knew each other from many previous encounters on the French wine circuit.

Standing along the wall and acting self-conscious were two young Frenchmen in their mid-twenties. One was Jean-Pierre Leroux, who was head of the dining room at the Paris Sofitel hotel, an elegant rival, although not at the same level as the InterContinental. The other was Gérard Bosseau des Chouad, the sommelier at the Sofitel, who had learned about the tasting while taking a course at the Académie du Vin. Bosseau des Chouad had told Leroux about it, and the two of them had come to the hotel uninvited on a lark. They were quiet in awe of the assembled big names of French wine and cuisine. Since no one asked them to leave, they watched the proceedings in nervous silence.

Shortly after 3:00, Spurrier asked everyone to give him their attention for a minute. Spurrier thanked the judges for coming and explained that he and Patricia Gallagher were staging the event to taste some of the interesting new California wines as part of the bicentennial of American independence and in honor of the role France had played in that historic endeavor. He explained that he and Patricia had recently made separate trips to California, where they had been surprised by the quality of the work being done by some small and unknown wineries. He said he thought the French too would find them interesting. Spurrier then said that although he had invited them to a sampling of California wines, in the tasting that was about to begin he had also included some very similar French wines. He added that he thought it would be better if they all tasted them blind, so as to be totally objective in their judgments. No one demurred, and so judges took their seats behind the long table, and the event began.

The judges wore standard Paris business attire. Odette Kahn of the *Revue du Vin de France* was very elegant in a patterned silk dress accented with a double strand of opera-length pearls. Claude Dubois-Millot was the most casual with no tie or jacket. The other men were all more formally dressed, and Aubert de Villaine, who sat at the far right end of the table, wore a fashionable double-breasted suit. Patricia Gallagher and Steven Spurrier sat in the middle of the judges and participated in the tasting. Spurrier was next to Kahn.

In front of each judge was a scorecard and pencil, two stemmed wine glasses, and a small roll. Behind them were several Champagne buckets on stands where they could spit the wine after tasting it, a common practice at such events since it would be impossible to drink all the wines without soon feeling the effect of the alcohol.

Spurrier instructed the judges that they were being asked to rank the wines by four criteria—eye, nose, mouth, and harmony—and then to give each a score on the basis of 20 points. Eye meant rating the color and clarity of the wine; nose was the aroma; mouth was the wine's taste and structure as it rolled over the taste buds; harmony meant the combination of all the sensations. This 20-point and four-criteria system was common in France at the time and had already been used by Spurrier and the others in many tastings.

Despite Spurrier's and Gallagher's attempts to get press coverage, it turned out that I was the only journalist who showed up at the event. As a result, I had easy access to the judges and the judging. Patricia gave me a list of the wines with the tasting order so I could follow along. And although the judges didn't know the identity of Chardonnay Neuf, for example, I did and could note their reactions to the various wines as they tasted them.

The waiters first poured a glass of 1974 Chablis to freshen the palates of the judges. Following the tradition of wine tastings, the whites then went first. I looked at my list of wines and saw that the first wine (Chardonnay Un) was the Puligny-Montrachet Les Pucelles Domaine Leflaive, 1972.

The nine judges seemed nervous at the beginning. There was lots of laughing and quick side comments. No one, though, was acting rashly. The judges pondered the wines carefully and made their judgments slowly. Pierre Tari at one moment pushed his nose deep into his glass and held it there for a long time to savor the wine's aroma.

The judge's comments were in the orchidaceous language the French often use to describe wines. As I stood only a few feet from the judges listening to their commentary, I copied into the brown reporter's notebook that I always carried with me such phrases as: "This soars out of the ordinary," and "A good nose, but not too much in the mouth," and "This is nervous and agreeable."

From their comments, though, I soon realized that the judges were becoming totally confused as they tasted the white wines. The panel couldn't tell the difference between the French ones and those from California. The judges then began talking to each other, which is very rare in a tasting. They speculated about a wine's nationality, often disagreeing.

Standing quietly on the side, the young Jean-Pierre Leroux was also surprised as he looked at the faces of the judges. They seemed both bewildered and shocked, as if they didn't quite know what was happening. Raymond Oliver of the Grand Véfour was one of Leroux's heroes, and the young man couldn't believe that the famous chef couldn't distinguish the nationality of the white wines.

Christian Vannequé, who sat at the far left with Pierre Bréjoux and Pierre Tari at his left, was irritated that those two kept talking to him, asking him what he thought of this or that wine. Vannequé felt like telling them to shut up so he could concentrate, but held his tongue. He thought the other judges seemed tense and were trying too hard to identify which wines were Californian and which were French. Vannequé complained he wanted simply to determine which wines were best.

When tasting the white wines, the judges quickly became flustered. At one point Raymond Oliver was certain he had just sipped a French wine, when in fact it was a California one from Freemark Abbey. Shortly after, Claude Dubois-Millot said he thought a wine was obviously from California because it had no nose, when it was France's famed Bâtard-Montrachet.

The judges were brutal when they found a wine wanting. They completely dismissed the David Bruce Chardonnay. Pierre Bréjoux gave it 0 points out of 20. Odette Kahn gave it just 1 point. The David Bruce was rated last by all the judges, and most of them dumped the remains from their glasses into their Champagne buckets after a cursory taste and in some cases after only smelling it. Robert Finigan had warned Spurrier and Gallagher that he'd found David Bruce wines at that time could be erratic, and this bottle appeared to be erratically bad. It was probably spoiled.

After the white wines had all been tasted, Spurrier called a break and collected the scorecards. Using the normal procedure for wine tastings, he added up the individual scores and then ranked them from highest to lowest.

Meanwhile the waiters began pouring Vittel mineral water for the judges to drink during the break. The judges spoke quietly to each other, and I talked briefly with Dubois-Millot. Even though he did not yet know the results, he told me a bit sheepishly, "We thought we were recognizing French wines, when they were California and vice versa. At times we'd say that a wine would be thin and therefore California, when it wasn't. Our confusion showed how good California wines have become."

Spurrier's original plan had been to announce all the results at the end of the day, but the waiters were slow clearing the tables and getting the red wines together and the program was getting badly behind schedule, so he decided to give the results of the white-wine tasting. He had been personally stunned and began reading them slowly to the group:

1. Chateau Montelena 1973
2. Meursault Charmes 1973
3. Chalone 1974
4. Spring Mountain 1973
5. Beaune Clos des Mouches 1973
6. Freemark Abbey 1972
7. Bâtard-Montrachet 1973

8.   Puligny-Montrachet 1972
9.   Veedercrest 1972
10. David Bruce 1973

When he finished, Spurrier looked at the judges, whose reaction ranged from shock to horror. No one had expected this, and soon the whole room was abuzz.

After hearing the results, I walked up to Gallagher. The French word in the winning wine's name had momentarily thrown me. "Chateau Montelena is Californian, isn't it?" I asked a bit dumbfoundedly.

"Yes, it is," she replied calmly.

The scores of the individual judges made the results even more astounding. California Chardonnays had overwhelmed their French counterparts. Every single French judge rated a California Chardonnay first. Chateau Montelena was given top rating by six judges; Chalone was rated first by the other three. Three of the top four wines were Californian. Claude Dubois-Millot gave Chateau Montelena 18.5 out of 20 points, while Aubert de Villaine gave it 18. Chateau Montelena scored a total of 132 points, comfortably ahead of second place Meursault Charmes, which got 126.5.

Spurrier and Gallagher, who were also blind tasting the wines although their scores were not counted in the final tally, were tougher on the California wines than the French judges. Spurrier had a tie for first between Freemark Abbey and Bâtard-Montrachet, while Gallagher scored a tie for first between Meursault Charmes and Spring Mountain.

As I watched the reaction of the others to the results, I felt a sense of both awe and pride. Who would have thought it? Chauvinism is a word invented by the French, but I felt some chauvinism that a California white wine had won. But how could this be happening? I was tempted to ask for a taste of the winning California Chardonnay, but decided against it. I still had a reporting job to finish, and I needed to have a clear head.

As the waiters began pouring the reds, Spurrier was certain that the judges would be more careful and would not allow a California wine to come out on top again. One California wine winning was bad enough; two would be treason. The French judges, he felt, would be very careful to identify the French wines and score them high, while rating those that seemed American low. It would perhaps be easier to taste the differences between the two since the judges knew all the French wines very well. The French reds, with their classic, distinctive and familiar tastes would certainly stand out against the California reds. All the judges, with the possible exception of Dubois-Millot, had probably tasted the French reds hundreds of times.

There was less chatter during the second wave of wines. The judges seemed both more intense and more circumspect. Their comments about the nationality of the wine in their glass were now usually correct. "That's a California, or I don't know what I'm doing here," said Christian Vannequé of La Tour d'Argent. I looked at my card and saw that he was right. It was the Ridge Monte Bello.

Raymond Oliver took one quick sip of a red and proclaimed, "That's a Mouton, without a doubt." He too was right.

Because of delays in the earlier part of the tasting, the hour was getting late and the group had to be out by 6:00 p.m. So Spurrier pushed on quickly after the ballots were collected. He followed the same procedure he had used for the Chardonnay tasting, adding up the individual scores of the nine judges.

The room was hushed as Spurrier read the results without the help of a microphone:

1. Stag's Leap Wine Cellars 1973
2. Château Mouton Rothschild 1970
3. Château Montrose 1970
4. Château Haut-Brion 1970
5. Ridge Monte Bello 1971
6. Château Léoville-Las-Cases 1971
7. Heitz Martha's Vineyard 1970
8. Clos Du Val 1972
9. Mayacamas 1971
10. FreemarkAbbey 1969

This time the stir in the room was even more pronounced than before. A California wine had won again! Who would have believed it! The judges sat in disbelief. To confirm that I had heard Spurrier correctly, I walked up to Gallagher again and asked, "A California wine also won the red?"

"Yes," she replied.

The results for the Cabernet wines were much closer than for the Chardonnays. Château Haut-Brion got the most first place votes of all the reds: three. French wines were rated first, in some cases tied for first, by seven of the nine judges. Stag's Leap was rated highly by most judges, but only Odette Kahn put it first and Raymond Oliver had it in a tie for first. In sharp contrast to the results in the white wines, the French red wines also rated much better overall than the California reds. French wines took three of the top four positions, while California wines were relegated to the last four slots. Based on the overall scores, the results were very close for the red wines. There was only a five-and-a-half-point difference between the top four finishers. Stag's Leap won by just a point and a half, with a total of 127.5, over second place Château Mouton Rothschild. But as the old saying goes, close only counts in horseshoes. Stag's Leap was the winner that day. It was the judgment of Paris.

Spurrier's suspicion that the judges would attempt to identify the French wines and score them higher while rating the California ones low appears to have taken place. In the Cabernet competition the judges had a significantly wider scoring range than with the Chardonnays. The judges may have honestly felt the quality differences were that great, but they may also have been out to make sure a French wine won. Odette Kahn, for example, gave two wines (Clos Du Val and Heitz Martha's Vineyard) only 2 points out of 20, one (Freemark Abbey) 5 points, and one (Ridge) 7 points. All her other Cabernet scores were double digits. But if she was trying to score California wines low, she didn't succeed. Her first two highest scores went to California: Stag's Leap and Mayacamas. Four other French judges also had the same pattern of rating several California wines in single digits, which is unusual in a fine wine tasting.

The California reds did very well on Spurrier's and Galla-gher's scoring cards. Spurrier in a moment of indecision had a four-way tie for first: Château Montrose, Château Mouton-Rothschild, Ridge, and Stag's Leap. Gallagher gave first place to Heitz Martha's Vineyard.

After the final results were announced, Odette Kahn marched up to Spurrier, gathering together all the force of her strong per-sonality, elegant presence, and aristocratic demeanor. As an editor, she realized better than probably anyone else in the room did the importance of what had just happened and the impact this wine tasting might have.

"Monsieur Spurrier, I demand to have my scorecards," she said.

"I'm sorry, Madame Kahn, but you're not going to get them back."

"But they are *my* scores!"

"No, they are not *your* scores. They are *my* scores!"

Spurrier and Kahn continued the sharp exchange over the own-ership of the scorecards, until she finally demurred, realizing there was no way to force him to give them to her. Spurrier then shoved the pieces of paper into the hand of his summer intern and told her to take them immediately back to the Académie du Vin.

The judges lingered for a while longer, sharing a glass of Cham-pagne and talking freely about the results of the tasting. I spoke with five of the nine. Their immediate reactions were candid. They were generally complimentary about the California wines they had just tasted. Most said they had heard that winemakers in California were doing interesting things, but they had little firsthand experience with the wines. Said Aubert de Villaine, "I tasted my first California wines in 1964, and since then there have been more and more good wine houses there."

Pierre Bréjoux told me, "I went to California in July 1974, and I learned a lot—to my surprise. They are now certainly among the top wines in the world. But this Stag's Leap has been a secret. I've never heard of it."

Pierre Tari said, "I was really surprised by the California whites. They are excellent. We clearly saw that the California whites can stand up to the French whites. They are certainly the best—after France. They have come a long way, but they have a long way to go."

Christian Vannequé told me, "The white wines approached the best of France without a doubt. California can almost do as well producing something like a Chassagne-Montrachet. The reds, though, were not as good and don't have the character of a Bordeaux. They are a bit minty, very strong in tannin and lack finesse."

There were also a few sour grapes among the judges. Tari complained, "French wines develop slower than California wines because of the climate, so the test was not completely correct." Added Aubert de Villaine: "In general there is still quite a difference. The French wines are still superior." Snipped Odette Kahn, "It was a false test because California wines are trying to become too much like French wines." Said Michel Dovaz, "In five or ten years, when the wines have properly matured, I'm sure the French red wines will do much better."

The InterContinental staff then hurried the group out of the room so they could get on with preparations for the wedding-party guests who would soon be arriving. As the judges walked out, Spurrier gave Dovaz the extra bottle of the winning Stag's Leap wine, which had not been opened. Dovaz thanked him and took it back to his apartment in Montparnasse on the edge of the student section of Paris. He opened the bottle a few weeks later, when a friend came for dinner. They each had a glass, but then Dovaz went to the kitchen and opened a bottle of French wine to serve with the meal. The Stag's Leap, he felt, was an admirable wine that had tested well, but it didn't quench his thirst.

After the tasting, Spurrier and Gallagher walked together back to the Académie du Vin. They chatted about the unexpected results, but didn't think much beyond that. From their trips to California, they knew Americans were making some good wines. After spending an hour or so at his business, Spurrier went home for dinner with his wife and two children. He told her about the interesting tasting they had held that afternoon and the unexpected outcome, but soon the conversation moved on to more mundane topics.

The day after the event, I called Gallagher at the Académie du Vin, looking for help in finding some of the Californians whose wines had been in the tasting. She had told me that the group was currently touring French wineries. Among them was the owner of Chateau Montelena, which had come in first among the whites. I asked if she could get a phone number where he could be reached, and a short while later she called back with the number. The Californians that day were supposed to be at the Château Lascombes winery in the Margaux region of Bordeaux. She couldn't guarantee anything, but perhaps I could track him down there.

At that exact moment at Château Lascombes, the California winemakers were having a glass of Champagne as an aperitif before lunch. One of the Château's staff members came up to group leader Joanne Dickenson and said that Monsieur Barrett was wanted on the phone. Dickenson's immediate reaction was that something must have happened at home to one of his children. Why else would anyone be trying to reach Jim Barrett in southern France in the middle of a wine tour? The only person in France who knew the group's itinerary was the travel agent in Paris.

Dickenson spotted Barrett across the room, walked over, and told him that he had a phone call. He also thought it must be bad news. The two Americans then followed the Château Lascombes staff member to another building and into a tiny office. The room was so small that Barrett had to kneel down on the floor to talk. All Dickenson heard was Barrett's end of the conversation, as he said, "No . . . Yes . . . Okay . . ." Barrett finally flashed Dickenson the okay sign and mouthed the words that everything was all right, so she went back to her hosts and the reception.

Once Barrett identified himself, I asked him, "Have you heard that your wine came in first in the tasting that was held on Monday in Paris?"

"No, I haven't. That's great."

"Well, you won in the white wine part of it. And a California red wine also won. So it was a California sweep. What's your reaction to beating the French at their own game and in Paris?"

Barrett's mind started racing, but the careful lawyer came to the fore. He thought quickly, "If I open my big mouth and say the wrong thing, it's going to seem arrogant, and they won't let me back into the Napa Valley." After a second's hesitation, Barrett said, "Not bad for kids from the sticks." He went on to add, "I guess it's time to be humble and pleased, but I'm not stunned. We've known for a long time that we could put our white Burgundy against anybody's in the world and not take a backseat."

I asked Barrett a few questions about his winery and the price of his wine in California. He said his winery was still a very new venture but that his "balance sheet has gone from a Pommard red to something like a rosé."

Following a few more exchanges, I knew I had a good reaction quote—"kids from the sticks"—and so I ended the conversation.

After talking with Barrett, I turned back to my old, gray manual typewriter to write my report. In those days, *Time* correspondents sent long files that gave the full story of an event, which was much more than ever appeared in the magazine. A report was then cut down to a much shorter piece by the magazine's New York staff. My report went on for eight pages and nearly two thousand words. It started: "Nine of France's top wine experts swirled and sniffed and sipped and spit Monday for over two hours at the Hotel InterContinental in Paris and rolled Bacchus over and awarded top prize in both red and white wines to two noble upstarts from California— Chateau Montelena for the white and Stag's Leap Wine Cellars for the red." I ended my report with a comment from the scorecard of Christian Vannequé about the Chateau Montelena Chardonnay, which he had ranked as the best white. I thought it summed up the attitude of the French judges toward all the California wines: "A very agreeable wine, which will blossom pleasantly and has a good equilibrium. To be followed."

After our conversation ended, Barrett returned to the pre-luncheon reception, which was just ending. He immediately told his wife about the call, so that she wouldn't be thinking the worst, as he had originally. Before sitting down he sidled up to Dickenson and said, "That was *Time* magazine. A reporter told me we won Steven Spurrier's tasting."

Barrett then sat down for lunch. Bob Travers, the owner of the Mayacamas winery, which also had a wine in the Spurrier competition, was sitting across the table and asked, "Is everything okay?" Travers also thought that something was probably wrong at home. Barrett looked at Travers with a smile as wide as a bottle of Chardonnay and said, "Yes, everything's fine."

The results of the Spurrier tasting soon began spreading quietly but quickly from Californian to Californian around the room.

Some ninety people attended the formal lunch, which was done in the best French style. Dickenson was seated to the right of Alexis Lichine, a part owner of Château Lascombes, while André Tchelistcheff was on his left. After lunch Lichine made a gracious, though condescending, speech, saying how nice it was that the Americans had come to learn from the French how to make great wine and how if they worked hard, someday they too might be successful. To Dickenson it was hard to take that speech, all the while knowing that California wines had just beaten some of the best French ones in Spurrier's tasting.

After lunch the California delegation politely thanked their hosts and got back into their bus. Everyone waved good-bye as the vehicle pulled away from Château Lascombes. As soon as it had passed the last pine tree and was safely out of sight of the main building, the group erupted like football fans whose team had just won the Super Bowl. Everyone was screaming; Barrett hugged Tchelistcheff. There were two more wine tastings that afternoon to bring the number of wines the Californians had tried in nearly three weeks in France to more than 250, but the group walked through the event in a dream. They were more excited about what had happened in Paris.

Once they arrived at their next hotel, Barrett sent a telegram to the staff at Chateau Montelena:

STUNNING SUCCESS IN PARIS TASTING ON MAY TWENTY-
FOUR STOP TOOK FIRST PLACE OVER NINE OTHERS WITH LE
PREMIER CRU WINE STOP TOP NAMES IN FRANCE WERE THE
BLIND TASTERS STOP

When the telegram arrived at Chateau Montelena, the staff wasn't sure what Barrett was referring to. They learned it was something important, when Grgich got a call from *Time* asking to send a photographer to take his picture. After that call, Grgich still didn't know what to do. So he started dancing around the winery shouting in his native Croatian, "I'm born again! I'm born again!" No one could understand a word he said, but who cared? Barrett's son Bo watched Grgich from a second-story window and thought he had gone bonkers.

The next day the Tchelistcheff group flew back to San Francisco. It was near dinnertime when André Tchelistcheff and his wife, Dorothy, reached their home in the city of Napa. Dorothy thought it might be a good moment to call Barbara Winiarski and tell her about the results of the Spurrier tasting. Barbara and the Winiarski children were already having dinner when the phone rang. When Dorothy Tchelistcheff told her that Stag's Leap had won the competition for the red wine, Barbara wasn't sure exactly which wine tasting that was, but thanked her for the message anyway. The children, though, became excited when they heard they had won something, and Barbara motioned to them to be quiet. Once her mother hung up the phone and told the children, Kasia and her younger sister Julia danced around the table with elation. They couldn't remember ever winning a wine contest before.

After dinner Barbara talked by phone with Warren, who was at his old family home in Chicago wrapping up some matters involving the estate of his mother, who had recently died. Barbara casually mentioned that their wine had won "that wine tasting in Paris." Warren also had a tough time remembering which tasting it was. Without realizing the profound impact the Paris Tasting would have on his life and his winery, he said simply, "That's nice."

color) such as, well probably all I could think of at that sta[...]
the Bordeaux grapes Cabernet and Merlot. I took a sniff[...]
enough, there were the telltale terribly well-mannered sme[...]
taught to describe as "blackcurrant" of young claret. "F[...]
ventured. Steve took a furtive look at the label. "That'[...]
year?" I tipped the glass away from me against my wh[...]
whether the wine had taken on any brick tinge wit[...]
been taught to in my wine classes. Still crimson b[...]
the rim, it must be young and probably not that[...]
(the best red wines tend to be very intensely col[...]
so I guessed it was probably some commercial b[...]
years old. "Yes, yes," said Steve impatiently, "[...]

Now this was a really tricky one. If it [...]
Château on the label, it was almost certainly[...]
one and could have been one of literally[...]
farms allowed to call themselves "Châtea[...]
ally, after a thoroughly unsatisfactory dia[...]
was revealed as the mass-market blend[...]
a drink meant to spread goodwill int[...]

Happily, although outsiders re[...]
insiders do seem to remember when[...]
they know how difficult it is. Notable feats[...]
odd bravura performance can cling flatteringly to[...]
for years and years. I will always remember Lindsay Hamilto[...]
wine traders Farr Vintners telling me that he had seen Oz Clarke,
fellow wine writer and extremely gifted blind taster, given a wine
that was actually a blend of Jaboulet's 1982 and 1983 Hermitage La
Chapelle, hesitate between identifying it as a 1982 or a 1983. Now
that's impressive.

On those rare occasions when I have managed to be more right
than wrong, it has usually been remembered and repeated back to me.
As the French wine writer (and once owner of Château Margaux)
Bernard Ginestet puts it, "I know of tasters who live by a reputation
forged on the basis of two or three inspired guesses." I sometimes
feel like that.

BLIND TASTING
Jancis Robinson

There is no doubt that guessing a wine's identity on the basis of taste alone is one of the most impressive tricks a human can perform. It is seen as the defining act of wine expertise. Wine outsiders seem endlessly fascinated by it, presumably because it demonstrates skills they have never developed themselves. Wine insiders call it blind tasting, and it always surprises me how many outsiders think this involves putting masks on the tasters (which would be a very danger-ous undertaking) rather than masking the identity of what is to be tasted, typically encasing the bottle in an opaque bag or cardboard sleeve.

I am more impressed by the possibly more common ability to identify music and performers from a short phrase, because I find it more difficult than blind tasting, but I suspect it involves a similar combination of one-third natural gift and two-thirds application guided by varying degrees of luck. Blind tasting for the purposes of identification is a very specialized sort of tasting of little practical use but great entertainment and a very specialized sort of tasting for the purposes of ing experience and a good memory were the most important elements[...] in blind tasting but experience can be a real blind, I have found[...] have never been as good at identifying wines as I was in the late 19[...] when my palate memory (and actual memory) were uncluttere[...] accumulation. Every new wine made a crystal-clear impressi[...] since I had experienced so few of these impressions, it was[...] to relate practically everything I tasted to just one of t[...]

The only time I have ever felt that I was being *tested* by a fellow professional was when I first visited Château Cheval Blanc, the great Saint-Émilion property whose wines have over the years become some of my absolute favorites for their grace and balance. I was researching my second book, *The Great Wine Book*, and wanted, fairly predictably, to include Cheval Blanc as one of thirty-seven properties profiled therein. The man who had been in charge of this first growth since 1970, after managing rubber and cocoa plantations in Africa and the Far East ("the same as vines really"), was the lofty Jacques Hébrard. His wife was one of the Heritiers Fourcaud-Laussac still prominently and proprietorially featured on the label of Cheval Blanc. When I turned up early one evening in 1981 as agreed, he was not particularly forthcoming. He answered my questions but volunteered not a word more. He made sure I realized that one of his jobs was to judge books written about Bordeaux. As I got up to go, he rather doubtfully invited me to stay for dinner. It must be a very small class of people who would refuse an invitation to dine at a first growth château and one which certainly does not include me, however reluctant the host.

The hostess, Madame Hébrard, turned out to be charming, as was their snow-white cat (Chaton Blanc?), and the table in the salon had already been laid for three. Before dinner we watched the landing of the first space shuttle on a television distractingly acting as plinth for a model of the plane which his father had piloted across the Atlantic half a century before. He was still distinctly gruff until he'd served the contents of the two decanters sitting on the sideboard. It is hardly a great feat to guess that at Cheval Blanc the wine they are most likely to serve is Cheval Blanc. My job was clearly to guess the vintages. The first wine was still very lively with a great thwack of Saint-Émilion warmth and sweetness. It was relatively concentrated in color still but had developed quite a brickish tinge at the rim. The smell, or "nose," was both fascinating and seductive and there was still lots of firm fruit. This must be a robust middle-aged vintage, but that rim looked too mature for it to be a 1970, yet it tasted too young to be any older than that. It was too good a wine to have been made in 1974, 1973 or 1972, so was it by any chance 1971? M. Hébrard smiled for the first time that evening and his wife looked approving. "Some more lamb perhaps?"

Now to the second decanter. Professional protocol dictated that it would be older than the first wine, and that was certainly confirmed by its lighter, browner color. Here was a fully mature wine I thought (although I thought the same when drinking it fifteen years later) which smelled so sweet, luscious and thoroughly charming that it could have been a 1966, but it was terribly impressive, very powerful and underneath all that charm something with enormous guts. Something, some divine intervention, made me plump for 1964, a great year for Cheval Blanc, rather than 1966, and then my host visibly melted. We all had a lovely time after that (and who wouldn't with these two decanters to help them?) and Jacques Hébrard was charm itself whenever I came across him subsequently.

My most embarrassing trial by tasting took place not long after this Cheval Blanc visit but in much more public circumstances. The broadcaster Terry Wogan was at the height of his fame, hosting a live, early evening chat show during which all he had to do was look coyly at the camera and raise an eyebrow to have the entire audience of the Shepherd's Bush Theatre and his millions of television viewers across Britain either swooning or chortling, depending on their sex. For some reason—the performing dogs principle, I suppose—Hugh Johnson and I were invited to appear together to taste some wine. Ever-generous Hugh, for neither the first nor last time, saw it as his duty to make sure we had some champagne to drink—bought from a dubious local off-license and drunk in a cramped dressing room. That bit was fine. But then eventually we were led, increasingly zombie-like in my case, to the set on stage and, under cover of some musical act, installed on the regulation sofa beside a coffee table on which were two wine glasses from hell. They were tall, narrow cones, heavy and ornately cut, just the sort of thing you would find in a boardroom but never in a wine lover's house because there was no bowl for the telltale aroma to collect in and no nice thin lip to put you in really close contact with the wine. And, as if that wasn't enough, the wine must have been sitting out since rehearsal time that afternoon under strong studio lights so that such smell as there had been had long since dissipated. Well, that's my excuse anyway, for failing, in front of probably five million people, to identify Château Lafite 1976, hailed as "the wine of the vintage."

Needless to say, I had been much more successful on a much less important show when asked to identify six wines for local TV in Newcastle several years previously very early in my career. The more of a nonentity you are, the more relaxed you can afford to be when blind tasting in public. It was the same sort of early evening show in Newcastle but a much more cramped studio. The stage manager tip-toed in with the wines on a tray as I sat watching the previous guest, a weatherman. I signaled to him that because he'd filled the glasses right up to the top rather than the usual tasting level of about a quarter full, he'd have to pour most of the six wines away. He signaled to me that he had nowhere to pour them, shrugged, and downed the equivalent of half a bottle in the thirty seconds before we were due to go on the air.

Blind tasting as performance art appeals to me less and less as I get older, for obvious reasons (although I see that I first made the analogy between it and crossword puzzle solving, both of them impressive but fairly useless, in 1980 when *The Sunday Times* tested our ability to identify our own recommendations and my palate was inexperienced enough to perform well).

There is another reason for blind tasting, however, which is invaluable for any wine professional: assessing the quality of a wine (as opposed to identifying it) without knowing what it is. Most of us consumer writers on wine acknowledge that the best way of testing a wine's real quality is to taste it blind with its peers, and we try to base our recommendations on that process as often as possible. Similarly, the best way of assessing a completely unfamiliar wine—some new offering from the hills of Attica, for example—is to taste it blind and try to work out what price you'd be prepared to pay for it. This was the basis on which the enlightened London wine merchant James

Rogers made all his wine-buying decisions. If only more retailers followed his example.

Blind tasting is a truly humbling experience and teaches us all just how heavily influenced we are by labels and reputations rather than inherent quality. If I had just half the cost of all the wines with a "Montrachet" in their name which have turned out to be expensive disappointments, I would be a very rich woman. The French are fiercely opposed to blind comparisons between their wines and those from other countries. They claim it is as senseless as comparing apples with pears. I'm not so sure. If you want to come to grips with, say, the essential Pauillac-ness of Pauillac, then of course it's a waste of time to taste five of them mixed up with five top California Cabernet Sauvignons. But if you want to test the hypothesis that Pauillacs are a better buy than California Cabernet Sauvignons, then such a blind tasting is one way to do it—especially since even quite experienced tasters can have difficulty telling some of them apart.

Just as the world of wine has been transformed in the last twenty years, so have the mores of blind tasting. When I started, blind tasting round a wine trade lunch table was a relatively simple matter. It was chiefly a question of deciding whether the red wine was bordeaux or burgundy. If it were burgundy, you progressed gently via Côte de Nuits or Beaune to whether it was a village wine, premier cru or grand cru and took in the vintage somewhere en route. If it were bordeaux you worked out which of the "Big Four" (Médoc, Graves, Saint-Émilion or Pomerol) and, if Médoc as it so often was, which of the "Little Four" (Saint-Estèphe, Pauillac, Saint-Julien or Margaux). Just occasionally someone served something really outré such as a Rhône or Château La Lagune or Cantemerle, a bordeaux from outside the little four communes of the Médoc.

Today all but the most conservative hosts serve wines from all over the world, many of them aping each other so successfully that they hardly carry a recognizable geographical origin at all, making blind tasting even more perilous. And a uniformity of aspiration has swept even the old stalwarts of the Médoc so that traditional com-munal differences are often subordinated to winemaking technique. In face, Professor Emile Peynaud of Bordeaux University, the grand seigneur of wine tasting and a winemaking consultant at numerous topflight châteaux, claims that such differences between villages are "really just the commercial styles which were followed when blend-ing in merchants' cellars years ago; the reality is quite different. For my own part, I would not claim to be able to identify the communes of a series of Médocs tasted blind. The problem is just as difficult in Burgundy where the distinction between wines from the Côte de Beaune and the Côte de Nuits is a matter for endless debate."

It is probably worth repeating the wine trade's most often told story here. The personnel change but the sentiment doesn't. A wine professional is asked when he, or she, last mistook bordeaux for bur-gundy. "Oh, not since lunch" is the answer—although nowadays it is getting harder and harder to find people who drink at lunchtime at all.

THE NOTION OF *TERROIR*

Matt Kramer

Always the beautiful answer who asks a more beautiful question
                                    —E. E. Cummings, *New Poems*

The "more beautiful question" of wine is *terroir*. To the English
speaker, *terroir* is an alien word, difficult to pronounce ("tair-wahr").
More frustrating yet, it is a foreign idea. The usual capsule definition is site or vineyard plot. Closer to its truth, it holds—like William Blake's grain of sand that contains a universe—an evolution
of thought about wine and the Earth. One cannot make sense of
Burgundy without investigating the notion of *terroir*.

Although derived from soil or land (terre), *terroir* is not just an
investigation of soil and subsoil. It is everything that contributes to
the distinction of a vineyard plot. As such, it also embraces "micro-
climate": precipitation, air and water drainage, elevation, sunlight,
and temperature.

But *terroir* holds yet another dimension: It sanctions what cannot be measured, yet still located and savored. *Terroir* prospects for
differences. In this, it is at odds with science, which demands proof
by replication rather than in a shining uniqueness.

Understanding *terroir* requires a recalibration of the modern
mind. The original impulse has long since disappeared, buried by
commerce and the scorn of science. It calls for a susceptibility to the
natural world to a degree almost unfathomable today, as the French
historian Marc Bloch evokes in his landmark work, *Feudal Society*:

The men of the two feudal ages were close to nature—much closer than we are; and nature as they knew it was much less tamed and softened than as we see it today. . . . People continued to pick wild fruit and to gather honey as in the first ages of mankind. In the construction of implements and tools, wood played a predominant part. The nights, owing to wretched lighting, were darker; the cold, even in the living quarters of the castles, was more intense. In short, behind all social life there was a background of the primitive, of submission to uncontrollable forces, of unrelieved physical contrasts.

This world extended beyond the feudal ages, as rural life in Europe changed little for centuries afterward. Only the barest vestiges remain today, with the raw, preternatural sensitivity wiped clean. The viticultural needlepoint of the Côte d'Or, its thousands of named vineyards, is as much a relic of a bygone civilization as Stonehenge. We can decipher why and how they did it, but the impulse, the fervor, is beyond us now.

The glory of Burgundy is its exquisite delineation of sites, its preoccupation with *terroir*: What does this site have to say? Is it different from its neighbor? It is the source of Burgundian greatness, the informing ingredient. This is easily demonstrated. You need only imagine an ancient Burgundy planted to Pinot Noir and Chardonnay for the glory of producing—to use the modern jargon—a varietal wine. The thought is depressing, an anemic vision of wine hardly capable of inspiring the devotion of generations of wine lovers, let alone the discovery of such natural wonders as Montrachet or La Tâche. *Terroir* is as much a part of Burgundy wines as Pinot Noir or Chardonnay; the grape is as much vehicle as voice.

The mentality of *terroir* is not uniquely Burgundian, although it reaches its fullest expression there. It more rightly could be considered distinctively French, although not exclusively so. Other countries, notably Germany and Italy, can point to similar insights. But France, more than any other, viewed its landscape from the perspective of *terroir*. It charted its vineyard distinctions—often called *cru* or growth—with calligraphic care. Indeed, calligraphy and *cru* are sympathetic, both the result of emotional, yet disciplined, attentions to detail. Both flourished under monastic tutelage.

Italy, for all of its ancient winegrowing tradition, never developed a mentality of *terroir* to the same or even similar extent as France. It lacked, ironically, the monastic underpinning of the Benedictine and Cistercian orders, which were represented to a far greater degree in France and Germany. An ecclesiastical map of western Europe during the Middle Ages (*Historical Atlas* by William R. Shepherd) shows hundreds of major monasteries in France and Germany, nearly all of them Benedictine or Cistercian. In comparison, Italy had less than a dozen.

The phrase "mentality of *terroir*" is pertinent. The articulation of the Burgundian landscape increased steadily long after the decline of the feudal ages. Ever-finer distinctions of site mounted along the Côte d'Or through to the Revolution of 1789, when the Church lands were confiscated and publicly auctioned. The monks and nuns, whose wines and vineyards remained the standard for nearly a millennium, never wavered in their devotion to *terroir*. If only by sheer longevity, their vision of the land became everyone else's. Wherever the Church shaped the viticultural landscape, *terroir* was the means by which that world was understood.

But in France there exists, to this day, a devotion to *terroir* that is not explained solely by this legacy of the Church. Instead, it is fueled by two forces in French life: a longstanding delight in differences and an acceptance of ambiguity.

The greatness of French wines in general—and Burgundy in particular—can be traced to the fact that the French do not ask of one site that it replicate the qualities of another site. They prize distinction. This leads not to discord—as it might in a country gripped by a marketing mentality—but consonance with what the French call *la France profonde*, elemental France.

This is the glory of France. It is not that France is the only spot on the planet with remarkable soils or that its climate is superior to all others for winegrowing. It is a matter of the values that are applied to the land. In this, *terroir* and its discoveries remind one of Chinese acupuncture. Centuries ago, Chinese practitioners chose to view the body from a perspective utterly different than that of the dissective, anatomical approach of Western medicine. Because of this different perspective, they discovered something about the body that Western practitioners, to this day, are unable to independently see for themselves: what the Chinese call "channels" and "collaterals," or more recently, "meridians." The terminology is unimportant. What is important is that these "meridians" cannot be found by dissection. Yet they exist; acupuncture works. Its effects, if not its causes, are demonstrable.

In the same way, seeking to divine the greatness of Burgundy only by dissecting its intricacies of climate, grape, soil, and winemaking is no more enlightening than learning how to knit by unraveling a sweater. Those who believe that great wines are made, rather than found, will deliver such wines only by the flimsiest chance, much in the same way that an alchemist, after exacting effort, produces gold simply by virtue of having worked with gold-bearing material all along.

Today, a surprising number of winegrowers and wine drinkers— at least in the United States—flatly deny the existence of *terroir*, like weekend sailors who reject as preposterous that Polynesians could have crossed the Pacific navigating only by sun, stars, wind, smell, and taste. *Terroir* is held to be so much bunk, little more than viticultural voodoo.

The inadmissibility of *terroir* to the high court of reason is due to ambiguity. *Terroir* can be presented, but it cannot be proven—except by the senses. Like Polynesian seafaring, it is too subjective to be reproducible and therefore credible. Yet any reasonably experienced wine drinker knows upon tasting a mature Corton-Charlemagne or Chablis "Valdese" or Volnay "Caillerets," that something is present that cannot be accounted for by winemaking technique. Infused in the wine is a *gout de terroir*, a taste of the soil. It cannot be traced to the grape, if only because other wines made the same way from the same grape lack this certain something. If only by process of elimination the source must be ascribed to *terroir*. But to acknowledge this requires a belief that the ambiguous—the unprovable and immeasurable—can be real. Doubters are blocked by their own credulity in science and its confining definition of reality.

The supreme concern of Burgundy is—or should be—making *terroir* manifest. In outline, this is easily accomplished: small-berried clones; low yields; selective sorting of the grapes; and trickiest of all, fermenting and cellaring the wine in such a way as to allow the *terroir* to come through with no distracting stylistic flourishes. This is where *terroir* comes smack up against ego, the modern demand for self-expression at any cost. Too often, it has come at the expense of *terroir*.

It is easier to see the old Burgundian enemies of greed and inept winemaking. The problem of greed, expressed in overcropped grape-vines resulting in thin, diluted wines, has been chronic in Burgundy, as are complaints about it. It is no less so today, but the resolution is easily at hand: lower the yields.

But the matter of ego and *terroir* is new and peculiar to our time. It stems from two sources: the technology of modern winemaking and the psychology of its use. Technical control in winemaking is recent, dating only to the late 1960s. Never before had winemakers been able to control wine to such an extent as is available today. Through the use of temperature-controlled stainless steel tanks, computer-controlled wine presses, heat exchangers, inert gases, centrifuges, all manner of filters, oak barrels from woods of different forests, and so forth, the modern winemaker can insert himself between the *terroir* and its wine to a degree never before achieved.

The psychology of its use is the more important feature. Self-expression is now considered the inalienable right of our time. It, thus, is no surprise that the desire for self-expression should make itself felt in winemaking. That winemakers have always sought to express themselves in their wines is indisputable. The difference is that today technology actually allows them to do so, to an extent unimagined by their grandparents.

Submerged in this is a force that, however abstract, has changed much of twentieth-century thinking: the transition from the literal to the subjective in how we perceive what is "real." Until recently, whatever was considered "real" was expressed in straightforward mechanical or linear linkages, such as a groove in a phonograph record or a lifelike painting of a vase of flowers. Accuracy was defined by exacting, literal representation.

But we have come to believe that the subjective can be more "real" than the representational. One of the earliest, and most famous, examples of this was Expressionism in art. Where prior to the advent of Expressionism in the early twentieth century, the depiction of reality on a canvas was achieved through the creation of the most lifelike forms, Expressionists said otherwise. They maintained that the reality of a vase of flowers could be better expressed by breaking down its form and color into more symbolic representations of its reality, rather than by straightforward depiction.

How this relates to wine is found in the issue of *terroir* versus ego. The Burgundian world that discovered *terroir* centuries ago drew no distinction between what they discovered and called Chambertin and the idea of a representation of Chambertin. Previously, there were only two parties involved: Chambertin itself and its self-effacing discoverer, the winegrower. In this deferential view of the natural world, Chambertin was Chambertin if for no other reason than it consistently did not taste like its neighbor Latricières. One is beefier and more resonantly flavorful (Chambertin) while the other offers a similar savor, but somehow always is lacier in texture and less full-blown. It was a reality no more subject to doubt than was a nightingale's song from the screech of an owl. They knew what they tasted, just as they knew what they heard. These were natural forces, no more subject to alteration or challenge than a river.

All of which brings us back to Burgundian winemaking. In an age where the subjective has been accepted as being more "real" than the representational, the idea of an immutable *terroir* becomes troublesome. It complicates ego-driven individualism, the need to express a personal vision. In an era of relativism and right of self-expression, Chambertin as *terroir* has given way to Chambertin as emblem. The notion of *terroir* as an absolute is rejected. All Chambertins therefore are equally legitimate. We have come to accept that a grower's Chambertin is really only his or her idea of Chambertin. The vineyard name on the label is merely as a general indication of intent.

How, then, does one know what is the true voice of the land? How does one know when the winemaker has interposed himself or herself between the *terroir* and the final wine? Discovering the authentic voice of a particular *terroir* requires study. The only way is to assemble multiple examples of a wine from a particular plot and taste them side by side. Ideally they should all be from the same vintage. This eliminates at least one distracting variable.

In seeking to establish the voice of a *terroir*, one has to concentrate—at least for the moment—not on determining which wines are best, but in finding the thread of distinction that runs through them. It could be a matter of structure: delicate or muscular, consistently lean or generous in fruit. It could be a distinctive *gout de terroir*, something minerally or stony; chalky or earthy. Almost always, it will be hard to determine at first, because the range of styles within the wines will be distracting. And if the choices available are mostly second-rate, where the *terroir* is lost through over-cropped vines or heavy-handed winemaking, the exercise will be frustrating and without reward. *Terroir* usually is discovered only after repeated attempts over a number of vintages. This is why such insight is largely the province only of Burgundians and a few obsessed outsiders.

Nevertheless, hearing the voice of the land is sweet and you will not easily forget it. Sometimes it only becomes apparent by contrast. You taste a number of Meursault "Perrières," for example, and in the good ones you find a pronounced mineraliness coupled with an invigorating, strong fruitiness. You don't realize how stony or fruity, how forceful, until you compare Perrières with, say, Charmes, which is contiguous. Then the distinction of Perrières clicks into place in your mind. It's never so exact or pronounced that you will spot it unerringly in a blind tasting of various Meursault *premiers crus*. That's not the point. The point is that there is no doubt that Perrières exists, that it is an entity unto itself, distinct from any other plot.

Such investigation—which is more rewarding than it might sound—has a built-in protocol. When faced with a lineup of wines, the immediate impact is of stylistic differences, a clamor of producers' voices. Once screened out, the lesser versions—the ones that clearly lack concentration and definition of flavor—are easily eliminated. Some are so insipid as to make them fraudulent in everything but the legal niceties. Then you are left with the wines that have something to say. At this moment, you confront the issue of ego.

The ideal is to amplify *terroir* without distorting it. *Terroir* should be transmitted as free as possible of extraneous elements of style or taste. Ideally, one should not be able to find the hand of the winemaker. That said, it must be acknowledged that some signature always can be detected, although it can be very faint indeed when you reach the level of Robert Chevillon in Nuits-Saint-Georges; Bernard Serveau in Morey-Saint-Denis; or the Marquis d'Angerville and Gerard Potel, both in Volnay, to name a few. The self-effacement of these producers in their wines is very nearly Zen-like: their "signature" is an absence of signature.

Such paragons aside, the presence of a signature is not intrinsically bad, as long as it is not too expensively at the cost of *terroir*. A good example of this is the winemaking of the Domaine de la Romanée-Conti. The red wines of this fabled property—Echézeaux, Grands-Échézeaux, Romanée-Saint-Vivant, Richebourg, La Tâche, and Romanée-Conti—all share a stylistic signature that becomes immediately apparent when the wines are compared with other bottlings from the same vineyards. (Only two of the properties are exclusively owned or *monopoles*, La Tâche and Romanée-Conti.) All of the wines display a distinctive silkiness, almost an unctuosity, as well as a pronounced oakiness.

Nevertheless, the wines of the Domaine de la Romanée-Conti do overcome this stylistic signature to display a full measure of their particular *terroirs*. This is confirmed when tasting other good examples of Richebourg or Grands-Échézeaux or the other properties. The reason is that the yields are admirably low; the clonal selection is astute; the harvesting punctilious in discarding rotted or unhealthy grapes; and the winemaking—stylistic signature aside—devoted to expressing the different *terroirs* to the fullest degree. The wines could be improved if the signature were less pronounced, in the same way that a beautiful dress could be improved if the designer's initials were eliminated.

This matter of signature only becomes apparent when tasting multiple examples of the same *terroir*. Although the ideal is what stereo buffs call a "straight wire," where the signal goes through the amplifier without any coloration, this simply is impossible given the intervention of both grape and grower. In this, winemaking in Burgundy really is translation. The poet W. S. Merwin maps out the challenge:

> The quality that is conveyed to represent the original is bound to differ with different translators, which is both a hazard and an opportunity. In the ideal sense in which one wants only the original, one wants the translator not to exist at all. In the practical sense in which the demand takes into account the nature of translation, the gifts—such as they are—of the translator are inescapably important.*

A good example of this would be the various Meursaults of the Domaine de Comtes Lafon and those of Jean-Francois Coche-Dury. Stylistically, the Lafon wines are more voluptuous, more apparently oaky when young, but impeccable in their definition and separation of flavors. There is no mistaking one *terroir* with another when tasting their wines. The same may be said of Coche-Dury, except that his style is more austere and somehow leaner, with distinctions of *terroir* that are almost painfully precise. The depth and concentration are the equal of Lafon, yet the delivery is slightly different. In both cases, the distinctions of site are preserved at all costs. Both accomplish what W. S. Merwin intends when translating someone else's poetry: "I have not set out to make translations that distorted

* *Selected Translations 1968–1978* (Atheneum, 1979)

the meaning of the originals on pretext of some other overriding originality."

Awareness of the existence of signature in a Burgundy is critical, if only because it is easy to be seduced by style at the expense of *terroir*. A surprising number of Burgundies, especially the white Burgundies, do just that. Character in a white wine is much more hard-won than in a red, if only because white wine grapes usually have less intrinsic flavor than red wine grapes. This is very much the case with Chardonnay compared to Pinot Noir.

Moreover, much of the flavor in a wine is extracted from the skins during fermentation. Where many red wines, and certainly Pinot Noir, are made with extended skin contact, most white wines see little or no skin contact. This is true for Chardonnay as it is produced in Burgundy, although there are exceptions. At most, a white Burgundy will see no more than twenty-four hours of its Chardonnay juice fermenting or simply macerating in contact with its skins; most Pinot Noirs are given anywhere from seven days to three weeks on the skins.

Because of this, the temptation is strong for the winemaker to infuse flavor into white wines by means of various winemaking techniques in lieu of winning it in the vineyard. The most common of these is the use of brand new oak barrels, which provide an immediately recognizable scent of vanilla and toastiness. Another approach is to leave the young but fully fermented wine on its lees or sediment while aging in the barrel and stir up this sediment from time to time. Here the winemaker is seeking to capitalize on the subtle flavorings of autolyzing or decomposing yeasts. Sometimes, though, the result is a wine with off flavors from microbial deterioration.

Too often, signature substitutes for insufficient depth. It is easier, and more ego-gratifying, to fiddle with new oak barrels and winemaking techniques than to toil in the vineyard nursing old vines and pruning severely in order to keep yields low. Character in a white Burgundy, even in the most vocal of sites, does not come automatically. One need only taste an overcropped Montrachet—it is too common—to realize how fragile is the voice of the land when transmitted by Chardonnay. As a grape, it is surprisingly neutral in flavor, which makes it an ideal vehicle for *terroir*—or for signature.

Character in a red Burgundy is just as hard-won as in a white, but its absence is not as immediately recognizable because of the greater intrinsic flavor of Pinot Noir. That said, it should be pointed out that flavor is not character, any more than a cough drop compares with a real wild cherry.

Where Chardonnay is manipulated to provide an illusion of depth and flavor, the pursuit with Pinot Noir is to make it more immediately accessible and easy down the gullet. An increasing number of red Burgundies now are seductively drinkable virtually upon release only two years after the vintage. Such wines can be misleading. Rather than improving with age, their bright, flashy fruitiness soon fades, like an enthusiasm that cools. The wine drinker is left stranded, stood up by a wine that offered cosmetics rather than character.

All of which underscores why *terroir* is the "more beautiful question" of wine. When the object is to reveal, amplify, and transmit *terroir* with clarity and resonance, there is no more "beautiful answer" than Burgundy. When it is ignored, wine may as well be grown hydroponically, rooted not in an unfathomable Earth that offers flashes of insight we call Richebourg or Corton, but in a manipulated medium of water and nutrients with no more meaning than an intravenous hook-up. Happily, the more beautiful question is being asked with renewed urgency by both growers and drinkers. A new care is being exercised. After all, without *terroir*—why Burgundy?

The WinefÜhrers

Donald and *Petie Kladstrup*

No region suffered more pillaging of its wine than Champagne. Nearly two million bottles were grabbed by German soldiers during the first weeks of the occupation alone.

It was, therefore, with immense relief that the Champenois learned that German authorities were sending in someone to oversee champagne purchases and, hopefully, end the looting and restore order. They were even more relieved when they found out who it would be: Otto Klaebisch of Matteüs-Müller, a winemaking and importing firm from Germany's Rhineland. "We were so happy we got someone from the wine trade, and not a beer man," Bernard de Nonancourt said. The Nonancourts knew Klaebisch well because he had been the prewar agent in Germany for a number of champagne houses, including Lanson, which the family of Bernard's mother owned.

Brandy, however, was Klaebisch's original background. He was born in Cognac, where his parents had been brandy merchants before World War I. When France confiscated all enemy-owned property during the war, the Klaebisch family lost its business there and returned to Germany.

Otto, however, retained his taste for the finer things in life, especially great champagne. He pursued a career in the wine and spirits industry, putting his French background to good use.

That background made Klaebisch's appointment as weinführer of Champagne easier to take. "If you were going to be shoved around, it was better to be shoved around by a winemaker than by some beer-drinking Nazi lout," said one producer.

Klaebisch began his "shoving" almost immediately. Unlike Heinz Bömers in Bordeaux, who had rented a small apartment, Klaebisch wanted something more impressive. A château, for instance. He found what he wanted when he saw where Bertrand de Vogüé, head of Veuve Clicquot-Ponsardin, lived. After one look, Klaebisch issued orders for the château to be requisitioned. An angry de Vogüé and family were sent packing.

"Klaebisch was very happy to be here," de Nonancourt remembered. "He did not like combat and the last thing he wanted was to be sent to the Russian front."

Given his family connections and professional contacts, Klaebisch landed the soft assignment without difficulty. His brother-in-law was none other than Foreign Minister Ribbentrop, whose father-in-law, Otto Henkel, was a good friend of Bordeaux's Louis Eschenauer. Eschenauer, in turn, was a cousin of German port commander Ernst Kühnemann. Eschenauer was also part owner of Mumm champagne, another property that had been confiscated from German owners in World War I. He had hired Ribbentrop to represent that marque in Germany.

Only a wine genealogist could unravel the complicated family and professional tree that entangled winemakers and merchants throughout France and Germany. It went a long way to explain how Klaebisch became weinführer of Champagne.

Klaebisch, however, was different from the other weinführers. He enjoyed the trappings of military life and almost always wore his uniform. He was also impressed with titles. When he first met Count Robert-Jean de Vogüé, the man whom he would be negotiating champagne purchases, he was deferential to the point of being obsequious, or, as one producer put it, "too anxious to please."

De Vogüé, head of Moët & Chandon, had a complicated family tree of his own. He was related to many of Europe's royal families as well as to many of France's leading wine producers. He even had connections with the Vatican. He also happened to be the brother of Veuve Clicquot's Bertrand de Vogüé, whom Klaebisch had just kicked out of his house.

Klaebisch ran into problems almost from the moment he moved in. The 1940 harvest was disastrous. The yield was 80 percent below average. Aware that Berlin expected him to supply a certain amount of champagne every month, Klaebisch visited the houses he had done business with before the war and asked them to make up the difference from their reserves.

De Vogüé thought that was a bad idea. He feared that other houses would be angry and jealous. With international markets cut off and sales to French civilians prohibited, those firms might easily go out of business.

Even the houses Klaebisch wanted to do business with were unhappy. Yes, their market was "guaranteed" but they also had to accept what the Germans were willing to pay, and it was not much. Producers feared that the huge quantities of champagne Klaebisch was demanding would soon deplete their stocks, leaving them stuck in the same economic morass they had been in during the 1930s.

Those years, more than anything, defined the almost militant mood that still prevailed in Champagne when Klaebisch arrived. In 1932, champagne houses had managed to sell only four and a half million bottles of the 150 million that were in their cellars. The mood among growers who sold their grapes to the houses was sour too. In 1933 and 1934, they were paid no more than one franc a kilo for their grapes. In 1931, they had been paid eleven francs, a loss of income that severely jeopardized their businesses. The picture improved in 1937 and 1938, but quickly turned bleak again when war was declared in 1939. In desperation, producers began walling up their champagne and shipping other stocks to the United States and Great Britain for safekeeping.

Now they faced massive requisitioning. Pol Roger, the house that made Prime Minister Winston Churchill's favorite champagne, was ordered to send huge quantities of its 1928 vintage to Berlin each month. "It was such a great vintage," said Christian de Billy, president of Pol Roger, who was born in that year. "We never had a lot and tried to hide what we could, but it was so wonderful and so well known that it was impossible to keep it out of German hands. Klaebisch knew it was there."

As German demands for champagne escalated—at times Klaebisch was demanding half a million bottles a week—de Vogüé feared, more than ever, that houses like Pol Roger would not survive. On April 13, 1941, he called together producers and growers to set up an organization that would represent the interests of everyone in the champagne industry. "We are all in this together," de Vogüé told them. "We will either suffer or survive but we will do so equally."

The organization they created was called the Comité Interprofessionel du Vin de Champagne, or CIVC, which still represents the champagne industry today. At the time, the goal of the CIVC was to enable producers to present a united front and speak with a single voice. De Vogüé, it was decided, would be the point man. "He had the courage and enough audacity to represent the interests of Champagne and to be the one and only delegate to the Germans," said Claude Fourmon, who was de Vogüé's assistant. "He never doubted the Allies would win the war, so his goal was to keep everything at an acceptable level. He wanted to make sure that everyone had something to start over with when the war ended."

Klaebisch was unhappy about the CIVC and did not want to deal with it; he preferred to stick with his prewar contacts. He knew that was how Bömers operated and he wanted to emulate the Bordeaux weinführer by taking complete control of the champagne business. Klaebisch summoned de Vogüé to his office in Reims.

There, he got right to the point. "Here are the ground rules. You can sell to the Third Reich and its military, and also to German-controlled restaurants, hotels and nightclubs, and a few of our friends like the Italian ambassador to France and Marshal Pétain at Vichy. The Marshal, by the way, likes to have a good quantity for his own personal use."

De Vogüé listened without interrupting as the weinführer outlined the conditions. "Nobody gets any free samples, there are no discounts no matter how large the order, and no full bottles of champagne may be sold unless empty bottles are first turned in." Then Klaebisch told de Vogüé how much champagne he wanted each month and what he was willing to pay for it. "You can spread the order out any way you wish among the major champagne houses just as long as I get my champagne," he said.

De Vogüé was taken aback. "There is no way we can meet those demands," he said. "Two million bottles a month? How do you expect us to do it?"

"Work Sundays!" Klaebisch shot back.

De Vogüé refused. To their credit, each man seemed to have an innate sense of how far they could push the other. After more heated exchanges, de Vogüé said champagne producers would work longer days to meet their quotas but only if the weinführer extended the number of hours they could have electricity. Klaebisch agreed.

De Vogüé, however, was not the only thorn in Klaebisch's side. In Berlin, Field Marshal Göring was demanding ever greater amounts of champagne for his Luftwaffe. The navy was also making huge demands. Buffeted from all sides, the weinführer went back to de Vogüé. This time, he was more conciliatory. "We've had our dis-agreements," he said, "but I've got a problem with Berlin and I hope you will see fit to help me." Klaebisch described how Göring was pressuring him to supply more champagne. He then proposed that if the CIVC would keep the champagne coming, he would make sure producers had all the supplies they needed such as sugar for their *dosages*, fertilizer for their vineyards, even hay for their horses.

De Vogüé said it was a deal.

It was an especially good deal for Pol Roger. Not long afterward, a spokesman from Pol Roger contacted the weinführer's office to say they were doing some repair work in their cellars and needed cement. Klaebisch arranged for its immediate delivery. Pol Roger used the cement to wall up and hide some of its best champagne from the Germans.

"The champagne houses did their best to perform a little sleight of hand," admitted Claude Taittinger, head of Taittinger Champagne. "Most tried to preserve their best wines and palm off the inferior blends on the enemy." They knew, for instance, that bottles whose labels were stamped "Reserved for the Wehrmacht" and often had a red bar running across it were unlikely to fall into hands of their regular customers. As a result, most of the houses did not hesitate to use them for their worst *cuvées*. "What they forgot," said Taittinger, "was that Klaebisch was a connoisseur and capable of cracking the whip now and then to show he was not always fooled by our tricks."

One day at lunchtime, Klaebisch called up Roger Hodez, secretary of the Syndicat des Grandes Marques de Champagne, an association representing the major champagne houses, and invited him for an aperitif. "We've never had a drink together," the weinführer said. "Why don't you drop by my office and we'll have one." Hodez felt he could not refuse.

When he arrived, Klaebisch invited him to sit down and poured him a glass of champagne. Then he poured one for himself. The weinführer seemed to be in a good mood and Hodez began to relax. Then, suddenly, Hodez's nose wrinkled as a ghastly odor rose from his glass. Bravely, he took a sip. The taste was only slightly better than the smell. There was no sign Klaebisch had noticed Hodez's discomfort. "What do you think?" he asked affably. Before Hodez could reply, the weinführer suddenly leaned across his desk and put his face inches away from Hodez's. "Let me tell you what I think," he snarled, his voice rising in crescendo. "It smells like shit! And this is what you want me to give the Wehrmacht to drink? I want the house that made this crap struck from the list of firms supplying champagne to Germany. I wouldn't dare send their stuff to Berlin!"

Hodez shrank back in his chair, fumbling for words as he tried to pacify Klaebisch. "I'm sure it was only an accident," he stammered, "a case of dirty bottles perhaps, or maybe . . ." Before Hodez could say anything else, however, he was ordered out of Klaebisch's office.

The shaken trade representative went straight to de Vogüé and told him what happened. De Vogüé immediately contacted the champagne house and warned officials of what Klaebisch had said. The head of the firm shrugged, saying he did not care. "We're not making much money from the Germans anyway. We'll be better off selling a little of our champagne on the black market and holding the rest until after the war."

De Vogüé shook his head. "That's not the point," he said. "We're all in this together and you have to provide your fair share." He instructed the firm to send its portion of champagne to several other houses, which agreed to bottle it under their own labels.

Klaebisch, however, was more suspicious than ever that champagne producers were trying to trick him. He began conducting spot checks of champagne bound for Germany, pulling out bottles, popping their corks, sniffing their contents and then tasting them. That is how François Taittinger ended up in jail.

François was twenty years old when he was brought in to help run the family firm after his uncle had become totally deaf. Like others, he underestimated Klaebisch's knowledge of champagne and thought he could outfox the weinführer by sending him champagne that was distinctly inferior in quality. When Klaebisch discovered it, he ordered François to his office.

"How dare you send us fizzy ditch water!" he yelled.

François, known for his quick temper, shot back, "Who cares? It's not as if it's going to be drunk by people who know anything about champagne!"

Klaebisch threw François into jail. In the same cell were a number of other champagne producers who had also tried to pass off bad wine.

A few days later, the eldest of the Taittinger brothers went to Klaebisch's office to plead François's case. Guy Taittinger was a former cavalry officer and a born diplomat. He regaled the weinführer with stories about his days in the French army. He described how he once had to "drink a bottle of champagne that had been decapitated with a saber and poured into a backplate of armor." Klaebisch was amused, so much so that finally he shook his head, put up his hand and said, "Okay, you win. Your brother can go."

Most people in Champagne saw Klaebisch not as a Nazi diehard but more as an arbitrator between the French wine community and Berlin. Never was that more evident than when Vichy launched a forced labor program, Service du Travail Obligatoire, or STO, to supply Germany with workers for its factories and industries. In one week alone, Pol Roger had ten of its workers hauled off to Germany; the next week, seventeen more.

"There's no way we can continue like this," de Vogüé warned Klaebisch. "We don't have enough people for our regular work, let alone for the harvest. If you do not get some of our workers back, you will have no champagne next year." The CIVC itself tried to keep the houses functioning by rotating experienced workers from one champagne maker to another. Still, the companies were falling far short of their imposed quotas.

The weinführer, who prided himself on his efficiency, quickly contacted authorities in Berlin. Faced with a choice between less champagne or less labor in their factories, the Germans chose the latter and allowed some of the more experienced and older workers to return to their cellars.

Each concession from Klaebisch, however, seemed to generate another edict. From now on, he said, a German officer must accompany every worker going into the *caves*. Producers thought it was ridiculous and completely impractical. When the weinführer backed off, there was a huge sigh of relief, for the chalk cellars, the *crayères* of Champagne, were being used by the Resistance, both as a place of refuge and as a place to stockpile arms and supplies.

In fact, the Resistance was doing a great deal more. It had picked up on the fact that champagne shipments were providing significant military intelligence. Through them, they could tell where the Germans were preparing a major military offensive. They first became aware of this when the Germans, in 1940, ordered tens of thousands of bottles to be sent to Romania, where, officially, there was only a small German mission. Within a few days, Romania was invaded by the German army. Afterward, bottles of bubbly were distributed to all the troops, a way of saying to the soldiers that "the Führer thinks of his men first."

From that time on, the Resistance, with help from the major champagne houses, kept meticulous track of where large shipments of champagne were going. Alarm bells went off toward the end of 1941 when the Germans placed a huge order and asked that the bottles be specially corked and packed so that they could be sent to "a very hot country." That country turned out to be Egypt, where Rommel was about to begin his North African campaign. The information was relayed to British intelligence in London.

As the war continued, relations between Klaebisch and de Vogüé deteriorated. Klaebisch felt more and more as though he were being taken advantage of and being "sandbagged" by de Vogüé. He was annoyed that de Vogüé always referred to him as Klaebisch, never Herr Klaebisch or Monsieur Klaebisch or even Captain Klaebisch, just Klaebisch.

But that was a mere irritation. Far more serious was that Klaebisch and other German authorities were becoming more and more convinced that de Vogüé and his colleagues at Moët & Chandon were actively helping the Resistance. Their suspicions were correct.

In the early days of the occupation, Moët & Chandon had been pillaged more than any other champagne house. The Chandon château on the grounds of Dom Pérignon's abbey had been burned down and many other buildings belonging to Moët were taken over to house German troops. To add insult to injury, the company had also been ordered to supply the Third Reich with 50,000 bottles of champagne a week, or about one-tenth of all the champagne the Germans were requisitioning.

"Under those conditions, I and others at Moët, the entire top echelon, couldn't help but resist," said Moët's commercial director, Claude Fourmon.

De Vogüé himself headed the political wing of the Resistance in the eastern region of France. In the early stages of the war, he had argued against an armed resistance that could endanger innocent lives. As the war ground on, however, his feelings began to change and he welcomed the Resistance into Moët's twenty-four kilometers of cellars. "At the very least," said his son Ghislain, "my father turned a blind eye to sabotage and subterfuge, and to tampering with champagne and its shipment."

On November 24, 1943, Robert-Jean de Vogüé asked his cousin René Sabbe to serve as translator for a meeting he and Claude Fourmon were scheduled to have with Klaebisch. Because the recently completed harvest had been so small—and so good—they were hoping to persuade Klaebisch to reduce the amount of champagne he was planning to requisition.

Shortly after they arrived, the telephone rang in an office next to Klaebisch's. A young officer interrupted the meeting to tell the weinführer that the call was for him. Klaebisch excused himself. Within minutes he was back and sat down at his desk, crossing his arms over his potbelly.

"Gentlemen," he said, "that was the Gestapo. You are all under arrest." On cue, several officers with pistols drawn burst through the door and took the three men into custody.

"We were completely stupefied," Fourmon later recalled. "De Vogüé had just persuaded Klaebisch to let houses sell more champagne to French civilians. I don't know exactly what triggered the call but I think the Gestapo wanted to take de Vogüé out of the line of command."

De Vogüé's first reaction was "Let Fourmon go; he knows nothing." He also pleaded for the release of Sabbe, saying he was there only to translate. De Vogüé's appeals were to no avail.

All three were charged with obstructing the trade demands of the Germans and imprisoned. Sabbe was released a few days later because of his age, but Fourmon was sent to Bergen-Belsen, a concentration camp in Germany.

De Vogüé was sentenced to death.

The sentence sent shock waves through Champagne. For the first time in history, the entire industry—growers and producers, labor and management—went on strike. Klaebisch was stunned and, at first, did not know what to do. He branded the strike an "act of terrorism" and warned that force would be used unless it ended immediately. The Champenois ignored him and stepped up their protest.

In the face of such unprecedented action, Klaebisch seemed paralyzed. Calling out troops, he feared, could result in even greater unrest and force the Germans to take over the production of champagne, something he knew they were ill prepared to do.

There was something else Klaebisch feared as well: the spotlight. The last thing he wanted to do was to call attention to himself, especially now when everything seemed to be falling apart. To make matters worse, his brother-in-law and mentor, Joachim von Ribbentrop, had fallen out of favor, and Klaebisch could all too easily picture himself suddenly freezing with other German soldiers on the Russian front.

After more fruitless appeals to the Champenois to end their protest, Klaebisch and the Germans gave in. They agreed to "suspend" de Vogüé's sentence but said they were only doing so because he had five children. Instead, he was put in prison.

Despite his clashes with de Vogüé, this was not what Klaebisch had expected or wanted. "I can well imagine Klaebisch was uncomfortable with my father's arrest," Ghislain de Vogüé said. "I suspect he was just obeying orders he had been given."

But punishment of the champagne industry had only begun. Champagne houses which had supported the strike were hauled before a military tribunal and given a choice. They could pay a heavy fine, 600,000 francs (about one and a half million francs in today's currency), or the head of each house could spend forty days in prison. Nearly all paid the fine.

Moët & Chandon suffered the worst. "They decapitated Moët," Claude Fourmon later said. Nearly all of the top management was sent to prison or concentration camps.

Hoping to discourage further disobedience and justify their crackdown against Moët, Klaebisch and other German authorities produced a propaganda film. It showed faked cases of Moët & Chandon champagne being seized and opened, all of them filled with rifles and other weapons. The film was distributed to movie theaters throughout France and Germany. The Germans also forced French newspapers to run an article saying de Vogüé had been helping "terrorists."

Within a few months, the German Occupation Authority had completely taken over the running of Moët. The man they put in charge was Otto Klaebisch.

My Fall

Roger Scruton

Growing up in the post-war England immortalized by Philip Larkin and Kingsley Amis I rarely encountered grapes or their divine by-product. But something called wine was familiar in our family, and the autumn seldom arrived without the gallon jars of sugared elderberry juice congregating before the brown enamel stove, our mother waiting for the day when the frenzied bubbling would dwindle to a whisper and the dark red liquid could be siphoned off and bottled. For three weeks the kitchen was filled with the yeasty scent of fermentation. Little clouds of fruit-flies hung above the jars and here and there wasps would cluster and shimmer on the spilled pools of juice.

The elder grows wild in our hedgerows, and produces the fragrant flowers which are at their headiest on midsummer nights—exhaling the perfume evoked in Act II of *Die Meistersinger*, as Hans Sachs sits before his cottage, meditating the great problem which, in my experience, wine does more than anything else to solve—the problem of how to turn *eras* into *agape*, how to give up wanting someone, so as to want her happiness instead. Steeped in water, thickened with sugar and citric acid, the elderflower makes an agreeable summer cordial. The dark red berries are almost sugarless, but rich in tannin and pectin. If you boil them, strain off the juice, add sugar and reduce it, the result is a jelly which keeps for years and which adds a sweet crimson halo to the taste of lamb.

However, it is for its wine that the elderberry has been most esteemed by the English. Plum, redcurrant, apple and gooseberry make excellent fruit-wines, still sold commercially in Austria. But none compares with elderberry wine, which, because of its quota of tannin, will mature for several years in bottle, acquiring its own splenetic English finish. The sugar is not provided by the fruit, but must be added to the initial must of water and bruised berries, three pounds to the gallon—to use the old and forbidden language—if you want the result to be dry. Although there are yeasts on the skins, they cause only a slow fermentation. Our mother would therefore stir in a quantity of brewer's yeast, which instantly caused the stalks of clustered berries to rise up and dance at the brim.

When enough colour had been leached from the berries she would pour the foaming torrent from the bucket into the jars, each sealed with a one-way valve to permit the escape of carbon dioxide while forbidding the inflow of oxygen. And the patter of the bubbles soothed our autumn evenings until bottling time, at the start of winter. We would keep the wine for two years, occasionally visiting it in the cellar under the kitchen and holding it to the light to admire the black deposit. When at last a bottle was opened we would take a glass after supper, much as our ancestors took their claret. And the resulting mixture of appreciative grunts and monosyllabic praise was the most interesting wine-talk that I have heard.

Those were happy days in our family: days before our mother's frail self-confidence had crumbled before our father's inexplicable rage. The bitter-sweet dust of elderberries on the tongue brings to mind her gentle face, her shy concern for her children, and the guilt that we rehearse together now, when we recall with tears her unswerving, suffering love for us. Elderberry wine belongs with her, in an England of quirky privations, of home-grown recipes and self-sacrificing kindness, a world in which the grape had yet to cast its spell over the suburbs. My two sisters and I were raised in the shelter of penury and puritanical restraint. And maybe we would have retained the meek decencies of our childhood, had it not been for the great transformation that our generation underwent when the Portuguese brand called Mateus Rosé burst on the scene, along with other breaches of English decorum, around 1963, 'Between the end of the *Chatterley* ban/ And the Beatles' first LP', as Philip Larkin famously put it (though in another connection). Then

> The earnest trumpet spake, and silver thrills
> From kissing cymbals made a merry din—
> 'Twas Bacchus and his kin!
> Like to a moving vintage down they came,
> Crown'd with green leaves, and faces all on flame;
> All madly dancing through the pleasant valley,
> To scare thee, Melancholy!

Maybe Keats should not have rhymed 'melancholy' with 'valley'; but he certainly knew something about the effects of wine. We rushed ignorantly into the stream that had suddenly bubbled up in our quiet streets; we bathed in its fresh aroma, and gulped down its gift of dreams. I went up to Cambridge, one of the lucky few with a college scholarship. And despite this financial resource, wine kept me in poverty.

But I drank without knowledge, ignorant of the priests that Bacchus has spread around our world, and who pursue their calling in places which can be discovered by accident but seldom by design. During my summer vacations from Cambridge I sometimes stayed with Desmond, a witty Irishman who had read everything, slept with everyone, spent whatever he could, and was recovering in a village near Fontainebleau. It took a little time to discover that Desmond was an ordained priest of Bacchus, since his doctor had advised restraint in the matter of alcohol. Desmond had interpreted this to mean first-growth clarets at dinner, and maybe second-growth at lunch. His doctor, he felt certain, would particularly approve of the Château Trotanoy 1945, made from the last grapes to escape the plague of phylloxera, which had such an improving effect on a frail constitution when drunk alone after dinner. Desmond held that such wines would be quite insulting to the medical condition of his young guest, whose untutored taste-buds and anaemic bloodstream were clearly crying out for Beaujolais. I gratefully drank what was offered, and felt sorry for Desmond, that his life was so bound by dreary medicinal routines.

Still, I couldn't help being a little curious about this bottle which Desmond would hug to himself in the library after dinner. The enigmatic name, the faded label, the frail tenacious hands that closed around the bottle, all emphasized the mystery. Finding Desmond asleep one day in his armchair, I quietly relieved him of his treasure and was granted for the first time the indescribable experience that comes when the aroma of a great vintage wafts above the glass, and the lips tremble in anticipation as though on the brink of a fatal kiss. I was about to fall in love—not with a flavour or a plant or a drug but with a hallowed piece of France. That bottle from which I had unfurled the loving hands contained a glinting, mahogany-coloured liquid, an intoxicating aroma, a subtle and many-layered flavour, but also something more precious than all of these, summarized in the ancient and inscrutable names of Trotanoy, the château, and Pomerol, the place. I was overwhelmed by the sense of this drink as the distillation of a place, a time and a culture.

I learned thereafter to love the wines of France, village by village, vineyard by vineyard, while retaining only the vaguest idea of the grapes used to make them, and with no standard of comparison that would tell me whether those grapes, planted in other soils and blessed by other place-names, would produce a similar effect. From the moment of my fall, I was a *terroiriste*, for whom the principal ingredient in any bottle is the soil.

By 'soil' I do not mean only the physical mix of limestone, topsoil and humus. I mean the soil as Jean Giono, Giovanni Verga or D. H. Lawrence would describe it: nurse of passions, stage of dramas, and habitat of local gods. The deities from which the villages of France take their names—whether pagan, as in Mercurey and Juliénas, or Christian, as in St Amour and St Joseph—are the guardians of vines that have acquired their character not only from the minerals that they suck from the rocks beneath them, but also from the sacrificial rites of lasting communities. That thought was intimated by my first sip of Ch. Trotanoy, and it is a thought that has remained with me to this day. But the concept of *terroir* has now become highly controversial, as more and more people follow the path to perdition that I trod those forty-five years ago. Poetry, history, the calendar of saints, the suffering of martyrs—such things are less important to the newly flush generation of winos than they were to us lower middle-class pioneers. Today's pagan drinkers are in search of the uniform, the reliable and the easily remembered. As for where the wine comes from, what does it matter, so long as it tastes OK? Hence the tendency to classify wines in terms of the brand and the grape varietal, either ignoring the soil entirely, or including it under some geological category like chalk, clay, marl or gravel. In short, the new experience of wine is that of drinking the fermented juice of a grape. But that was not my experience on that fatal day in Fontainebleau: with my nose rubbing the nose of Trotanoy I was coming face to face with a vineyard. There in the glass was the soil of a place, and in that soil was a soul.

Wine criticism, as we know it today, was the invention of a literary critic, Professor George Saintsbury, who published his pioneering *Notes on a Cellar-Book* in 1920. Not a single grape varietal is mentioned in that book, which dwells on the vineyards, villages and vintages represented in the Professor's cellar over a full drinking life. Saintsbury does not treat his reader to 'tasting notes', which he dismisses as 'wine slang'. A wine, for him, was an individual, not to be assimilated to a type or a brand; each taste was the inimitable signature of a place and the traditions established there, among which the choice of grape is only one. And in my view (which I shall later try to justify) wine should always be approached in this way, if it is to open the way to serious meditation. 'Nothing makes the future so rosy,' Napoleon remarked, 'as to contemplate it through a glass of Chambertin', and we instantly respond to the sentiment. But suppose he had said 'nothing makes the future so rosy, as to contemplate it through a glass of Pinot Noir'? The word 'contemplate' would have lost its resonance, and the remark, no longer associating the greatest risk-taker of his day with a tranquil plot of earth in Burgundy, would have been flushed clean of its pathos and its spiritual truth.

Desmond owned a flat in an inner courtyard off the Rue Molière.
The sun never penetrated into this courtyard, and Desmond's windows opened onto dark gullies which would fill each midday with
the smell of fried garlic and the shouts of homecoming men. On my
visits to Paris I occupied the inner room. It had no windows, and I
would spend the day lying on the bed that filled the space, holding
under the bedside light one or other of the books that lined the walls.
I became as lost in French literature in that darkened room as I had
been lost in French wine in the darkened library at Fontainebleau.
The literature and the wine seemed to me to be different manifes-
tations of the same idea. The bohemian poet, weaving his *paradis
artificiel* in the city garret, was connected by unseen spiritual threads
to the walled garden of sun-swollen grapes—the natural paradise
from which he had fled.

But why had he fled? What did this city bring that the countryside lacked—that countryside so exactingly described by Balzac
and Zola? Turning the leather-bound pages of Baudelaire, Verlaine,
Nerval and Rimbaud, and then those of Apollinaire, Leiris, Eluard
and Pouge in their plain white Gallimard covers—covers so flattering to the reader, in their implication that there is no need to
explain what he will find between them—I arrived at an idea of
Paris. I associated this idea with Desmond, believing that it had
brought him to the city many years before, in search of the thing
that can be found only where solitude and society flourish side by
side, where erotic dreams compete with weary disillusion, and where
the sounds and sights of ordinary bourgeois life prick the observing
consciousness with sudden sharp regrets—and that thing is the self.
Desmond had come to Paris after the war, with the remains of a
squandered fortune, and an omnivorous sexual appetite, in order to
waste his inheritance and confront himself. And, because for all his
profligacy he had a heart of gold, he was rescued by the good woman
who could care for him, who took him down to Fontainebleau, to
make a home for him and the children of his failed marriages—and
a home too for me, who had fallen for one of those children and
then been dumped by her.

And maybe that was what I too would find in Paris—this elusive thing, myself, the thing that Rimbaud sent in his *bateau ivre* across imaginary seas, though in fact to Paris and into the arms of Verlaine, the thing that Desmond had confronted in that sombre, windowless closet in the city's heart, and which I too hoped to confront, maybe while reading Baudelaire in that very closet or through some encounter achieved in the zinc-topped bar by the *porte cochère* below.

And then one day a living poet came to stay in Desmond's flat. His name was Yves de Bayser:* a distillation of the erotic and the aristocratic that ought to have marked out a place for him in any literary circle. He was still young, tall and good-looking. He had been befriended by René Char and Albert Camus. But his *Églogues du Tyran* had attracted no notice from the critics, his love-life was in disarray, and he sat motionless in the corner, wearing dark glasses from under which the tears made snail-tracks down his large red cheeks.

It was clear that Yves had come to stay and, on my visits from Fontainebleau, I did my best to talk to him. When at last I broached the question of his troubles, he responded with a description of his childhood in the Valois, imbuing it with the claustrophobic atmosphere of Châteaubriand's *Memoires d'outre-tombe*. He got as far as the quarrel between mother and father and then said '*mais tout ça c'est bien loin*' and left off with a sigh. Each time I broached the topic the response was the same: a careful narrative, breaking off at that impassable point, with the words '*tout ça c'est bien loin*'. After a while I began to think of him as the soul of Desmond's flat. He did not read or write, but sat among the books as though personifying their meaning. He acknowledged all my opinions with a gentle nod of the head, as though he had for a long time struggled against the orthodox view of Baudelaire, Rimbaud, Aragon or whoever and finally admitted defeat. He was a symbol, to me, of literary suffering; and if anyone was on the way to discovering himself, in the peculiar circumstances made available by Paris, it was surely Yves, who seemed to have everything needed for the task. He had suffered and

* Pronounced *baisère*, not *baiser*, for obvious reasons.

was suffering; he was absorbing the ineffable Parisian loneliness in the quality darkness of Desmond's *echt-*bohemian flat; he was in the middle of the city, surrounded by the cries and rumbles of bourgeois normality; and he never ventured into the street. He had published a book of poems, in one of those plain white covers which are such incontrovertible proof of a distinguished soul. He had loved, and been loved by, both men and women. And he had created his childhood on the models of Châteaubriand and Proust. Yet there was something missing.

It didn't take much to understand what it was. I had seen Yves make himself a sandwich or a cup of coffee. But I had never seen him drink a glass of wine. I reported this to Desmond, who informed me that Yves was a reformed alcoholic, who would not touch the demon drink in any form. In consequence his melancholy had become static, congealed, an immovable deposit in the base of his mind, with all ideas and longings trapped beneath it.

By now I had advanced my apprenticeship to the point of rounding off each day in Paris with a glass of white wine, and developing a certain taste for Muscadet. I kept a bottle of it in the refrigerator at Rue Molière and, visiting the flat one day, Desmond was appalled to discover me pouring this slug-coloured liquid into a glass. He hurried to the nearest Nicolas, returning with a bottle of Puligny-Montrachet, and some ice to cool it. This wine proved as great a revelation as that stolen glass of Trotanoy, rising to meet me like a flower in the glass, its buttery petals enclosing a crystal radiance of apple-flavoured fruit. And once again I associated this complexity and clarity of flavour with the soul of the soil. The name of the wine too had charm, though it was a long time before I learned the meaning of that hyphenated 'Montrachet'. All other white wines that I had encountered seemed insignificant in comparison with that simple Puligny from Nicolas, and indeed my nose-to-nose encounter with the village of Puligny-Montrachet was far more influential even than my visit in the glass to Trotanoy. On returning to Cambridge I brought with me a love of white Burgundy and a belief in its attributes which was in no way diminished by my ignorance of the grape, the way of life and the viticulture inherent in the place to which I was attached. Like one who has fallen in love at first sight, I had full and privileged knowledge of the object of my affections, and needed no information from any source beside my own intoxicated senses. And if, in my subsequent travels in France, I have never visited Burgundy this love of mine is the explanation. I know the place too well to be able to face what it has no doubt suffered from the trampling of affluent tourists.

Desmond was an affectionate rouè, who did much to loosen in me the restraints of a puritan upbringing. But during my under-graduate years I encountered another of Bacchus's priests who was, by contrast, as buttoned up as a priest can be. Coming from our local grammar to a college dominated by self-confident boys from Eton and Harrow, bearing a scholarship in a subject that I abhorred, and finding myself in a suite of chill bare Victorian rooms at the start of the coldest winter on record, my first instinct had been to run away. It was an instinct that I could not act upon since there was nowhere to run to, I having already run away from home nine months before in one of those definitive adolescent gestures which I was planning at some stage to revoke, though I never in fact got round to it. There was nothing for it but to go to this old geezer who had been appointed *in loco parentis* and to tell him that I was not going to read natural sciences, that the thought of crystallography, biochemistry and microbiology filled me with disgust, that there must surely be some other subject—Chinese, for instance—that would answer to my bohemian yearnings without damaging my brain, and that in any case if he didn't come up with something better I was leaving the college that night, so there.

My agitated knock was greeted with silence. Listening carefully I discerned a faint, mouse-like scraping somewhere behind the door. After a while I realized that the sound was music—though music played so softly that it was like music remembered, rather than music heard. I knocked again and, after a short pause, was greeted with a quiet 'come in'. Bursting through the door like the proverbial bull I found myself in a china shop, surrounded by precious vases, delicate musical instruments and a hundred polished and fragile things, among which none appeared more fragile or more polished than the *loco* himself—a large porcelain head which turned faint blue eyes in my direction from behind a clavichord, on the keys of which his beautiful ivory hands were resting.

'You are my tutor,' I blurted out, overcome with confusion.

Dr Picken looked at me silently.

'I feared as much,' he said at last.

'I need to talk to you.'

He got up from the clavichord and quietly closed the lid. With slow studied gestures, like a bomb-disposal expert, he turned and tiptoed to his desk, from where he gestured me towards an armchair. I stood by it, not sitting, and delivered my prepared speech. He winced every now and then at some particularly coarse turn of phrase, but otherwise remained seated, motionless behind a neat array of pens, papers and green jade dragons. When I had finished and after a moment's silence during which he studied me apprehensively, he quietly addressed the problem, as though speaking to himself and in a voice so soft that I had to strain to overhear him.

'I cannot recommend Chinese,' he said. 'It is a language I happen to know, collection of languages I should say, and requires an immense amount of work and dedication. We can rule out English since obviously you will read those books in any case, and that really leaves no choice save history or moral sciences. Not that I approve of either.'

'What,' I asked, 'are moral sciences?'

'Well may you ask. It is the traditional Cambridge name for philosophy.'

'Moral sciences, then,' I instantly decided.

Dr Picken sighed reproachfully.

'We admit you young men to read the natural sciences, which are, you know, the greatest legacy of this university, and you can never stay the course.'

'Would *you*?' I asked, looking around at the books and instruments, the scrolls and vases, and assuming myself to be in the presence of a distinguished orientalist.

'I did,' he replied.

'You mean you are a scientist?' I asked incredulously. He nodded. 'I branched out a bit,' he added. 'But I stayed the course.'

I eagerly accepted the glass of sherry which he poured from a decanter. He told me about his work in cytology, concerning which he had written a large book. I asked to see it, and turning over the pages I saw that the last chapter was entitled 'Envoi', a word that I knew from Ezra Pound's Cavalcanti translations. I looked across at Dr Picken with renewed interest. This old geezer was clearly not *loco* at all; nor was he so very old. I asked him what he thought of Ezra Pound. He responded with a shy but authoritative lecture on the Confucian Odes. Pound's inaccuracies in the translation, he told me, were off-set by some real felicities in the feeling. He went on to talk about the Noh plays, indicating without stating it that he knew Japanese as well. And when at last I was convinced that this man was quite the most learned person I had ever met and that I ought to take his advice, he got up slowly, and said,

'Moral sciences it is, then. I will send you to Dr Ewing.'

His manner was somehow precarious, and it became clear to me that I was intruding, that I had been intruding all along, that only a carefully nurtured veneer of politeness had enabled him to carry on a conversation with me, and that his interrupted session at the clavichord had probably been going on in his mind throughout our talk. I left with a note for Dr Ewing, and so began my career as a philosopher.

Dr Picken was a conscientious tutor, who refused quite categorically to make favourites of his pupils, and who invited us all to dinner, five at a time, once a year. I know that I was a trouble to him, often visiting him at unauthorized hours for an emergency *exeat*, which he would grant while looking at me from distant and fearful eyes, as though not sure whether I was tricking him into complicity in some crime about which he would rather not know. He retreated from emotion, and would not allow me to express it. And sometimes, passing his room in the evenings, and seeing him seated at the clavichord, or at the lovely old chamber organ on which he played the Chorale Preludes of Bach, I would have the sense of a creature so fragile that merely to touch him would cause him to fall in fragments to the floor.

I can still remember the conversation with which Dr Picken advanced me to the next stage of my career as a wino. He had cheered me up with some Burgundy left over from one of his dinners and we were standing in his little kitchen, as neat and clean as every other part of his museum-like rooms, as he carefully washed up—it being intolerable to him to see a dirty glass polluting the chair-side table. He turned to look at me—which he rarely did—and all of a sudden his round face shone with a divine radiance.

'I should tell you,' he said, 'that the Burgundy you have just drunk was not very good. In fact commercialization has more or less destroyed the region, and people of your generation will probably never know Burgundy as we knew it. With one exception. There is a small Domaine in Vosne-Romanée called Domaine de la Romanée-Conti. If you ever come across it you should drink it. It has the perfect balance of stalk and fruit, and the soil speaks through it too. Nobody else now knows how to make wine like that.' And after holding my astonished gaze for a moment, he as suddenly looked away, clearly wondering whether he should have made so blatant a display of his apostolate.

This opinion was delivered to me in 1964, when Romanée-Conti was probably twice as expensive as other *grands crus*. In this as in everything Dr Picken's opinion was also knowledge.* The Domaine, whose 4 acres of ancient vines have been prayed over for centuries by the monks of St Vivant, is now recognized, following seven centuries of mortal determination and divine intervention, as the greatest vineyard on the Côte d'Or. I remembered Dr Picken's little speech, and was able to repeat it at all kinds of gatherings where knowledge about good wine was rewarded with a glass of it. But it

---

* Saintsbury was of the same opinion as Dr Picken: 'It is the fashion . . . to put Clos-Vougeot at the head of all Burgundies, and very delicious Clos-Vougeot can be; but I never drank any specimen thereof equal to the 1858 Romanée Conti for the combination of intensity and delicacy in bouquet and flavour, for body, colour and every good quality of wine'. *Notes on a Cellar-Book*, London 1920, pp. 54–5.

was forty years before I tasted Romanée-Conti, and by this time it was fifty times the price of other serious Burgundies.

I found myself at a professional tasting organized by Corney and Barrow, the London merchant with exclusive British rights to the Domaine's wines. I stood among silent, long-faced Masters of Wine, in a room of hospital aspect, with clean white shelves, decanters, glasses and each wall lined with taps and sinks. I watched the expert Adam's apples trembling on the expert necks, and listened in awe to the wine as it slurped and gurgled around those distinguished palates, to be suddenly and peremptorily spat into the sink—a hundred quid's worth with every gob!

I encountered for the first time the real suffering of the wine writer. For how can you swirl something around in your mouth with a beatified expression on your face, knowing that its going price is £1,500 a bottle, and then just scribble 'damned good' on your note-pad? I saw the crumpled brows as they strove to lengthen their paragraphs, to Parkerize here and cauterize there, and in one way or another to excuse the horrible crime of throwing the entire monthly cost of the family mortgage down the sink. I struggled for a long time to describe the Grands Échézeaux, and eventually came up with: 'Saint-Saëns's 2nd cello concerto: deep tenor notes behind a sylph-like veil'. I looked at the description for a while, and then crossed it out, revolted by its affectation, and wrote 'damned good' instead. And whether those paragraphs of flimsy winespeak, with their mixed metaphors and far-fetched analogies, ever mean more than that is one of the deep and difficult questions that I address in Chapter 6.

How can anyone afford this wine? 'Easy,' said Corney and Barrow's Adam Brett-Smith, 'Romanée-Conti is the only wine you can reliably drink for free: just compare the *en primeur* price with the price today.' Sure enough, it was on sale in 2003 for £3,500 for six, and a year later, on the day when I drank it, for £8,400. You could have bought a dozen in 2003, sold six in 2004, keeping six bottles for yourself and £1,400 profit. And you would have the added comfort of knowing that you were robbing the rich. The only problem, of course, is to find that initial £7,000.

Dr Picken, I am sure, could never have spent on wine the money needed to buy the last extant example of the Anatolian reed-flute; and in any case, in his day Romanée-Conti was affordable (sort of). Dr Picken was, in fact, frugal in his habits, and the very image of the bachelor don, who had retreated from life in order to immerse himself in learning. Wine was part of that learning, and the pleasure that he took in it was inseparable from the knowledge that shone from the meniscus. For those who have dedicated their lives, and who have put *eros* to one side, wine provides a solace that endows the hard-edged armour of scholarship with a soft lining of pleasure.

Dr Picken typified the osmotic process whereby a cultural and intellectual inheritance was transmitted within college walls. Provided you approached him with a humility equal to that which he constantly displayed, you could pick up from him any amount of knowledge on any number of subjects—from the wave structure of the benzene ring to the translation of Dante, from Frazer's theory of magic to the chronology of the Upanishads—and the very irrelevance to the surrounding world of everything he knew made the learning of it all the more rewarding. He justified, in my eyes, the rigorous monasticism that had been nurtured by the Cambridge colleges, living as he did in permanent retreat from ephemera. His attitude to learning was the very opposite of that which has come to dominate the schools and universities today. He did not believe that the purpose of knowledge is to help the student. On the contrary. For Dr Picken, the purpose of the student is to help knowledge. He was throughout his life the willing and self-sacrificing trustee of an intellectual inheritance. Young people mattered to him because they had the brains into which his reservoir of learning could be poured, along with the wine. He looked at us students sceptically, but always with that underlying hope that, in this or that undisciplined young face, there was yet the outward sign of a brain large enough and dispassionate enough to capture some of the accumulated knowledge of mankind, and which could carry that knowledge through life without spilling it, until finding another brain into which it might be discharged.

I learned from Dr Picken, therefore, that wine is not just an object of pleasure, but an object of knowledge; and the pleasure depends on the knowledge. Unlike every other product that is now manufactured for the table, wine exists in as many varieties as there are people who produce it. Variations in technique, climate, grape, soil and culture ensure that wine is, to the ordinary drinker, the most unpredictable of drinks, and to the connoisseur the most intricately informative, responding to its origins like a game of chess to its opening move. And precisely because there is nothing—nothing *immediate* that is—to be done with the knowledge contained in wine, Dr Picken had acquired it, just as he had acquired knowledge of Japanese *gagaku*, of the semantics of modal logic, of the metrical structure of the Andalusian *qasida*, and of quantum effects in the pre-frontal cortex. He taught me not just to think without relevance, but to drink without it too. Only in that way do you subvert the rule of mere opinion, and place knowledge on its throne.

It is thanks to people like Dr Picken that Bacchus has been duly honoured in our colleges, and it was to one of those colleges, Peterhouse, that I proceeded in due course as a Fellow, bringing with me, however, the disreputable baggage of a bohemian life that included everything, from guitar to girlfriend, that Dr Picken would have observed with distress. Peterhouse had an excellent cellar, where classed-growth clarets lay dreaming through the years, to be made available to the Fellows at a fraction of their market value. I arrived there in 1969, fresh from the *événements de mai* which I had witnessed in Paris, and in response to which I had discovered my vocation as an intellectual pariah. The long march through the institutions was proceeding apace, the Marxizing of the curriculum had been more or less achieved, and the only good thing remaining about collegiate life, so far as I could see, were the cellars—though these too were threatened, the office of Peterhouse Cellar-Master having been bestowed on a cheery American leftist who was rapidly auctioning off these symbols of class privilege and capitalist decay.

At the end of my first year there arrived among the Fellows another pariah called David Watkin, an architectural historian notorious for his habit of wearing a collar and tie. He had been described to me as an evil reactionary, an enemy of social progress and enlightenment, who would do his best to thwart the ambitions of those Fellows who were striving to meet the educational challenges of the twentieth century. This description so warmed me to the unknown Dr Watkin that I immediately went to call on him in the rooms which he had been assigned in St Peter's Terrace, on the staircase next to mine. I was astonished to discover that he had already transformed the day-quarters of the dingy don who had previously occupied them to the chambers of a Regency gentleman, with furnishings, prints and ornaments that might have been rescued from a great estate, and a great disaster. It had the air of someone who had fallen from the heights of inherited affluence and who was struggling to maintain himself in elegant decline.

The impression was enhanced by the presence of my third priest of Bacchus, the former Catholic chaplain to the university, Monsignor Gilbey, meticulously dressed in the style of an Anglican clergyman of Jane Austen's day, crouching forward in a bergère chair as though interrupted in the course of a confessional. Dr Watkin himself was dressed in a three-piece suit and starched collar, from which his thin neck rose like a fluted column, bearing a head of Doric severity which, however, on my explaining my identity, broke into a thin Ionic smile. I was introduced to the Monsignor, who confined his adverse judgement of my bohemian dress to a rapid sweep of the eyes, and then rose to take me by the hand as though welcoming the Prodigal Son. The two of them began to talk with a kind of Firbankian allusiveness of the appalling nature of Dr Watkin's new surroundings, and the dialogue between them, in which I was included as a sympathetic audience, could have been conducted by two out-of-work actors, consoling themselves with their favourite Noel Coward roles.

And indeed, as I came to know them better, I came to understand both of them as accomplished thespians, who had chosen their roles and chosen to be meticulously faithful to them. To say this is not to make a criticism. On the contrary, it is testimony to their great strength of character that, having understood the moral and aesthetic chaos of the world into which they were born, they each of them recognized that there is only one honest response to it, which is to live your life as an example. This is what Alfred Gilbey was to David Watkin; and it is what David Watkin has been to me. As I got to know him, and as the smile with which he greeted me advanced from that original Ionic thinness to a positively Corinthian gaiety, I found myself roused first to admiration and then to wonder that a person should be able to live as David lived, his deeply romantic sensibility confined in a dramatic role entirely devoted to the classical idea. He had absorbed that idea from the Monsignor, who taught that chaos lies all around us, and that our first duty is to impose upon it whatever order—spiritual, moral, aesthetic—it can bear. The alternative to order is not freedom, which is a form of order and its highest purpose, but disorder, randomness and decay. This was a thought that I too had retrieved, though from the smoke-filled, glass-spattered streets of Paris in 1968 rather than the country mansion, now an estate of council houses, in which the Monsignor had been raised. When David and I sat down—as we often did thereafter—over a bottle of claret, it was to drink to the divine orderliness that sped from the bottle, and to lament the chaos all around. David's room was a refuge from the modern world; and no refuge, he believed, is complete without claret: a theorem which we proved conclusively, and many times over, from the premises provided by Peterhouse cellar, which included a sublime Château Palmer 1962, a Château Léoville-Lascases from the same year and a Grands Échézeaux 1961 which David would drink only if there was no claret on offer, believing that gentlemen do not drink Burgundy after dinner.

David was one of many friends made in my brief time as a don. However, in all respects relevant to the donnish life I was abnormal: right-wing, proletarian, heterosexual—any one of those defects would have raised suspicion, but to possess them all suggested a reckless disregard for proprieties. I left as soon as I could for London, taking with me a few cases of 1961 claret. But I kept in touch with Monsignor Gilbey, and would sometimes dine with him. And under his tuition my understanding of wine took another great leap forward.

Although the Monsignor was a priest of Bacchus, he was also an apostle of Christ and a devotee of order in all its forms. He spent less time seared at his special table than kneeling in his private chapel (both situated, as it happens, in the Travellers' Club in Pall Mall). Convinced that it is in the nature of truth to give offence, he lived in a small, charmed circle of recusants, secure in the belief that 'in my Father's house there are many mansions', so that death would not, after all, be a social disaster.

Two sounds above all, he remarked, attach us to this vale of tears: the cry of beagles on a lively scent, and the pop of claret from the bottle. He was as unmusical as he was politically incorrect; but he was right about claret. The shape of the bottle combines with the texture of the wine to produce a sibilant bubbling, somewhere between a murmur and a kiss. Maybe this justifies claret's otherwise peculiar English name (applied to the wines of Gascony when Gascony was the merrier part of England, and when it was only the light red *clairet* that was shipped).

Gilbey held that claret is to be drunk for preference after a meal. The wine should fall onto a full stomach, and rise again as discourse. This idea originates in the symposium of the Greeks, to whom we owe the proverb *oinos kai aletheia*, wine and truth, which became *in vino veritas* when the Romans took over. Claret still has this aura for me, of a wine to be not swilled but meditated, and always in good company—which does not, of course, preclude drinking it alone, if your own company reaches the required standard (which, after a glass or two, I find, mine does).

The Gilbey family is famous for its gin; but they also own Château Loudenne, a bourgeois growth in the Médoc, acquired in 1875, a few years after the Rothschild family acquired Château Lafite and a few years before the whole region was devastated by phylloxera. The Monsignor, in dedicating his life to Christ, had never doubted that his soul had also been improved by claret, and by the civil dialogue that claret induces in its devotees. His second priesthood therefore fitted naturally behind the first. He knew exactly how to choose from a wine list the unassuming claret which, like his own Loudenne, would make no boastful claims for itself, either on the label or in the glass, which would suggest neither wealth in the purchaser nor ignorance in the guest, and which would rise from the glass with that fresh savour and smiling address that is never more evident than in the better *crus bourgeois*—not Loudenne only, but the exquisite Château Villegeorge or the robust Château Potensac, with their simple *appellations* of Haut-Médoc and plain Médoc. It is, Gilbey taught, in the inner landscape created by these modest clarets, that the soul of the drinker most often encounters the soul of the drink. They are conversational wines, wines to be listened to; and they provided the 'third that walked beside us' when the Monsignor explained to me the orthodoxies of the Catholic faith, and the hierarchies which they seemed, in his beatific vision, to demand of us. I did not go along with what he said, but I wrote of his character and philosophy much later, in *Gentle Regrets*, remembering with gratitude and affection a man who, on the narrow path marked out for him, went always forward, his bright eyes fixed on the horizon where his Saviour stood.

Of the 1961 clarets that I brought with me to London, I drank only a single bottle. Following marital breakdown they accompanied me, my sole capital, to a flat in Notting Hill, to be stored in the damp cellar beneath the road. The labels fell off, so that it proved impossible to auction them when divorce and the taxman required it. Luckily, however, a good friend and fellow lover of white Burgundy, Antonia Fraser, was at the time initiating her husband to be, Harold Pinter, into the higher liturgy of Bacchus. She was able to persuade Harold that no cellar would be complete without a stock of 1961 clarets, even if their identity had to be taken on trust from a far from trustworthy philosopher. Harold bought the lot, and generously invited me to share the first of them—a Croizet-Bages. We sat together for an hour, on either side of the only thing we ever agreed about, our thoughts fixed on the ambrosial liquid in which we hid our awkward smiles.

One treasure from my Cambridge years, however, remained with me. Somehow I had managed to acquire a bottle of 1945 Château Lafite—the greatest year from the greatest of clarets. I judged it too good to share, except with that special person whom I had never met, and too good to drink alone unless to mark some new beginning, some break in the scheme of things which I could hardly hope to recognize before it was past. So the bottle accompanied me through life's turmoils like a talisman. I sank often, and drank much. But at a certain point began the steady upward climb that I describe in *On Hunting*—the climb which led from my initial position, as an arrogant outcast in a university whose name I disgraced, to my final destination as a contrite and undistinguished follower of foxhounds. I learned of a tiny sheep farm in Wiltshire, whose lady owner wished to sell. It was autumn when I visited the place. Before the hearth sat a woman with a gentle face and quiet demeanour, tending the gallon jars that stood by the cast-iron stove. I listened to the bubbles as they danced in the valves, and studied the wasp-edged puddles on the tiles. I had come home.

A month later the farm was mine, and I celebrated this unexpected good fortune by sitting alone to drink my treasure, looking in amazement across an ancient pasture towards Sam the Horse, the one creature whose opinions were reliably more conservative than mine.

It is fruitless to attempt to describe the flavour of Lafite. Its effect on the nose, the tongue and the palate cannot be captured in words, nor should we view with anything but contempt the new habit, associated with American wine critics like Robert Parker, of assigning points to each bottle as though in a hard-run race to victory. To assign points to a claret is like assigning points to symphonies—as though Beethoven's 7th, Tchaikovsky's 6th, Mozart's 39th, Bruckner's 8th all hovered between 90 and 95. So let me conclude this brief survey of my apprenticeship with the real reasons for esteeming that bottle of 45 Lafite. Not only was it priceless and irreplaceable, so that pulling the cork was a final goodbye to a mistaken path. It also prompted me to order and unfold my thoughts, to take things gently and in proper sequence, to look back over failure in a spirit of forgiveness and to face the future with no thought of success. The wine catalysed those thoughts, but it did not cause them: for they had their origin in me, and in all that I had been holding within myself and forbidding, until this moment, to take shape as *Selbstbestimmung*. I came to see that we receive by giving, and that my good fortune would be incomplete if not shared. I needed to shake myself free of pettiness and resentment, and to count my blessings, whose flavour was distilled in the glass from which I sipped. And I was permitted, now, to cast my thoughts back, beyond the years of foolish self-assertion, to those evenings of peace and penury, when the fruit flies hung above the gallon jars, and our mother busied herself with the small rituals of home. Was it surprising that, with my mind so softened, I was soon to meet the special person with whom this bottle might have been shared?

WINE

Jim Harrison

I have seventy-seven wine stories; better yet, call them modest epiph-
anies. As the century wanes into the banality of a new millennium
(who holds what watch?), I consider the great inventions of the past.
Naturally one must include electricity and toilet paper, and exclude
computers of all varieties, but near the top of the products of the
human imagination, like an ancient deity that is so omnipresent it
has become invisible, is the corkscrew.

Of course, we all know that some vintners are so greedy they
would rather use old rags than the sacred cork tree, but then people
of intelligence have had quite enough of this economic fascism, this
trough of venality that is the global economy, and have resisted.
The simple physical act of opening a bottle of wine has brought
more happiness to the human race than all of the governments in
the history of the earth. Even organized religions are mere spiritual
mousetraps compared to the *pop* of the cork, the delicious squeak
when you loosen it from the firm grip of the corkscrew. And then
the grandeur of the burble as we fill the glass, the very same sound
we hear at the source, the wombs of all the rivers on earth.

That said, we must go to the particular; it is fruitless to keep
chattering about women in general when they can be comprehended
only on an individual basis, and then partially at best. Whether it
is women or wine our gifts of intelligence are limited, but it is this
specific charm of the immutable that fuels our existence. Taste is a
mystery that best finds its voice in wine.

At this very moment I'm a bit nervous because there is a gale on Lake Superior, and the wind is so severe that a large white pine has toppled in the backyard of my cabin. The marine forecast on the radio states that the waves will reach between twenty and twenty-four feet and that the gale will last another full day. Stepping outside for a moment, I can hear the roar of Lake Superior though it is three miles downriver from this cabin. What can I do about the surrounding forest that is now twisting in the wind? Why, have my first glass of wine of the day. I pull the cork of a Lirac, the gift of a friend. The cork sound counters the shuddering walls of the log cabin. As I drink the first glass rather quickly, my metal Weber grill is blown over in the yard. The Lirac is very good, if a bit midrange, but such is its power that the storm becomes acceptable. At least I'm not in a boat. Another smaller tree falls and my dog barks. I'd offer her a glass but she doesn't care for wine. I read from a volume of Chinese poetry. The bottle slowly empties itself. Now the gale is only a gale. It's outside, and I'm inside. Three blue jays at the feeder are ignoring the storm and its sixty-knot winds. If I went outside with a full glass there would be waves on the surface of my wine. Instead, I prepare some duck confit for my dinner.

Acute fear is a peculiar emotion, always a surprise in it suddenness and power. Several years ago, flying home from Montana with my wife, we boarded a small propeller plane in Minneapolis much delayed by thunderstorms. Finally, the impatient pilot took off and half-way through the flight, when we were out over Lake Michigan, we collided with the storm, which couldn't be avoided by flying north or south. The plane twirled on an invisible pivot, bucked like a rodeo horse, then stood on its tail with wings flapping like the rare anhinga bird, which resembles an airborne serpent. The passengers moaned and hooted and vomited like doomed owls. I'd like to say I was fearless but it would be a pointless lie. I'd planned on strangling the impetuous pilot, but when we reached Traverse City he emerged from the cockpit soaked with sweat and with an utterly tortured expression of apology.

We reached home after midnight and my wife went promptly to bed. I was still trembling from having kissed death's ass and fetched two wines from the cellar, a Migoua and a Tourtine Bandol from Lulu Peyraud's Domaine Tempier. I slowly drank both of these superb bottles while meditating on the essential criminality of flight and on how even birds have the wit not to fly into thunderstorms. After a short while, this blessed Bandol began to take over and I again realized that we are only flowers for the void. Finally the wine swept me back to Provence in late April, where I had eaten and drunk so happily at Lulu Peyraud's house after we'd knelt in the courtyard by the grave of her husband, Lucien, who had created this splendid wine. By the time I went to bed, the flight had become merely another tidbit of horror to file in the brain, detoxified so nobly by the wine. Despite their frequent strikes, I fly Air France to Europe because it serves interesting wines, the only palliative for the blasphemy of flight.

Naturally, we save our best bottles to celebrate or commemorate. Some twenty years ago, by sheer luck, I was able to buy a private collection for a modest price. A man had a liver problem, but for personal reasons he did not want to sell his wines to a restaurant. I heard about it and moved quickly, and have placed the experience up near funding my remote cabin in Michigan's Upper Peninsula and our little winter casita near the Mexican border. Buying this collection, now mostly dissipated, allowed me to drink some wines that writers are only rarely allowed to approach for financial reasons, and also to treat friends. Guy de la Valdene, a dear friend and the primary wine guide of my life, was at my house for bird hunting on the eve of going off for very serious surgery. We sat at my kitchen counter and gently drank two bottles of 1953 Richebourg. On another occasion, when Guy made *salmis de bécasse*, we drank several bottles of Grands-Échezeaux, his father's favorite wine. And just a week ago, the night before Guy left following our annual grouse and woodcock hunt, we had a splendid 1967 Latour, the best Latour of my life except for the 1949 I shared with my daughter on the night before she was married, along with the 1961 Lafite-Rothschild we had had earlier with dinner.

Such bottles truly resonate in the memory, growing even more overwhelming as they distance themselves with the years. I close my eyes and let my taste memory become vivid, somewhat like a sex fantasy that makes your hair stand on end and goose bumps rise on your arms. Now that I no longer write screenplays, my tastes have necessarily had to become more modest, and I have to depend on the kindness of friends and strangers with bigger wallets. I have in the past few years developed a taste for about thirty different Côtes-du-Rhônes, though naturally some of the most expensive ones, like Crozes-Hermitages and Gigondas, are the tastiest. Côte Rôtie is, of course, off to the side, all by itself in lonely splendor. Last fall when my latest novel, *The Road Home*, had begun doing quite well in France, I shared several celebration bottles of old Côte Rôtie with my friend and publisher Christian Bourgois. Success in itself can be quite disturbing, hard to accommodate, and I have spent as much time as possible alone in my room, where a number of good bottles have consoled me, including two Côte Rôties sent over by Dominique Bourgois's father, and two bottles of a fine year of Château Beychevelle, which were a gift from Jeanne Moreau, whose gorgeous voice obviously has been nurtured by wine.

Sometimes a humbler wine totally fits the situation. One day last fall in Paris, when I was angry from doing so many interviews, I left the hotel lobby and walked over to the Select on Montparnasse, a café I visit every day when in the city, and had a simple but delicious bottle of Brouilly. My anger subsided when the resident cat allowed me to pat it, and by tilting my head I had a good look at a woman's legs in the corner. I shall ever after think of thighs when I drink Brouilly.

I have left out American wines because I can think of only one truly great one, the 1968 Heitz Martha's Vineyard, and I have no story attached to it. Doubtless there are some considerable American wines, but most are too thickish and oaky for my taste.

I shouldn't forget how wine can assuage grief. Once, my phenomenal bird dog, an English setter named Tess, over whom I shot more than a thousand birds, got a stick caught in her throat and began to hemorrhage. After two late-night trips to the veterinarian she was finally pronounced out of danger. I had been so shattered I hadn't been able to eat dinner, and after she finally slept I remembered that on this very day a friend had sent a fresh foie gras from D'Artagnan. It was 2:00 A.M. when I finished steaming the foie gras over Sire de Gouberville cognac. I ate it with a baguette and my best remaining bottle of Margaux. I don't recall the year of this fine wine, but I raised my glass to my sleeping dog, who had been nearly lost but was found again.

Lastly, but perhaps most important because we do not know what happens after death, I owe to wine the fact that I'm still alive. Some years ago I was in bad health and several doctors learned that I was utterly addicted to V.O., a Canadian whiskey that, though delicious, is a poor substitute for water or wine. I explained the mortal problem to my friend Michael Butler, who works for that great importer of French wines Kermit Lynch. We decided that some magnums of Châteauneuf-du-Pape Vieux Telegraphe might help me through the harrowing ordeal I was facing. One evening in our little casita, I set out a bottle of the V.O. and sat down in a rocker, staring at this dread potion for four hours, drinking nothing but the spirits of denial. If I couldn't stop whiskey I'd have to give up alcohol altogether, and what then would become of the lonely bottles in my cellar? I rocked like an autistic child. Tears formed, but I won. I dumped the bottle of whiskey in the sink, had a glass of the Vieux Telegraphe, petted my dog, and went to bed, a new man in an old bottle.

from SIDEWAYS

Rex Pickett

The sun poured bright parallelograms of mote-swirling light through the venetian blinds of my rundown, rent-controlled house in Santa Monica. I was moving frenetically from bedroom to living room packing for a road trip with my best friend, Jack Cole. We were headed for the Santa Ynez Valley and a week of wine tasting before he was to be married the following Sunday. Though I couldn't afford this impromptu excursion, I desperately needed to get out of L.A. The place was suffocating me, fueling paralyzing panic attacks that had been a chronic affliction of mine over the years.

The phone rang, but the number that materialized on my caller ID didn't register so I stood frozen over the answering machine, waiting.

"Miles, is Roman," my landlord began in his Transylvanian-sounding drawl. "It is the fifteenth of September and I still not receive rent. Every month we go through this. If I don't get check by tomorrow I have no choice but to begin eviction. I don't like this. You are my friend. I know you are starving writer . . ."

I levered the volume on the answering machine to 0, the hair on my forearms tingling. The rest of Roman's exhortation I could recite from memory. He would warm up with how lenient he had been, then he would launch into a foaming-at-the-mouth diatribe about how my financial shortcomings were the cause of his elevated blood pressure and a host of other onuses that daily racked him on the property owner's cross. His jeremiads were worthy of Job and their intent was to make me feel guilty and scrape together the $850 in question.

I resumed packing, the call pecking away at the edges of my already frayed psyche. Into my travel-scarred suitcase I threw a couple of bleak-themed novels I knew I would never crack. For good measure I added *The Oxford Companion to Wine*, Jancis Robinson's brilliant and exhaustive tome on everything you ever wanted to know about the universe of wine. It was the perfect book to calm the nerves at three in the morning when you wake in an unfamiliar motel room in a cold sweat, trembling from excess. After all, Jack and I were journeying to wine country, and I wanted to have the one book that had supplied me with all the basics of my one undying passion—besides, of course, the unrepentant penning of two unpublished novels and scores of unproduced screenplays.

As I was about to shutter the house the phone rang a second time, jangling my nerves. I raced over to the caller ID, expecting it to be my disgruntled landlord again, amplifying on his first message with another warning salvo. But the number that came up on the display was a 212 area code so I lunged for the phone. "Hello," I answered breathlessly.

"Miles," sang a cheery woman's voice. "It's Evelyn, your favorite agent." She was the sixth in a long line of backstabbing sharks, but so far she seemed to be the rare exception: an agent who believed in me.

"Evelyn, what's up? You sound upbeat for a change." In fact, she had that uncharacteristic lilt in her voice that promised argosies, ships of fortune that would diminish the pain of the thirty-five rejection letters from the who's who of major publishing houses that I had arrayed on my living room walls: a festoon of failure, I proudly told everyone.

"Some *potentially* good news," Evelyn said. "Richard Davis at Conundrum liked your book."

My jaw dropped. The novel she was referring to had been shopped around New York for nearly a year now with no takers. There had been the first tier of submissions to the cream of the crop, when excitement was high and optimism exaggerated. Then there was the second tier: less prestigious houses, which meant less advance money, and considerably less budget for promotion once I got published, which I still assumed I would. The slow morphine drip continued as more rejection letters sluiced through Evelyn's New York office and were shunted to me in L.A. Bringing up the rear was the third tier: boutique houses on the periphery seeking a home run and a move into the second tier. Short of vanity presses and the Internet self-publishing venues, this was where Evelyn disembarked and moved on to the BBD—bigger and better deal. We were clinging to tattered ribbons and we both knew it.

"Great," I replied, almost not wanting to hear the qualifications for fear they would put a damper on my excitement.

"He's passing it to the other senior editors to read over the weekend. I'm expecting a decision toward the end of next week. Of course, he recommended some revisions."

"Of course," I replied. "A publishing deal would certainly have that galvanic effect on me."

Evelyn laughed heartily, the gallows laugh of a hardworking agent who wasn't getting any younger. "So, we're in pretty good shape," she said. "I've got my fingers crossed."

"Terrific," I replied, glancing at my watch. "I'm getting ready to take off for a little trip."

"Oh? Where?"

"Santa Ynez Valley. An hour north of Santa Barbara. The poor man's Napa/Sonoma. My friend Jack is getting married and we're going to go out in style. It's research for my next book," I added.

"Sounds like a blast," she said. "Are you writing anything new, Miles?"

"Well, um," I began haltingly. I glanced around at the rejection letters thumbtacked to my walls, their stinging words glaring reminders of why I had been unproductive recently. Of course, there was also the divorce, the dwindling bank account, the renewed wave of panic attacks, the loss of my film agent to the St. Vitus's dance, and the sudden departure of a short-lived girlfriend who couldn't put up with my occupational moodiness. "I've got something brewing," I said finally. "Something epic."

"Well, keep writing," she encouraged. "And I'll call you when I hear something."

We signed off and I stood still for a moment, a hundred thoughts crisscrossing in my head. I had almost given up the book for dead—two years down the toilet and all the bad debts that backed up with it—but I was thrilled Evelyn had not. I made a mental note not to give up all hope in humankind.

I locked up my house, threw my suitcase into the back of my Toyota 4Runner, and headed off to the weekly Friday afternoon wine tasting at Epicurus, where I was to rendezvous with the incorrigibly late Jack.

Epicurus was a long railcar-shaped wine emporium wedged in between a mattress store and a spa that specialized in high colonics. Wine bottles were racked halfway up both walls and down the middle of the long rectangular space, arranged according to varietal and country of origin.

The familiar crowd was packed into the small cordoned-off tasting area, affectionately dubbed The Bullpen, in the rear of the shop. In recent years The Bullpen had been witness to many wild Fridays after the owner had gone home, leaving the store entrusted to James, his English wine guru. Usually James would uncork bottle after bottle, recklessly cherry-picking the store's inventory in retaliation for what he referred to as his *insulting* salary. It was the place to be on Friday for the Westside wine cognoscenti.

This afternoon they were pouring Gary Farrell, a high-end vintner whose winery is smack in the middle of the Russian River Valley. Pinot Noir country. My grape. The one varietal that truly enchants me, both stills and steals my heart with its elusive loveliness and false promises of transcendence. I loved her, and I would continue to follow her siren call until my wallet—or liver, whichever came first—gave out.

There was a buzz in The Bullpen when I arrived. A few people called out hellos and waved as I squeezed into the small space and found a clean glass. Most of the regulars were already holding court in their customary positions, arms crooked with wineglasses held below their noses. They included: Carl, an electrician at Warner Brothers, a small roly-poly man with a thirst for Bordeaux and a private cellar stocked with some of France's finest (and the burst capillaries in his face to prove it); Jerry, a reptilian-faced, paunchy man in his forties, dentist by trade, oenophile by avocation, who used the Friday tastings as a way to meet prospective new paramours even though we all knew he was married; Eekoo, a wealthy Korean real estate entrepreneur who boasted a temperature-controlled bedroom stacked floor to ceiling with the finest California Cabernets, Chardonnays, and Pinots, the highly allocated ones, the mythical bottles you don't find in wine stores. Eekoo's trademark was the varietal-specific Riedel stemware he lugged around in a wooden case from tasting to tasting. Then there was Malibu Jim, a slender, sallow-faced man in his fifties who sampled the wines, then typed in tasting notes on a laptop, research for a book he probably would never get around to writing. Recent newcomers, I noticed, were a pair of pleasantly plump office assistants who had discovered the best $5 party in the city and were fast becoming regulars. They didn't know much about wine, and they came reeking of perfume—a wine tasting no-no—but they were a load of laughs once they got a few tastes under their belts. And then there were the walk-ins, the one-timers, the curiosity seekers who heard the convivial banter in the back of the store, noticed wine being sampled, and thought it would be fun to join in. Sizing up the fresh dramatis personae, I became aware of three attractive women in their early thirties, huddled together, demarcating a proprietary space, conscious of the leering stares but determined to enjoy their afternoon outing.

"Miles," Carl called out, raising his glass, already flush in the face. He tended to arrive early and get a head start on the festivities. "Didn't think you were going to make it."

"Gary Farrell, are you kidding?" I said as I elbowed my way over to the lineup. Manning the bottles was a matronly woman with a pie-shaped face and a friendly but strained smile. As disembodied arms snaked in between jostling bodies she tried to monitor the amounts that were being poured. It usually began politely, then slowly deteriorated into a help-yourself-to-all-you-can-drink line of attack. We were still in the polite phase of the afternoon when I held out my glass to her.

"Would you like to begin with the Chardonnay?" she asked over the din of voices.

"Absolutely," I said.

She picked up an open bottle of the Farrell Sonoma and poured me a splash. I put my nose in the glass, inhaled deeply, and got a whiff of honeydew and underripe pears. On the palate the wine was indelicate, slightly oaky, very tropical-fruity, a little on the flabby side: a fairly typical California Chard for the Chard-swilling masses. I compared notes with Carl and he readily agreed.

As I waited for Jack, I edged my way nearer the three women who were making their first appearance. They were deep into the reds and I sensed they were getting ready to head for the hills.

"What do you think of the Farrells?" I asked the one in the middle, a pretty, dark-haired slip of a girl.

"Mm." She wrinkled her forehead. "I guess I like the Merlot the best." Her pals concurred with her assessment, nodding and *mmm-ing*.

I grimaced. Merlot, a quintessential blending grape, when left to its own devices almost always—Pétrus notwithstanding—results in a bland, characterless wine. "What about the Pinots?" I asked, smiling what I hoped was a charming and knowing smile.

"I didn't like 'em." She formed her mouth into a tight little O trying to describe her displeasure with my favorite grape.

Disenchanted, I backed my way toward the lineup of bottles, sensing I had struck out. As the crowd shifted and reshifted in the cramped space, I quickly sampled the second Chard, a single-vineyard wine with a better balance of fruit and acidity and subtler oak overtones that imparted a slightly smoky, almost nutty taste.

"Excellent," I said to the wine rep, when she asked if I liked it. I rinsed my glass and held it back out. "Let's get serious."

She reached for the first Pinot and poured me a splash. It was Farrell's Sonoma standard, blended from a selection of vineyards. It gave off that unmistakable Pinot nose of cassis and blackberry, but it wasn't distinguished, drifting in the mouth like a rudderless boat. The second Pinot was a single-vineyard from the nearby storied Rochioli property. It had notes of cardamom and exotic berries, and it pinwheeled around on my palate, deliciously lingering. *Mm*, I thought to myself, rolling the wine around in my mouth, *this is more like it*.

I shuffled my way through the crush of bodies back to where the three neophytes were winding up with the Cabs, hoping for one last shot. I was beginning to feel a little high and it emboldened me to re-approach them.

"You don't like this Rochioli Pinot?" I asked.

The dark-headed one shook her head again.

"Really?" I sipped and took another spin around the block. "I think it's close to dazzling."

Jerry the dentist, face florid from having already traipsed through the lineup several times, butted in. "I don't think it's that dazzling," he contended, hoping to curry favor with women I didn't think would give him the time of day. They all smiled at him and I drifted away for a second and final time. Ten minutes later he had the darkheaded one buttonholed against the wall and—more appallingly—she seemed fascinated by his ineloquent winespeak.

Dispirited, I kept returning to the Rochioli as if to a trusted friend. As the rep poured me more, Carl sidled over to solicit my opinion. I barraged him with hyperbolic hosannas, reaching deep for the metaphors and the poly-syllabics, which always made him chuckle.

"You're right," he said, after I had finished reeling off my lyrical account, the wine liberating my tongue to new heights of glibness. "Absolutely first-rate Pinot."

"How was Spain?" I asked.

"Excellent," he said. "Had a great time."

"Drink any good Riojas and Riberas?"

"Yeah, some really tasty ones." He winked, then filled me in about a big feast at a winery where they roasted lambs over flaming vine cuttings.

While listening to Carl's chronicle of his Spain trip, I bypassed the Merlot and reached for the Zin, not wanting the rep to think I was hogging the Pinot. I refilled Carl with a scandalously healthy splash that drew an admonitory stare from the rep. We clinked glasses and laughed, delighting in our naughtiness.

Then Carl bent close to my ear and whispered, "Woman in the black shirt and blond hair is checking you out."

I shot a furtive glance in the direction Carl was indicating. One of the dark-headed one's friends was not just looking at me, but smiling. I didn't know if she was flirting or had simply discovered the slippery pleasures of Pinot at my urging.

"They don't like the Rochioli," I told Carl. "I can't date a woman who doesn't like Pinot. That's like getting involved with someone who's disgusted by oral sex."

Carl laughed. "How long's it been since you've had a girlfriend?"

"I can't remember. A while." I sipped the Zin. It was spicy and full-bodied, but it didn't transport me. "But it's been a welcome break. I can feel the creative juices starting to flow again."

Carl screwed his face up in disbelief. Suffering months without sex was unimaginable to him. Indiscriminate in his own tastes, he often came to the Friday tastings accompanied by the lees of womankind. "Maybe it's time to reevaluate the pleasures of Merlot," Carl suggested, tipping his head toward our three novices.

"I'm not going to journey from the sublime to the pedestrian for a phone number," I said, shaking my head. "What's the deal with Jerry?" I noticed that the dentist was still locked in conversation with the dark-headed one.

"Flatters them, doesn't put them down for not liking Pinot," Carl affectionately criticized me.

"Imagine getting a root canal from that guy." I affectedly staggered in place, imitating a drunk. "He's probably one of those drill-and-fillers who anesthetizes his patients and then feels them up in the chair."

Carl laughed, goading me on. We loved the mordant humor that the combination of wine and gossip evoked in both of us.

Eekoo edged into our cabal, his Riedel Sommeliers glass cradled in his hand like the Hope Diamond. "What do you think of the Farrells?" he said, his speech hobbled by the series of tasting events he had strung together beginning early in the day.

"Rochioli is nice," I said.

He sipped the wine from his bulbous stemware and worked it professionally around in his mouth. "Not as good as the '99 Kistler."

Carl and I rolled our eyes at the same time. Of course, nobody but Eekoo could find—let alone, afford—the '99 Kistler, so the reference was a no-win one-upmanship, but we humorously tolerated his elitism all the same.

"Heard you were taking a little trip," Eekoo said to me, blinking like a gargoyle through the thick lenses of his glasses.

"My friend Jack's getting married a week from Sunday. We're going to do a little Santa Ynez wine tour."

"Ah," Eekoo said, smiling benignly as if recalling fond memories of just such a trip.

"Where *is* Jack?" Carl suddenly wondered.

I glanced at my watch. "Should be here pretty soon. You know Jack, he's always late."

"I miss that guy. Haven't seen him here in quite a while."

"His fiancée is holding him to the straight and narrow. That's what happens when you get into a *real* relationship."

Carl tilted his head back and laughed. Eekoo shot his arm between us in pursuit of one of the bottles, but his aim was off and he sent the Sonoma Pinot crashing to the cement floor. The explosion of glass produced a collective hush for a moment, but the silence was quickly swamped by a chorus of amiable catcalls. The party was in full swing now and the wine rep looked anxious, her eyes darting warily about the swelling, unmanageable crowd.

At the sound of shattering glass, Graham, the balding, barrel-chested proprietor, broke away from the cash register and strode toward us. "You animals," he boomed, squatting down to help the rep clean up the mess. It wasn't the first time and he was armed and ready with dustpan and brush.

"We've almost killed the Rochioli Pinot," I said. "Open another bottle."

Graham rose on the other side of the partition. He had a large, bowling-ball-shaped face created exclusively to intimidate. "This is a tasting, Miles, not a public service."

"Without us, you'd be in Chapter 11."

"If you didn't get so sideways on Fridays you might be on the last chapter of that novel of yours."

I smiled and pointed my finger at him. Touché. He returned the gesture.

"Come on. Open another bottle," I urged.

"Yeah," Carl said. "More people are coming."

Graham shook his head in mock disgust. He didn't like the Friday tastings, but he tolerated them because they were good for business. At their conclusion, the oenophiles, their wallets liberated in direct proportion to the amount of wine they had consumed, were usually in the mood to carry on elsewhere and would ring up extravagant purchases, sometimes solely to impress one another.

As Graham finished sweeping up the broken glass, arms reached indiscriminately for the remaining bottles. The Farrell rep, realizing that she had lost control, quickly filled a glass of the Rochioli for herself and hoarded it in her corner. Graham, aspiring to be the wine mensch of Santa Monica, waved the dustpan theatrically and said in defeat, "Open another Rochioli, Carol."

The rep looked stricken for a moment, but she reluctantly reached down and unzipped her wine satchel and emerged with a second bottle. Raucous, but genial, cheers welcomed the sound of its uncorking. Glasses were refreshed all around and the *ooh*-ing and *aah*-ing started all over again.

Soon, I felt a warm glow spread through me. Voices overlapped and muddled into one another. As evening crept up on us, the light grew soft and the faces shadowed. Then, as if entering through the backdoor of a dream, Dani, a statuesque Aussie with a runner's physique—graphic designer by profession—came bounding down the back stairs, her braless breasts rising and falling inside a tight, midriff-revealing T-shirt. She circled into The Bullpen, a smile on her ruddy, sunburned face, eager to sample.

"Dani," I called out, happy to see my favorite regular.

"Miles!" She shoehorned her way through the throng and greeted me with a tight hug. With so much woman pressed against me, I nearly fainted. When she finally released me I had the presence of mind to right a clean glass and fill it half full of the second Chardonnay from a new, cold bottle the rep had also uncorked.

"I'm taking you right to the Allen Vineyard. None of this mediocre wine for you," I said.

"Oh, you are, are you?" she said, cocking her head coquettishly. She accepted the glass, took a sip, closed her eyes gently for a moment, and savored the wine. "Thanks, Miles. I needed that."

"My pleasure."

Carl, inebriated enough now to test the waters, had drifted over and was making small talk with the blond friend of the dark-headed one who was, judging by her expression, apparently in the process of getting the pants charmed off her by Jerry. Occasionally she even *laughed* at what the dentist was saying. I turned away. A wobbly Eekoo was staring bleary-eyed over Malibu Jim's shoulder at his laptop, critiquing his wine-tasting notes, stabbing a finger—which Jim kept shooing away—at his screen. The Farrell rep, having long since worn out her function as a pourer and explicator of Gary's winemaking methodologies, retreated deeper into her corner with a second—full(!)—glass of the Rochioli, resigned now to the pleasurable fact that she might as well get looped with the rest of us. The Bullpen had, in its inimitable way, collectively reduced our zeitgeist to a tribal low common denominator.

I leaned into Dani's apple red face. "Do you think it's unreasonable not to want to date anyone who doesn't like Pinot? It's the burning question for me this afternoon."

"Who's that?" Dani asked, her antennae tuned now to the horde in The Bullpen. She grabbed a fistful of my shirt and maneuvered me over to the bottles so we wouldn't have to keep reaching through the crowd to refresh our glasses.

"Dark-haired one over there talking to Jerry," I said, nodding in their direction.

Dani squinted and glanced over my shoulder. She shrugged. "You're too critical, Miles."

"Someone's got to have standards around here."

She laughed and we touched glasses. "Where's Jack?"

"Should be here any minute." I reflexively checked my watch. An hour had disappeared like the flare of a match. *Have to slow down*, I cautioned myself.

"Are you leaving from here?" Dani asked. Her voice sounded a little like it was trying to reach me from underwater.

"Yeah. I'm getting an early start." I raised my glass to the impending trip, the promising news from my agent, and the feeling of warmth that had by now blanketed me. "I'm taking a week off and doing nothing but tasting wines and breathing fresh air."

"Sounds like fun. Wish I could come."

"When are you and Roger getting married?" I asked, referring to her handsome investment banker fiancé.

"This December."

"Really? That's great." I tried to offer my congratulations with conviction, but even I could faintly make out a tinge of disappointment in my voice. Maybe I was infatuated with Dani because the only times I ever interacted with her were when I had a wine buzz going, but even on paper she was something special: wine lover, athlete, gourmet cook; what more could a guy want?

"Yeah," she was saying, her words coming back into my consciousness, "we're going to take the plunge." Without looking, she reached around for more of the Rochioli and topped both of us off, eliciting a snort of disdain from the beleaguered rep. We ignored her and carried on.

"Like this Pinot, Dani?"

"Mm hm." Dani made a face that underscored her pleasure. Her attention was drawn over my shoulder again. "Some woman keeps looking over here."

"Really?" I didn't bother to look. "Probably because she thinks I'm with you, her interest has rekindled." I stole a quick glance at the blonde Carl was chatting up. "Carl'll try to seduce her with his '97 Caymus Special Selection. If that doesn't get her excited, he'll go deep and offer to pop one of his *premiers crus* Bordeaux."

Dani threw back her head of short auburn hair and laughed hard. "So, what's happening with your novel?"

"Thirty-five rejections and counting. They just keep pouring in."

"No," Dani empathized.

"But thirty-six might be the charm. Just spoke to my agent. Editor at some small publishing house expressed serious interest. He's passing it upstairs to the button-pushers as we drink."

"I want to read it," Dani insisted, a weekly refrain she never followed up on.

"She's got a good feeling this time," I said.

Dani bent closer to me until our faces were almost touching. Her breath smelled piquantly of wine and stinky French cheeses. I misinterpreted her gesture and turned my mouth toward hers for the kiss that I delusively thought she was offering.

"He's going for the kill," she whispered instead, thwarting me mid-kiss.

I threw a backward glance and glimpsed Jerry the dentist brushing the dark-headed woman's hair back off her forehead and gazing into her eyes in a way that could only be described as adoringly. Next to them, roly-poly Carl appeared to be making headway with her blond cohort. I flashed to a vision of a frolicking foursome, whisked off to Carl's nearby condo to partake of his small, but well-stocked, cellar. As if it hadn't been clear already, now it was a fait accompli that I was out of the picture. No doubt Jerry had already informed his mark that I was a chronically unemployed writer, which was usually about all it took to get desirable women to steer clear of me at all costs. That was one of the liabilities of getting hammered every Friday and unburdening yourself on people you thought were your friends. The personal revelations always came back to haunt you.

I turned back to Dani, shaking my head scornfully. "Amount of wine those guys have been drinking, I doubt either of them could get an erection."

Dani poured off more of the Rochioli, filling our small tasting glasses to the rim, before the others could get their mitts on it. As the tastings drew to a close, and the bottles grew depleted, selfishness became the common mantra of the afternoon.

"I'm happy for you and Roger," I heard myself say. "But if it doesn't work out, I want you to call me, okay?"

Dani dipped her head to one side and smiled.

"I'm serious," I blundered on, aware that I was spewing drunken nonsense, feeling that cavernous loneliness welling up in me again but oblivious of the consequences and determined to hurtle forward with abandon.

Dani placed a sympathetic hand on my shoulder. Then, unexpectedly, she planted her lips on mine and held them there for what seemed like an eternity. I felt her tongue hot and moist inside my mouth. It wasn't an affectionate kiss, but rather a showy display to flout propriety and draw attention.

From behind me, a chorus of rowdy, counterfeit hoorays erupted. On cue, Dani unstuck herself and chased the kiss with the last of her Rochioli. In one movement, she reached indiscriminately into the field of dead bottles to grab one that had anything sloshing around on the bottom. She fished out the Allen Chard, veering recklessly backward in the order—my girl! I held out my glass and she topped me off. I was light-headed from the wine, the unexpected kiss, and the clamor of laughter and indistinct voices. Our eyes sank into each other for a brief moment. I had a fantasy of Dani dragging me across the street to her apartment and granting me a sympathy pop while her fiancé, leaving her unattended on yet another lonely weekend, jetted around the globe. But looking into each other's bloodshot eyes, I knew it was a rotten idea, and I could tell she knew it, too, and we quickly dispelled it with a pair of awkward laughs.

I was eager for Jack to arrive and call it a tasting when, out of nowhere, Jerry the cavity filler directed something at me he probably intended as a harmless joke. I didn't exactly catch all of it, what with the riot of competing voices and my diminishing auditory faculties, but I was in a mood just askew enough, inspired by the swell of laughter that followed his remark, to whirl around and retort: "Where's your wife this week, Jerry? We miss her."

His goofy, mirthful face instantly imploded into a bilious scowl. The dark-haired woman, whose head he'd been filling with more than porcelain, broke into an aghast hand-to-the-mouth-oh-my-God! expression. She mouthed something to the dentist while simultaneously starting to back away. Out of earshot one could reasonably assume it was a follow-up to my derogatory comment. Gesticulating a little wildly and visibly flustered, Jerry was clearly trying to explain away my remark. He held up his left hand to show her he didn't wear a wedding ring, but that was hardly convincing to a smart woman at a wine tasting where lies flowed freer than Chardonnay.

A few moments later, the three newcomers regrouped and fled The Bullpen, vowing no doubt never to return. Carl held up two empty arms to me as if he had fumbled a pass in the end zone, an innocent victim of collateral damage. Next to me, Dani, who maintained a proprietary death grip on the Chard—one of the only bottles with any wine remaining—was bent double, poleaxed with laughter.

Jerry the dentist, ditched and publicly humiliated, stormed out of The Bullpen into the main part of the store where he paced the Italian section and glowered at the Brunellos. Our eyes locked for a quick, spiteful moment. He straightened his middle finger and shook it in and out in front of his scowling face. That ignited me.

"Hey, Jerry," I called out, cupping my free hand around the corner of my mouth. "Get a bottle of the Muscadet, it'll pair perfectly with your wife's pussy!"

The Bullpen exploded into laughter. The mood was once again giddy and arms crisscrossed the ledge to check for dregs in the few remaining bottles. The Farrell rep quailed in her corner and sipped her wine, resigned to the carnage. The two tittering office assistants, totally liquored up, bumped hips to a tune only they heard.

I turned away to refresh myself with more wine when the dentist charged into The Bullpen and shoved me backward. I lost my balance and a half glass (damn!) of the Chard went flying.

"Hey, hey," I heard Dani soothe as though she were calling from another room. I was semiafraid for the dentist that Dani was going to physically come to my assistance. She owned a brown belt in martial arts and would have kicked his ass, only adding to Jerry's humiliation.

"That wasn't funny," Jerry screamed, his face malignantly red with bile and tannin.

"It's because of lecherous jerks like you that more single women don't come to these tastings," I shot back.

Jerry was the type in whom alcohol raises the level of violence. He rushed at me and wrapped his arms around my waist like some junior varsity wrestler and attempted to take me to the floor. The office assistants scrambled for their purses. Malibu Jim swiftly folded up his laptop and skulked off like a garter snake. Eekoo, in full panic mode, retrieved his wooden case of handblown Riedels and clutched it protectively to his chest. Carl darted over to save the precious few bottles, now teetering on the narrow ledge where they had once stood pristinely unopened. Graham angrily disengaged himself from a customer and rumbled into view.

As I grappled with the hysterical dentist, Dani, in an inspired move I don't think Gary Farrell had in mind when he vinified his '99 bottling, hoisted the silver spit bucket aloft—full from a long afternoon of tasting—and upended it on Jerry's head.

A fetid mixture of wine and cheese-infused saliva splattered everywhere. Jerking erect, Jerry flailed at his face, his arms scissoring back and forth like windshield wipers gone berserk.

"Try the Meritage, Jerry," I said, getting to my feet. "Fruit forward and drinkable now!"

Graham elbowed his way into The Bullpen. "All right, everybody, the tasting's over."

A scowling Jerry, his polo shirt stained with wine, started to advance on me again, but the heftier Graham stepped in between us. "Come on, Jerry," Graham warned. "I don't want to have to ban you from coming here."

Jerry brandished his middle finger at me again as Graham coaxed him out of the tasting area.

The buzz in The Bullpen gradually quieted. Dani, Carl, and I made small talk as the Farrell rep started to gather up her brochures and tote bags. A moment later, as if on cue, Jack materialized at the top of the back stairs, haloed by the late-afternoon sun. He was a tall, ursine man with movie-star good looks, fashionably unshaven, with a mop of sandy brown hair that shot in all directions on his large head. He was attired in his trademark black bowler's shirt with JACK embroidered in white lettering over the pocket, a pair of colorful Hawaiian shorts, and matching flip-flops.

"Miles," he declared.

"Jack! You made it!"

Jack was outsized in every way. When he broke into laughter, it rattled the shackles of your unconscious and demanded that you join in. When he walked into a movie theater he swallowed the entire aisle. He was the guy who got hired on the spot because of his infectious charisma, the guy who didn't have to work to get the girl. Unlike me, any weaknesses he had were secreted and any negativity painted over with broad strokes of optimism. Truth for Jack was what he could touch and smell and taste at any given moment. Self-reflection was generally too deep for him. He was a meat eater, a problem solver, a spirit lifter after a tough day, the guy everyone would want to rub shoulders with in a foxhole while mortars rained down. He seemed an unlikely candidate for marriage. Given his personality and looks, opportunities for long nights with the opposite sex were limitless, and another man not so endowed would wonder why Jack wouldn't want to live the Casanova life until his privates gave out. But Jack had a sentimental side, too, and I could—if I tried hard enough—envision him with a brood of children, sprawled in a La-Z-Boy with a six-pack on ice, spinning anecdotes about his colorful past.

Jack came down the stairs and wheeled into The Bullpen with his familiar swagger, which always lightened the mood instantly.

He greeted Dani with a devouring hug, slapped Carl heartily on the shoulder, then slung an arm around me and poured himself what was left of the Zin, indiscriminate as always about his choice of quaff as long as it was red as blood and potently alcoholic.

A few minutes later everyone was laughing again. Graham returned, having successfully shooed Jerry out of his store.

Jack was getting up to speed on the melee. "The guy's married," I was explaining, "and he knew I was hitting on her."

Jack looked at me dismissively. "You overreacted, Miles."

"I made a little joke and the fucker got physical," I said.

"So what's the problem between you and Jerry?" Graham asked.

"I'll tell you my problem. A couple of weeks ago I brought a date here. He chats her up. That's cool—I know she's not going to go for him. Middle of the week he tracks her down on the set of a film she's working on, flatters her with a load of poppycock, then asks her out."

"What's wrong with that?" Graham said.

"What's *wrong* with *that*?" I echoed. "The guy tried to do an end run around. The woman thinks I hang out with creeps. You ought to ban him from these tastings."

Graham just screwed up his face in response.

Jack, bored with the argument, picked up one of the remaining bottles, but only managed a few dribbles of wine when he upended it. "Hey, Graham. How about opening another bottle? I need a glass for the road. Miles and I are officially on vacation."

"Where're you going?"

"Santa Ynez Valley," I answered. "Do the winery tour, then stuff Jack in the monkey suit and get him hitched a week from Sunday."

"It's a little bachelor week blowout," Jack elaborated. "Miles is going to educate me on wines and I'm going to educate him on life."

"Someone should call the cops," Graham said. Everyone laughed. "All right," he said. "What're you guys in the mood for?"

"Let's sample some champagne," I said. "Get in the matrimonial mode."

Graham beetled his brow and thought for a moment. Then he slapped his thigh. "I've got an idea." He strode upstairs, where he kept his private stash, and reappeared a minute later with a cold bottle of '92 Byron sparkling wine.

I set four clean glasses on the terrazzo ledge. Graham expertly uncorked the bottle and poured them foaming half full. We all toasted and sampled. It had the beautiful gold color of an aged champagne, appropriately yeasty and rich on the palate.

"What do you think?" Graham asked.

"Luscious," I remarked, taking another sip. "I didn't know Byron made a sparkling wine."

"Hundred percent Pinot Noir," Graham said. "I figured since you guys are doing Santa Ynez and Miles is a Pinot freak, this would be right up your alley."

"Why do you call it a sparkling wine and not champagne?" Jack asked.

"The term 'champagne' is trademarked by the French, and if it's not from the Champagne region of France, then it can't be called champagne—at least not on the label," I explained. "But because I'm sick of the French and their proprietary ways, Spumanti, Cava, California sparkling, they're all champagne to me. Right, Graham?"

"Whatever you say, Miles."

Jack nodded thoughtfully. "I'll remember that."

"I've only got one case left," Graham said. "They don't make it anymore. Two forty a case."

I looked at Jack with widened eyes and nodded vigorous approval.

"All right, we'll take it," Jack said.

Dani drained her glass. "I've got to be going. Roger's supposed to call."

"No, come with us," I said. "Roger won't mind. Take a week off."

Dani wagged a finger at us. "You two guys in the wine country for a week. Sounds like a hen's night out. Bye." She waved as she made her way out of The Bullpen. "Thanks for the champers." And then she was gone, leaving a rectangle of harsh orange sunlight in her wake.

Jack shook his head in an exaggerated manner. "Man, that chick's got it going on. Would I ever love to strap her on."

"Hey, don't talk about Dani like that. She's a good girl," I said.

"Yeah, right," Jack said, laughing. "Good to the *bone*."

"Hey, I saw your ex in here the other day," Graham said, referring to Victoria, the woman I had been married to for eight years. I hadn't seen or talked to her in some months.

"Oh, yeah?" I said, my mood changing abruptly. "What was she doing on the West Side?"

"Came over to fuck me," Graham replied, deadpan.

"Yeah, right. She'd remarry *me* before she'd mount you. Fucking goat."

Graham and Jack both laughed.

"Was she with anyone?" I probed.

"Yeah, some guy I've never seen before. Tall, good-looking, well dressed. Pretty much your opposite."

"Hah, hah. What was she buying?"

"Case of Krug."

"Oh, yeah?" I said, eyes widening. "What was the occasion?"

Graham started to respond, but abruptly halted mid-sentence, his eyes darting furtively over my shoulder in the vicinity of Jack.

I turned quickly and snatched a brief glimpse of Jack raking his hand through his mop of hair as if he had just short-circuited a gesture to Graham behind my back.

Getting the message, I said, "Okay, okay, I'm over it, all right? I'm a very happily single man. A glass of wine, a crusty piece of baguette, a good book, and I'm fine."

Jack and Graham exchanged smirks, and refrained from digging the needle in any deeper. It had been over a year since the divorce, and I had to admit I missed the little things that marriage provided, the routines that kept my life in check and prevented me from going off the deep end.

"All right," Jack said, sensing the seismic pitch in my mood. "This place is dead. Let's get on the road."

We dispatched Graham upstairs to fetch the case of Byron. For good measure, we augmented the purchase with a case of Veuve Clicquot. We said our good-byes to Graham and Carl and then headed out to the parking lot, each with a case weighing down our arms. We piled them into the back of my 4Runner, the vehicle we had designated for the trip. I started automatically for the driver's side, but Jack grabbed hold of my shirt collar and yanked me around.

"Whoa, whoa, whoa, where're you going? I'm driving, Homes."

"What?"

"I don't want to spend the first night bailing you out of the tank."

"Give me a break. I've hardly wet my whistle."

Jack exploded into laughter. "You're sideways, brother. Scuffling with Jerry, asking Dani to come with us. Goodness gracious."

"What's wrong with asking Dani to come with us?"

"Give me the keys, Miles." Jack extended his hand and cocked his head to the side. Chastened, I surrendered the keys, then circled around to the passenger side and climbed in.

Jack fired up my 4Runner, turned onto Seventh Street and headed north. I rolled down my window, poked out my head, and let it loll on my arm. It was an unseasonably warm evening. The sky was an uncursed expanse of deepening blue and the air was pungent with the smell of the ocean. We cruised through ritzy Brentwood, whose sprawling, tree-shaded homes depressingly reminded me of my station in life, then turned on to San Vicente Boulevard. My gaze followed the wide grass median, where entertainment people jogged back and forth to maintain their ageless physiques and vent their frustrations with the movie business. It fled past me in a blissful wine-hazy blur.

PERILS OF BEING A WINE-WRITER

Auberon Waugh

I have a cousin who lives near me. He is much richer than I am, with an acreage of fat fields in Somerset and Devon which puts him well into the millionaire class. For some reason, although he is a generous host in other ways, he always serves filthy wine—the cheapest jug reds from Spain which he buys in ten-gallon plastic containers. On one occasion he produced a drink of such stupendous horror that I was inspired to write a column in the *Tatler*—then edited by Tina Brown—denouncing the English upper-class habit of serving cheap wine at meals. They would never dream of serving inferior cuts of beef, or scrag-end of lamb. Why did they think they could get away with nasty wine?

The trouble was that although there is a well-worn vocabulary of praise to describe good wine—it can be muscular, well-knit, complex, fragrant, etc.—there is no equivalent glossary to describe what is bad. The foul beverage itself tasted of vinegar, blue ink and curry powder, but such a bald description gave no hint of the shock, or disappointment, even the sadness of such a discovery. After playing with the idea of comparing it to a collapsed marquee fallen into a rotting silage pit, I eventually decided that it reminded me of a bunch of dead chrysanthemums on the grave of a stillborn West Indian baby. It was in that form that my cousin's wine was used as an object lesson for the readers of *Tatler*.

Shortly after my article appeared, Tina Brown received a letter from the Press Council saying it had received a complaint from a midwife in the London borough of Camden, which complaint was being backed by her local representative on the Race Relations Board. In due course, we were summoned to appear before the Council in full session—Tina in a ravishingly elegant grey knitwear two-piece, I in a dark blue suit and white collar.

Was I suggesting that the wine was nastier by virtue of reminding me of a West Indian baby? Not at all, I said. The metaphor of a dead piccaninny was used for the greater poignancy of the image it evoked. The West Indian connection was also explained by reference to curried mangoes which, although admirable things in themselves, were out of place among the tastes in a bottle of wine. After due deliberation, the Press Council acquitted us both of any intention to excite racial hatred, or to affront the sensitivities of any ethnic group. So we walked free. It was the first time any editor of the *Tatler* had appeared before that august body. I suspect it will be the last time any wine correspondent is summoned to explain and justify his comments on a particular bottle of wine.

The results of this episode were two-fold. First, and most important, my cousin started taking slightly more trouble over the wine he served. Second, another brave publishing initiative bit the dust:

> One task more declined, one more footpath untrod, One more triumph for devils and sorrow for angels, One wrong more to man, one more insult to God!
>
> —Robert Browning

In other words, Tina has learned her lesson, and wine-writing has resumed its former course. No more collapsed marquees or poignant grave-markers. Looking at a recent edition of *Vanity Fair*, where she now reigns, I found an interesting and informative article on the Pinot Noir varietal wines of California and Oregon, by Joel L. Fleishman. I was particularly interested in this article because I have been searching for some time for a good Pinot Noir from anywhere except Burgundy, so far with very little success. My cellar has perhaps 500 or 600 red Burgundies quietly maturing, but it occurred to me after completing my purchase of the 1983 vintage that red Burgundy prices have become so high in the better communes and domaines that I will probably never buy any more. Hence the desperate search for a substitute. Mr Fleishman tasted twenty-one American Pinot Noirs, and picked out seven of them as especially worthwhile. Of these seven, five were described in the following terms:

(a) 'A bouquet of tobacco infused with a beautiful perfume and a flavor of ripe cherries . . .'
(b) '. . . powerful dark-cherry fruit, slightly smoky in taste . . .'
(c) 'a bouquet of ripe berries, with hints of rose petals and lavender, and intense, complex, fruit flavors'
(d) 'an intense flavor of cherries, dry, not sweet, with a "chewiness" not detected in any of the other wines'
(e) 'A closed-in bouquet but lush, well-knit, and well-balanced smoky cherry flavors'

The overwhelming impression seems to be of cherries and smoke. I am not criticising Mr Fleishman's taste or vocabulary. Plainly cherries and smoke are the things to look for in American Pinot Noir. When describing tastes, one is bound to use some sort of shorthand, in any case, unless one is to embark on some baroque poetic fantasy on every occasion. It reads oddly to me only because neither cherries nor smoke have yet reached Europe as a way of describing wine. I have been eating cherries all my life, and breathing in smoke for much of it, but I have never found a Burgundy which tasted of either—let alone of tobacco, perfume, rose petals or lavender. If I found one of my wines tasting of any of those things I would send it back and demand an explanation. It is true that I once thought I detected a hint of cigar smoke in a Joseph Phelps Chardonnay I was given at a British Academy of Gastronomes lunch. But I had been told to look for it, and decided eventually that the smell probably came from my neighbour, a nice fat *Sunday Times* journalist called Godfrey Smith, who was smoking a cigar.

But we wine buffs talk of Burgundy as being 'velvety' or 'silken' and use an entire alternative glossary which is every bit as misleading or meaningless. In fact, the number of words which can usefully be used to describe or assess wine is limited. Apart from the obvious words of appreciation or dismissal—good, bad; sweet, sour; too little taste or too much—it can be fined down to about six technical considerations. These are the strength and balance of alcohol, acid, tannin, fruit, sugar, the degree of concentration and state of maturity. We all know—the wine buffs, that is—what sort of taste should be produced by each grape varietal or blend, and this is assessed in discussion of the 'fruit'. But not everybody who drinks wine is a wine buff, and wine articles would be unreadable if writers confined themselves to these technical measurements. Hence the clusters of cherries, the bottles of perfume and wads of tobacco, the baskets-full of strawberry, raspberry, gooseberry, pomegranate, passion fruit and mango called in to help the poor wine-writers describe a taste. I am not sure how helpful any of them are. It is one thing to be discussing a wine with various friends who are drinking it too—some of the most enjoyable conversations I have ever had have been on that basis—but quite another when you are trying to describe the taste of a particular wine to someone who probably is reading your piece immediately after breakfast or under the hair dryer.

My own feeling, despite several unhappy experiences, is that wine-writing should be camped up: the writer should never like a wine, he should be in love with it; never find a wine disappointing but identify it as a mortal enemy, an attempt to poison him; sulphuric acid should be discovered where there is the faintest hint of sharpness. Bizarre and improbable side-tastes should be proclaimed: mushrooms, rotting wood, black treacle, burned pencils, condensed milk, sewage, the smell of French railway stations or ladies' underwear—anything to get away from the accepted list of fruit and flowers. As I say, I am not sure that it helps much, but it is more amusing to read.

Until fairly recently, it was considered rude in polite upper-class society to make any comment at all on food or wine. To praise it was as boorish as to hint at criticism. Anything offered was assumed to be of the best. It was even ruder to notice a hostess's furniture or pictures. This is changing now, as servants disappear and the hostess herself is usually responsible for cooking, but old-fashioned and grand people, living in the country, still tend to look a bit startled when guests start praising their food, wine or appointments. This polite convention may explain why the food and wine in many country houses were so foul, why all the carpets were bald, the chintzes covered in dogs' hairs. But one of the perils of being a wine-writer is that guests always expect to be given something memorable in the way of wine when they come to your home.

The trouble with this expectation is that the best wines are now prodigiously expensive. Where even fifteen years ago any reasonably well-off person could reckon to fill his cellar with premiers crus Bordeaux, and grands crus Burgundies, now only the very rich indeed can even think of drinking such wines—starting, as they do, at about £30–£35 the bottle for a wine which will not be ready to drink for another fifteen years.

My own solution is to search for unusual wines which provide guests with something to talk about—even a sense of discovery—without ruining the host. Very few people realize how cripplingly expensive the best wine is nowadays. They will think it quite normal to be served a Château Haut-Brion, and reckon themselves short-changed if they are given a Beychevelle or a Léoville–Las Cases. Instead, I search the world to find examples of pre-phylloxera Cabernet from Chile, rare and honeyed Chardonnays from Australia or Gewürztraminers from New Zealand, Chenins Blancs from South Africa, even Zinfandels from California. Perhaps my most successful discovery has been a Cabernet from Lebanon called Château Musar, made by a genius called Serge Hochar who trained in Bordeaux at Château Léoville–Barton. This is a really superb wine . . . as soon as the Americans discover it, its price will go through the roof.

Then I will have to go on my travels again—to Provence, where they are beginning to make some seriously good, thick red wine from such Bordeaux grapes as Cabernet Sauvignon, Merlot and Malbec, as well as importing Syrah from the northern Rhône and Cinsault from the South. Or Bulgaria, whose heavily subsidised Cabernets are beginning to be discovered, unfortunately, at the cheap end of the market. There are many good minor wines from the Loire, too, while Spain and northern Italy are both making huge strides in the quality of their production.

EAST OF EDEN, 1963–1965

Julia Flynn Siler

In 1963, the tense relationship between the brothers would explode over a mink coat. Robert and Marjorie received a gold-embossed invitation from President Kennedy and his glamorous wife, Jackie, to join them at a state dinner at the White House in honor of the president of Italy, scheduled for November. The Mondavis had been invited as prominent Italian-Americans and Robert, to the dismay of the rest of the family, had assumed the honor was only meant for him and his wife. After they had accepted the invitation, it quickly became a source of concern: What would Marjorie wear? And how would Robert, who then earned around $24,000 a year, be able to afford it?

The couple went shopping together at what was then the most sophisticated department store in San Francisco: I. Magnin and Company. Initially, they didn't find anything that was quite right—until a saleslady suggested that Marjorie try on a mink coat, with the wildly expensive price tag of $5,000. It fit beautifully and the Mondavis felt it was just the right thing for the event—but the couple decided against buying it because it was so expensive. As weeks passed, Marjorie still hadn't found a coat to wear, and they returned to I. Magnin to discover that it had gone on sale and its price had dropped 50 percent. Even so, the $2,500 price tag was a huge amount for a family with three young children.

Robert decided to buy the coat and put it on his company expense account, with the intention of scrimping and saving in other areas to pay back Charles Krug. While that decision may have been defensible in the sense that it was important for the couple, as representatives of the family business, to look their best at the White House, Robert's decision to expense the coat without getting approval from the rest of the family first was hardly diplomatic.

When Peter and his wife, Blanche, heard about the purchase, they were stunned. Blanche, who was a divorcée with a young daughter when Peter married her, rode her second husband hard on how his brother seemed to get all the invitations and take all the glamorous trips while she and Peter stayed at home. On top of Robert and Marjorie's trip to Europe and their lunch at La Pyramide, this seemed to be more evidence of Robert's irresponsible spending. Envy, too, may have played a role in Peter and Blanche's perspective on the purchase: Why, after all, had Robert and Marjorie been invited and they had not? And why had the company paid for Marjorie's expensive mink coat while not paying for one for Blanche?

The issue simmered as Robert and Marjorie's trip to the White House for dinner was postponed after President Kennedy's assassination. Robert and Marjorie did eventually attend a state dinner in honor of the slight, white-haired president Antonio Segni of Italy and his wife two months later in the company of such notables as baseball star Joe DiMaggio, composer Gian Carlo Menotti, and pundit Walter Lippmann. As the first state dinner hosted by the new president Lyndon Johnson and his wife, Lady Bird, the White House presented what one observer described as a "musical program of probably the greatest extremes ever witnessed at a presidential dinner"—a rendition of Verdi, followed by a rousing hootenanny. Marjorie looked elegant in the mink coat that would later touch off a family furor.

Despite the mounting tension between their fathers, Rosa held the family together, and her grandchildrens' memories of the 1960s are happy ones, particularly of the summers they spent together on the ranch and in Lodi. The extended family stayed in touch with its Central Valley roots, even after Cesare's death. During Lodi's annual harvest festival, the Mondavis would gather at Rosa's home on West Pine Street to watch the festival parade. The grown-ups would sit on the porch and steps, while the cousins would perch on the roof above them to get a better view.

The families spent much of the summer together in Lodi, where the heat could rise to an oppressive 103 or 104 degrees during the day. But when they were on the family compound at the Krug Ranch, they'd head to the Napa River, where they'd catch frogs, and fish for sunfish and perch with bobbers. On the Fourth of July, the Mondavis often spent the evening with the Martini family at their nearby winery, the children running around the woods in the pitch-dark night while their parents sipped their drinks and had their own supper, serenaded by the sound of crickets and bullfrogs. For a night out, both Peter and Blanche and Robert and Marjorie were regulars at the square dancing clubs that thrived in St. Helena in the 1960s, a vestige of rural simplicity.

Prunes were still the primary crop and St. Helena's schools sometimes closed during those years to allow children to help out with the harvest. The town's population was just a few thousand people and while it was safe—the Mondavi kids would ride their bicycles to school along St. Helena's elm-lined Main Street and gather after school and on weekends at the A&W Root Beer stand—it also had its prejudices. Robert's eldest son, Michael, was a little embarrassed to tell people his family was in the wine business, because it was then still mostly an immigrant occupation.

Whether she was in Lodi or at the ranch, Rosa spent most of her day in the kitchen, humming happily as she made delicious homemade gnocchi—potato dumplings—with dark, rich sauces made from the quail, duck, and even robins that the boys would shoot from the trees for her. She would strip the meat from the jack rabbits that the boys caught for her: They considered them pests since they'd nibble from the low-hanging grapes. Rosa would also sometimes kill a chicken herself. She'd swing it above her head and then stab it with an ice pick, draining its blood into a pot. Always frugal, she would boil the blood and serve it as a side dish with bacon and onions.

"Nonna," as she was known, never got her driver's license and so, to do her marketing, she would have her sons or grandsons, once they were old enough, drive her to St. Helena to visit the butcher, the baker, and the other merchants in town.

During the Christmas season, the Mondavi cousins would take turns driving Rosa to St. Helena's Main Street, where the shopkeepers would offer their customers cookies, punch, and wine in the back of their stores. "Everyone was speaking Italian" back then, Peter Jr. recalls. Peter, who is known in the family as "Pete," had begun working at the winery when he was eight, unwrapping wineglasses from tissue paper that would be part of the Christmas gift baskets that the winery sold. His older brother, Marc, would assemble gift baskets on the third floor of the creaky and vast Redwood Cellar as a kid.

Every Easter, the Mondavis would stage elaborate egg hunts on the grounds of the ranch—with the older cousins hiding eggs in the gardens or in the Redwood Cellar if it was raining. With catwalks, spiderwebs, and a cupola with 360-degree panoramic views of the vineyards, the winery offered plenty of places for the children to hide and search for colored eggs. The extended family gathered around the table at three P.M. every Sunday for a large home-cooked meal Rosa prepared. The adults might not lay their napkins on their laps and wipe their mouths to finish until four or five hours later. In between courses, the kids would play bocce ball on the lawn. After the meal, someone would usually bring out an accordion; they'd literally roll up the rugs and dance on the wooden floors.

One summer, Timothy and his cousin Marc built a track for Timothy's new gas-fired go-cart. They raced it around the ranch. "We tore up the lawns and got chewed out for it," says Marc. "It's a wonder nobody got killed." Marc says that Nonna, his father, Peter, and Robert seemed to take turns disciplining the boys. Nonna would pull out her yardstick and wave it around threateningly, thwacking the boys with it every now and then.

The cousins spent hours each day during the summer in the swimming pool. And while the Mondavi kids were not brought up to feel they were wealthy, they enjoyed certain amenities. Although

Rosa did all the cooking, she had a full-time housekeeper who would serve the family, many of whom worked at the winery, their several-course lunch each day. In good weather, they'd eat under the spreading oaks, on a rollaway table covered in a red-and-white checked tablecloth, near the front door of Nonna's home. If woodpeckers began making a racket during lunch, Peter, Michael, and sometimes their cousin James would get their BB guns and try to shoot them—at least until their grandmother put a stop to that practice.

"Stop shooting the house, boys," she'd admonish, gesturing with both hands, with a smile on her lips. By then in her seventies, Rosa was broad-hipped and full-bosomed, favoring wash-and-wear jersey dresses and plain, comfortable shoes. She kept the waves of her thick gray hair pinned behind her ears and wore a thin wedding band. She cooked, gardened, and ran the home where she and her brother, Nazzareno Grassi, lived together after Cesare's death. For fun she'd play *scopa*, an Italian card game, and black jack, occasionally cheating to win. When she was dealing, she'd stack the cards in her favor, then slap her winning combination down and proclaim, "Blacka Jacka!" She also loved to watch Lawrence Welk, and attended the monthly dinner dance at the Native Sons of Italy Hall in St. Helena.

Not every aspect of the Mondavi grandchildren's lives was so idyllic. Michael struggled as a student in St. Helena's public school system and spent little time with his father, who traveled constantly. "I was a bad student in a bad school system," Michael says, explaining why his parents decided to send him to a boarding school in the Ojai Valley in the sixth grade. From that time on, Michael traveled back and forth between school and the Krug Ranch.

Michael moved on to Bellarmine Preparatory, a Jesuit high school, where he joined the football team and played offensive guard. He was a fearless player who wouldn't hesitate at going up against boys much bigger than he was, even though by his final years in high school he was a well-put-together six-footer with an athletic build.

Although Michael was outgoing, he didn't often let on that he was from a family that was well off.

Bellarmine was an academically rigorous prep school, with two to three hours of homework per night. Perhaps because of the heavy workload, students liked to blow off steam by pulling pranks, such as lifting up someone else's VW and sticking it between two trees. The acronym for the school disciplinary approach was JUG—an acronym for "Judgment Under God." Students would say they "got JUGged," meaning they'd been disciplined by a teacher. Most of the time punishment entailed memorizing a passage of a text or an obscure snatch of poetry. Day students, who made up about half of Bellarmine's student body, were known as "day dogs."

At his graduation from Bellarmine, Michael recalls receiving several awards, including one for being his class's most improved student. When his father, who attended the ceremonies, learned of the award, he commented, "Oh, my God, I didn't think you had it in you." Robert's cruel remark stung his son, though later Michael would say he didn't think his father intended to wound him. "I think it was his lack of understanding of how to be a father," Michael says now. "One thing you can say is my father never had an excess of sensitivity. It just was not in his DNA."

By 1965, all three of Robert and Marjorie's children were away at college or boarding high schools. Michael, then in his early twenties, was in his final year at the University of Santa Clara, a Jesuit college on the Peninsula just south of San Francisco. Marcia, eighteen in 1965, was completing her senior year at Santa Catalina School for Girls in Monterey, a boarding school, and had been accepted into the University of Santa Clara. Timothy, just fourteen then, was in his first year of Bellarmine Prep.

Michael, Marcia, and Timothy were all boarders. But during the summers, they would return to the ranch and work at the winery. Michael, in particular, began working in Krug's repair shop from eighth grade on and then, when he turned eighteen, worked for several summers alongside his cousin Peter Ventura as a "cellar rat," as Cesare had—doing the toughest, dirtiest jobs there were in the winery. "My father's instructions to Mike Bertolucci, who was the cellar master then, was to give me the dirty jobs and the hard jobs and if I came home and complained, then Mike was doing a good job," Michael said.

Wearing boots and coveralls, they'd scrub the tops, insides, and underneath the huge redwood tanks, encrusted with years of layered sugars, yeast, and mold, where many of Krug's wines were still made. They also played the occasional prank, particularly on the staffers in lab coats who tested the wine. One time, they took the car of one of the lab workers and, with the help of six or eight other workers, lifted it and placed it sideways on a truck ramp so the owner couldn't drive off. Another time, the cousins poured the contents of their buckets over the side of a tank they'd been cleaning on one of the main tour alleys, accidentally drenching a female tourist in the fermenting juice and muck. After their paychecks were docked to pay to clean the dress, the cousins never did that again.

Robert was ambitious for his children and particularly for Michael. But that may not have been the only reason they were off at boarding schools and college during this time. Robert and Marjorie's marriage was strained by his intense focus on work. At family dinners, Robert would spend the entire meal talking about the winery, despite his sister Helen's suggestion that he leave work behind for a few hours and talk about something other than business. But she seldom succeeded in shifting the conversation away from the family business.

Robert was also a perfectionist who held his family to what they saw as impossibly high standards. Always very sparing with compliments, Robert would focus on the one gold medal out of ten that Peter's production innovations at Krug had not won—rather than on the nine that they did. He'd begin with a compliment, saying, "Gee, Peter, this wine is wonderful, but . . ." followed with criticisms.

His children and wife didn't escape his barbed comments either. Indeed, it took a long time for Michael to understand why his father was so harshly judgmental. "He wasn't picking on you; he was measuring everything against the image of perfection that he carried in his mind—but had never experienced." To Robert, what others viewed as his critical eye, he viewed as his drive to raise the business and the family to a higher level.

Marjorie, to all outward appearances, seemed to simply absorb or ignore her husband's criticisms. With an apron tied around her waist and dressing a salad on the oilcloth-covered kitchen table, Marjorie worked hard to develop her skills as a cook, which could never match those of Robert's mother, Rosa. She'd spend hours in her modest kitchen, with curtained windows and a view out to the garden, tidying up the dishes before calling the family to gather around the dinner table for the evening meal. Robert would take his place at one end of the table and Marjorie at the other, and Robert would begin carving the roast. Marjorie was hoping the meal would please her husband.

"An absolutely beautiful dinner, Marj, but the prime rib could have used more salt," he would say. Or, if she'd prepared a leg of lamb, he'd begin by saying, "Gee, Marj, it was great but . . ." and then launch into wide-ranging criticism for twenty minutes.

Always elegant, Marjorie would look at Robert and smile, maintaining her composure. Around the dinner table, with family and friends present, Marjorie would not strike back. Her restraint in the face of her husband's criticism earned her a reputation for being gracious and ladylike. But Marjorie coped with her hurt feelings in other ways. As early as the 1950s, she was drinking heavily and at one point, family members staged what would now be called an intervention to try to help her with the problem. By the 1960s, people outside the family began to realize Robert's wife was an alcoholic. "Marj was an alcoholic because Robert pushed her that way," says the wine historian William Heintz, echoing the sentiments of other people in the valley, particularly those who ended up siding with Peter in disputes between the brothers. "She couldn't keep up with her husband."

Meanwhile, a vivacious Swiss woman named Margrit Biever, who wore her hair in a thickly braided blond pigtail draped over one shoulder, had joined Krug in the early 1960s, leading tours and helping with public relations. Because the winery was a small operation at that time, Margrit (pronounced Margaret) caught Robert's eye. They danced together at Krug's annual employee Christmas party and Margrit remembers that one of the false eyelashes she was wearing had fallen off without her knowing it and was resting on her cheek. Margrit, who was married and had three children of her own, was also able to connect with the Mondavi family through her interest in food and wine as well as her ability to speak Italian. In some respects, she had gifts similar to Rosa's, including her ability to prepare a beautiful meal and to bring people together at the table.

The tension at the Mondavis' dinner table during those years may have been heightened by Robert's roving eye. Michael, for one, believes his mother had sensed the attraction between her husband and his sparkling, buoyant employee almost from the beginning. Peter's wife, Blanche, noticed, too, her brother-in-law's cocky behavior. That gave her another reason to be critical of most everything that her husband's older brother did—including his constant traveling and tendency to focus almost solely on work even at home, which seemed to amount to neglecting his wife and children. Meanwhile, Marjorie's drinking problem worsened as her marriage began to unravel. So when Peter, Rosa, and other members of the family expressed their views that Robert was uncontrollable, they may have meant his private life as well as his expense account.

In early October of 1965, Robert went to Lodi to talk with Peter. The headlines were dominated by Pope Paul VI's visit to the United States and the airwaves were filled with the Beatles' new hit, "Love Me Do." To protest the Vietnam War, student activists had staged the first public burning of a draft card.

Closer to home, there were also big changes taking place; Lodi, the once sleepy town where the Mondavi boys had spent much of their youth, was growing explosively. Highway 99, the site of Cesare's tragic accident in the 1950s, had become a four-lane expressway. A new middle school had opened earlier that year to accommodate the waves of newcomers to the area. In June, voters had passed the first municipal bond measure in forty-four years to fund a new building for the police and fire departments, as well as a new courtroom and sewage treatment plant. But despite the growth, Lodi kept up some of its oldest traditions, including the harvest-time grape festival, which had been held almost every year since 1907.

But on that crisp autumn morning after harvest, as the leaves on the grapevines were reddening, the brothers began to argue over Robert's spending and, specifically, his decision to put Marjorie's mink coat on his company expense account. Peter had once again accused Robert of spending too much company money on travel and promotion. Then Peter, uncharacteristically, exploded and accused Robert of taking money from Charles Krug in order to buy the mink coat, since he doubted that Robert could afford to repay it. Robert was enraged by the implication; his younger brother had dared to call him a thief and a swindler.

"Say that again and I'll hit you," Robert warned him.

Peter said it again.

Then he gave him a third chance. "Take it back."

"No."

Robert swung and struck his younger brother hard. Then he did it again.

By one account, the brothers—both in their fifties by then—ended up wrestling on the ground, dust and curses flying. At some point, Robert had his hands around Peter's neck and throttled him, leaving purple marks on his throat.

When Rosa saw the bruises, she demanded he tell her where he'd gotten them. At first, Peter insisted he didn't know. Then he claimed he had run into a door. Although he was a grown man with children of his own, Peter would always be Rosa's youngest child, in need of her protection as she saw it. Eventually Peter told his mother about how Robert had hit and tried to choke him. That news was the breaking point for Rosa.

After all the years of mounting conflict, the fact that the broth-ers had come to blows precipitated a family crisis. If this had been merely another argument between the Mondavi boys that had gotten out of hand, that would have been one thing. But it was much more. It was the future of the business itself.

Both sides gathered their armies. Rosa, in her role as matriarch, quickly conferred with the rest of the family about what to do about Robert. She also turned to a prominent San Francisco lawyer, Joseph L. Alioto, who would eventually serve as that city's mayor. A year or two earlier, Alioto had joined the board of the Mondavi family's company at Robert's suggestion. One of his key skills was speaking Italian, which helped in communicating with Rosa, whose Italian was better than her English. As well, the family had brought in Fred Ferroggiaro, who was then chairman of the finance committee of the Bank of America and was a member of the family company's board, to try to mediate the dispute between her sons. Rosa also tapped the well-known management consultancy McKinsey and Company to help the family through the crisis.

Robert had met the McKinsey consultant Douglas Watson on a transcontinental Pan Am flight earlier that year from San Francisco to New York. The men spent the entire six-hour flight talking about the wine industry and how it was changing. Watson was struck at the time by Robert's almost evangelical conviction that Krug's future lay in transforming itself into a high-quality, premium wine producer.

Watson quickly grasped that the young vintner's ambitious vision was sharply at odds with the philosophy of some of his other wine clients, including the California Wine Association, a trade group of mostly Central Valley wine producers who shipped their wines back east. Soon after that conversation, Robert hired McKinsey to review Krug's marketing strategy and prepare a ten-year growth plan. He hoped that the white-shoe firm would agree with him that Krug's future was in the fine-wine business.

Watson and his team interviewed the winery's employees and examined Krug's costs. In 1965, the company had earned a pretax profit of $201,000—almost ten times greater than a year earlier. That fact alone would seem to have bolstered Robert's position as head of the family business, since Krug was booming. Robert had asked McKinsey to weigh in on a relatively simple strategic question: whether Krug should drop its less expensive CK label, which sold most of its wines in half-gallon and gallon jugs, and focus instead on its higher-end Charles Krug wines. McKinsey concluded that the winery should focus on its more profitable Charles Krug label wines.

In the course of that study, the McKinsey consultants discovered a swirling cauldron of bitter family emotions. They soon saw that Robert's brash style had alienated the other family members. It didn't take long before they discovered that a majority of Krug's shareholders, Rosa, Peter, Mary, and at that point Helen, believed that Peter should replace Robert as general manager. And although McKinsey's initial assignment was to see if they could find a better way to structure Krug, when Robert punched Peter in Lodi in the fall of 1965, they ended up in the midst of a war, since the majority of Robert's family had turned against him.

Several months after their final report had been delivered and the engagement completed, Watson and his team again met with members of the Mondavi family. This time, though, he met only with Rosa and Henry Ventura at McKinsey's offices on 100 California Street in the heart of San Francisco's financial district. The meeting took place on a Saturday morning. Rosa had turned to Watson and the other consultants because she wanted advice on how to handle her battling sons. Over several hours, the McKinsey men talked through the various possibilities to end the feud once and for all.

To Watson, it seemed as if Rosa had already made up her mind to fire Robert. Diplomatically, the consultant suggested that the family instead ask Robert to take a paid six-month "leave of absence." Watson was hoping that that might cool the family's heated emotions down, allowing Rosa and the rest of her children to see that Robert's contributions to the business outweighed his mistakes in family diplomacy. Rosa decided to take his advice.

A day or two later, Rosa summoned Robert and other members of the family to her home on the ranch. Joining them was Fred Ferroggiaro. As the other members of the family filed out of the room without asking Robert about the dustup between him and Peter, Ferroggiaro delivered the news: Robert must take a six-month leave of absence with pay and would no longer be general manager of Krug. Although Ferroggiaro attempted to present the leave as a "cooling-off period," Robert was furious and shocked at having been blindsided by his mother and siblings. He felt betrayed by his family.

Robert's ouster was formalized at a board meeting of Krug that took place on November 11, 1965, in the main dining room of Rosa's home, with its enormous dining table that could seat twenty. It was a stormy event, with shouting and fists pounding on tables. After hearing the news that all the shareholders of the company with the exception of Robert had decided that Peter should become general manager and Robert should be put on leave, two directors— the company lawyer Webster Clark and an auditor named Harry Meade—objected to Robert's removal. Out-voted, they both ended up resigning in protest instead.

Not long after that meeting, Robert's son Michael learned that there would be no position for him at Krug either. As a senior at the University of Santa Clara, Michael had been planning to join his father and uncle at Krug after a trip to Europe in the summer after his graduation. Instead, Rosa had let it be known that Michael would not be working for the family business. It was a crushing blow—made worse coming from his grandmother. In later years, Michael would struggle to understand why Rosa would do such a hurtful thing to him. The explanation he came up with was that Rosa, for many years, had herself been excluded from any business matters by her chauvinistic husband and was not equipped to handle it when she was forced into that role. Cesare's attitude had been that business was not for women. Indeed, when one of the women in the family would go into Cesare's office in Lodi, all conversation would stop.

Robert, in turn, interpreted Rosa's decision to ban Michael from working in the business less charitably. He simply saw it as her way of making sure that Peter's children would inherit the ranch.

Rosa later denied that she had banned any of her grandchildren from working for Charles Krug. She explained in a court deposition, through an interpreter, that the tensions between her sons had begun years earlier.

"Before dying, my husband asked me to go in between the two brothers and try to make them agree," she said in the deposition. "I answered him: You are not able to do that. How do you think I will be able?" Cesare urged her to try anyway, but her efforts failed. Three and a half months later, her husband died.

To be sure, Rosa was more comfortable preparing food in the kitchen and feeding her family and guests than mediating disputes between her sons. Barely literate and with little or no formal education, she was ill equipped to halt the feud that was brewing. She developed the habit of sucking breath in through her thin lips and letting it out again in a staccato fashion that signaled to her family that she was upset or anxious. At night, she would weep in her bed.

Outwardly, her response to their fighting over the years had been to insist that the boys try to get along, as if they were school-children again. She was a forceful, hardworking person who didn't fear much in her life. Indeed, a few months before Robert and Peter had their tussle, a fire started on the third floor of the winery. Neither of her sons was around at the time. In a moment captured by *The St. Helena Star*, Rosa donned a fireman's jacket and hose to help put out the blaze.

But after the fisticuffs in Lodi, she realized that she could no longer cope on her own with her sons fighting. So she picked one son over the other. Rosa's choice: Peter, the baby of the family who she felt needed more of her protection. Recalling that decision during her deposition, she would explain that she tried to consider all of her children's interests, and perhaps she felt that Robert was better able to fend for himself. "With everybody, because I was—for everything. Sometime I am a mother to everybody. I am the mother of all of them."

Yet, what the Mondavi brothers needed at Charles Krug was not a mother, but a mediator who could help them work out their disagreements quietly and quickly. That didn't happen, despite the efforts of Joe Alioto and others.

However he might rationalize Rosa's reasons, Robert was especially furious that Michael had been banished from working at Charles Krug. Like his own father, he had implicitly embraced the idea that his eldest son would follow in his footsteps and inherit his role as leader of the family business. It was an echo of the ancient system of primogeniture—land going to the firstborn son—that still exists in many rural societies and was certainly the norm in Sassoferrato at the turn of the century, when Cesare and Rosa emigrated to the U.S.

From Robert's perspective, his father's idea had been to build a business for the entire family, including his son Michael. He tried to explain to his mother that his son had wanted to join the business since he was a boy, but Rosa told him he couldn't because of what she termed a "difference of opinion." Rosa refused to be specific with Robert about what that difference was, but, of course, it was Robert and Peter's inability to get along with each other at Krug.

"I then said to her, 'If that's the case, Mother, what I will do, I'm going to build a winery.'"

Afternoon at
Château D'Yquem

Joseph Wechsberg

*No man is born a connoisseur, but with patience and talent you may
become one.*

Monsieur K., Sr.

Monsieur K. lived in a fine old house across from an old park. There
was the smell of marble and wood, and the fragrance of wine that
seems to hover over the old houses of Bordeaux, whose owners have
wisely invested their wealth in fine wines.

Monsieur K. was sitting in the salon as I came in. His armchair
was covered with blue velvet, and his head rested on a needlepoint
lace, like a gem in the jeweler's case. He was a fragile, white-haired
man with a finely shaped head, delicate features, and the hands of
an artist. His art was the wine of Bordeaux. In this city, where fake
experts don't last long, Monsieur K. has been respected for decades
as one of the great artists of wine. I'd known him for years. He told
me how pleased he was to see me again.

"Sit down, sit down," he said, pointing vaguely into space with
no chair in it to sit on. "I've been trying to decide about the wines
that we are going to have with our lunch."

In the adjoining dining room the table was set up in bourgeois
style. Long sticks of white bread, hors-d'reuvres, and olives were
already prepared. Several decanters and wine bottles were standing
on the buffet.

"Sometimes my wife can't make up her mind what to cook, and naturally I can't make up my mind before she's made up hers. People make much fuss about great vintages and fine *crus* but they pay too little attention to the relationship of food and wines. They commit the heresy of serving older, full-bodied wines before younger, elegant ones. They serve the liqueurish wines of Sauternes, Barzac, Monbazillac, Anjou, and Vouvray at the beginning of the meal. Afterward, of course, all other wines appear dull and as mild as milk. People waste fine wines by serving them with salad, the enemy of wine. The only liquid that goes with salad is a glass of mineral water."

Monsieur K. shook his head in resignation. *Rien à faire*, he said, the world was going to the dogs. People would enjoy wines much more if they would follow the simple rules—rules that have been set by the palate, not by wine growers or professional gourmets. With fish, oysters, other seafood, and hors-d'oeuvres, serve Chablis, Pouilly-Fuissé, Puligny-Montrachet, Chassagne-Montrachet, Sancerre-Sauvignon, Vouvray *sec*, Graves *sec*, Tavel, Hermitage *blanc*, Montrachet, Alsace. With white meat and fowl, serve red Bordeaux from the Médoc or Graves region; Beaujolais and light red Burgundies; Chinon, Arbois, Bourgeuil. With red meat, game, *foie gras* and cheese, serve Pomerol, Saint-Émilion, Néac; Beaune, Pommard, Volnay, Corton, Nuits-Saint-Georges, Clos Vougeot, Musigny, Romanée, Chambertin; Moulin-à-Vent, Morgon, Juliénas; Hermitage *rouge*, Côte Rôtie, Châteauneuf-du-Pape.

"People serve white wines ice-cold when they ought to be moderately chilled," said Monsieur K. "Cold wine never offers its full taste. Even here in Bordeaux some people don't know that red wines need time and warmth to release their flavors. They bring their bottles up from the cellars ten minutes before the meal. Sometimes they place them near the stove. *Ah, mais ça se casse!* The sediments fall down, the wine breaks. A few weeks ago a dinner was given here for some ships' captains. I was asked to select the wines. The following day no one called to commend me on my choice—which was unusual. So I investigated. The stewards had put the bottles into a bathtub filled with warm water to bring them up to room temperature. *Right here in Bordeaux!*"

Monsieur K. put the tips of his fingers together and gave the ceiling a contemplative stare. "People treat wine as if it were a soulless liquid. But wine is a living organism. Its cells act like the cells of a human being. Wine lives even when it seems to be dead in the bottle. Believe me, I've stopped going out to restaurants. I just can't stand the sight of a *type* called *sommelier* who wears around his neck a chain that ought to be tied to his leg. He's a criminal, a murderer! He swings a fine old bottle as though it were a soft-ball. He's never heard of the sediments, a sign of maturity and age, which develop over years of careful storing and must not be disturbed. He doesn't know that the cork must be drawn slowly and steadily, without haste or jerking. He forgets to clean the inside lip of the bottle with a white cloth and to sniff at the cork. Perhaps he knows that wine bottles are stored horizontally, and Cognacs and Armagnacs are not, because they would burn the cork. But does he know what a wine cellar should be like—clean, dark, well aired, but without drafts, and in a place that has no street trepidations. Ah, it is all very, very sad."

He got up, and returned with a file containing charts and statistics.

"My little treasure chest. Charts for every year since 1847, giving the exact number of rainy days, the summary of medium temperatures for each month of the year, and the hours of sunshine. There seems to be a sort of recurrent parallelism between certain vintages, every thirty or fifty years. Either they cross one another or they meet in pairs. The cycles would be almost perfect if the war years hadn't created disturbances that were not to be expected. Take, for instance, 1895 and 1945. Both vintages have the same characteristics. The red wines were full-bodied and "roasted," as we call it, having been produced from overripe grapes. The wines were sweet, oily, round, and full of sap. The white wines were sweet, flavory, *savoureux*. Similar analogies exist between 1896 and 1946. Both years produced wines that were harmonious, elegant, deep-colored."

Mme K. came in, a white-haired woman of great dignity, dressed in black. She said lunch was ready. Her husband didn't look up from his charts.

"The wines of 1868 and 1869 are similar to those of 1898 and 1899, exactly thirty years later, and again to those of 1928 and 1929. Always an outstanding year followed by a great one. The years of 1868, 1899, and 1929 have produced wines that are almost strikingly similar: round and oily, soft, yet with lots of life, near-perfect wines. Note too that the 1898 and 1928 are still growing in quality, while the 1899 and 1929 are either at their height or declining. *Ça c'est vraiment curieux!* The charts don't lie, my friend. With the help of those charts my father would be able to forecast the quality of the future harvest as early as June. He made a fortune that way. He made only one mistake, in 1858, when he didn't know that mildew can ruin a harvest. Almost broke him."

Monsieur K. gazed fondly at a framed portrait on the wall. It showed a sumptuously bearded gentleman radiating the confidence that comes from having remade one's fortune after being broke. Mme K. took advantage of the momentary lull in her husband's monologue to point at the table, with the desperate urgency of the hostess who knows that the roast in the oven is getting drier every moment. As we walked into the dining-room, Monsieur K. was reminiscing about his father.

"He used to say: 'No man is born a connoisseur, but with patience and talent you may become one.' But it takes years, many years. When I was four years old, my father let me taste some wine and asked me how I liked it. There never was a meal in our house when wine wasn't discussed at great length. You can't help learning that way."

Lunch was good and the wines were superb. There was a Margaux 1900 which Monsieur K. had decanted a few hours earlier, holding the neck of the bottle against a candle to see when the sediments started to come and it was time to stop pouring. The Margaux was served with a Roquefort that was not too strong in flavor.

Monsieur K. gazed thoughtfully at the robe of the wine, holding his glass against the light. "This Margaux gives me great satisfaction. Back in 1901, when I was a young man, my father and a friend of his went out to the vineyards of Margaux to buy some of the young wines. I was permitted to go along. They tasted this wine, which was then only a few months old. Must have been quite hard on the tongue. My father's friend said: '*Il est bon mais trop gentil.*' My father shook his head. 'This wine will be great in fifty years,' he said. How right he was! Papa was a genius."

The wines of Margaux have always been my favorites for their delicacy, aroma, and beautiful color, and this Margaux seemed to combine all their virtues. It was round and flavory, soft and elegant, truly a great wine.

"I gave a little dinner a few months ago for twelve friends," Monsieur K. said. "All of them are lovers of fine wine. I served them a Château Guiraud 1875, without showing them the label. They were to guess the origin and the year. All came pretty close. Some voted for the Pontet-Canet 1875, and some thought it was a Léoville-LasCases 1871. Everybody agreed that the 1875 was *une exquise jeune fille*. Still, these days some people make much too much fuss about vintages. After all, there have been only four unforgettable vintages in the past hundred years: 1847, 1875, 1900, and 1929."

Mme K., who, in the tradition of long-suffering French wives, had not spoken up while her husband was holding forth, asked me to take another piece of the *tarte aux fraises*. Her husband poured the wine, a liqueurish Château d'Yquem 1899.

"No matter what some people may say about Bordeaux wines, they can't say anything about Yquem," he said, with some asperity. "Yquem is perfection. I chose this wine forty-five years ago. It was the month before we got married."

"That was the Armagnac," said Mme K.

"Oh, yes. I'm sorry, *ma chère*. It was the Armagnac. We will have it later. It is pure perfume—all the sharpness and fire have gone." He gently placed his hand on the arm of his wife. "Forty-five years isn't so long in Bordeaux. At a banquet at Château d'Yquem, a few months ago, they had twenty couples, each of them older than eighty years. . . ." He looked at me and said: "Why don't we drive out to Yquem? The afternoon is pleasant."

An hour later we arrived at the gravel-covered courtyard of Château d'Yquem, a large, medieval stone structure with walls a yard thick and a round watchtower overlooking the gentle slopes of the Sauternes district. A heavy-set, elderly man with a blue beret and heavy bedroom slippers welcomed us. He seemed to be a friend of Monsieur K., who introduced M. Henriot, the *régisseur*. It must be true, as they say in Bordeaux, that people take on the color of the wine that they "work" and drink. M. Landèche's face had had the reddish color of the grapes of Château Lafite-Rothschild. And M. Henriot's hue reflected the golden glow of the wines of Château d'Yquem.

We walked past the administration buildings inside the courtyard. A white-haired patriarch in bedroom slippers came out and vigorously shook hands with Monsieur K. He was the château's bookkeeper and had been employed here fifty-nine years.

"I came in 1893," he said, and rubbed his hands. He seemed none the worse for wear. "It was a golden age. A bottle of Château Yquem cost fifty sous."

"Fifty *gold* sous," Monsieur K. explained.

"Yes," said the bookkeeper. "How easy it was to keep books! Today one needs so much space to write down all the large figures. Did the gentlemen taste our new wine, Léopold?"

"I was just going to take them there," said M. Henriot. "Why don't you come along?"

We walked over a graveled path. In front of a small house a parchment-faced, toothless woman was knitting.

"She was ninety-three last Easter," said the bookkeeper. "Last year, at the dance that Monsieur le Marquis gives at the end of the harvest, she was dancing with me and the other young men. She has her glass of Yquem every night after dinner."

"Maybe a couple of glasses," said M. Henriot. The young men smiled and Monsieur K. clucked his tongue appreciatively.

Presently we were in the cellar. I saw rows of barrels of wine forming straight lines, like soldiers at a parade. M. Henriot, moving about silently in his heavy slippers, brought us samples. The one-year-old wine was still somewhat dry and rough-cornered, but the two-year-old was sweet and luscious, and already had the peculiar flavor of Yquem. I took a swallow, and then I drank up my glass.

M. Henriot chuckled. "*Doucement, doucement*," he said.

"This wine is made of overripe grapes. *La pourriture noble*, we call it. It contains more alcohol than any of the red wines in the Médoc. Ah, our wonderful, wonderful Sauternes!"

His face was brightened up by the supreme bliss that I had noticed earlier on M. Landèche's and Monsieur K.'s faces when they tasted *their* wines. "Isn't it a ray of sunshine, caught in the glass—a bowl of liquid gold?"

We moved to another barrel, and then to the one behind, sampling more wines. A mood of contentment seemed to settle down over the cellar, and us. The old bookkeeper talked of the Cardinal de Sourdis, an archbishop of Bordeaux in the seventeenth century, who had greeted a bottle of Sauternes with the words: "*Je te salue, oh, roi des vins*," and Monsieur K. sat on a barrel, dangling his thin legs, quoting Baudelaire,

> *J'allumerai les yeux de ta femme ravie,*
> *A ton fils je rendrai sa force et ses couleurs . . .*

From the château's chapel came the sound of the Angelus bell. Through the open door of the cellar I saw the sun go down behind the softly rounded slopes of Sauternes with their rows of Semillon and Sauvignon vines. The sky took on the golden glow of the liquid in my glass, and the air had a mellow fragrance. M. Henriot shuffled around in his slippers, refilling our glasses with the liquid gold of Yquem.

from A LONG FINISH
Michael Dibdin

'Barolo, Barbaresco, Brunello. I am a purist, Dottor Zen. I also happen to be able to afford that classical austerity which is the ultimate luxury of those who can have anything they want. In wine, as in music, the three Bs suffice me.'

'I see,' said Aurelio Zen, who didn't see anything except the bins of bottles stretching away into the gloomy reaches of the vast, cold, damp cellar, its vaulted roof encrusted with a white mesh of saltpetre.

'Barolo is the Bach of wine,' his host continued. 'Strong, supremely structured, a little forbidding, but absolutely fundamental. Barbaresco is the Beethoven, taking those qualities and lifting them to heights of subjective passion and pain that have never been surpassed. And Brunello is its Brahms, the softer, fuller, romantic afterglow of so much strenuous excess.'

Aurelio Zen was spared the necessity of answering by an attack of coughing which rendered him speechless for almost a minute.

'How long have you had that cough?' the other man asked with a solicitude which was all too evidently feigned. 'Come, let us go back upstairs.'

'No, no. It's only a touch of chestiness. A cough won't kill me.'

Zen's host looked at him sharply. To someone who did not instantly recognize him—no such person was known to exist—he might have appeared an unremarkable figure: trim and fit for his sixty-odd years, but distinguished mostly by the layers of expensive tailoring which clad him like a second skin, and by a face whose wrinkles and folds seemed an expression not of calendar age but of inheritance, as though it had been worn by countless other eminent and powerful members of the family before being bequeathed to the present owner.

'Kill you?' he exclaimed. 'Of course not!'

With an abrupt laugh, he led the way further into the labyrinth of subterranean caverns. The only light was provided by the small torch he carried, which swung from right to left, picking out stacks of dark brown bottles covered in mildew and dust.

'I am also a purist in my selection,' he announced in the same didactic tone. 'Conterno and Giacosa for Barolo, Gaja and Vincenzo for Barbaresco. And, until the recent unfortunate events, Biondi Santi for Brunello. *Poco ma buono* has always been my motto. I possess an excellent stock of every vintage worth having since 1961, probably the best collection in the country of the legendary '58 and '71, to say nothing of a few flights of fancy such as a Brunello from the year of my birth. Under these exceptional circumstances, vertical tastings acquire a classical rigour and significance.'

He turned and shone his torch into Zen's face.

'You are Venetian. You drink fruity, fresh *vino sfuso* from the Friuli intended to be consumed within the year. You think I am crazy.'

Another prolonged outburst of coughing was the only reply, ending in a loud sneeze. The other man took Zen by the arm.

'Come, you're unwell! We'll go back.'

'No, no, it's nothing.'

Aurelio Zen made a visible effort to get a grip on himself.

'You were saying that I don't understand wine. That's true, of course. But what I really don't understand is the reason why I have been summoned here in the first place.'

His host smiled and raised one eyebrow.

'But the two are the same!'

He turned and strode off down the paved alley between the bins. The darkness closing in about him, Zen had no choice but to follow.

The instruction to attend this meeting at the Rome residence of the world-famous film and opera director, whose artistic eminence was equalled only by the notoriety of the rumours surrounding his private life, had come in the form of an internal memorandum which appeared on his desk at the Ministry of the Interior a few days earlier. 'With respect to a potential parallel enquiry which the Minister is considering regarding the Vincenzo case (see attached file), you are requested to present yourself at 10.30 hrs on Friday next at Palazzo Torrozzo, Via del Corso, for an informal background briefing by . . .'

The name which followed was of such resonance that Giorgio De Angelis, the one friend Zen still had in the Criminalpol department, whistled loudly, having read it over Zen's shoulder.

'*Mamma mia!* Can I come too? Do we get autographs? I could dine out on this for a year!'

'Yes, but who'll pay the bill?' Zen had murmured, as though to himself.

And that was the question which posed itself now, but with renewed force. The celebrity in question clearly hadn't invited Zen to his *palazzo*, scene of so many widely reported parties 'demonstrating that the ancient tradition of the orgy is still not dead', merely to show off his wine collection. There was a bottom line, and the chances were that behind it there would be a threat.

'I can appreciate your point of view,' his host's voice boomed from the darkness ahead. 'I myself grew up in the estuary of the Po, and we drank the local rotgut—heavily watered to make it palatable—as a sort of medicine to aid digestion and kill off undesirable germs. But perhaps there is some other way I can make you understand. Surely you must at some time have collected something. Postage stamps, butterflies, first editions, firearms, badges, matchboxes . . .'

'What's that got to do with wine?'

The famous director, known to his equally famous friends as Giulio, stopped and turned, admitting Zen back into the feeble nimbus of light.

'The object of the collection is as unimportant as the quantities inserted in an algebraic formula. To the collector, all that matters is selection and completeness. It is an almost exclusively male obsession, an expression of our need to control the world. Women rarely collect anything except shoes and jewellery. And lovers, of course.'

Zen did not reply. His host pointed the torch up at the curved ceiling of stone slabs.

'The nitre! It hangs like moss upon the vaults. We are now below Via del Corso. Young men, my sons perhaps included, are racing up and down in their cars as they once did on their horses, yet not a murmur of that senseless frenzy reaches us here. The wine sleeps like the dead.'

'I used to have a collection of railway tickets,' Zen remarked. Giulio flashed a smile.

'I knew it!'

A dry rustling amongst the bottles to his left made Zen start.

'Rats,' said the famous director. 'You were saying?'

'My father . . .'

Zen hesitated, as though at a loss, then started again.

'He worked for the railways, and he used to bring them back for me, little cardboard tickets with the name of the destination printed on them, the class and the fare paid. By the end I had one to all the stations as far as Verona, Rovigo, Udine and Trieste . . .'

He paused again, then clicked his fingers.

'All except Bassano del Grappa! I remember someone making a joke about having to wait until I was older before trying grappa. I didn't understand at the time. I was just annoyed at having that gap in my collection. It ached like a pulled tooth.'

'Excellent! Perfect! Then no doubt you will understand how I felt when I heard about this dreadful business involving Aldo Vincenzo.'

Zen frowned, returning reluctantly to the present.

'Vincenzo?' he echoed.

The famous director shone his torch around the neighbouring bins, lifted a bottle and held it out to Zen. The faded label read: BARBARESCO 1964. VINIFICATO ED IMBOTTIGLIATO DAL PRODUTTORE A. VINCENZO.

'Aldo Vincenzo was one of the producers I selected more than thirty years ago as worthy of a place in the cellar I then decided to create,' he declared solemnly, replacing the bottle on the stack with as much care as a baby in its cot. 'And now he's dead and his son is in prison, all on the eve of what promises to be one of the great vintages of the century! That's the reason why you have been "summoned here", as you put it.'

'You want to complete your collection.'

'Exactly!'

'To continue your horizontal tastings.'

His host regarded Zen sharply, as if suspecting some irony.

'They might be that,' he remarked, 'if one actually swallowed all the wines on offer. Such, of course, is not the way in which a *vertical* tasting is conducted. But in any case, if you imagine that I have any chance of personally enjoying this year's vintage at its best, you credit me with the longevity of a Methuselah. The patriarch, not the bottle.'

Zen struggled mutely with some internal paroxysm, then sneezed loudly, spraying gobs of sputum over the adjacent wine bins. The famous director grasped him once again by the arm and led him back the way they had come.

'Enough! We'll continue this talk upstairs.'

'I'm all right,' Zen protested. 'It's just this cold I've felt coming on for . . .'

'I'm not worried about *you*! But sneezing in a cellar risks half the bottles turning out corked. So they say, at any rate. As for the presence of a menstruating woman, forget it! The whole business of wine is full of that sort of lore. I both believe and disbelieve, but with an investment like this I can't afford to take chances.'

Giulio closed and locked the massive door giving into the vaults and led the way up a long, winding staircase and through an archway leading to the ground floor of the *palazzo*. They passed through several suites of rooms to the book-lined study where he had received Zen on the latter's arrival, and gestured him into the armchair which he had occupied earlier.

'As I was saying, the idea that I'm collecting the Vincenzo wine of this year—assuming there is any—for my own benefit is, of course, absurd. If the vintage is even half as good as has been predicted, it will not be remotely approachable for ten years, and won't reach its peak for another ten. By which time I will be, if not defunct, at least "sans teeth, sans eyes, sans taste, sans everything", as Shakespeare says.'

'Then why should you care?' demanded Zen, lighting a cigarette, which induced another massive fit of coughing. The other man eyed him keenly.

'Do you have children, *dottore?*'

'No. That's to say . . . Yes. One.'

'Boy or girl?'

'A boy. Carlo.'

'How old?'

There was a long pause.

'He's just a baby,' Zen replied at length.

'Congratulations! But they grow up rapidly. Hence my interest in this year's Vincenzo wines. I have two sons, both in the most repulsive period of their teens. At present they regard my interest in wine as just another example of their father's dotage. If they drink at all, it's some obscure brand of imported beer, although Luca at least shows promising signs of becoming a *collezionista* about that, too, hunting down limited-release Trappist brews and the like.'

He set about the meticulous business of cutting and lighting a massive cigar.

'I believe—I *have* to believe—that in time they will come to appreciate what I have bequeathed them, and perhaps even set about extending the cellar far into the next millennium as a heritage for their own children.'

A triumphant puff of blue smoke.

'But that is to look too far into the future. For the moment, all that concerns me is this harvest! Unless we act now, the grapes will either be sold off to some competitor or crudely vinified into a parody of what a Vincenzo wine could and should be.'

Aurelio Zen tried hard to look suitably concerned at this dire prospect.

'But what can I do about it?' he asked. 'If the son is already under arrest . . .'

'I don't believe for a moment that he did it,' the famous director exclaimed impatiently.

Zen produced a crumpled handkerchief from his pocket and blew his nose.

'Nevertheless, I've been given to understand that the Carabinieri have concluded their investigation. They have pressed charges against Manlio Vincenzo and the case is now in the hands of the judiciary. I don't see where I come in.'

His host exhaled a dense barrage of smoke.

'Perhaps you should be more concerned about where you go out,' he said.

Zen frowned.

'Go out? You mean, from this house?'

For the first time, Giulio smiled with what appeared genuine amusement.

'No, no! All appearances to the contrary, I am not planning to immure you in some lost recess of my cellars. Nevertheless, a not dissimilar fate might well await you.'

He eyed Zen keenly.

'I refer to your next professional posting.'

'That is a matter of departmental policy,' Zen replied, drawing on his cigarette.

Another smile, a shade more meaningful.

'Exactly. And in that regard I wish to draw your attention to various facts of which you are aware, and to another which is as yet privileged information. I shall be brief. Firstly, the current Minister is a man of the Left. Many of his friends and associates in the former Communist Party dedicated their lives to the struggle against organized crime. Some of them were killed as a result.'

His eyes met Zen's, and slid away.

'In addition, you have recently been reassigned to work for Criminalpol after your brilliant exploits in Naples where, as the whole country knows, you were instrumental in smashing the terrorist organization known as *Strade Pulite*.'

'But that was . . .'

'A major coup! Indeed. All this you know, *dottore*. What you do not know—what no one outside the Minister's immediate circle knows—is that he is in the process of forming an élite pool of senior officers who are to be drafted to Sicily to spearhead the coming campaign against the organization which took the lives of his comrades.'

Giulio waved his hand negligently.

'We've all heard this before, of course, every time some judge or police officer was gunned down or blown up. But that was in the days when the Mafia had its men here in Rome, in the highest circles of power. Everyone understood how the game worked. Any over-zealous official who looked like he was doing some worthwhile work was transferred or killed, the government put up a token show of force, the Mafia made a token show of backing off, and in a few months it was back to business as usual.'

He glanced at Zen, who stifled a cough.

'But this time, so I am assured, it will be different. A fight to the finish, with no quarter offered. The Mafia's links to Rome have all been cut, and the new government is eager to show that it can deliver on what its predecessors endlessly promised. As a result, a process of internal head-hunting has been going on for officers of proven experience, ability and—shall we say?—independence.'

He broke off to relight his cigar, holding the tip at a respectful distance from the flame.

'Your dossier, Dottor Zen, revealed you to have been severely compromised in the eyes of the former regime. This fact, needless to say, put you at the top of the list under the new management. Add to this your evident astuteness and ability to get things done, and you became a natural candidate for the new squad.'

'They're sending me to Sicily?' gasped Zen.

His host nodded.

'Oh, yes. I'm afraid there's nothing we can do about that. There's promotion in it, of course, and a substantial pay rise, but you're definitely going to have to go south. The only question is when and where.'

For a moment Zen looked as though he was about to burst into tears, but all that emerged was another massive sneeze.

'*Salute!*' said his host. 'Speaking of which, Sicily is notoriously insalubrious, particularly for newly arrived policemen who might well be drafted straight to the capital. If one were to arrive a little later, on the other hand, once the central command structure had been set up and all posts in Palermo filled, it might prove possible to secure an assignment in some relatively pleasant spot. Do you know Syracuse? An ancient Greek settlement in the least troubled portion of the island, possessing all the charm and beauty of Sicily without being tiresomely . . . well, *Sicilian.*'

Zen raised his eyes to meet those of his interlocutor.

'What guarantees do I have?'

A look of pain, almost of shock, appeared on the famous director's face.

'You have the guarantee of my word, *dottore.*'

'And your interest is?'

'I thought I'd made that clear. I want Manlio Vincenzo released from prison in time to make the wine this year.'

'Even if he murdered his father?'

A shrug.

'If he turns out to be innocent, so much the better. But let's assume that he did kill Aldo. It's absurd to believe that Manlio Vincenzo poses a threat to any other member of the community. And in the meantime there's a potentially great wine—maybe *the* great wine of the century—which demands the skill and attention only he can provide.'

He shrugged again, more expansively.

'After that, I don't really care what happens to him. In a year the estate will have had time to reorganize, to get another wine-maker or sell out to Gaja or Cerretto, either of whom would be only too glad to get their hands on the Vincenzo vineyards. But for now, Manlio's my only resource. Just as I'm yours.'

Zen sat trying to catch his breath through the layers of phlegm which had percolated down into his lungs.

Why me?' he demanded point-blank.

The famous director waved the hand holding his cigar, which left a convoluted wake of smoke hanging in the still air.

'I made various enquiries, as a result of which someone mentioned your name and sketched in the details of your record. Most promising, I thought. You appear to be intelligent, devious and effective, compromised only by a regrettable tendency to insist on a conventional conception of morality at certain crucial moments—a weakness which, I regret to say, has hampered your career. In short, *dottore*, you need someone to save you from yourself.'

Zen said nothing.

'In return for the services which I have outlined,' his host continued seamlessly, 'I offer myself in that capacity. I understand that at one time you enjoyed the favour of a certain notable associated with the political party based at Palazzo Sisti. His name, alas, no longer commands the respect it once did. Such are the perils of placing oneself under the protection of politicians, particularly in the present climate. They come and go, but business remains business. If you do the business for me, Dottor Zen, I'll do the same for you. For your son, too, for that matter. What was his name again?'

'Carlo.'

The famous director leant forward and fixed Zen with an intense gaze, as though framing one of his trademark camera angles.

'Do we have a deal?'

Zen was briefly disabled by another internal convulsion.

'On one condition,' he said.

The man known to his friends as Giulio frowned. Conditions were not something he was used to negotiating with the class of hireling which Zen represented.

'And what might that be?' he asked with a silky hint of menace.

Aurelio Zen sniffed loudly and blew his nose again.

'That when you next give a party here, I get an invitation.'

There was a moment's silence, then the famous director roared with what sounded like genuine laughter.

'Agreed!'

THE ASSASSIN IN THE VINEYARD

Maximillian Potter

The winter-night sky above the Côte d'Or countryside of Burgundy, in eastern France, is cloudless, with just enough moon to illuminate the snow-covered ground and silhouettes. From dense woods atop a hill, a man emerges. He moves from the trees and starts down the gently sloping hillside—and almost immediately he is surrounded by vineyard. The vines are frost-dusted and barren, twisted and vulnerable, like the skeletons of arthritic hands reaching for spring.

The vineyard is within a sea of vineyards that stretches seemingly without end to the man's left and right: row after row after row they unfurl, barely separated from one another by ribbons of fallow land or narrow road. In the direction he walks, easterly, the vines flow with him down the hill, continuing as the ground flattens, until off in the distance they end at a small village. The hamlet, Vosne-Romanée, is constructed of ancient stone and topped with shake shingles, its humble, storybook skyline marked by a church steeple. At this late hour, in early January 2010, shutters are closed, and no one stirs.

As the man descends the hill, navigating the vines, he exudes the purpose of someone who knows precisely where he's headed and what must be done when he gets there. All around him the vine rows are so uniformly straight it's evident they have been meticulously arranged, painstakingly cultivated. At one particular vineyard, the man stops. Unlike the vineyards around it, this one is marked by a monument: a tall, gray, stone cross that towers over the vines like a sacred scarecrow. In the base of the cross are engravings; there's a date: 1723. The cross is perched atop a section of a low stone wall, and affixed to the wall is a sign in both French and English. It reads:

MANY PEOPLE COME TO VISIT THIS SITE AND
WE UNDERSTAND. WE ASK YOU NEVERTHELESS
TO REMAIN ON THE ROAD AND REQUEST THAT
UNDER NO CONDITION YOU ENTER THE VINEYARD.
THANK YOU FOR YOUR COMPREHENSION.

Here, in the vineyard called La Romanée-Conti, the man drops to his knees. For a moment, it appears that he might pray, that he might be one of the thousands of devotees who every year for decades now have come from around the world to see this patch of earth that oenophiles regard as a kind of mecca-Xanadu.

"A fabulous thing"—so begins one of the books about this vineyard. "Mysterious, sensuous, transcendental, the greatest wine in the dukedom of Burgundy, once reserved for the table of princes, its origins blurred in the mists of time—cannot help but spawn fabulists. For two centuries, no wine—no vineyard—has so deeply and so consistently motivated man's mythologizing instinct as La Romanée-Conti."

But the man has come for other reasons entirely. His breath puffing into the frigid night air, he reaches to his forehead, and a headlamp flicks on. From his shadow of a shape, he produces a cordless drill and a syringe. He begins to drill into the *pied de vigne*—the foot of the vine—the low whir of the drill's motor lost in the cold, smothered by the overwhelming quiet. He moves to a neighboring vine, less than a yard away, and does the same.

He takes up the syringe. He plunges it into the hole he has drilled in one of the vines and injects some of the syringe's contents. He performs the same procedure on the other vine. The man collects his drill and syringe, turns off his headlamp, and makes his way up the hill. He steps from the sea of vineyard and disappears back into the trees.

The Holy Grail

Burgundy's Côte d'Or is arguably the world's most enigmatic wine-growing region. About a three-hour drive southeast of Paris, it is a 30-mile-long-by-two-mile-wide slice of countryside between Dijon in the north and Beaune to the south. Within Burgundy—or Bourgogne—there are dozens of subregions, and within those, numerous towns and villages. Vosne-Romanée is a village in the Côte d'Or. And in this relatively tiny sliver of Burgundy there are literally hundreds of vineyards, or *climats*.

Although the region cultivates almost exclusively one type of red grape, the Pinot Noir, the wines of each *climat* are distinctive. This is not the hype of wine marketers or the sales pitch of French wine brokers—*négociants*—but rather a geological fact. Abrupt, dramatic changes in fault lines and other natural phenomena unique to the Côte mean the characteristics—the *terroir*—of individual *climats*, even ones side by side, can be wildly different. So, too, then are their Pinot grapes. Along with the hundreds of *climats*, there are almost as many wine-making *domaines*, and most every *domaine* has its own viticulture techniques. Therefore, to refer to a wine from this area as a "Pinot Noir" means nothing and discounts everything.

All of these same factors are what draw discerning oenophiles and savvy collectors to Burgundy. The diversity, the complexity, the romantic alchemy of it all, when done well, when uncorked and dancing over the palate, are what make Burgundies . . . well, so divine. As the writer Matt Kramer put it in his critically acclaimed guide to the region, *Making Sense of Burgundy*, "Even the most skeptical are willing, after savoring a genuinely great Burgundy, to concede that there may well be—dare one say it?—a Presence in the universe beyond our own."

The fact that Burgundy has such a small wine-growing region and produces, comparatively speaking—in relation, say, to the expansive French Bordeaux region—so few bottles only makes the quest for the finest Burgundies all the more worthwhile. One would be hard-pressed to find an educated wine-lover who would disagree with

Robert Sleigh, one of Sotheby's leading wine experts, when he says, "Romanée-Conti is hands down the best and rarest Burgundy in the world—the Holy Grail." The legendary vineyard is a postage stamp of soil at 4.46 acres, producing roughly 500 cases annually, which is less than one-fiftieth the production of Bordeaux's Château Lafite Rothschild.

Indeed, whatever superlatives can be ascribed to a wine apply to the eponymous wine from the Romanée-Conti vineyard. It ranks among the very top of the most highly coveted, most expensive wines in the world. According to the Domaine de la Romanée-Conti's exclusive American distributor, Wilson Daniels, acquiring or purchasing a bottle is as simple as calling your local "fine-wine retailer." However, because D.R.C. is produced in such limited quantities, and because the high-end wine market is such an intricate and virtually impenetrable web of advance orders—futures—and aftermarket wheeling and dealing, it's not as simple as the distributor suggests. Wilson Daniels's own Web site points would-be D.R.C. buyers to wine-searcher.com, which is a worldwide marketplace for wine sales and online auctions. There, the average price for a single bottle from 2007 (excluding tax and the buyers' premium) is $6,455—and that's the most recent vintage available.

A bottle of 1945 Romanée-Conti would be a steal at $38,000. Last October, in Hong Kong, Sotheby's Sleigh staged a record-setting sale of Romanée-Conti. The 77 bottles, which included three magnums, were divided among 18 lots, spanned relatively recent vintages between 1990 and 2007, and fetched a total hammer price of $750,609. A single bottle of 1990 Romanée-Conti went for $10,953—which was a few hundred dollars more than the sale price that day for an entire 12-bottle lot of 1990 Château Lafite.

Only a few months before that Hong Kong auction, word of the attack on the vines of Romanée-Conti began seeping into the world beyond Burgundy. Very little news of the incident—what in reality was an unprecedented and remarkable crime—had been reported in the French media. In the United States, there was nothing other than small blurbs in the wine press. Clearly, no one in

Burgundy—including the patriarch in charge of the family-owned-and-operated Domaine de la Romanée-Conti—wanted to talk about it publicly. By way of explaining the silence, a former mayor from the Côte and a wine-maker there, Jeanine Gros, summed it up succinctly: " 'Wine' and 'poison,' these two words do not belong in the same sentence."

The Slope of Gold

'There are no great vineyards produced by predestination, by divine providence," the French observer Pierre Veilletet wrote. "There is only the obstinacy of civilization." The obstinate one in charge of the great Romanée-Conti today is 71-year-old Aubert de Villaine. Over two rainy days this past fall, he allowed me into his Domaine de la Romanée-Conti and discussed, albeit most reluctantly, the plot against his wine. However, as de Villaine pointed out, he does not feel that the vineyard is his family's per se; rather, it belongs to Burgundy, to history—and to fully appreciate the crime, the sacrilege, one must understand all of the holiness and hedonism that flow through Romanée-Conti.

The Benedictine monks of the medieval Catholic Church were the original obstinate ones who civilized Burgundy's Côte. They were the *défricheurs*, or "ground clearers," who married the fickle Pinot Noir grape to the ostensibly inhospitable terrain. They discovered that a narrow strip of land about halfway down the gently sloping hillside produces the very best wines—the grands crus. "The Slope of Gold," it was called. While the monks first cultivated the vineyard that would become Romanée-Conti, it was the Prince de Conti, centuries later, who gave the wine its name and infused it with nobility and naughty.

The worthless forest and fallow land that the Duke of Burgundy had deeded to the monks in the 1100s were by the late 1500s profitable *climats*, and the monarchy wanted in. Taxation compelled the priory to sell a "perpetual lease" on their finest *climat*, the first incarnation of Romanée-Conti: Cros des Cloux. Between 1584 and

1631, Cros des Cloux had three owners, before it was transferred to the Croonembourg family. Under this owner, Cros des Cloux blossomed in the marketplace. As it did, for reasons historians can't fully explain, the family changed the name to La Romanée. By 1733 the Croonembourgs' La Romanée was going for prices as much as six times those of most other reputable growths of the Côte. Still, when the Croonembourg patriarch died, in 1745, the family over the next 15 years slipped into debt and La Romanée was sold to Louis-François de Bourbon—the Prince de Conti.

A noble, and a magnet for intrigue, drama, and a good party, Louis-François was married and had a mistress by the time he was 16. His mother-in-law caught wind of the affair and to punish him persuaded the monarchy that her young son-in-law ought to serve in King Louis XV's army. During France's 1733 war with Austria, Louis-François earned the rank lieutenant general and the king's admiration.

The king came to cherish the prince. He not only gave de Conti his own army but knighted him into the Order of Malta, one of the highest honors of the time (which excused him from the otherwise required vow of celibacy). The king grew so close to the prince that the king's mistress, Madame de Pompadour, came to despise de Conti. It so happened that when the Croonembourg estate offered La Romanée for sale in July 1760, she, too, desired it. Perhaps knowing that if Madame de Pompadour learned of his interest in the vineyard she would surely outbid him, the prince hired a proxy who successfully represented him in the sale.

The Order of Malta appointment gave Louis-François claim to the Palais du Temple, in Paris. He and his mistress turned the palace into something of a party compound for intellectuals and artists—Mozart was a regular guest. Immediately upon purchasing La Romanée, the prince removed the wine from the market and kept it for himself, for entertaining at the palace. The La Romanée that had been first cultivated as God's work, and that was then sold for six times more than other grands crus, was now exclusively for nobles and their V.I.P. dinner parties, out of reach for mere mortals.

Rooted in the Domaine

The Prince de Conti died as America was born, in 1776. His son, Louis-François Joseph, the next prince, carried on his father's partying and aristocratic ways. And this did not serve him well in the wake of the French Revolution. "His house is filled with plotters and conspirators" is how one historical record describes the prince in 1790. "It is easy to see . . . that it is he and he alone who conceives and guides aristocratic plots." The prince was arrested, and the government auctioned his vineyard, which for the first time was billed at sale as La Romanée-Conti.

The vineyard passed through three families between 1794 and 1869, the year that Aubert de Villaine's ancestor Jacques-Marie Duvault-Blochet took over. Upon Blochet's death, shares of Romanée-Conti splintered among his heirs, and no one thought much about the vines until 1910, when Aubert's grandfather Edmond Gaudin de Villaine, who had married into the family, took on the role of managing the D.R.C.

Edmond was the architect of the modern D.R.C. He unified the parcels of Romanée-Conti that had fractured among the heirs. In 1912 he trademarked "Domaine de la Romanée-Conti," and in 1933, Edmond acquired all of the La Tâche vineyard, which is but a few yards from Romanée-Conti. Acquiring sole ownership of Romanée-Conti and La Tâche gave the D.R.C. *monopoles* over the two best vineyards in Burgundy, and for that matter two of the best vineyards in the world.

Of course no success is without struggle. World War I destabilized Europe's wine market. America, with its Prohibition and Great Depression, was not yet a market that could be counted on. Fortunately, Edmond found a like-minded partner in a local *négociant*, Henri Leroy, who bought a 50 percent share in the Domaine. Thanks to their collective leadership and financial resilience the Domaine's *monopoles* of La Tâche and Romanée-Conti remained whole and strong. What's more, even as other *domaines* had to sell and divide their *climats*, Leroy and de Villaine maintained parcels of other top-tier vineyards—Échézeaux, Romanée-St.-Vivant, Richebourg, and Grands Échézeaux—all very near one another, under the banner of the Domaine de la Romanée-Conti. These *climats*—along with the lone D.R.C. Chardonnay Montrachet, which the Domaine acquired between 1964 and 1980—produce grands crus that are second in quality, reputation, and price only to La Tâche and Romanée-Conti.

Growing up and watching his grandfather, and then his own father, Henri, give so much of themselves to the D.R.C., young Aubert was not sure wine-making would be for him. One of six children, he went to Paris, the big city, where he studied political science. In the early 1960s he moved to America and hung out for a year in Northern California, wine country of all places. He wrote a couple of articles about California wines for *La Revue du Vin de France*. He fell in love with an American girl from Santa Barbara with a *Gatsby*-esque name, Pamela Fairbanks, who would become his wife.

It was after moving about, leaving the D.R.C., that a 26-year-old de Villaine came to realize that his life, his soul, was indeed rooted in the Domaine, and in 1965 he asked his father if he could begin working at the vineyard. Ever since, de Villaine's reverence for the D.R.C. has been absolute. He and Pamela do not have children, so in the fall of 2010, he turned over his shares in the Domaine to his nieces and nephews. He tried to make them understand that the shares were not gifts from him and were much more than shares in a company. He impressed upon his young relatives that the shares derived from people they had loved dearly: one of de Villaine's two brothers, who died very young, and his own father, who died years ago. He told his nieces and nephews, too, that the shares were fruits from vines cultivated by people they never knew, who gave the best of themselves for many generations.

Wine and Poison

On the top of Aubert de Villaine's otherwise tan, bald head there is a doily-size pinkish splotch. When he takes a moment to give something consideration, he scratches this spot, just as he does when he has to decide when the harvest ought to begin—and just as he did on that day in early January 2010 when he found himself reading an unsigned note informing him that the D.R.C. must prepare to pay a ransom or Romanée-Conti would be destroyed.

It was not so much a note as it was a package, delivered to his private residence. (A similar package arrived at the home of Henry-Frédéric Roch, who holds the title of co-director of the D.R.C. and represents the Leroy family's interest in the Domaine.) Inside the cylindrical container, the type an architect might use for blueprints, was a large parchment. Unrolled, the document was a detailed drawing of Romanée-Conti. While the 4.46-acre vineyard is essentially a rectangle, there are nuances to its shape. De Villaine noticed that whoever had sent this letter and sketched the vineyard knew its every contour, and what's more, the author had noted every single one of its roughly 20,000 vine stocks. In the center of the vineyard sketch this person, or persons, had drawn a circle. There was a note, too, which conveyed that the vineyard would be destroyed unless certain demands were met; the note stated that another letter with further instructions would be coming in 10 to 15 days.

De Villaine viewed the letter as a hoax, some kind of sick joke. Really, if he has to admit it, he chose to see it that way. That was easier, *much* easier, than to think it was real. Then, in mid-January 2010, he received another package at his home. It was in the same type of cylindrical container, and inside was the same sketch of the vineyard. Only this time there were two circles. In addition to the circle in the center, there was another, much smaller circle in the upper left corner of the vineyard.

The correspondence instructed de Villaine to leave one million euros in a suitcase in the corner of the Romanée-Conti vineyard, right near the area represented by the small circle on the drawing. By way of proof that he—she, they, whoever they were—meant business, the letter informed de Villaine that some 82 vines of Romanée-Conti had already been poisoned. According to the note, the two vines in the area marked on the sketch by two X's in the small circle had been killed by poison. The other 80 vines were marked by X's in the much larger, center circle; however, those could be spared with an antidote—that is, provided de Villaine paid up.

This time, de Villaine called the authorities. He did not call the local police. Burgundy is too small, too full of gossips and competitors who might use this fact or fiction against his Domaine. True or not, if the world thought the D.R.C. vineyards had been compromised . . . Well, de Villaine could not begin to imagine, or, rather, he *could* imagine what that might mean. He could not afford for this to be mishandled, and so he called a police official he'd met in Dijon who was now a senior official with the police based in Paris. Investigators arrived at the D.R.C. The two vines supposedly poisoned were removed. Quickly, it was determined they had been poisoned, and were dying. The other 80 or so vines in the large circle—while they had been drilled—in reality had not been poisoned. That part, at least so far, was a bluff.

Whoever was responsible, de Villaine was convinced, knew exactly what he was doing by targeting the D.R.C. It was clearly someone who had been sneaking around in his vineyard, and for quite some time, to produce such a detailed sketch. What's more, it appeared to de Villaine that whoever it was likely knew a great deal about wine. The second letter included sophisticated wine-making terms, like *décavaillonnage* and *démontage*.

And there was this fact: from what the police had discovered, the criminal, or criminals, used a syringe to inject the poison. This was especially significant—over the centuries, *vignerons* had used such a *pal* or syringe-like technique to inject liquid carbon disulfide into the soil and save the vineyards from devastating infestations by the phylloxera insect. Meaning, the very methodology that had been used to preserve the vines was now being employed in an attempt to kill the vineyards of Romanée-Conti.

On the advice of investigators, de Villaine did not drop off the money as directed. Instead, a trusted employee, in the dark of night, left a note in the vineyard on the specified day, February 4. In the note, de Villaine relayed that he would pay as demanded, but it would take time to muster the euros; he'd have to call an emergency meeting of the shareholders from the Leroy and de Villaine families. Within a matter of days, de Villaine received another mailing—what would be the third and final piece of correspondence. The tone of this letter was polite, even grateful that payment would be made. It instructed de Villaine to *please* deliver the money in a valise to the cemetery in the neighboring town of Chambolle-Musigny. The suitcase was to be left inside the cemetery gates at 11 P.M. on February 12, 2010.

The week of the arranged drop-off, de Villaine was scheduled to be out of the country, in America, on a promotional tour for the D.R.C.'s 2007 vintages. The investigators assigned to the case encouraged de Villaine to go about his normal business. They told him it was important to act as if nothing unusual were afoot. They reminded him, too, that the same D.R.C. employee who had left the note at the vineyard could serve as the drop-off man. Jean-Charles Cuvelier, the deputy manager of the D.R.C., the police said, appears to "be capable and cold-blooded." The latter part of the description was wry cop humor, for Cuvelier is about as cold and hard as a freshly baked croissant.

Cuvelier has been de Villaine's indispensable lieutenant since 1993. The two met at a party in Dijon. Cuvelier, then in his early 30s, had mentioned that he was a schoolteacher who worked with at-risk kids and that the job was wearing on him. De Villaine mentioned he was looking for an assistant. Ever since, Cuvelier has been at de Villaine's side, or, rather, quietly anticipating his needs. As Étienne Grivot, himself a respected wine-maker in the Côte, puts it, Cuvelier is considered "the guardian of the Temple."

Cuvelier is a stocky man, now in his late 50s, with bifocals perched on the end of his nose, which he tends to wrinkle. He has a gap-toothed smile and fidgets a great deal, but with a nervousness that's endearing. Evidently he easily perspires through a dress shirt and a wool sweater on a cold day, but only because, it seems, he is sweating the details of the D.R.C.

Not all that long ago, Cuvelier became a widower. After a prolonged battle against cancer his wife of 33 years died in June 2008. And so, who would have blamed Cuvelier if, on that night of

February 12, 2010, he had allowed himself to wonder what his wife would have said if she could see him now, walking into a cemetery in the black of night, carrying a suitcase filled with one million in fake euros. Not knowing who or what was behind this plot and what might be in store, he could only hope she would watch over him and keep him safe.

The ancient village of Chambolle-Musigny is only about two miles north of Vosne-Romanée, if you take the right dirt road through the vineyards of the Côte. Like Vosne-Romanée, Chambolle-Musigny has no more than 600 full-time residents. The cemetery is on the outskirts of the town. You pass it on the way in and out; it's square, surrounded by a stone wall, and not much bigger than a public pool. The entrance is an arching, green wrought-iron fence. Just as the criminal had directed, it was 11 P.M. when Cuvelier pushed through the squeaking gates.

Earlier in the day, Cuvelier had traveled to the police station in Dijon, where he was briefed on the night's plan. There would be about a dozen armed police officers hidden about the cemetery, with their eyes on him and everything around him. In the bag, along with the fake euros, there'd be a transmitter—a tracking device—that would be activated when the bag passed by a sensor embedded in the threshold of the cemetery archway. Cuvelier was instructed to keep the earpiece for his cellular phone in his ear and activated, as a police officer would be in constant communication with him. Cuvelier, breathing heavily, trembling, perspiring, his heart pounding, entered the cemetery. It was cold and dark, with frost on the tombstones. He dropped the bag in the flower box just inside the gate and exited. He got into his car and drove off. No more than 30 minutes later, he received a call from the police: *We got him.*

Crime and Punishment

Cuvelier immediately phoned de Villaine in the United States and passed along the information police had thus far. The man's name was Jacques Soltys; he was in his late 50s. Stunningly, catching him had been a snap. After Cuvelier left the bag, police spotted Soltys coming down a hillside on foot, then heading toward the cemetery. He retrieved the bag and walked off. He was caught less than 200 meters from the cemetery, on his way to a nearby train station. In the days that followed, as police learned more, so did Cuvelier and de Villaine.

The D.R.C. had not been Soltys's only mark. He had simultaneously orchestrated a similar plot against another very highly regarded vineyard, Domaine Comte Georges de Vogüé, in Chambolle-Musigny. Police discovered this because the first package mailed to de Villaine had a Paris postmark. Footage from the surveillance cameras at that Paris post office revealed that another package, very similar to the ones mailed to de Villaine, had been mailed to the owners of de Vogüé. That vineyard, too, had lost two of its vines to poison.

As de Villaine and Jean-Luc Pépin, the director of de Vogüé, suspected, based on the extortion notes and sketches, Soltys indeed knew about wine-making. When Soltys had been about 12 or 13 years old, his parents sent him to the Lycée Viticole de Beaune, a boarding trade school that specializes in wine-making. According to the current principal, Pierre Enjuanès, who still has Soltys's file, Soltys was raised in the Épernay area, a region known for champagne. His parents were wine-makers there, overseeing a modest vineyard. And, Enjuanès says, Soltys was trouble from the start. He was at the school for only a few months before he was expelled, for offenses including smoking, cursing, and staying up all night. In the file at the school, there's a black-and-white picture of young Soltys: dark hair, starched white collar, furrowed brow. A headshot for a boy that would have a life of mug shots.

Soltys went from delinquent to career criminal. He'd committed a string of armed robberies and even attempted a kidnapping. During one of the crimes, shots were exchanged with the police, and Soltys ended up hit in the chest. In all he'd been sentenced to at least 20 years. Though he served only a portion of that time, he'd spent most of his adult life behind bars. Soltys figured that there were easier jobs to pull off, like extorting wine-makers.

Soltys had done a considerable amount of planning and preparation. He'd built a makeshift shack deep in the woods atop the hills overlooking the vineyards. In the shack, among other things, police found a sleeping bag, a couch, a hot plate, a change of clothes—the clothes of a vineyard laborer—batteries, a headlamp, a cordless-drill kit, syringes, many bottles of the weed killer Roundup, and a handgun.

Soltys had not been operating alone. He'd been able to mail the package to de Villaine's home because, according to what the police told de Villaine, Soltys had his son, Cédric, follow the winemaker and learn his address. Unlike his father, Cédric, who according to sources is in his late 20s or early 30s, didn't have a record but, according to several sources, is mentally fragile. Perhaps because of the way his father had raised him, or, rather, didn't raise him. Regardless, the portrait of the son that emerges is one who relied heavily on his father. Soltys Sr. may have treated his son poorly, but he also looked after him. It was an *Of Mice and Men* George-and-Lennie bond. According to a central character in the investigation, Soltys's life of crime had left his wife, Cédric's mother, struggling to get by. If anything, it seems, she too was a victim.

To show his thanks to the investigators, when de Villaine returned from his trip to America he invited them to the Domaine and uncorked a few bottles of 2006 Vosne-Romanée Premier Cru—along with a tasting of a 1961 Romanée-Conti—to toast their work. In the weeks following the arrest, as word of the crime leaked into the French press, de Villaine began hoping that the whole matter could be bottled up quietly, that whatever criminal proceedings there needed to be would be resolved without trial.

De Villaine was concerned that a trial would generate media attention, which in turn might inspire copycat crimes. Also, why would he want the world to think about the fact that weed killer had been injected into vines of Romanée-Conti? Five months after the arrests, the prosecution's case against Jacques and Cédric Soltys became extremely difficult to pursue, because in July 2010, Jacques turned up dead in a Dijon prison. According to prison officials, he'd hung himself in a bathroom.

Burgundy's Heritage

The French legal system is unlike America's. Among the many differences, once a suspect is in custody, the matter is turned over to a
juge d'instruction. Akin to a one-person grand jury, this judge takes
over the investigation, overseeing both the defense and the prosecution, *and* the police, and decides whether official charges—"formal
accusations"—should be filed. Until a trial begins, there are no public
records of the case. No police reports are made public, not even mug
shots. Defense attorneys can be fined or worse for speaking to the
media. Officially, the only officer of the court empowered to discuss
the Soltys matter is Éric Lallement, the equivalent of the district
attorney of Dijon.

On an afternoon late last year, Lallement showed me into his
office and through an interpreter fielded questions about the matter. A man in his early 50s, dressed in a blue suit, he sat with his
legs crossed and fiddled with his cuff links while he spoke. On the
coffee table between us was a file filled with information about the
Soltys case. He kept this file to himself but referred to it periodically
throughout our conversation. Soltys, he said, left behind a suicide
note, but in it he did not, as a father might do, attempt to absolve his
son of responsibility. Cédric, he said, had been released from prison,
but not cleared of charges.

Lallement suspected the judge *would* determine formal accusations were warranted against the son. After all, he said, Romanée-
Conti is not only a Burgundian treasure but a national one, and it is
important for the government to send the message that such crimes
will not be tolerated.

Of particular interest to Lallement is that the Soltys plot to
poison the most storied vineyard in the world is unprecedented.
While there have been crimes of vandalism, agriculture terrorism,
and extortion on vineyards in France and elsewhere, never before has
there been a poisoning of the vines. The top wine-makers of the most
storied *domaines* and families in Vosne-Romanée—Étienne Grivot,
Louis-Michel Liger-Belair, Jean-Nicolas Méo-Camuzet, Jeanine and

Michel Gros—all say that they have never seen a crime like this before.

Yes, they are concerned. Quite frankly, they all would rather not discuss such a vulnerability. Like de Villaine, they are concerned about the possibility of copycat attempts. They quietly support his wish that there be no trial, that there be no further talk of the Soltyses and poison in the vines, as there is nothing anyone could do, or at least *wants* to do, to prevent such crimes. "A Burgundy with fences and lights and patrolled by German shepherds," says Cécile Mathiaud, press director for the association of Burgundy wine-makers. "This is something I cannot imagine. This would not be Burgundy."

According to a law-enforcement official, when Cédric found out about his father's suicide, he sat in a chair, staring into space, looking lost. This same source said that while the judge may determine formal accusations may be warranted against Cédric Soltys, experts hired to determine his mental competency would likely declare he is not fit to stand trial, and the matter would never reach a public trial. Thus far, Lallement's prediction for the legal proceeding is the correct one. Early this year, according to Jean-Luc Chemin, a prosecutor colleague of Lallement's, the French courts had determined that Cédric will face trial. Chemin says he has been assigned to prosecute the case, which he suspects will begin "sometime after September."

Such a trial might solve a lingering mysery: on the surveillance tape the police obtained from the Paris post office, the person mailing the Soltys packages was not Jacques or Cédric, though it was unclear who exactly the person was. Perhaps whoever it was was an ignorant pawn, simply someone asked to mail a few parcels. Or perhaps not. According to Jean-Luc Pépin, the director of the Domaine Comte Georges de Vogüé, the police found evidence of plans to carry out similar plots against other vineyards. "Oh, yes," he says, "it appeared there would be more vineyards targeted."

Outwardly, at least, Aubert de Villaine seems to have moved on. After all, the two tainted vines have been removed, and all traces of the Roundup are gone. Ultimately, no other vines were harmed—the *terroir* has been preserved, there will be no impact on future harvests.

In addition to producing the world's finest Burgundy, de Villaine is at the forefront of a campaign to have the United Nations Educational, Scientific and Cultural Organization recognize all of the Côte as a World Heritage site. Currently there are 911 sites around the world that have received this rare distinction. World Heritage status means that, among other criteria met, the site has "outstanding universal value." The Great Barrier Reef, the Great Wall of China, the Tower of London, the Statue of Liberty, and the banks of the Seine in Paris are but a few on the list. It would, undoubtedly, be a fitting tribute for the D.R.C., the de Villaine family, the larger Burgundian family, and France. Such an honor, Aubert de Villaine understandably hopes, would make it easier for everyone to forget all of this talk of wine and poison.

BURGUNDY ON THE HUDSON

Bill Buford

Last month, Daniel Johnnes, the wine director at one of New York's most expensive restaurants, Montrachet (which is French for "Give me your wallet"), persuaded eighteen winemakers from Burgundy to come to New York to show off the subtleties of their stuff. There was a wine tasting in the afternoon, and a grand meal in the evening, and, in addition to the many wines on offer, in varying flamboyant sizes of extravagance (magnums, Methuselahs, and an unknown thing, poured by two people at once, that looked like a small tanker truck), there were bottles brought by the guests, a hidden admission cost that resulted in there being quite a lot to drink.

The evening, which was called La Paulée de New York, and was inspired by the harvest festival in France (it remains unclear what harvest was being celebrated in midtown in the month of February), was organized around the cooking of several notable chefs. The entertainment was provided by Les Cadets de Bourgogne, and consisted of a dozen old men singing an oompah-pah song every ten or fifteen minutes, which sounded like a French interpretation of the hokey-pokey. In their version, you stand up, and then, rather than putting your left foot in, or your right foot out, you merely flash your hands in one direction, and flash your hands in another, and then clap a few times. It didn't seem particularly subtle, given that subtlety was the theme of the evening. Red Burgundy is made from the Pinot Noir grape, and its qualities are not always immediately apparent, especially to Americans, who tend to like wines made with the much heartier Cabernet Sauvignon. Cabernet has American virtues—forthright, not fancy, and distinguished by its irrepressible sunny disposition. Cabernet also has the distinction of smelling like a grape. Pinot Noir, which is grown in misery and mildewy dampness and tends to rot, is altogether different. Its distinction is not in what it tastes like but in what it smells like, and in its greatest examples that smell is described euphemistically as "barnyard." Great Burgundies, that is, smell of cow shit.

Any of this could be learned from one of the great winemakers scattered around the room. The most distinguished was Dominique Lafon, the cool, blond, thin, aristocratic son of René Lafon, who was, in turn, the grandson of Jules Lafon, who was, as it happens, the inventor of this very festival. The Lafons make a Burgundy so exquisite that you can't find it in New York. In any case, subtlety turned out not to be the theme of the evening, which was evident to anyone lucky enough to be seated next to one of the great winemakers. ("Psst," Daniel Johnnes was overheard saying, "you're next to Dominique Lafon. Congratulations. I'm counting on seeing some party tricks in return.") Party tricks? The real objective of the evening, it was becoming evident, was not to educate anybody in anything but merely to take work-obsessed, mineral-water-drinking, gym-going New Yorkers and render them blotto and legless.

It would be impossible to know how many different wines were drunk, and for a very good reason: by the end of the evening, few people could count. There were scorecards in evidence (pieces of paper with scratch marks), and every now and then a label that, in the damp, gurgled air, had fallen off one of the bottles. For instance, there was some sprayed-upon wrinkled thing from one of Dominique Lafon's ancient bottles, a 1967 something, or maybe it was a 1917 something—whatever it was, it was blurry, or somebody was. Or slurry. Something. Furry, maybe. And there was Dominique Lafon himself, no longer looking quite so aristocratic, standing on his chair and leading everyone in a new round of the French hokey-pokey, which was starting to sound impressively subtle after all. "It's a bit like Chopin, innit?" somebody said. The wine, though, seemed to be losing some of its subtlety. In fact, by that point in the evening, after fifty different examples of the stuff (or was it sixty?), it was a bit like stewed fruit. Stewed fruit that smelled of cow shit.

The education of the evening turned out to be in the benefit auction at the end. Now, there's a strategy: get a bunch of wealthy New Yorkers blindingly blitzo-blotto and then sell them something. The bidding started off sensibly enough. A magnum of Montrachet was sold for eight thousand dollars. That's about seven hundred dollars a glass. The purchaser was an eye surgeon, who made so much money that he worked only on Mondays and Tuesdays and read wine catalogues the rest of the week. Nice life. Things started to get a little crazy when a lunch with the wine guru Robert Parker went for twenty thousand dollars. But that was only lunch. The next item was a dinner, cooked in your home by the chef Daniel Boulud. That was it: dinner at home. The first bid was ten thousand dollars, placed by a big bald man with a long cigar, who then thumped his chest and made a kind of *ugh* sound. This was raised immediately to twenty thousand dollars by a man with an even larger chest. He then high-fived his neighbor and roared. This was raised—well, you get the idea. There was a lot of manly noise. Unusually, it ended in a draw (very gentlemanly), with the two barrel chests offering forty thousand dollars each.

By the close, there was a feeling that a moment in European-American relations had been witnessed, in which the French behaved like the French and the affluent New Yorkers were irretrievably themselves. There were other feelings, too—illness, double vision, and a furry, slurry, blurry thing that was not a good feeling at all.

JUST ENOUGH MONEY

A.J. Liebling

If, as I was saying before I digressed, the first requisite for writing well about food is a good appetite, the second is to put in your apprenticeship as a feeder when you have enough money to pay the check but not enough to produce indifference to the size of the total. (I also meant to say, previously, that Waverley Root has a good appetite, but I never got around to it.) The optimum financial position for a serious apprentice feeder is to have funds in hand for three more days, with a reasonable, but not certain, prospect of reinforcements thereafter. The student at the Sorbonne waiting for his remittance, the newspaperman waiting for his salary, the freelance writer waiting for a check that he has cause to believe is in the mail—all are favorably situated to learn. (It goes without saying that it is essential to be in France.) The man of appetite who will stint himself when he can see three days ahead has no vocation, and I dismiss from consideration, as manic, the fellow who will spend the lot on one great feast and then live on fried potatoes until his next increment; Tuaregs eat that way, but only because they never know when they are going to come by their next sheep. The clear-headed voracious man learns because he tries to compose his meals to obtain an appreciable quantity of pleasure from each. It is from this weighing of delights against their cost that the student eater (particularly if he is a student at the University of Paris) erects the scale of values that will serve him until he dies or has to reside in the Middle West for a long period. The scale is different for each eater, as it is for each writer.

Eating is highly subjective, and the man who accepts say-so in youth will wind up in bad and overtouted restaurants in middle age, ordering what the maître d'hôtel suggests. He will have been guided to them by food-snob publications, and he will fall into the habit of drinking too much before dinner to kill the taste of what he has been told he should like but doesn't. An illustration: For about six years, I kept hearing of a restaurant in the richest shire of Connecticut whose proprietor, a Frenchman, had been an assistant of a disciple of the great Escoffier. Report had it that in these wilds—inhabited only by executives of the highest grade, walking the woods like the King of Nemi until somebody came on from Winnetka to cut their throats— the restaurateur gave full vent to the creative flame. His clients took what he chose to give them. If they declined, they had to go down the pike to some joint where a steak cost only twelve dollars, and word would get around that they felt their crowns in danger—they had been detected economizing. I finally arranged to be smuggled out to the place disguised as a *Time-Life* Executive Vice-Publisher in Charge of Hosannas with the mission of entertaining the advertising manager of the Hebrew National Delicatessen Corporation. When we arrived, we found the Yale-blue vicuña rope up and the bar full of couples in the hundred-thousand-dollar bracket, dead drunk as they waited for tables; knowing that this would be no back-yard cookout, they had taken prophylactic anesthesia. But when I tasted the food, I perceived that they had been needlessly alarmed. The Frenchman, discouraged because for four years no customers had tasted what they were eating, had taken to bourbon-on-the-rocks. In a morose way, he had resigned himself to becoming dishonestly rich. The food was no better than Howard Johnson's, and the customers, had they not been paralyzed by the time they got to it, would have liked it as well. The *spécialité de la maison*, the unhappy *patron* said when I interrogated him, was jellied oysters dyed red, white, and blue. "At least they are aware of that," he said. "The colors attract their attention." There was an on-the-hour service of Brink's armored cars between his door and the night-deposit vault of a bank in New York, conveying the money that rolled into the *caisse*. The wheels, like a juggernaut's, rolled over his secret heart. His intention in the beginning had been noble, but he was a victim of the system.

The reference room where I pursued my own first earnest researches as a feeder without the crippling handicap of affluence was the Restaurant des Beaux-Arts, on the Rue Bonaparte, in 1926–27. I was a student, in a highly generalized way, at the Sorbonne, taking targets of opportunity for study. Eating soon developed into one of my major subjects. The franc was at twenty-six to the dollar, and the researcher, if he had only a certain sum—say, six francs—to spend, soon established for himself whether, for example, a half bottle of Tavel *superieur*, at three and a half francs, and braised beef heart and yellow turnips, at two and a half, gave him more or less pleasure than a *contre-filet* of beef, at five francs, and a half bottle of *ordinaire*, at one franc. He might find that he liked the heart, with its strong, rich flavor and odd texture, nearly as well as the beef, and that since the Tavel was overwhelmingly better than the cheap wine, he had done well to order the first pair. Or he might find that he so much preferred the generous, sanguine *contre-filet* that he could accept the undistinguished *picrate* instead of the Tavel. As in a bridge tournament, the learner played duplicate hands, making the opposite choice of fare the next time the problem presented itself. (It was seldom as simple as my example, of course, because a meal usually included at least an hors d'oeuvre and a cheese, and there was a complexity of each to choose from. The arrival, in season, of fresh asparagus or venison further complicated matters. In the first case, the investigator had to decide what course to omit in order to fit the asparagus in, and, in the second, whether to forgo all else in order to afford venison.)

A rich man, faced with this simple sumptuary dilemma, would have ordered both the Tavel *and* the *contre-filet*. He would then never know whether he liked beef heart, or whether an *ordinaire* wouldn't do him as well as something better. (There are people to whom wine is merely an alcoholized sauce, although they may have sensitive palates for meat or pastries.) When one considers the millions of permutations of foods and wines to test, it is easy to see that life is too short for the formulation of dogma. Each eater can but establish a few general principles that are true only for him. Our hypothetical rich *client* might even have ordered a Pommard, because it was listed at a higher price than the Tavel, and because he was more likely to be acquainted with it. He would then never have learned that a good Tavel is better than a fair-to-middling Pommard—better than a fair-to-middling almost anything, in my opinion. In student restaurants, renowned wines like Pommard were apt to be mediocre specimens of their kind, since the customers could never have afforded the going prices of the best growths and years. A man who is rich in his adolescence is almost doomed to be a dilettante at table. This is not because all millionaires are stupid but because they are not impelled to experiment. In learning to eat, as in psychoanalysis, the customer, in order to profit, must be sensible of the cost.

There is small likelihood that a rich man will frequent modest restaurants even at the beginning of his gustatory career; he will patronize restaurants, sometimes good, where the prices are high and the repertory is limited to dishes for which it is conventionally permissible to charge high prices. From this list, he will order the dishes that in his limited experience he has already found agreeable. Later, when his habits are formed, he will distrust the originality that he has never been constrained to develop. A diet based chiefly on game birds and oysters becomes a habit as easily as a diet of jelly doughnuts and hamburgers. It is a better habit, of course, but restrictive just the same. Even in Paris, one can dine in the costly restaurants for years without learning that there are fish other than sole, turbot, salmon (in season), trout, and the Mediterranean *rouget* and *loup de mer*. The fresh herring or sardine *sauce moutarde;* the *colin froid mayonnaise;* the conger eel *en matelote;* the small fresh-water fish of the Seine and the Marne, fried crisp and served *en buisson;* the whiting *en colère* (his tail in his mouth, as if contorted with anger); and even the skate and the *dorade*—all these, except by special and infrequent invitation, are out of the swim. (It is a standing tourist joke to say that the fishermen on the quays of the Seine never catch anything, but in fact they often take home the makings of a nice fish fry, especially in winter. In my hotel on the Square Louvois, I had a room waiter—a Czech naturalized in

France—who used to catch hundreds of *goujons* and *ablettes* on his days off. He once brought a shoe box of them to my room to prove that Seine fishing was not pure whimsey.) All the fish I have mentioned have their habitats in humbler restaurants, the only places where the aspirant eater can become familiar with their honest fishy tastes and the decisive modes of accommodation that suit them. Personally, I like tastes that know their own minds. The reason that people who detest fish often tolerate sole is that sole doesn't taste very much like fish, and even this degree of resemblance disappears when it is submerged in the kind of sauce that patrons of Piedmontese restaurants in London and New York think characteristically French. People with the same apathy toward decided flavor relish "South African lobster" tails—frozen as long as the Siberian mammoth—because they don't taste lobstery. ("South African lobsters" are a kind of sea crayfish, or *langouste*, but that would be nothing against them if they were fresh.) They prefer processed cheese because it isn't cheesy, and synthetic vanilla extract because it isn't vanillary. They have made a triumph of the Delicious apple because it doesn't taste like an apple, and of the Golden Delicious because it doesn't taste like anything. In a related field, "dry" (non-beery) beer and "light" (non-Scotchlike) Scotch are more of the same. The standard of perfection for vodka (no color, no taste, no smell) was expounded to me long ago by the then Estonian consul-general in New York, and it accounts perfectly for the drink's rising popularity with those who like their alcohol in conjunction with the reassuring tastes of infancy—tomato juice, orange juice, chicken broth. It is the ideal intoxicant for the drinker who wants no reminder of how hurt Mother would be if she knew what he was doing.

The consistently rich man is also unlikely to make the acquaintance of meat dishes of robust taste—the hot *andouille* and *andouillette*, which are close-packed sausages of smoked tripe, and the *boudin*, or blood pudding, and all its relatives that figure in the pages of Rabelais and on the menus of the market restaurants. He will not meet the *civets*, or dark, winy stews of domestic rabbit and old turkey. A tough old turkey with plenty of character makes the best *civet*, and only in a *civet* is turkey good to eat. Young turkey, like young sheep, calf, spring chicken, and baby lobster, is a pale preliminary phase of its species. The pig, the pigeon, and the goat—as suckling, squab, and kid—are the only animals that are at their best to eat when immature. The first in later life becomes gross through indolence; the second and third grow muscular through overactivity. And the world of tripery is barred to the well-heeled, except for occasional exposure to an expurgated version of *tripes à la mode de Caen*. They have never seen *gras-double* (tripe cooked with vegetables, principally onions) or *pieds et paquets* (sheep's tripe and calves' feet with salt pork). In his book, Waverley Root dismisses tripe, but he is no plutocrat; his rejection is deliberate, after fair trial. Still, his insensibility to its charms seems to me odd in a New Englander, as he is by origin. Fried pickled honeycomb tripe used to be the most agreeable feature of a winter breakfast in New Hampshire, and Fall River, Root's home town, is in the same cultural circumscription.

Finally, to have done with our rich man, seldom does he see even the simple, well-pounded *bifteck* or the *pot-au-feu* itself—the foundation glory of French cooking. Alexandre Dumas the elder wrote in his *Dictionary of Cuisine*: "French cooking, the first of all cuisines, owes its superiority to the excellence of French bouillon. This excellence derives from a sort of intuition with which I shall not say our cooks but our women of the people are endowed." This bouillon is one of the two end products of the *pot*. The other is the material that has produced it—beef, carrots, parsnips, white turnips, leeks, celery, onions, cloves, garlic, and cracked marrowbones, and, for the dress version, fowl. Served *in* some of the bouillon, this constitutes the dish known as *pot-au-feu*. Dumas is against poultry "unless it is old," but advises that "an old pigeon, a partridge, or a rabbit roasted in advance, a crow in November or December" works wonders. He postulates "seven hours of sustained simmering," with constant attention to the "scum" that forms on the surface and to the water level. ("Think twice before adding water, though if your meat actually rises above the level of the bouillon it is necessary to add boiling water to cover it.") This supervision demands the full-time presence of the cook in the kitchen throughout the day, and the maintenance of the temperature calls for a considerable outlay in fuel. It is one reason that the *pot-au-feu* has declined as a chief element of the working-class diet in France. Women go out to work, and gas costs too much. For a genuinely good *pot-au-feu*, Dumas says, one should take a fresh piece of beef—"a twelve-to-fifteen-pound rump"—and simmer it seven hours in the bouillon of the beef that you simmered seven hours the day before. He does not say what good housekeepers did with the first piece of beef—perhaps cut it into sandwiches for the children's lunch. He regrets that even when he wrote, in 1869, excessive haste was beginning to mar cookery; the demanding ritual of the *pot* itself had been abandoned. This was "a receptacle that never left the fire, day or night," Dumas writes. "A chicken was put into it as a chicken was withdrawn, a piece of beef as a piece was taken out, and a glass of water whenever a cup of broth was removed. Every kind of meat that cooked in this bouillon gained, rather than lost, in flavor." *Pot-au-feu* is so hard to find in chic restaurants nowadays that every Saturday evening there is a mass pilgrimage from the fashionable quarters to Chez Benoit, near the Châtelet—a small but not cheap restaurant that serves it once a week. I have never found a crow in Benoit's *pot*, but all the rest is good.

A drastically poor man, naturally, has even less chance than a drastically rich one to educate himself gastronomically. For him eating becomes merely a matter of subsistence; he can exercise no choice. The chief attraction of the cheapest student restaurants in my time was advertised on their largest placards: "*Pain à Discrétion*" ("All the Bread You Want"). They did not graduate discriminating eaters. During that invaluable year, I met a keen observer who gave me a tip: "If you run across a restaurant where you often see priests eating with priests, or sporting girls with sporting girls, you may be confident that it is good. Those are two classes of people who like to eat well and get their money's worth. If you see a priest eating with a layman, though, don't be too sure about the money's worth. The fellow *en civil* may be a rich parishioner, and the good Father won't worry about the price. And if the girl is with a man, you can't count on anything. It may be her kept man, in which case she won't care what she spends on him, or the man who is keeping her, in which case she won't care what he spends on her."

Failing the sure indications cited above, a good augury is the presence of French newspapermen.

The Restaurant des Beaux-Arts, where I did my early research, was across the street from the École des Beaux-Arts, and not, in fact, precisely in my quarter, which was that of the university proper, a good half mile away, on the other side of the Boulevard Saint-Germain. It was a half mile that made as much difference as the border between France and Switzerland. The language was the same, but not the inhabitants. Along the Rue Bonaparte there were antiquarians, and in the streets leading off it there were practitioners of the ancillary arts—picture framers and bookbinders. The bookshops of the Rue Bonaparte, of which there were many, dealt in fine editions and rare books, instead of the used textbooks and works of erudition that predominated around the university. The students of the Beaux-Arts were only a small element of the population of the neighborhood, and they were a different breed from the students of the Boulevard Saint-Michel and its tributaries, such as the Rue de l'École de Méde-cine, where I lived. They were older and seemingly in easier circum-stances. I suspected them of commercial art and of helping Italians to forge antiques. Because there was more money about, and because the quarter had a larger proportion of adult, experienced eaters, it was better territory for restaurants than the immediate neighborhood of the Sorbonne. I had matriculated at the Faculté des Lettres and at the École des Chartes, which forms medievalists, but since I had ceased attending classes after the first two weeks, I had no need to stick close to home. One of the chief joys of that academic year was that it was one long cut without fear of retribution.

I chanced upon the Restaurant des Beaux-Arts while strolling one noon and tried it because it looked neither chic nor sordid, and the prices on the menu were about right for me: *pâté maison*, 75 centimes; sardines, 1 franc; artichoke, 1.25; and so on. A legend over the door referred to the proprietor as a M. Teyssedre, but the heading of the bill of fare called him Balazuc. Which name represented a former proprietor and which the current one I never learned. I had a distaste for asking direct questions, a practice I considered ill-bred. This had handicapped me during my brief career as a reporter in Providence, Rhode Island, but not as much as you might think. Direct questions tighten a man up, and even if he answers, he will not tell you anything you have not asked him. What you want is to get him to tell you his story. After he has, you can ask clarifying questions, such as "How did you come to have the ax in your hand?" I had interrupted this journalistic grind after one year, at the suggestion of my father, a wise man. "You used to talk about wanting to go to Europe for a year of study," he said to me one spring day in 1926, when I was home in New York for a weekend. "You are getting so interested in what you are doing that if you don't go now you never will. You might even get married."

I sensed my father's generous intention, and, fearing that he might change his mind, I told him that I didn't feel I should go, since I was indeed thinking of getting married. "The girl is ten years older than I am," I said, "and Mother might think she is kind of fast, because she is being kept by a cotton broker from Memphis, Tennessee, who only comes North once in a while. But you are a man of the world, and you understand that a woman can't always help herself. Basically . . ." Within the week, I had a letter of credit on the Irving Trust for two thousand dollars, and a reservation on the old *Caronia* for late in the summer, when the off-season rates would be in effect. It was characteristic of my father that even while doing a remarkably generous thing he did not want to waste the difference between a full-season and an off-season passage on a one-class boat. (He never called a liner anything but a boat, and I always found it hard to do otherwise myself, until I stopped trying. "Boat" is an expression of affection, not disrespect; it is like calling a woman a girl. What may be ships in proportion to Oxford, where the dictionary is written, are boats in proportion to New York, where they nuzzle up to the bank to feed, like the waterfowl in Central Park.)

While I continued to work on the Providence paper until the rates changed, Father, with my mother and sister, embarked for Europe on a Holland-American boat—full-season rate and first class—so that my sister might take advantage of her summer holiday from school. I was to join them for a few days at the end of the summer, after which they would return to the United States and I would apply myself to my studies. Fortunately, I discovered that the titulary of a letter of credit can draw on it at the issuing bank as easily as abroad. By the time I sailed, I was eight hundred dollars into the letter, and after a week in Paris at a hotel off the Champs-Elysées I found, without astonishment, that I had spent more than half of the paternal fellowship that was intended to last me all year. The academic year would not begin until November, and I realized that I would be lucky to have anything at all by then. At this juncture, the cotton broker's girl came to my rescue in a vision, as an angel came to Constantine's. I telegraphed to my parents, who were at Lake Como, that I was on my way to join them. From my attitude when I got there—reserved, dignified, preoccupied—my father sensed that I was in trouble. The morning after my arrival, I proposed that we take a walk, just the two of us, by the lake. Soon we felt thirst, and we entered the trellised arbor of a hotel more modest than ours and ordered a bottle of rustic wine that recalled the stuff that Big Tony, my barber in Providence, used to manufacture in his yard on Federal Hill. Warmed by this homelike glow, I told my father that I had dilapidated his generous gift; I had dissipated in riotous living seventy-two per cent of the good man's unsolicited benefaction. Now there was only one honorable thing for me to do—go back to work, get married, and settle down. "She is so noble that she wouldn't tell me," I said, "but I'm afraid I left her in the lurch."

"God damn it," he said, "I knew I should never have given you that money in one piece. But I want you to continue your education. How much will you need every month?"

"Two hundred," I said, moderately. Later, I wished I had asked for fifty more; he might have gone for it. "You stay in Paris," he said—he knew I had chosen the Sorbonne—"and I'll have the Irving send you two hundred dollars every month. No more lump sums. When a young man gets tangled up with that kind of woman, they can ruin his whole life."

That was how I came to be living in Paris that academic year in a financial situation that facilitated my researches. Looking back,

I am sure my father knew that I wanted to stay on, and that there was no girl to worry about. But he also understood that I couldn't simply beg; for pride's sake, I had to offer a fake *quid pro quo* and pretend to myself that he believed me. He had a very good idea of the value of leisure, not having had any until it was too late to become accustomed to it, and a very good idea of the pleasure afforded by knowledge that has no commercial use, having never had time to acquire more than a few odd bits. His parents had brought him to America when he was eight years old; he went to work at ten, opened his own firm at twenty-one, started being rich at thirty, and died broke at sixty-five—a perfect Horatio Alger story, except that Alger never followed his heroes through. At the moment, though, he had the money, and he knew the best things it would buy.

The great day of each month, then, was the one when my draft arrived at the main office of the Crédit Lyonnais—the Irving's correspondent bank—on the Boulevard des Italiens. It was never even approximately certain what day the draft would get there; there was no air mail, and I could not be sure what ship it was on. The Crédit, on receiving the draft, would notify me, again by ordinary mail, and that would use up another day. After the second of the month, I would begin to be haunted by the notion that the funds might have arrived and that I could save a day by walking over and inquiring. Consequently, I walked a good many times across the river and the city from the Rue de l'École de Médecine to the Boulevard des Italiens, via the Rue Bonaparte, where I would lunch at the Maison Teyssedre or Balazuc. There were long vertical black enamel plaques on either side of the restaurant door, bearing, in gold letters, such information as "Room for Parties," "Telephone," "Snails," "Specialty of Broils," and, most notably, "Renowned Cellar, Great Specialty of Wines of the Rhône." The Great Specialty dated back to the regime of a proprietor anteceding M. Teyssedre-Balazuc. This prehistoric *patron*, undoubtedly an immigrant from Languedoc or Provence, had set up a bridgehead in Paris for the wines of his region of origin.

The wines of the Rhône each have a decided individuality, viable even when taken in conjunction with *brandade de morue*—a delightful purée of salt codfish, olive oil, and crushed garlic—which is their compatriot. *Brandade*, according to Root, is "definitely not the sort of dish that is likely to be served at the Tour d'Argent." "Subtlety," that hackneyed wine word, is a cliché seldom employed in writing about Rhône wines; their appeal is totally unambiguous. The Maison Teyssedre-Balazuc had the whole gamut, beginning with a rough, faintly sour Côtes du Rhône—which means, I suppose, anything grown along that river as it runs its three-hundred-and-eighty-mile course through France. It continued with a Tavel and then a Tavel *supérieur*. The proprietor got his wines in barrel and bottled them in the Renowned Cellar; the plain Tavel came to the table in a bottle with a blue wax seal over the cork, the *supérieur* in a bottle with a purple seal. It cost two cents more a pint. I do not pretend to remember every price on the card of the Restaurant des Beaux-Arts, but one figure has remained graven in my heart like "Constantinople" in the dying Czar's. A half bottle of Tavel *supérieur* was 3.50; I can still see the figure when I close my eyes, written in purple ink on the cheap, grayish paper of the *carte*. This is a mnenonic testimonial to how good the wine was, and to how many times I struggled with my profligate tendencies at that particular point in the menu, arguing that the unqualified Tavel, which was very good, was quite good enough; two cents a day multiplied by thirty, I frequently told myself, mounted up to fifteen francs a month. I don't think I ever won the argument; my spendthrift palate carried the day. Tavel has a rose-cerise *robe*, like a number of well-known racing silks, but its taste is not thin or acidulous, as that of most of its mimics is. The taste is warm but dry, like an enthusiasm held under restraint, and there is a tantalizing suspicion of bitterness when the wine hits the top of the palate. With the second glass, the enthusiasm gains; with the third, it is overpowering. The effect is generous and calorific, stimulative of cerebration and the social instincts. "An apparently light but treacherous *rosé*," Root calls it, with a nuance of resentment that hints at some old misadventure.

Tavel is from a place of that name in Languedoc, just west of the Rhône. In 1926, there were in all France only two well-known wines that were neither red nor white. One was Tavel, and the other Arbois, from the Jura—and Arbois is not a rose-colored but an "onion-peel" wine, with russet and purple glints. In the late thirties, the *rosés* began to proliferate in wine regions where they had never been known before, as growers discovered how marketable they were, and to this day they continue to pop up like measles on the wine map. Most often *rosés* are made from red wine grapes, but the process is abbreviated by removing the liquid prematurely from contact with the grape skins. This saves time and trouble. The product is a semi-aborted red wine. Any normally white wine can be converted into a *rosé* simply by adding a dosage of red wine* or cochineal.

In 1926 and 1927, for example, I never heard of Anjou *rosé* wine, although I read wine cards every day and spent a week of purposeful drinking in Angers, a glorious white-wine city. Alsace is another famous white-wine country that now lends its name to countless cases of a pinkish cross between No-Cal and vinegar; if, in 1926, I had crossed the sacred threshold of Valentin Sorg's restaurant in Strasbourg and asked the sommelier for a *rosé d'Alsace*, he would have, quite properly, kicked me into Germany. The list is endless now; flipping the coated-paper pages of any dealer's brochure, you see *rosés* from Bordeaux, Burgundy, all the South of France, California, Chile, Algeria, and heaven knows where else. Pink champagne, colored by the same procedure, has existed for a century and was invented for the African and Anglo-Saxon trade. The "discovery" of the demand for pink wine approximately coincided with the repeal of prohibition in the United States. (The American housewife is susceptible to eye and color appeal.) In England, too, in the same period, a new class of wine buyer was rising with the social revolution. Pink worked its miracle there, and also in France itself, where many families previously limited to the cheapest kind of bulk wine were beginning to graduate to "nice things."

---

* "Some [peasants] will give you a quick recipe for *rosé* which shall not pollute these pages."—The late Morton Shand's classic, *A Book of French Wines*, Jonathan Cape, Ltd., London, 1960 edition.

Logically, there is no reason any good white- or red-wine region should not produce equally good *rosé*, but in practice the proprietors of the good vineyards have no cause to change the nature of their wines; they can sell every drop they make. It is impossible to imagine a proprietor at Montrachet, or Chablis, or Pouilly, for example, tinting his wine to make a Bourgogne *rosé*. It is almost as hard to imagine it of a producer of first-rate Alsatian or Angevin wines. The wines converted to *rosé* in the great-wine provinces are therefore, I suspect, the worst ones—a suspicion confirmed by almost every experience I have had of them. As for the *rosés* from the cheap-wine provinces they are as bad as their coarse progenitors, but are presented in fancy bottles of untraditional form—a trick learned from the perfume industry. The bottles are generally decorated with art labels in the style of Robida's illustrations for Rabelais, and the wines are peddled at a price out of all proportion to their inconsiderable merits. There is also behind their gruesome spread the push of a report, put out by some French adman, that while white wine is to be served only with certain aliments, and red wine only with certain others, *rosé* "goes with everything," and so can be served without embarrassment by the inexperienced hostess. The truth is, of course, that if a wine isn't good it doesn't "go" with anything, and if it is it can go in any company.* Tavel though, is the good, the old, and, as far as I am concerned, still the only worthy *rosé*.†

---

* Mr. Frank Schoonmaker, a writer on wine and a dealer in it who has done much to diffuse *rosé* in this country, wrote to me after the first appearance of this statement that I "surely wouldn't want to serve a good claret with sardine or a Montrachet with roast beef." To this I must answer that I wouldn't serve a Montrachet or any other good wine of *any* color with sardines, since they would make it taste like more sardines. Beer might be a better idea, or in its default, *rosé*, and I offer, without charge, the advertising slogan "*Rosé*, the perfect companion for fish oil."
† The eminent Shand, in 1960 (*A Book of French Wines*), wrote with more authority but no less bitterness of the Pink Plague: "Odd little *rosés* were belatedly exhumed from a more than provincial obscurity to set before clamorous foreign holiday parties; or if none such had ever existed steps were speedily taken to produce a native *rosé*."

At the Restaurant des Beaux-Arts, the Tavel *supérieur* was as high on the list as I would let my eyes ascend until I felt that the new money was on its way. When I had my first supersensory intimation of its approach, I began to think of the prizes higher on the card—Côte Rôtie, Châteauneuf-du-Pape, and white as well as red Hermitage, which cost from three to five francs more, by the half bottle, than my customary Purple Seal. Racing men like to say that a great horse usually has a great name—impressive and euphonious— and these three wines bear similar cachets. The Pope's new castle and the Hermitage evoke medieval pomp and piety, but the name Côte Rôtie—the hillside roasted in the sun—is the friendliest of the three, as is the wine, which has a cleaner taste than Châteauneuf and a warmer one than Hermitage. Châteauneuf often seems to be a wine that there is too much of to be true, and it varies damnably in all respects save alcoholic content, which is high. Red Hermitage is certainly distinguished; as its boosters like to say, of all Rhône wines it most resembles a great Burgundy, but perhaps for that reason it was hardest for a young man to understand. It was least like a *vin du Rhône*. As for the scarce white Hermitage, of which I haven't encountered a bottle in many years, it left a glorious but vague memory. Côte Rôtie was my darling. Drinking it, I fancied I could see that literally roasting but miraculously green hillside, popping with goodness, like the skin of a roasting duck, while little wine-colored devils chased little nymphs along its simmering rivulets of wine. (Thirty years later, I had a prolonged return match with Côte Rôtie, when I discovered it on the wine card of Prunier's, in London. I approached it with foreboding, as you return to a favorite author whom you haven't read for a long time, hoping that he will be as good as you remember. But I need have had no fear. Like Dickens, Côte Rôtie meets the test. It is no Rudyard Kipling in a bottle, making one suspect a defective memory or a defective cork.)

On days when I merely suspected money to be at the bank, I would continue from the Restaurant des Beaux-Arts to the Boulevard des Italiens by any variation of route that occurred to me, looking in the windows of the rare-book dealers for the sort of buy I could afford

only once a month. Since on most of my trips I drew a blank at the
Crédit Lyonnais, I had plenty of time for window-shopping and for
inspection of the bookstalls on the quays. To this I attribute my possession of some of the best books I own—the *Moyen de Parvenir*, for
example, printed at Chinon in the early seventeenth century, with
the note on its title page: "New edition, corrected of divers faults
that weren't there, and augmented by many others entirely new."

On the *good* day, when I had actually received the notification,
I had to walk over again to collect, but this time I had a different
stride. Simply from the way I carried myself when I left my hotel on
the Rue de l'École de Médecine, my landlord, M. Perès, knew that
I would pay my bill that night, together with the six or seven hundred francs I invariably owed him for personal bites. He would tap
cheerfully on the glass of the window that divided his well-heated
office and living quarters from the less well-heated entrance hall, and
wave an arm with the gesture that he had probably used to pull his
company out of the trenches for a charge at Verdun. He was a *grand
blessé* and a Chevalier of the Legion of Honor, *à titre militaire*, with
a silver plate in his head that lessened his resistance to liquor, as he
frequently reminded Madame when she bawled him out for drinking
too much. "One little glass, and you see how I am!" he would say
mournfully. In fact, he and I had usually had six each at the Taverne
Soufflet, and he convived with other lodgers as well—notably with
an Irishman named O'Hea, who worked in a bank, and a spendthrift
Korean, who kept a girl.

At the restaurant, I would drink Côte Rôtie, as I had premedi-
tated, and would have one or two Armagnacs after lunch. After that,
I was all business in my trajectory across Paris, pausing only nine or
ten times to look at the water in the river, and two or three more to
look at girls. At the Crédit, I would be received with scornful solem-
nity, like a suitor for the hand of a miser's daughter. I was made to sit
on a bare wooden bench with other wretches come to claim money
from the bank, all feeling more like culprits by the minute. A French
bank, by the somber intensity of its addiction to money, establishes
an emotional claim on funds in transit. The client feels in the moral

position of a wayward mother who has left her babe on a doorstep and later comes back to claim it from the foster parents, who now consider it their own. I would be given a metal check with a number on it, and just as I had begun to doze off from the effects of a good lunch, the Côte Rôtie, the brisk walk, and the poor ventilation, a *huissier* who had played Harpagon in repertoire at Angers would shake me by the shoulder. I would advance toward a grille behind which another Harpagon, in an alpaca coat, held the draft, confident that he could riddle my pretensions to the identity I professed. Sometimes, by the ferocity of his distrust, he made me doubt who I was. I would stand fumbling in the wrong pocket for my *carte d'identité*, which had a knack of passing from one part of my apparel to another, like a prestidigitator's coin, and then for my passport, which on such occasions was equally elusive. The sneer on Harpagon's cuttlefish bone of a face would grow triumphant, and I expected him to push a button behind his grille that would summon a squad of detectives. At last, I would find my fugitive credentials and present them, and he would hand over the draft. Then he would send me back to the bench, a *huissier* would present me with another number, and it all had to be done over again—this time with my Kafka impersonation enacted before another Harpagon, at another grille, who would hand out the substantive money. Finally, with two hundred times twenty-six francs, minus a few deductions for official stamps, I would step out onto the Boulevard des Italiens—a once-a-month Monte Cristo. "Taxi!" I would cry. There was no need to walk back.

from SWEETBITTER

Stephanie Danler

There were tables in the back dining room set with stainless steel sheet trays and bowls so big I could bathe in them. Macaroni and cheese, fried chicken, potato salad, biscuits, an oily green salad with shredded carrots. Pitchers of iced tea. It looked like food for a large catered event, but my trailer handed me a white plate and started helping himself to family meal. He went and sat at a table in the corner without inviting me to follow. The staff had taken over the back dining room. They came from every department: the servers in aprons, people in white coats, women removing headsets, men in suits, tugging at ties. I sat near the servers, at the very last chair—it was the best seat if I needed to run.

Preshift turned out to be a turbulent affair. A frazzled, skittish manager named Zoe was looking at me, and it seemed like it might be my fault. She kept calling out numbers or names—things like "Section 6" and "Mr. Blah-blah at eight p.m." but the servers talked right through her. I nodded deafly. I couldn't touch my food.

The servers looked like actors—each perfectly idiosyncratic, but rehearsed. It all felt staged for my benefit. They wore striped shirts of every color. They were performing, snapping, clapping, kissing, cutting each other off, layers of noise colluding while I sank into my seat.

Howard walked up with wineglasses hanging like spokes from his hand. A young man in a suit trailed behind him with a bottle of wine wrapped in brown paper. The servers passed around the glasses with tastes of wine, but one never made it to me.

When Howard clapped his hands everyone went silent.

"Who would like to begin?"

Someone called out, "Pinot, obviously."

"New World or Old?" Howard asked, scanning the room. His eyes fell on me for a second and I dropped my face to my plate. I remembered every time a teacher had called on me and I didn't know the answer. I remembered wetting my pants in the fourth grade and thought that if he called on me I would again now.

"Old World," a voice called out.

"Obviously," someone else said.

"It's old. I mean, it's got age—look, it's beginning to pale."

"So we're talking Burgundy."

"It's just a matter of deduction now, HR." This man lifted his glass and pointed it to Howard. "I'm onto you."

Howard waited.

"A little austere to be Côte de Beaune."

"Is it off?"

"I was thinking it might be off!"

"No, it's perfect."

They stopped talking. I leaned forward to see who had said that. She was in the same row as me, behind too many people. I saw the bowl of her glass as she pulled it away from her nose and then brought it back. Her voice, low, ponderous, continued:

"Côte de Nuits . . . hmm, Howard, this is a treat. Gevrey-Chambertin, of course. The Harmand-Geoffroy." She put the glass down in front of her. From what I saw, she hadn't taken a sip. The wine caught the light rebelliously. "The 2000. It's actually showing really well."

"I agree, Simone. Thank you." Howard clapped his hands together. "Friends, this wine is a steal, and don't let the difficult 2000 vintage put you off. Côte de Nuits was able to pull off some stunning wines and they are drinking well, today, right now, this minute. As far as this gift goes, pass it on to your guests tonight."

Everyone stood up together. The people around me stacked their plates on top of my full one and left. I held them to my chest and pushed through the swinging doors in the kitchen. Two servers walked by on my right and I heard one of them say in a false singsong, "Oh, the Harmand-Geoffroy, of course," and the other girl rolled her eyes. Someone walked by on my left and said to me, "Seriously? You don't know what a dishwasher looks like?"

I moved toward a trough that ran the length of the room, laden with dirty dishes. I set them down apologetically. A tiny, gray-haired man on the other side of the trough huffed and took my stack, scraping the food off of each one and into a trash can.

"Pinche idiota," he said, and spit into the trough in front of him.

"Thank you," I said. Maybe I had never actually made a mistake before in my life and this is what it felt like. Like your hands were slipping off of every faucet, like you didn't have the words or directions and even gravity wasn't reliable. I felt my trailer behind me and spun around to grab him.

"Where do I—" I reached out for an arm and noticed too late that it wasn't striped. It was bare. There was a static shock when I touched it.

"Oh. You're not my person." I looked up. Black jeans and a white T-shirt with a backpack on one shoulder. Eyes so pale, a weatherworn, spectral blue. He was covered in sweat and slightly out of breath. I inhaled sharply. "My trailer person I mean. You're not him."

His eyes were a vise. "Are you sure?"

I nodded. He looked me up and down, indiscreetly.

"What are you?"

"I'm new."

"Jake." We both turned. The woman who knew the wine stood in the doorway. She didn't see me. Her gaze distilled the kitchen light to its purest element.

"Good morning. What time does your shift start again?"

"Oh fuck off, Simone."

She smiled, pleased.

"I have your plate," she said, and turned into the dining room. The doors swung back violently. And then all I could see was his feet pounding the last few stairs.

*   *   *

She stopped me on my first steps into the dining room, holding a glass of wine in her hand. I had the fleeting impression that she had been waiting for me a long time.

"Open your mouth," Simone said, her head raised, imperious. Both of us looked at each other. She painted her lips before each service with an unyielding shade of red. She had dark-blond hair, untamable, frizzy, wisped out from her face like a seventies rock goddess. But her face was strict, classical. She held the glass of wine out to me and waited.

I threw it back like a tequila shot, an accident, a habit.

"Open your mouth now," she commanded me. "The air has to interact with the wine. They flower together."

I opened my mouth but I had already swallowed.

"Tasting is a farce," she said with her eyes closed, nose deep in the bowl of the glass. "The only way to get to know a wine is to take a few hours with it. Let it change and then let it change you. That's the only way to learn anything—you have to live with it."

"All right. What is Sancerre?" Simone's brown eyes, serpentine.

"Sauvignon Blanc," I answered, my hands crossed in front of me on the table.

"What is *Sancerre?*"

"Sancerre . . ." I shut my eyes.

"Look at France," she whispered. "Wine starts with the map."

"It's an appellation in the Loire Valley. They are famous for Sauvignon Blanc."

"More. Put the pieces together. What is it?"

"It's misunderstood."

"Why?"

"Because people think Sauvignon Blanc is fruity."

"It is not fruity?"

"No, it is. It's fruity, right? But it's also not? And people think you can grow it anywhere, but you can't. Popularity is a mixed blessing?"

"Continue."

"The Loire is at the top. It's colder." She nodded and I continued. "And Sauvignon Blanc likes that it's cold."

"Colder climates mean a longer growing season. When the grape takes a longer time to ripen."

"It is more delicate. And has more minerality. It's like Sancerre is the grape's true home?"

I waited for affirmation or correction. I did not know half of what I'd said. I think she pitied me, but I received a grim smile and, finally, a half glass of Sancerre.

NORTHERN RHÔNE

Kermit Lynch

Nowadays, when heading north from Provence, I hear Paul Tardieu's passionate exclamation, "Once you know Provence, you don't ever want to leave it. No one ever goes back north, no one!" If over the years I have grown attached to Provence, in terms of wine itself my heart belongs to the great reds of the northern Rhône. The best combine a reminder of the sunny Mediterranean with the more self-conscious, intellectual appeal of the great Burgundies farther north, which is not a bad combination. And these prized wines of the northern Rhône are France's rarest: Hermitage has 300 acres planted in vines compared to 7,900 at Châteauneuf-du-Pape. Gigondas has 2,600; Cornas, only 130. To bring it into perspective, Vieux Télégraphe, a single *domaine* at Châteauneuf-du-Pape, has the same surface in vines as all of Cornas. Vieux Télégraphe's vineyard can be cultivated by tractor despite the stones, whereas at Cornas a tractor would topple sideways down the hillside. Yet Châteauneuf-du-Pape and Cornas sell at about the same price, which explains why so many of the northern Rhône's best vineyards have been abandoned: they must be worked by hand, and the pay stinks.

By *autoroute*, Cornas is only one hour from Châteauneuf-du-Pape, but everything changes.

That vast luminous Provençal skyscape is gone, and with it the expansive feeling it engenders.

In the north, you see what spawned the name Côtes du Rhône in the first place, the "hillsides of the Rhône." Most vineyards have a view down to the river.

The talismanic olive and cypress trees disappear, and though one sees aromatic herbs like rosemary and thyme in the northern Rhône, they do not grow wild but must be cultivated.

Butter and cream replace olive oil in the cuisine of the northern Rhône. Garlic and tomato play a lesser role. This is the midlands, so the fish markets exude a less appetizing odor.

The northerners are supposedly harder workers, and more cerebral. They accuse their neighbors to the south of being lazy and superficial. But the southerners pity the uptight northerners, who are thrashed this way and that by their cold winter wind.

Those stonework walls that define the northern vineyard landscape are not to be found in the southern Côtes du Rhône, although farther south at Bandol the hills are once again adorned with them, so let no one slander the Provençaux for being lazy. The hand-made walls transform the landscape to an extent the artist Christo would envy. Painstakingly constructed over the centuries, the dry-stone terraces bear witness to the value the ancients accorded these viticultural sites.

After the dizzying number of *appellations* in the south, the northern Rhône is easy. There are but a handful, including some of France's noblest: Saint-Péray, Cornas, Saint-Joseph, Hermitage, Crozes-Hermitage, Condrieu, Château Grillet, and Côte Rôtie. And in contrast to the numerous grape varieties permitted down south, the northern Rhône reds are the result of a single variety, the Syrah. One would think that a blend of grapes could create a more complex range of aromas and flavors than a lone variety, yet the Syrah juice eked out from one of those steep hillsides can produce wines of dazzling complexity, wines whose exotic aromas seem to shimmer and change like the flashes of color gleaming from a jewel.

The first wine village encountered as one enters the northern Rhône produces white wine exclusively. Old wine books mention Saint-Péray's "taste of violet," boast that Pliny and Plutarch both regarded it highly enough to single it out in their writings, and that it was a favorite of composer Richard Wagner. What more could you ask?

No one can argue with past appreciations because we cannot taste the Saint-Péray they were obviously enjoying, but in our day and age something has gone haywire. Saint-Péray is full of subterranean cellars. Someone must be making good wine because the ingredients exist: hillside vineyards and the same grape varieties that make white Hermitage. But each time I go to Saint-Péray I am so indifferent to what I am offered that it takes two or three years to overcome the taste memory and convince myself to return and try again. It is useless to discuss whether Saint-Péray has a taste of this or a taste of that. The problem is finding any taste at all. The wines seem to have been concocted by freshmen students trying to pass an enology exam in sterilization. A+ ! No one is going to write a *Parsifal* with a glass of technological Saint-Péray for inspiration.

As you survey the terraced slopes from below, the boundary between Cornas and Saint-Péray is indiscernible. It is weird, because in terms of what you find in your glass the two are opposites. Unlike its neighbor, Cornas does not produce white wine, but calling Cornas red does not do it justice. Should your pen run dry, fill it with Cornas, but this is not the wine to uncork the evening of the day you paid to have your teeth cleaned. Actually, there are wines as dark and darker, but rarely as remarkably vivid.

Because the vinification has remained old-fashioned, there are several excellent producers at Cornas. For some reason, *Invasion of the Enologists* has yet to appear at the Cornas cinema. Underground in one of the several cellars it might as well be 1885 or 1785. And with a dense, vibrant Cornas in your glass, you are tasting a wine not unlike what was poured in 1885 or 1785. The curé of the parish wrote in 1763, "The Mountain of this village is nearly all planted in vines which produce a very good black wine which is sought after by the trade because it is so heady [*fort capiteux*]."

This is Syrah country. Cornas is the first village where the grape shows its true colors, so to speak, and it does not start off timidly. The taste of Cornas is as bold as its appearance. You chew it around in your mouth and it seems to stain the palate. There is nothing like it.

Why, then, is there so little of the stuff? Why are there only 130 acres planted when there are 1,300 acres of Cornas available for planting? Is there not enough demand worldwide to sop up 1,300 acres of Cornas?

Auguste Clape, the best-known grower in Cornas, regrets that there has never been a *négociant* of importance with vines at Cornas, someone who understands commerce better than the small local growers, someone who could help the *appellation* become better known, as Guigal has done for Côte Rôtie. It is a point well taken; after importing Cornas for years, as recently as 1982 I felt obliged to offer an "introductory price" in order to tempt my clients to try Cornas.

Then again I think I would just as soon Cornas stay lost lest the twentieth century take notice and decide to sophisticate this monumental relic. And yet, if it remains unknown, if its price does not soar, the Cornas slopes will not again be covered with vines.

Even if the price becomes more interesting to the growers, replanting the abandoned terraces is not certain. Once untended, oak and pine trees seem to multiply and sprout up like weeds. In order to replant vines, the trees would have to be uprooted, but most of those terraces are too narrow to permit the kind of earth-moving equipment necessary. Manually? Today? Forget it. A recent menace is the appearance of several new homes in the heart of the Cornas *appellation*. In the old days, the villagers worked the slopes and lived on the plain. Now they want to live on the slopes for the breeze and the view and cultivate the flatlands because it can be done by tractor. But, God help us, the results are not the same, and the difference between the two wines is not subtle. One is Cornas and one is not. Auguste Clape has Syrah growing on both terrains, and he says of his flatland wine, "It makes a decent table wine, but nothing more, and yet it is exactly the same Syrah clone that makes my Cornas. The only difference is the *terroir*."

Qualms aside, let us consider how Cornas is drunk, once one has mastered the art of bending one's elbow and swallowing. In the wine literature, it is repeatedly advised that Cornas must be aged several years before it is worthwhile, but there is something about a brand-new Cornas that should not be missed. Muhammad Ali may have grown more savvy as he matured, but who can forget the young Ali, that dazzle and explosiveness? A bottle should be uncorked when it appears on the market, in order to experience its youthful extravagance of color and size. But then Cornas shuts down for three or four years, after which its aromas begin to develop. For some reason, a perfect Cornas is never as aromatic as a perfect Hermitage or Côte Rôtie. When asked how else Cornas differs from Hermitage, Auguste Clape answered with a trace of a smile that Cornas is more *rustre* (loutish or brutish), while his friend up the road, Gérard Chave, who makes Hermitage, used the polite word *ruslique* (rustic).

Both agreed that Cornas is less elegant and more tannic than Hermitage.

Clape advised following Hermitage with Cornas at table. "I have often been to meals where the order was Saint-Joseph, Côte Rôtie, Hermitage, then Cornas. When we tried the reverse, Cornas followed by Hermitage, the Hermitage did not stand up well. A rustic wine," he concluded, "will overwhelm a finer wine."

Yes, normally when several wines are served, the progression is from light to heavy, following the theory that a heavyweight will knock a lightweight out of the ring. By the same token, the progression should go from simple to complex, from rustic to aristocratic, from young to old, the guiding principle being: one's judgment is going to be influenced by whatever went before. The question is of some import because you do not want to diminish your appreciation of a perfectly good wine by serving it inappropriately. Hermitage is no lightweight, but we do not want it to *seem* so in the rough, tannic presence of a Cornas; a lighter wine following a heavier wine can actually seem thin. Likewise, a perfectly lovely country quaffer served after a noble growth might seem ignoble, or a young wine raw after a mellow old bottle. Cornas after Hermitage? To me, there is something jarring about the notion. Might not the Cornas seem *rustre* rather than *rustique?*

The dilemma helps bring into definition the difference between these two great Syrahs. A proper Hermitage will have a stronger, more eloquent bouquet. It is more distinguished, more the aristocrat. It sings like a chorus of several parts. Cornas sings great bass.

The solution is to give some attention to the vintages chosen, once it has been decided to serve Cornas and Hermitage at the same meal. I would refrain from serving the two at the same stage of maturity. Cornas 1980 could lead into Hermitage 1971, or Cornas 1976 into Hermitage 1966, and so on. A progression toward the older, more aristocratic bottle is a safe guideline to follow, but improvisations are not forbidden. An old Hermitage with roast bird could be followed by a purplish blast of young Cornas with cheese to wake up your party.

Saint-Joseph *rouge* possesses neither the dimensions of a great Hermitage nor the substantiveness (there is a lot of there there) of Cornas. Consequently, it is not respected to the same degree. But in reality Saint-Joseph is not a substitute that fails to measure up. Here Syrah can be enjoyed in another role. When in doubt about anything, it can be helpful to turn to Mozart, who in *Don Giovanni* provides an analogy: Zerlina (Saint-Joseph) may not match the emotional dimensions of Donna Elvira (Hermitage), nor is she as "heavy" as Donna Anna (Cornas), but Don Giovanni certainly finds Zerlina's "farmer's daughter" seductiveness distracting enough. Then Zerlina sings a playfully erotic song of comfort to her poor, bruised fiancé, Masetto. No self-respecting music critic would start throwing rotten eggs merely because her song lacks the emotional extremes of Donna Elvira's passionate outbursts, but I believe today's wine critics would. For them, big means good, light means less good; serious means good, playful is less good. What a humorless way to look at things. Which deity handed down the law that serious, heavy wines are better than gay, playful wines? It certainly was not Bacchus. Was it America's Puritan God, who refuses to accept that wine can be pure unadulterated *fun*? When ranking Syrahs, the critics want us to believe that you can apply the same standard to all of them, as if when you uncork a bottle of Syrah you are always looking for the same qualities. The truth is, if a perfect Hermitage deserves an A+, or 20 points, or 100, or five stars, so does a perfect Saint-Joseph. Perfection is perfection, even if the wines taste different. Thank God they taste different! One of the miracles of French wine, one reason it is so endlessly enchanting, is its diversity, even within the same region employing the same grape variety. Rather than belittling it, exalt Saint-Joseph for being different. Here one can breathe in that wonderful, wild, hillside Syrah aroma without waiting years for the wine to soften or open up. And Saint-Joseph *rouge* is the one Syrah that might even be placed in an ice bucket on a summer day and served cooled down a bit with lunch, outdoors.

The white wine from Saint-Joseph is not easy to obtain because little is produced. It is a white that must be aged in wood in order to be worthwhile. In stainless-steel tanks, which have all but taken over in the cellars, the wine's wonderful pit-fruit flavors do not develop. It remains closed and unpleasantly aggressive on the palate. But if it is vinified in used oak and if it has not been emasculated by efforts to clean it up or stabilize it, Saint-Joseph *blanc* can be a gorgeous, expressive dry white that ages well. A 1972 tasted in 1985 had a quincelike aroma, a chalky edge on the palate, and a fleeting suggestion of apricot skin in the aftertaste.

Originally, Saint-Joseph referred to a single hillside between Mauves and Tournon which is now the property of the Chapoutier family. Then the name Saint-Joseph began to be applied to the wines from the series of terraced slopes between Châteaubourg and Vion, which included the exceptional vineyards of Mauves, Tournon, and Saint-Jean-de-Muzols, whose wines had once been marketed under their own names, such as *vin de Mauves* and *vin de Tournon*. In those days, prices varied from parcel to parcel even within the same village because the ancients knew the lay of the land and the quality of the juice it gave.

And what of Saint-Joseph today? How did it grow from 240 acres in 1970 to over 700 today? Why, when the quantity produced is increasing, is Saint-Joseph an *appellation* in decline? The answer is to be found on the abandoned hillsides, grown over with weeds and straggly remnants of vines.

The French wine bureaucrats of the INAO (Institut National des Appellations d'Origine) enlarged and redefined Saint-Joseph, lumping together practically everything on the west bank of the Rhône from Cornas to Ampuis, approximately forty miles, including flatland soil along the riverbanks that had never been planted with grapes. They allow bottles of this stuff to sashay out onto the marketplace decked out in a Saint-Joseph label. Never mind the consumer or truth-in-labeling. Never mind some possible twinge of responsibility to our predecessors who labored to carve those steep hillsides into a shape hospitable to the vine, who left behind thousands of miles of hand-built stone walls because the wine was finer from up there. Nothing is sacred to these officials of the INAO who continue to devalue these historic sites even though they were hired to protect them.

Think about it. *Côte* means "slope," or "hillside." *Rôtie* means "roasted." Today, wine from the flat plateau above the "roasted slope" can legally call itself Côte Rôtie.

In Celtic, Cornas meant "roasted slope." Now the INAO is considering allowing the plateau above Cornas to be planted in vines whose wine will be sold wearing a Cornas label. Welcome to our brave new world of French wine in which there may be no *côte* in your Côte Rôtie and no *cornas* in your Cornas.

When I praised the wine of Saint-Joseph, I did not mean the ordinary wine whose grapes were mechanically harvested on flat terrain thirty miles from the original Saint-Joseph hillside.

But let them plant the plateaus, the hollows and sinks, let them grow grapes in their belly button if they want to, laissez-faire, but do not call it Côte Rôtie, Saint-Joseph, or Cornas.

The French are capable of such *noblesse*. At its inception, the system of *appellation contrôlée* was elaborated with admirable rigor. Here was a noble idea. But when they set their minds to it the French can outwhore anybody. Imagine someone trying to convince you that red is green, or a square, round. The current bunch in control of the

INAO would have us accept the notion that a slope is flat. This is more than preposterous, it is legalized fraud.

Crozes-HERMITAGE? Here we go again. Hermitage is that one majestic hillside tilted south like a solar receptor. If there is any single vineyard that the Creator obviously designed expressly for wine production, it is Hermitage.

I suppose someone might be inspired to try a Musigny after tasting a good Chambolle, or a Montrachet because of a good Puligny, but would sampling a bottle of Crozes-Hermitage motivate anyone to try an Hermitage? It is as likely as Muzak leading someone to Bach.

Crozes-Hermitage is by far the largest *appellation* in the northern Rhône. It includes terrain that does not even deserve to be called Côtes du Rhône. Where's the *côte*? Since the *appellation* was redrawn and expanded to include sandy flatland soils, that is where most of the growers have moved because they can attack with tractors and harvesting machines and because the yield per acre is so much higher. Profit! Facility! The best of all possible worlds!

In other words, by changing the legislation the INAO has, purposefully or not, encouraged the growers to abandon the sites that give the best wine.

The grape variety at Crozes, at least, remains the same as at Hermitage. However, Syrah without a hillside is like Saint George without a dragon: boring.

In reality, Crozes is a sleepy village just behind the Hermitage crest. There are vineyards near Crozes, above the Rhône at Gervans, for example, which provide an environment for the vine similar to that at Hermitage. In olden days the wines from certain of these sites even commanded the price of the lower parcels at Hermitage, and their wine can indeed be reminiscent of Hermitage, thus the reason for coupling Crozes to Hermitage in the first place.

The best parcels of Crozes, of Saint-Joseph, Cornas, and Côte Rôtie include some of the world's finest vineyards, yet many of them lie fallow. It is a twentieth-century failure. Two thousand years ago, a Roman chronicler observed that the slopes on both sides of the Rhône were covered with vines! One way to encourage replanting these historic sites would be to permit certain wines to have more specific information on their labels. As a wine buyer, you should have the right to know whether your Saint-Joseph comes from one of the great hillside sites or from a flat one. The INAO should permit growers to specify: Saint-Joseph, *vin de Tournon* or *vin de Mauves*, or Crozes-Hermitage, *vin de Gervans* or *vin de Mercurol*, for example. As time passes and the consumer begins to distinguish and judge the different qualities, the price of the wines produced from the best sites would rise (just as in Burgundy a Pommard "Rugiens" is pricier than a Pommard), perhaps making the tremendous task of replanting the hillsides a profitable venture.

> Once upon a time I imported a *vin de Gervans* from a producer whose vines were well situated. His soil was granitic; his exposition was almost as south-facing as l'Hermitage; he had the old Syrah, not one of today's superproducer clones; and his vinification was traditional.

I purchased 1970, 1973, 1974, and 1976. His red lacked elegance and so did he, but it was always a big wine, stuffed full of Syrah flavor. And he was a big-boned Porthos-like figure with a red bulbous nose. An ordinary wineglass looked like a thimble in his hands.

The first danger sign that my Crozes source might be drying up appeared in 1977. There was a disturbing lack of consistency from cask to cask. One exploded with wild raspberry, the next approached vinegar, the next was beginning to oxidize. He downed his glass of each, nonetheless. Then he uncorked a 1970 and filled our glasses to the brim. Well, it is difficult to smell well when your glass is too full to swirl, but one whiff was all that was necessary to see that we had a corked bottle. It happens. There will be an occasional off bottle no matter how expensive the wine or how fancy the label. You pour it down the drain and fetch another. But he seemed not to notice, and he drained his glass in one go.

The next time I drove up the hill, his wife came out to meet me. Her nose had the same colorful glow as her husband's. When I asked how things were going, she moaned, "We don't have enough wine to satisfy the demand." Then she added brightly, "We're getting twenty-two francs per bottle now." That was not far from the price of Hermitage itself! Madame was re-creating a scene French wine families must be taught in school: tell your buyer he will be lucky to get any wine at all, and should he be so lucky he will pay dearly for the honor.

Her husband hulked through the doorway. He had a faraway look in his eye, which suggested that he had been a trifle too attentive to his wine's evolution, and evidently he had had his fill, because instead of taking me directly to the cellar for business as usual, he led me to his garage, which he opened with one of those electronic gadgets. Inside, there was a spanking new car. He invited me to seat myself in front of its majestic dashboard. For the next twenty minutes I sat there watching him demonstrate accessories. Things glowed and twinkled. The windshield wipers click-clacked. Water sprayed. The seat retreated, advanced, and tilted with a purring vibration. The air conditioner exhaled. The roof slid open. Finally he shifted into reverse, gunned it, and backed out a few yards, then he nosed it back into the garage. I glanced over at the odometer: 18 kilometers. I asked when he had purchased it. "Six months ago," he answered, which meant a drive up the hill from the dealer, and an in-and-out-of-the-garage every day for six months.

I miss the great Crozes that he used to make. It is as if a chapter were missing from my favorite book. I have never been back. Years later I noticed his Crozes *blanc* on a restaurant list and ordered it with hope and curiosity. It was not *blanc* at all, however, but brown, oxidized, and undrinkable.

When asked what people should know about Hermitage itself, winemaker Gérard Chave replied, "When people think of the Côtes du Rhône, they always imagine huge *domaines*. They should know that the surface area of the Hermitage vineyard totals only three hundred acres. It is tiny, even smaller than Côte Rôtie or Saint-Joseph. And it should also be known that the area planted in vines has remained the same for centuries. An *appellation* that has not been altered is an extremely rare thing, especially in the Rhône."

Gérard Chave's Hermitage appears under his father's label, Jean-Louis Chave. The label will once again be perfectly appropriate when Gérard's son Jean-Louis takes over, continuing a succession of winegrowing Chaves which began in 1481! The family still possesses the original document showing that a property was given to Charles Chave by the Seigneur d'Yserand in return for an unstated service rendered. That property, however, was not at Hermitage itself. Vineyards at Hermitage were acquired much more recently, in 1890.

Some might think the métier would grow a little stale after five hundred years, but no, you could not design a better, more enthusiastic Chave than Gérard. During the centuries there must have been several flowerings of talent in this winegrowing family, but it would be difficult to surpass the impact Gérard has had. Guigal, the *négociant* at Ampuis, has also had a tremendous influence on the Rhône market. Chave's impact has been less flamboyant, less commercial than Guigal's, very much like the difference between their wines. There is a moral force behind Gérard Chave's respect for tradition and tireless search for quality. Here is a man who comprehends the heritage left behind in those mountainsides, one after another along the Rhône River, carved and sculpted and planted over the centuries in order to produce an annual flowering and fruition and finally a thing of liquid beauty. Chave is capable of communicating the responsibility that heritage imposes, and he does it not like a preacher handing down commandments but with a questioning mind, the smile of a man who loves a good joke, and a contagious joie de vivre. On top of all that, it is not easy to name a finer winemaker. Whatever qualities we might include in a listing of what makes a wine great, they all seem present at once in a glass of Chave Hermitage.

The Chave winery is a few miles from Hermitage in cellars under their home in Mauves, a thin strip of a town that supports itself growing fruit and making wine. Nowhere in Mauves is there evidence of the French flair for storefronts, or any outward flair at all for that matter.

Main Street is the Route Nationale 6, pinched in size by the buildings of the village, which, according to old postcard photos, were constructed with narrower horse-drawn vehicles in mind. This circumstance does not slow down the lead-footed French truck drivers who blast past, full throttle, an arm's length from where I must stand waiting for a Chave to answer the doorbell. The diesel fumes are trapped between the buildings on each side of the highway, coloring Mauves not mauve but a charmless sooty gray.

All is instantly forgotten when Gérard Chave appears in the doorway with a bright smile. He is a good-looking man in his early fifties, a cross between Gene Kelly and Buster Keaton, with candid, friendly eyes and a nose designed for wine sniffing. Often he greets me with his glass thief in hand, and before I can even pay respects to his wife, Monique, we are descending into the cellar. Suddenly I stand with a glass of the current white Hermitage vintage in hand and I am gazing into one of wine's most magical colors. It is golden, with much nuance, from glints of green and straw yellow to just a suspicion of something like peach skin. Even if we start tasting at nine in the morning, it always looks good enough to drink, but that first taste is only the downbeat of a lengthy set of variations to follow, so spitting is mandatory if I want to make it back up the steep dirt path out of the cellar.

One taste of white is drawn from a glass-lined tank, another from a large chestnut oval, another from an oak barrel gray with age. One was fermented in new *limousin* oak, the next in *vosges* from Alsace. There is also an experimental batch to taste and compare, some new technique that Gérard had heard about and wanted to try in order to see the results for himself.

Here is a place to study the influence of wood on white Hermitage. I always voice my alarm at the success the *négociant* Guigal enjoyed with one batch of Hermitage *blanc* because I am terrified Chave might be tempted to follow the current new oak fad. Guigal's bottling inspired a French journalist to write, "It is the best white Rhône I have ever tasted, and a lesson in vinification for the other winemakers of the Rhône." Guigal wines do seem to drive wine writers to daffy extremes. The irony is, according to the story I heard in a cellar in Tain l'Hermitage, the white Hermitage in question was purchased, not vinified, by Guigal. The actual producer sold it off in barrel as a failed *cuvée* because it was so oaky. I had the chance to taste it. It showed no Hermitage character. It had one smell: new oak. It is a dull, monotonous odor, but it is amazing how many tasters fall for it. I say if you are going to pay the price for an Hermitage it might as well smell like Hermitage. Chave uses new oak as a seasoning whose presence is one of the many facets in the aroma of his bottled wine. He likes the analogy of a chef using salt in the kitchen: a little can improve a dish, but too much covers up all the other flavors.

On the other hand, there are Hermitage growers who have begun bottling their white without any wood aging at all, and some now prevent their white Hermitage from undergoing its malolactic fermentation, which necessitates a supertight filtration and a good dose of SO_2 lest the wine follow its natural inclination and burst into a stinky, bubbly "malo" after it is bottled.

"Such wines," Chave says, "are not bad, but they are not in the style of the classic Hermitage. Vinification in wood," he says, "allows a better development of the aromas because there is a phenomenon of osmosis in the wood that you don't have in glass or metal. In stainless steel, the wine remains more anonymous. It does not reflect the originality of the *appellation*, by which I mean those characteristics that make Hermitage Hermitage. The definition of Hermitage's character does not date from yesterday. Winemaking methods that have been employed over the decades also contribute to a wine's identity. Here is where the rules of the INAO are altogether incomplete. The INAO regulates the grape varieties, the number of buds to leave on each branch, the form of the pruning, all sorts of things, but on the subject of making the wine, they say nothing. You can do whatever you like. If I decide tomorrow to make my red Hermitage by carbonic maceration, no one can tell me I don't have the right. It would still be considered Hermitage."

The multiple *cuvées* of his newest white Hermitage are followed by a procession of bottled vintages reaching back over several years. Today, from all the *appellations* of the northern Rhône that produce white wine, there is only one sure thing year in and year out, and that is the quality of the Chave Hermitage *blanc*. Be it 1986, 1985, 1984, 1983, 1982, 1981, or 1980 (picking the decade I know best), it is a white to be enjoyed young, old, and in between. And there is a pleasure to be obtained by laying down enough bottles of one single vintage to be able to observe its evolution over ten, twenty, or thirty years.

These descents into Chave's inner sanctum are the ultimate thrill for a wine taster. Deep underground you hear nothing from the outside world, and never are those professional tastings disturbed unless there is an emergency. His cellar is composed of several chambers. One in particular is unforgettable. It is filled with barrels and, in bins along the walls, the family treasury of old bottles, some of which are completely engulfed in mold. The wisps, webs, and curls of mold are colored from velvety black to silvery white and everything in between. Some have a green tinge, some blue. Some patches glisten with droplets of moisture. The stuff hangs from the ceiling, the walls are draped with it, and while it is not exactly teeming, it does appear to be taking over. Thus, the visual backdrop as you regard the robe of the wine in your glass. The cool, damp air is pleasantly thick with aroma. There is the rowdy, backward smell of new red wine in barrel, the mysterious hoary/fresh smell of the fungus, and the continual evaporation of all the wines that have been spit onto the dirt and gravel floor since who-knows-when. It is a setting in which you feel a lineage with the ancients who preceded you, who made the same clinking sounds with a glass thief as the glasses are filled, the same slurping, chewing, spitting sounds, the same lip-smacking, murmurs, and grunts of approval.

Chave has vines growing in several parcels scattered over the Hermitage *appellation*, and his bottled red is always a blend of them. In the wine literature we find the names of these separate parcels cited well before we come across any reference to Hermitage itself.

A document from 1389 mentions Bessards, Méal, Rocoules, Baumes, and others, but the earliest appearance unearthed so far of Hermitage as Hermitage is from 1598.

In April 1983 I arrived to taste Chave's 1981 Hermitage *rouge*. He had not yet assembled and bottled his various *cuvées*, so we wandered from one part of the cellar to another, taking tastes from various *foudres, demi-muids*, barrels and casks.

"We will start with Les Dionnières," he said, plunging his thief through the bunghole of one of his barrels, drawing out some purple wine and, aiming carefully, splashing a bit of it into my glass and his. "Les Dionnières is at the bottom of Hermitage, below Les Rocoules. It always gives a fine, elegant wine, never very tannic. You mustn't think that the higher slopes always give a wine better than those down below. In fact, when we have a dry year, the lower slopes will give the better wine because the vines are less stressed. In a normal year, yes, the higher, steeper slopes are better. But in terms of the different parcels, to have a good balance, a little of each is essential. In 1981 the higher slopes *are* better, but you can see that the lower parcels give an elegant, fruity wine. Still, it is certain that if it were bottled as is, separately, it would not be completely representative of the *appellation* Hermitage."

I asked if the lower parcels like Les Dionnières were flat.

"At Hermitage there is no flatland. It is not like Crozes-Hermitage. But the soil is lighter at the base of the hill, which favors the grape's maturity.

"Here, this is Les Baumes. It always has finesse as well as being tannic. Fine but strong. Les Dionnières has a perfume like little red fruits, raspberry and cherry, but Les Baumes is more like wildflowers. The aromas can change from year to year, however. It depends on the maturity of the grapes and above all if the year was dry or not. It would be too simple if every vintage were alike. Then I could put the same blend into bottles every year. Ten percent Baumes, twenty percent of this, fifteen percent of that . . . It would not hold the same interest for me."

I gave him my impression of Les Baumes, that it seemed fuller and richer but also shorter on the palate.

"That shortness is due to the astringence of the tannin. It dries out the mouth so it seems shorter. For aging, it has more strength than Les Dionnières. You could make a good *little* Hermitage by blending the two.

"Here we have Peléas. It has more depth. There is an aroma of violets.

"And this is Les Rocoules. There is not much red grown there. Les Rocoules is almost entirely white."

I asked how he decided whether to plant red or white grapes in the different parcels.

"Oh, there is not much of a decision to make," he answered. "That decision was made centuries ago. The nature of the soil decides for you. The sections of limestone and clay are destined to be white, but white in granite won't work, the result is not elegant enough. This was all determined a long time ago. But I've experimented and learned for myself that granitic soil is not suitable for white wine. On the other hand, Syrah grown in white-wine soil works better. See how it gives a fatter wine with more glycerine, more like a white.

"Now, Le Bessard. Can you smell the hawthorn blossom? I pointed it out to you up on the hill yesterday. It grows around here and we often find its aroma in our wine. Bessard has a more tannic structure than the others, without having higher alcohol. There are elements here that you do not find in the others. It is less floral, but longer on the palate. . . . For me, none of them can stand alone."

I asked if the differences between the wines was a question of exposition, or the level of the hill, or the soil.

"It is always the soil. At Hermitage the exposition is practically the same everywhere on the hillside. But Bessard is essentially granitic."

"Is it the same clone of Syrah as Peléas and the others?"

"They are all the same. I graft from our old vines when I replant."

He hesitated and glanced down a row of large oval casks. "We have another *cuvée* of Bessard to taste, but we'll get to it later because it is so tannic. First, let's taste Le Méal."

Le Méal seemed solidly structured, but less aromatic, less rich than the others. I asked what in particular it imparts to his final *assemblage*, or blend, in bottle.

"It is a combination of tannins. In the *assemblage* there is the tannic side to consider, and the floral or aromatic side. Some *cuvées* bring a certain finesse, a perfume or aroma to the blend, others a tannic support. And then some tannins are harsh; others finer, smoother."

When I asked him what he thought of Le Méal's aroma, he said it reminded him of cherry. "But that can change," he added. "One day you find black currant, and shortly afterward it is more like cherry or vanilla."

"You don't find cherries year after year in Le Méal?"

"Absolutely not. It is too simplistic, saying a wine is like this, this, or that. Only the journalists get away with that. They might taste it once or twice a year at most, but when you taste a wine several times a year, you perceive that it is not as easy and definitive as all that!

"Now, here is that other *cuvée* of Le Bessard I told you about. Notice that this one is in *foudre*. There is a huge difference between the *foudre* and the barrel. This is less mature. Less finished. What a difference! Leave the same wine in two different containers and two months later you have two different wines."

I asked if they had been precisely the same wine at the outset.

"Absolutely, so one can conclude that a wine 'makes itself' more rapidly in barrel than in *foudre*. That is why I like to have a little of each. I'm going to transfer this one into barrels and the other one will go into these *foudres* before I make my *assemblage*."

But why not leave it all in *foudre* in order to have a slower evolution once it is in bottle, a slower aging process?

"No, there is a different kind of oxidation in bottle. What is aging? It is an oxidation. But the sort achieved in wood you will never achieve in a glass bottle."

I told him about my experience in Raymond Trollat's cellar in nearby Saint-Jean-de-Muzols. "He has fifty-year-old *demimuids*. Some are chestnut, some oak. After fifty years, of course there is absolutely no taste of wood imparted to the wine, yet the character of the wine from each kind of wood differs."

"And fifty years from now there will still be a difference," Chave said, "because the pores of the wood are different. Oak is tighter, more compacted, so the exchange with the air is slower, resulting in a firmer, more closed-in wine. The pores of chestnut are larger. It breathes more easily, resulting in a wine that is more supple, more advanced."

After we had tasted each *cuvée* of 1981 separately, we revisited each one and Chave carefully squirted out a bit of this, a bit more of that, a touch of Peléas, until he presented me with a glass of red Hermitage and declared, "Today, this is my conception of what the 1981 *assemblage* will be."

If Betty Grable was able to insure her legs, Chave should be able to insure his nose. He lowered it into his glass. "No, it needs something floral . . . here, a little more Les Baumes . . . there, see . . . the nose comes out better." Then he counted down a row of barrels and took out a few drops of another wine which he added to his composition. "Just a bit more Peléas to soften that tannin. I don't know. It is imprecise like this, without a measuring device. And it would be simpler if there were only three or four wines to blend, but it is fascinating because here there are so many possibilities. Imagine a composer who had only three or four tones to work with. But wait now, see if a touch more Bessard . . . from the *foudre* . . . no, it isn't any more satisfying, is it? Before I bottle the 1981 I will spend two weeks working to find the proper *assemblage*. Afterward, you won't be able to recognize any of these *cuvées* we tasted, but there will be a certain harmony on the palate. Today is like a first sketch."

Afterward the corks began popping. We tasted his 1980, 1979, 1978, and 1977.

The vintage chartists had made the 1977 difficult to market in the United States. I asked Chave if he had some sort of chart or system for rating his different vintages.

"For me, once a wine is in bottle, I have another conception of its quality which is not at all of wine as wine alone. Once you have a sound wine in the glass, your reasoning must be different, and each time you taste a wine you've got to imagine it with a dish. Otherwise, you are just saying you prefer this wine a little more than that wine, which is not very interesting. And this is where one can reproach most wine critics. You must be knowledgeable about cuisine in order to recommend a wine, in order to say this wine would go well with game, for example. The ultimate destination of a wine is on the table, with food. Serve the same wine with two different dishes and you will have two different opinions of it."

Chave then pulled the cork on his 1976 *rouge*, 1975, 1974, 1969, then the 1942. Blissful appreciation replaced the immense effort of concentration required to appraise the younger *cuvées*. Going back through the decades of Chave's Hermitage, you witness as wild, turbulent youth evolves into something sophisticated and profound.

"Here, let's change everything," Chave said, turning once more to what his English importer Robin Yapp has called "that sinister sea of fungus." He pulled out a bottle and scraped a thick puff of mold off the top of the cork before twisting in his corkscrew. There was no vintage on the bottle because no label can survive that humidity, so Chave announced its vintage, Hermitage *blanc*, 1952. Against the dark background, the deep golden color of the wine was stunning to the eye. The nose was old, thick, honeyed, alive, marvelous. Something about it, perhaps the sensation of immense depth, recalled those lordly bouquets of an old Yquem or an Alsatian *vendange tardive*, but the Hermitage seemed even more impressive for being dry. It dazzles without the advantage of sweetness or noble rot.

At harvest, the Hermitage hillside is a colorful scene bathed in a soft sunlight in which there is a suggestion of autumn's arrival. The vine's green foliage cascades from wooden stakes, but the impetuous growth of late spring and early summer has passed and the plant looks spent. The Syrah clusters are dark purple and so small, few, and far between you wonder (trying to get a foothold on the steep slope) at the effort that went into producing them. And then suddenly a bottle of Hermitage seems cheap.

Because of the positioning of the hill, the view is spacious, bound by the distant Alps to the east, the Massif Central to the west, and to the south it always seems that if the sky were just a little clearer there would be a view all the way to the Mediterranean. And at the base of the hill there is the mighty Rhône executing an unusually graceful curve.

In 1986, Chave gathered his team of thirty harvesters on October 2, and they began picking the white grapes, which were not white at all. Some Marsanne grapes were golden, some almost purple, others dark and shriveled. The Marsanne was delicious eating right off the vine, and Chave said that he knows it will be a good vintage when he sees the pickers munching on grapes as they work.

Strangely enough, Chave's team was practically the only one on the hillside. Then I looked closer and noticed that the neighboring plots had already been stripped of their treasure.

"Almost everyone has finished harvesting," Chave said. He had a big grin. "They were afraid it might rain, afraid to gamble. Some of them finished eight days ago and we are just beginning. They won't have enough natural sugar in their grapes, so they will have to add sugar. Oh yes, even at Hermitage now they have granted us the right to chaptalize. It is scandalous. So these enologists tell everybody to harvest early in order to have more acidity and avoid the risk of rot. They tell them to pick early, that they can add the sugar later. Here, taste a green grape. You see, it has no flavor, no character. Now taste a golden one. See the difference? They want to make what I call a *vin technologique*. It is fruity, but they all taste the same whether they are from the Loire, the Rhône, or wherever. That is not what I want. Grapes are a fruit just like a pear or a peach. If they are ripe, they have a lot more flavor and aroma. People forget that a grape is a fruit. They would never eat a green peach, but they harvest green grapes. If they didn't chaptalize, some growers would have a white

Hermitage at 11 degrees alcohol this year. We are harvesting ripe grapes which will produce a wine with 13 degrees alcohol! The flavor of the two wines will be totally different."

When I left, Chave was instructing his foreman to mix water into the harvesters' wine supply because at the end of the previous day one of them had stumbled and hit his head on a rock and an ambulance had to be called. They mulled over the subtle insurance question: was he still on the job, or was he on the way home *after* work? The worker had just finished washing his hands, the foreman said. Then he argued that if he diluted the wine some of the crew would be angry. "What about the guys who only take a sip from time to time? Are we going to penalize the moderate ones because of the two or three who overdo it?"

Chave said that the wine is too strong. He serves his harvesters Hermitage, a blend of the press wine, the wine from younger vines, and from the less successful *cuvées* that he does not want in his *assemblage*. "Hermitage is too strong to drink out in the hot sun."

It is an argument which must have a five-hundred-year history in the Chave family.

If Hermitage appears to have been created expressly for the vine, with only a few tucks and folds needed to perfect it, Côte Rôtie is obviously man's painstaking creation. The steep slopes are a sloppy patchwork of stone walls and terraces, often barely wide enough for a single row of vines. There are parts of the hill where the earth looks more like some jagged extraterrestrial metal than soil fit for cultivation, but the ancients tamed these slopes, and Côte Rôtie, along with Hermitage, is where the Syrah is capable of magnificence.

Syrah, serine, sarine, syrrah, sirah, syras, schiras, schirac, sirac. In 1868, after more than twenty centuries of winegrowing, someone noticed that the *serine* of Côte Rôtie and the *sirrah* of Hermitage were the same grape, an indication of how provincial this part of France was, and is. When I arrived in 1976, I was struck by how rustic the cellars and equipment remained, even though the

Paris–Marseilles *autoroute* and railway line is never more than a few kilometers away.

Given the similarity between the wines of Côte Rôtie and Hermitage, it is unbelievable that it took so long for someone to deduce that they are born of the same parent vine. There is a difference between the two wines, but describing that difference has proven to be a problem. Gérard Chave says Côte Rôtie is less heady than Hermitage, a statement that invites charges of chauvinism (or Chavinism) because the aroma of a well-vinified Côte Rôtie from old vines grown upon the original roasted slope has no peer in terms of headiness. There is a difference between these two Syrahs, but to explain it I would have to dredge up notes from a literature class years ago in which my professor tried to simplify Nietzsche's distinction between Apollonian and Dionysian qualities. It went something like this:

Apollonian. Master of oneself, harmonious, a beauty that is more formal, more architectural, as in the wine of Hermitage.

Dionysian. A wilder force, instinctive, immediate, a beauty that is more passionate than cerebral, as in the wine of Côte Rôtie.

In fact, were Côte Rôtie's carriage less regal, its aroma might seem ostentatious. Only royalty can wear plumes and glittering jewels and white fox robes and get away with it.

The village that hosts the Côte Rôtie spectacle is Ampuis. Each wine village in France seems to boast Roman artifacts, but when it comes to claims of antiquity, Ampuis is the undefeated champion. Some wine books repeat the unproven story that Ampuis was the site of France's first vineyard. It is perhaps the name of the place that prompts such nonsense. They say that the name evolved from *ampelos*, Greek for "vine," proving that the Greeks cultivated wine grapes at Ampuis even before the Romans showed up. Well, why not?

But what about the theory that Ampuis comes from *empoisser*, "to make sticky"? Plutarch wrote about the wine of the region and called it a *vin empoissé*, or at least that is the French translation of what he said. Some are convinced that the Romans added pitch to their Côte Rôtie, which presumably would have made it sticky. Pitch = *poix* in French, and it is not far from *em-poix* to Ampuis. It is difficult to imagine anyone adulterating a Côte Rôtie with pitch, but in our era, adulterating it with an overpowering smell of new oak seems to be considered acceptable behavior, so who knows?

Or, *am* can mean "around," and *puits*, which is pronounced exactly like *puis*, means "well." Following this theory, Ampuis means "around the well." To support this theory one can cite the Beaujolais village Amplepuis, meaning "generous well."

Or *am* might have been shortened over the centuries from *aimer*, meaning "to like" or "to love," or *aimable*, meaning "happy" or "lovable." Ampuis = the lovable well? I'll drink from that.

If *am* comes from *amoeba*, we may have a stagnant well.

Or *am* could have come from the Greek root *amph*, which can mean two hillsides or a rounded shape as in amphitheater.

The French word *puy* is also pronounced like *puis*, and means "mountain" or "height."

Then there is the theory that *puis* evolved from the Greek and Latin *podium*, which referred to the large wall that circled an amphitheater, on which were situated the seats of honor. This is not inconceivable if you visualize the stone walls which follow the rounded shape of the hillsides of Côte Rôtie; however, it does seem quite a drastic case of mispronunciation going from Ampodium to Ampuis.

Theories and legends also abound regarding the initial vine plantings. Many believe that the Syrah arrived via the Greeks, who had settled Marseilles (Massalia) at the mouth of the Rhône, and whose trade took them north via the river. There is no evidence of Greeks settling at Ampuis; however, Greek amphorae have been found downriver at Tain l'Hermitage. It is curious that the cultivation of the Syrah in Provence and in the southern Rhône is only a recent, twentieth-century occurrence, when it was imported from the northern Rhône with the farfetched idea of ennobling the southern wines. Had it worked its way north from Marseilles, would there not have been traces left in the south? While I have absolutely no historical foundation for supposing it, my nose tells me that the Syrah came from the east, via the Alps. A young Syrah has more in common with a young Nebbiolo from Piemonte than it does with a wine from the Matseilles region.

Terracing the hillsides of Ampuis could have taken centuries. It is doubtful that a Greek or Roman winemaker gazed up, nodded sagely, and decreed them the perfect site for Syrah. In the beginning the vines must have been planted at the bottom of the hill, where farming was easier and where there was plenty of water from the river nearby. And it must be remembered that the Rhône was not stationary. Only in the nineteenth century did man begin to control the course of the Rhône. Before, it changed course almost by whim, and a terrain that was farmed on the plain one year might have been submerged the next, another reason to cultivate the slopes. But when people began tasting wine from the roasted slope someone must have noticed that it produced finer wine, so the vineyards were expanded upward to meet the demand. All this is conjecture; perhaps the Creator installed the terraces on the sixth day in order to drink well on the seventh.

Constructing the stone walls served two purposes. It removed the large rocks from the soil, facilitating cultivation, and it prevented the remaining soil from washing down the hill in a rainstorm.

The walls are handmade, and some workers could not help expressing themselves by creating patterns as they labored. Therefore, some of the walls are random collections of stones, while others form eye-catching designs.

We know that in the seventh century Saint Eloi wrestled with a demon in the church at Ampuis, but as far as I can tell, and I am not the historical researcher needed here, the first documented statement, the first outright proof that there were vines at Ampuis, dates from A.D. 889. Before that, Côte Rôtie was always referred to as a *vin de Vienne*, or "wine of Vienne," the more important city a few kilometers north of Ampuis. An act dated "a Friday in the month of April in the second year after the death of Charlemagne" certifies that a certain Monsieur Rostaing and his wife, Andelmonde, donated to the church at Vienne two parcels of vineyard situated *"in villa Ampusio,"* reserving at the same time, however, their right to the actual fruit from those vines for the rest of their lifetime. Rather than leave the vineyard to some ne'er-do-well relative, they fixed it so the Good Lord would come into possession of some prime Côte Rôtie grapes just as He was deciding whether to send Rostaing and Andelmonde upward to paradise or down into the fiery pit.

Eleven centuries later, there is still a Rostaing with vines at Ampuis. I have neglected to ask him if he is a descendant of Rostaing and Andelmonde, because I cannot risk ruining such a perfect transition. Today's Rostaing, René Rostaing, was born in 1948 and vinified his first Côte Rôtie in 1970 at age twenty-two.

"In order to understand Côte Rôtie, you must climb up through the vineyards," he said one day. "Looking out the window of a car is not enough." He turned out to be a passionate guide who seems to know every nook and cranny, every stone's mineral composition and geological origin.

The different slopes of Côte Rôtie, such as the two most famous, Côte Blonde and Côte Brune, are separated by deep, stream-eroded ravines. According to Rostaing, the erosion over the millennia created dramatically diverse soils. "Ampuis is a small vineyard, one of France's smallest," he said. "We have less than three hundred acres planted in thirty different soils, and no more than a dozen acres share the same exact soil composition."

As one sees in Chave's cellar, different soils create different wines, especially when the plant is Syrah.

Hiking up his parcel of Côte Blonde, Rostaing said, "It is this siliceous base of chalk and quartz that gives Côte Blonde's wine its elegance and refinement. The Blonde is a wine that needs time. For the first few years it seems relatively muted, but with age it begins to express itself. It has a tannin that seems almost delicate, a tannin that is well-integrated into the wine. It has finesse."

We went back to his car in order to go have a look at La Landonne.

"La Landonne starts here, just beyond the creek," he said. "La Landonne is not part of the Côte Brune. I insist upon this point because the error has been repeated again and again. There are more slopes to Côte Rôtie than Brune and Blonde. Côte Brune and Blonde make up ten percent of Côte Rôtie and no more. This tendency to call the southern slopes Blonde and the northern Brune is an inaccurate simplification. From south to north you have Côte Mollard, Blonde, Brune, Moutonnes, Landonne, and Vieillière."

As we slipped and huffed and puffed our way up the stony incline, Rostaing shook his head sadly. "Look at this. La Landonne starts here, where there is nothing growing but weeds. Over here, a few vines. More weeds over there . . . La Landonne lies fifty percent fallow! Here is my parcel. Here is Rostaing's La Landonne! Three thousand square meters. Fifteen hundred bottles per year! The vines over there belong to my uncle, Marius Gentaz. He has five thousand square meters. It's steep, isn't it? He has old vines, at least sixty years old. See how they were trained? Beautiful vines! The soil here has more clay. There is very little quartz, so the wine it gives is more rustic, less elegant than Côte Blonde.

"My grandfather made wine here after World War I and sold it in barrel to the local café-bars. Five francs per liter. Côte Rôtie was the everyday wine for the people of Ampuis. You know, a glass while they played their game of *boules* outdoors in the square. Then, closer to World War II, life began to change, the cost of living began to increase. People wanted more comforts. Before, they would go fishing on Sundays, they wore the same clothes day after day, but later everyone had to own a car, then a second car, a new freezer, a vacation. Meanwhile, Côte Rôtie was selling no better. So what happened? The people decided it was not worth the effort to work the hillsides. They abandoned them. Half of La Landonne lies fallow, and it dates from that period. That was when they planted the flatlands below us, but they planted apricots because they were more profitable than selling Côte Rôtie. Apricots, lettuces, peas . . ."

Later that day, Rostaing's uncle, Marius Gentaz, continued the story. A relaxed man in his sixties, dressed in the traditional French worker's blue coveralls, he said that some of those farmers on the plain

had to sell their land to the government in the early 1960s when the
Paris–Marseilles *autoroute* was built. Some used their money to buy
vineyard land back on the slopes.

Many of the northern Rhône winemakers think that Gentaz is
making the most typical, traditional Côte Rôtie of our day. I asked
him what his secret is.

"In order to make a good Côte Rôtie," he said with unfeigned,
almost naïve modesty, "the vines must be planted in the right place
and you must bring in healthy grapes. And you cannot make great
wine here with young vines. They must be fifteen to twenry years
old before they begin to give a pretty wine."

I said surely there must be something in the vinification, some
secret method to explain his wine's quality.

"Well, you've got to take good care of it, keep the barrels filled
up to the top." (My apologies to any winemakers looking for the trick
to making good Syrah!) Then Gentaz smiled and said, "You raise the
wine the way it has to be raised. I haven't changed anything. I make
my wine the way my father-in-law taught me, the way he made it
eighty years ago. Exactly the same way!"

Fifty percent of La Landonne barren! And, according to René Rostaing, 60 percent of the wine harvested at Ampuis now comes from
the plateau, which the ancients more appropriately devoted to corn
and wheat. What a tragedy for one of the world's finest vineyards.

Ironically, in our time the very factor that might mean renewal
for the original Côte Rôtie vineyards has an attendant risk, which is
that it could alter so drastically the taste of Côte Rôtie as to render
it unrecognizable to those who know the taste of the real thing. The
various Côte Rôtie bottlings from Guigal, the *négociant* at Ampuis,
dominate blind-tasting events, dominate the wine journals, newspapers, and magazines to a degree that has become dangerous. The
public is very close to deciding a Côte Rôtie is by definition oaky
and alcoholic, and the next step is the rejection of the traditional
Côte Rôtie, which is not oaky or alcoholic.

By no means do I blame Guigal for this state of affairs. He has great commercial instincts and his oaky wines with their blistering alcoholic content are crowd pleasers. It requires talent to so enrapture the public and the critics. Ah, the critics. Never have I seen one single discouraging word about Guigal's Côte Rôtie, even though it is a very anonymous-tasting wine, easily mistaken for a big, oaky Gigondas or even a Bordeaux. I want my Côte Rôtie to taste like Côte Rôtie. This all reminds me of an acquaintance who always seemed to have a new girlfriend. His girlfriends all had two things in common: huge breasts. His choices might be pretty or not, intelligent or not, interesting or not. Nothing seemed to matter to him as long as the breasts were enormous. It was such an impractical way to assess the quality of a woman that it began to seem almost perverse. And I have an identical reaction to those who go gaga over an inky, oaky, monster wine that has, it might as well be by accident, a Côte Rôtie label. I cannot begin to communicate how profoundly the critics' embrace of such freak wines depresses me.

Why ask that a wine be jarring to the senses, a criterion that we do not apply to other arts like music or painting in which delicacy is valued, where shading, nuance, even silence or empty space can be considered remarkable. But keep an eye on the wine critics' ratings. If a wine is black, packs an alcoholic, tannic wallop, and smells like a lumberyard, it receives high points.

Traditional Côte Rôtie does not have a thick, heavy quality, as if it had been applied with a brush. A description from 1786 says Côte Rôtie is "*un vin flatteur et fort delicat*" (a seductive, highly delicate wine).

A later description says that Côte Rôtie is distinguished by "*la finesse de sa sève*" (the finesse of its sap) and its unique bouquet, which makes it "one of the most delicate and agreeable wines of France."

"The finesse of its *sève*." Consider the phrase. It is not bad at all. *Sève*, the sap or lifeblood of a plant, conveys an impression of vigor, of intensity. A Côte Rôtie is by no means light stuff; it is a substantial wine, but what is unusual is this saplike quality combined with a certain finesse, a certain delicacy. Top it off with that amazing perfume of Syrah fruit grown in this special *terroir* and you have a wine set apart from all others. Anyone can make a heavy, oaky wine. All you need is a new barrel and sugary (or sugared) grape juice. But a Côte Rôtie that tastes like Côte Rôtie can come only from the *terroir* of the roasted slope and from the traditional vinification developed over the centuries in the cellars of Ampuis.

How ironic that a heavy, oaky wine should be the object of such acclaim and desire that, thanks to it, the small Côte Rôtie growers are now obtaining a just price for their wine, and consequently land that had been abandoned is beginning to be replanted. I suppose I could be compared to a classical music fan who cannot stand the fact that the public is listening to Elvis or the Beatles instead of Haydn and Mozart, but I fear the day when the classic Côte Rôtie like that of Marius Gentaz disappears completely to be replaced by the Guigal recipe. In more and more cellars I see new oak barrels as the northern Rhône growers try to copy his success.

The Importance of
Being Humble

Eric Asimov

I don't particularly enjoy calling attention to myself, a characteristic that served me well when I was reviewing restaurants. While many people imagine restaurant critics donning wigs, false beards, and costumes before heading out into the lively night, it never occurred to me to disguise myself in pursuit of anonymity. I thought of a disguise as the last resort of the exhibitionist. Instead, my technique was to fade into the background. It's a lot easier to be nondescript if you sincerely don't want to be noticed, although it may not make as good a story.

Modesty may cause one to be overlooked, but in my restaurant job, that was the idea, right? In the field of wine, modesty is a great strength as well, although in this bombastic world of ours, it can cause people to be discounted or just plain ignored. In fact, some of the greatest, most inspirational winemakers I've met have been some of the most modest, humble individuals I have known. Without egos? Not at all. They all had a very healthy sense of themselves. But they had perspective as well.

In wine—good wine, at least—modesty and humility stem from recognizing that humans will never have the ultimate power. In winemaking, that role belongs to nature. Humans can do their best to manage their vineyards to counteract whatever curveballs nature throws their way. They can anticipate. They can compensate. But they cannot control, not, at least, if they want to make great wine.

To control means to eliminate as many variables as possible. But great wines are made by bowing to the inevitability of variation and accepting the special characteristics that each vintage offers. To put it in plainer terms: Shit happens. As a winemaker, you can recognize that and try to manage things well enough so that your wine survives whatever shit comes its way, and maybe is even better for it. Or you can do your best to ensure that shit never affects your wine, which, like a life free of bumps and bruises, may make for a smoother countenance but a far less interesting one.

What kind of shit? From the initial decision of where to plant a vineyard, control is an issue. Great wines tend to be made from vineyards planted in risky places, perhaps in a climate that is barely warm enough to ripen the grapes, or on slopes so steep that only mountain goats would be foolhardy enough to try to climb them, or on soil so poor that the vines have to struggle to find enough nutrition to survive. This was the kind of wondrous natural adaptation that might make even the most committed atheist ponder a possible intelligence behind the design of the universe. In the agrarian local economies of long ago, the most nutritious soils, which were the easiest to farm, were reserved for the food crops most crucial for sustaining life. Meanwhile, grapevines, which improve the quality of life but are not exactly necessary for sustenance, did not compete for space because they were adapted to poor soils and sites that were difficult to farm. Wine was in a sense a luxury for those willing to make the laborious effort, but judging by the vast number of ancient vineyards put in difficult, inaccessible places, wine must have been considered worth the work.

Nowadays, we no longer have to decide which soils are suitable for food crops and which are best for grapevines. For better or worse, modern technology permits food to be grown pretty much wherever it is convenient to do so, which gives modern grape growers far more freedom in deciding where to plant their vines. This is not so true in the Old World, where many of the decisions on the best places to plant vines were made and codified centuries ago in agrarian societies, when the need for each community, sometimes each family, to grow sufficient amounts of its own food was imperative. Sadly, some of the greatest, most difficult-to-farm vineyard sites were abandoned in the twentieth century. After the scourges of phylloxera, the ravenous aphid that attacked the roots of grapevines, and the two world wars, the economics in places like the northern Rhône Valley offered little incentive to continue farming these sites. What's more, labor-saving automated equipment, introduced after World War II, offered a powerful inducement to war-weary farmers to abandon steep hillside sites, where such equipment could not be used, in favor of inferior but flat sites. Fortunately, some of these historical vineyards are now being recovered, as the modern economy beckons with newly attractive rewards to people who can make distinctive wines.

Not every Old World vineyard is in an ideal place, obviously. For centuries, far more bad wine than good was made in Europe, which everybody ought to acknowledge regardless of a desire to romanticize winemaking of the past. But without the ancient imperatives guiding the selection of vineyard sites, New World growers have had far more freedom in deciding where to create vineyards, and far more options.

In California once, as I was driving south on Highway 101 through the Salinas Valley toward Paso Robles, I saw an absolutely astounding vineyard. It was an extraordinary flat expanse that started first on the east side of the highway, then jumped over to the west side across from a series of oil rigs. This vineyard extended for miles, covering thousands of acres. If you told a worker to go prune a row of vines, and not to come back until he finished, you might not see him again for months.

Nobody hoping to make great wine would conceive of such a vineyard. This is a modern-day creation planted for the purpose of control. The climate is predictable. The crops can be managed with the help of fertilizers and irrigation. Threats are parried with pesticides and herbicides. Harvests are automated, and winemaking is industrial. These wines won't be exciting, or even interesting, but they will be cheap and palatable.

Of course, the managers of vineyards like this are not trying to make fine wine. Their aim is profit and little else. But the same

questions of control come up for more ambitious winemaking projects. Anybody trying to grow great grapes and make fine wine will face
crucial issues in the vineyard, like water management. Leaving aside
questions of conservation, growers could insure a healthy crop by
irrigating the vines, but the grapes are less likely to make interesting
wine than if growers take the riskier approach of not irrigating at all
or minimally, forcing the roots of the vine to dig deep into the earth
in search of moisture. The same is true with fertilizers, pesticides,
and herbicides. Using these chemical products insures predictable
results, though they may cause long-term harm to the vineyard as
well as to the planet. The wines, alas, will suffer for it, too.

The more labor-intensive approach of farming organically or
biodynamically can lead to better-quality grapes and healthier vineyards, but they are riskier and more expensive. Relying on cover
crops and mulching for nutrition, and supporting beneficial insects to
control pests in the vineyard requires more work as well as a leap of
faith and a recognition that things may not go exactly as you plan. In
other words, great growers cede certitude. Instead, through hard work
they try to stack the odds in their favor. But nothing is ever assured.

The issue is perhaps easier to understand by looking at it in
restaurant terms. On the one side you have fast-food franchise restaurants that make a profitable virtue out of consistency and predict-
ability. With occasional exceptions, ingredients are prefabricated
and recipes are codified. Consumers will always know what they are
getting, regardless of regional or seasonal differences. Many people
take comfort in that. The food is simple, satisfying basic desires for
savory warmth, and people who do not spend a great deal of time
thinking about what they are eating, which may be the vast majority,
are content with that.

On the other side are certain individual chefs who shop daily
and allow their menus to be dictated by what they find in the market.
Their customers may not know exactly what they are going to get
when they come to the restaurant. Whatever it is, though, if they
know and trust the chef, they can assume that the quality will be
high and they will be satisfied. Just as the chefs cede control of their

menus to the ingredients that beckon, these customers relinquish control of their experience to the chef.

I leave you no doubt about which sort of experience I prefer. But while the fast-food industry may be repugnant in many ways, I have no problem with people who simply prefer a predictable consistency in their food. Just as with wine, nobody is obliged to care about the experience of eating. Oh, sure, one can make a case about the moral and political consequences of eating, as people like Michael Pollan and Eric Schlosser have done so convincingly. That's not my point. You can think of food simply as fuel and satisfy the need to eat in many politically acceptable ways, just as you can drink wine without being curious as to how it's made, where it comes from, and whether it's any good. You get no points in life for caring about wine or food. If whatever you pick up in the supermarket on the way home does the trick for you, that's fine.

But if you do care about what you eat and what you drink, and you take pleasure in being intrigued, then you appreciate the other qualities that are far more important than consistency. You cede control, and essentially allow yourself to take a journey with a restaurant or a wine producer.

Of course, the idea of letting go can easily be abused. Marketers, bless their crafty little minds, understand both sides of the issue. Just as they know how to appeal to those craving consistency, they have targeted the other end, those who see the winemaker as kind of a hands-off farmer merely allowing the grapes to make themselves into world-class wines. For these people, the marketers coined the clumsy buzzword *non-interventionist.*

What is a non-interventionist winemaker? A successful producer of bird food and vinegar! Seriously, if you stick around the wine business you hear all sorts of clichés, like "good wine is made in the vineyard." Of course, the gist is true: you must have excellent raw materials to make excellent wine. But the truth is, winemakers must intervene all the time. Every decision they make—how to prune the vines, how to position them relative to the sun as they grow, how to handle the fermentation, how and where the wine will settle and age before bottling—each of these decisions requires intervention. This sort of intervention, however, is not the same as control. It's a form of guidance in which you do your unstinting utmost to grow the best possible grapes and make the best possible wines, but nonetheless remember your place.

Even the best grapes can be made mediocre or ruined in the cellar. Again, it's an issue of control and power. Very good wines can certainly be made by the most controlling of winemakers, those who might choose all sorts of manipulative techniques to ensure a predictable outcome. They might choose a specific kind of yeast to initiate fermentation and guarantee that the fermentation completes, because the behavior of the indigenous yeasts that populate the grapes is not quite as certain. They might add particular bacteria to spur the malolactic fermentation; that is, the transformation of malic acid into lactic acid, so that it takes place when the winemaker prefers, rather than when it might occur naturally. These winemakers might add water to reduce the amount of alcohol in the wine, or they might add sugar before fermentation to produce more alcohol. They might add enzymes to darken the color if it's red wine, since the public seems to associate darker wines with higher quality. They might add tartaric acid if it's lacking in verve and vitality. They might use microoxygenation technology to make the wine more supple, or send it through a concentrator to intensify it. To a lesser extent, they might use temperature control to manage the fermentation process. Many winemakers use one or another of these techniques. The more they employ, the greater their control over the wine.

If winemakers start off with great grapes, as I said, they may make very good wine. But in general to make great wine, winemakers must again cede control. They must have, in the proverbial words of a legendary Burgundian, "the courage to do nothing." Instead of overtly manipulating the wine to achieve a desired result, they try merely to shepherd the wine along its way, guiding it for sure but ultimately allowing nature to take its course. If fermentation with indigenous yeast doesn't begin right away, well, they wait. If the cold of winter impedes the malolactic fermentation, well, they wait until spring for it to occur. Sometimes wine is not ready to leave the cellar on schedule. This can be a real problem in small facilities, which might have only enough space to store and age one or two vintages at a time. Then commercial considerations trump the winemaker's heart—the wine is bottled and it departs. But with enough space, that stubborn vintage will simply be stored to age until it is ready to go.

Regardless of the status of the wine in question, Beaujolais or Grand Cru Burgundy, Contra Costa zinfandel or Napa Valley cabernet, barbera or Barolo, Cru Bourgeois Bordeaux or first-growth Bordeaux, the more the winemaker plays shepherd rather than dictator, the more interesting the wine will be.

It takes modesty and humility for winemakers to cede control, because they realize that ultimately they are subject to the whims and fortunes of nature. I particularly notice this sense of modesty and humility in people who have a long history of association with their vineyards and wine. Aubert de Villaine of Domaine de la Romanée-Conti is one of the most humble individuals in wine. So is Maria-José López de Heredia, one of the proprietors of the great and venerable Rioja producer R. López de Heredia. Roberto Conterno of Giacomo Conterno, the great Barolo producer, is modest about his role in the winemaking process, as was Bartolo Mascarello, who kept the faith that old-school Barolo, produced using the methods he learned from his own father, was worth preserving even as others ridiculed him.

I will emphasize again that being modest and humble does not preclude having a strong ego. All of these winemakers I've mentioned have a sure sense of themselves and their worth. Some might even be described as more than sure of themselves. But when it comes to their wines they understand the limitations of the human role.

Josko Gravner, the relentlessly experimental wizard of Friuli–Venezia Giulia, has always gone his own way and does not suffer fools gladly. But in his relation to his vineyards and his role in the greater scheme of winemaking, I would describe him as modest and humble. I would say the same of Anselme Selosse, who makes wonderful Champagnes labeled with his father's name, Jacques Selosse, and Aleš Kristančič of Movia, whose family has farmed its estate in Slovenia, just over the border from Italy, since 1820. None of these men are shy—they are most definite in their opinions—and they are not coy about their own abilities. But their well-earned pride does not place them above the natural processes of great winemaking. "The greatest danger is man, who can upset the balance," Anselme Selosse once told me, discussing his vineyard work. His job, he said, is to guide with a gentle hand, but to stay out of the way.

A powerful sense of self-worth is not at odds with a humble approach toward wine. Gianfranco Soldera, who makes one of the great Brunellos di Montalcino, is most definitely not a modest individual. He will tell you without prompting why his wines are so much better than those of many of his peers. He nonetheless subordinates himself to his vineyard and his wines, which are sublime. I never met Robert Mondavi in his prime, but my impression was that humility was not one of his primary virtues. Still, I was always struck by something he told Rémi Krug, of the Champagne Krugs, back in 1983. "Rémi, I believe we can say that, in only a few years, we have been able to make great quality wines," Krug recalled Mondavi saying, as he spoke to me twenty years later. "But they still lack subtlety, and this will take generations to achieve." Regardless of how Mondavi felt about his own abilities, this indicates a recognition of the inherent limitations of a winemaker's power.

Without a long history of successful winemaking in the New World, it's not as easy for American winemakers to display their modest sides as perhaps it is for their Old World counterparts. In both Napa and Sonoma, I've met many people in the wine trade who relentlessly put forth the message that as far as wine goes, they live in God's country. There's a sort of manifest destiny to their attitudes that I find unattractive, as it indicates the insecurity that so often is at the root of arrogance.

Nonetheless, California is not without its share of modest individuals who manage to produce great wines. I would cite Bob Travers of Mayacamas, who makes wonderful cabernet sauvignons on Mt. Veeder, as a man who sees his role as a steward of the land, and who perhaps has paid a critical price for not being a louder advocate for his own wines. Paul Draper of Ridge Vineyards will strike nobody as lacking an ego, but when it comes to his wines, I think he keeps the human role in a proper perspective. The same is true of Ted Lemon of Littorai, Wells Guthrie of Copain, and Ehren Jordan of Failla.

Jim Clendenen of Au Bon Climat is a larger-than-life personality, and he is proud of his wines, but he does not mistake his ambition for his achievements. Kevin Harvey of Rhys Vineyards, like a lot of newcomers to the American wine business, made his fortune doing something else. He is now spending a good deal of it establishing vineyards in the Santa Cruz Mountains. He is highly ambitious, and hopes to achieve greatness, but he also recognizes that the wine business moves at an agricultural pace, and that there is a huge difference between claiming greatness and achieving it. He makes the best wines he can make while acknowledging that his estate is in its infancy.

Just as the attitudes of the winemakers and grape growers can play a significant role in what people eventually consume, I believe that the attitudes of the people who think and write about wine for a living contribute significantly to how consumers feel about what they are drinking. Wine writers are not by nature the most modest and humble individuals. After all, we are confident enough of our opinions to imagine the public will find them at least useful, and possibly even entertaining and inspiring. Yet ultimately, consumers would be far better served if wine writers were less certain and less defensive, and more willing to concede the possibility of errors and mistakes.

I don't mean that critics should not be assertive in their opinions. Nobody wants a wishy-washy approach to wine. But again, it comes down to recognizing the ambiguities of wine, and the possibility that differences of opinion might be legitimate and mistakes occur in part because wine is temperamental.

This is a difficult point, because wine writers must make a living, and that requires selling oneself or one's publication. Demeaning one's competitors while exalting number one may not be so much an accurate expression of one's beliefs as it is a concerted if unconscious effort to maintain one's earning power. Nonetheless, I believe many people would feel more comfortable with wine if the authorities in the field were less concerned with seeming godlike and all-knowing.

Harry Waugh, the great British wine merchant, is today best remembered for his response to the question "Have you ever mistaken Bordeaux for Burgundy?" His answer: "Not since lunch."

This quip is often cited as a reminder of how even the most knowledgeable in the wine trade can be easily fooled, yet the wisdom in it seems to have been lost. The joy of wine is not about getting the right answer in a guessing game. It's not memorizing soil compositions and the weather characteristics of old vintages. It's most certainly not identifying peculiar aromas to see who has the keenest sense of smell, or the most florid imagination. These activities may all be rewarding pastimes for wine professionals—a bunch of sommeliers amusing themselves after hours, or merchants gathering at a Bordeaux tasting. But for ordinary people who may yearn to experience the pleasures that wine has to offer, the idea that one must engage in and master these rituals before one can enjoy wine contributes greatly to the anxiety that so many feel.

I'm willing to 'fess up right now: My career in wine has been riddled with mistakes. I've mistaken syrah for pinot noir at dinner. In blind tastings, I've harshly judged wines that seemed too tannic or too dense, only to learn later that they were bottles that I ordinarily love. Did that demonstrate that my beloved wines are in fact not so good? No. But I believe it demonstrates the limits of blind tastings. I've indeed guessed wrong when I've been given a glass of something and been asked to identify it. It's a silly game of fool the wine writer, and I don't mind playing along. You know what? I'm not ashamed at all.

All of these activities, assumed to measure one's connoisseurship, instead have more to do with ego gratification than they do with understanding the important things about wine. Personally, I feel I can contribute far more to the public discourse on wine by showing how wrong I can be rather than demonstrating that I'm infallible.

One area where I can safely say I've never been wrong is in conveying the pleasure that I get from a good bottle of wine. I may not be adequate to the task. I might not be able to communicate the depths of emotion I feel or the sense of awe that washes over me when consuming a great wine, and sometimes even a good wine. But it's not a matter of right or wrong. It's simply a feeling. Being open to these feelings is much more important than mastering a list of wine facts. If you fall in love with wine, you may be inspired to learn things that you never imagined you would care about. But it's the rare individual who is force-fed the dry facts about wine first, and then falls for what's in the glass.

THE SECRET SOCIETY

Bianca Bosker

My initial interactions with Morgan were, admittedly, strange.

We first bumped into each other at a wine festival, the Wine Bar War, where Morgan skipped the pleasantries to recite an ode to the virtues of his wine fridge. His station was the only one serving red wine cooled to cellar temperature in a blistering Brooklyn warehouse, and he took immense pride in this bit of forethought. I admire that level of obsessive-compulsive hedonism, plus I'd heard some intriguing things about Morgan, so I emailed him to ask if he'd be free to chat about how and why he became a sommelier.

"I have done a lot of thinking and writing about this for myself, to work out why what I do is actually of cultural and social importance, rather than just being an intermediary in moving widgets through a distribution channel," he replied, by way of "yes." He suggested drinks at Terroir, a snug wine bar in the East Village that blasts Iggy Pop and the Who and keeps its wine list in graffiti-covered binders. He called it one of his "'spiritual homes' in the wine world."

Morgan arrived on his bike in a hipster uniform of jeans, a vintage T-shirt, a gray beanie, and battered Saucony sneakers, which he'd lifted from his dad's closet. He'd rather drink his money than wear it, he explained, folding his long legs under the narrow bar counter. He yanked off his hat, shaking loose a single curl that dangled and danced on his forehead like a fuzzy exclamation point. Morgan was bike messenger from the neck down and Hugh Grant from the chin up: lazily, rascally handsome, with blue eyes, a well-defined jaw, and poofy waves of dramatic hair.

Before I could express a preference, he summoned two glasses of sherry for us to share. "Sherry is one of the most complicated things," he began. He launched into a lecture, delivered at a speed usually reserved for reciting drug side effects on TV commercials, about the biological and oxidative aging process for Amontillado sherry; the nuances of Fino, Manzanilla, Amontillado, and Oloroso sherries; the killer pairing of an Oloroso with olives and eighteen-month-old *jamón*; the "umami-type flavors that are more of that oxidation"; the widespread confusion of dryness and tannin; and wine trends of the 1800s. He soon had both feet propped up on the legs of my stool and was pounding the counter under my chin for emphasis, his curl bouncing along excitedly. Did I know about Thomas Jefferson's love for Madeira? That Barolo wasn't dry until 1870? The stomach-churning richness of nineteenth-century meals? "You look at those historic menus from the 1880s from, like, Delmonico's, it's, like, hol-ee *shit*!" He threw his head back and waved both hands in the air for emphasis, or maybe he just couldn't control himself. "These people were just trying not to *die*!" He wanted me to know that the most expensive wines on the *Titanic* had all been German Rieslings. He declared tasting notes "fundamentally evil." He admitted to lusting after a $1,400 bottle of Champagne—"a steal!"—that would be "a borderline religious experience." He rattled off the strengths and weaknesses of his palate with the ease of a basketball star ticking off stats for a recruiter: rotundone-deaf, mixes up Nebbiolo and Sangiovese, suspected supertaster status. He was working on his own oeuvre about wine—"more manifesto or religious tract than it is a wine book"—that was meant to "occasion a sea change to adjust America's metanarrative about how they see themselves relative to wine."

"The greatest lie that's been sold to the American populace is that they're not in control of their own tastes," he preached, curl quivering as if in agreement.

This was typical Morgan: borderline professorial, a tad hyperbolic, and extremely long-winded. "There's a propensity towards my confidence and my comfort with certain things shortchanging me actually listening to people," he told me later, far past the point at which I'd figured that out.

Morgan ordered us another two glasses of wine, and plowed through his personal history. He was twenty-nine, had studied theater at Emerson (a small liberal arts college that appropriately started as a "school of oratory"), and had abandoned acting to pursue sommelierdom. (You might remember Morgan's knuckles from *21*, the movie about card counters in Vegas casinos. Morgan played a hand double.) In seven years, he had worked his way up from serving just-okay wine at a red-sauce joint in Boston to helping powerful men with large expense accounts pick out bottles at Aureole, Chef Charlie Palmer's Michelin-starred restaurant on the edge of Times Square. Morgan joined Aureole after being fired from Jean-Georges, the crown jewel of French chef Jean-Georges Vongerichten's international empire. Morgan, never one to deny himself liquid pleasure, had helped himself to a margarita one evening while reviewing order forms in the back office. And that was the end of that.

He was in his second year of trying to pass the Master Sommelier Exam, the highest rank restaurant wine pros can reach. In terms of difficulty and prestige, attaining it is the dining-room equivalent of being made a Navy SEAL. But while there are 2,450 active SEALs, only 230 people have ever become Master Sommeliers. To put that in perspective, 200 people sit for the exam annually. Ninety-five percent of them fail. On average, in the years leading up to the test, Master candidates will taste more than 20,000 wines, study for 10,000 hours, make more than 4,000 flash cards, and affix 25 laminated maps to the walls of their shower stalls. The theory section of the test is often used to weed people out. (What's the altitude of the Fiano di Avellino appellation? Didn't think so.) Morgan had nailed theory on his first try, which left the tasting and service portions for him to pass. He would be attempting both sections in the late spring, around the same time I aimed to take my own Certified exam. I felt a tug of kinship for this guy who was also turning his life upside down for one of the Court's tests, would be prepping on the same time line as me, and maybe—possibly, hopefully—would let me join him in his training regimen.

I could also relate to him because I too am an exceptionally nerdy person. I am so hopeless when it comes to physical activity and so content being bathed in the LED glow of the computer screen that my husband introduces me to his friends as an "indoor kid." I mean, I was the *technology* editor for a website. My job was to commune with fellow nerds. And I met them, in every shape and size, by the dozens—programmers, hackers, futurists, roboticists, you name it. But even I, surely one of the world's foremost connoisseurs of geekery, was awestruck by Morgan. He had accomplished a remarkable feat: He'd gone so far in the direction of nerdy that he came back around to cool, or something like it that I found even more compelling. The air around him practically vibrated with the intensity of his passion for wine. His enthusiasm was magnetic.

Our first evening together lasted almost three hours. Unable to squeeze a word in edgewise, I had to wait until Morgan had disappeared into the bathroom to request the check. I was running half an hour late for dinner with a friend.

"Whatever you want to parse out of the experience, just let me know because I'm there to help you process it," Morgan said as we parted.

I knew just what to ask him—and Plato would never have approved.

Our collective distaste for taste (and smell) begins with Plato. To the great Greek philosopher, these were the no-good degenerates of the five senses. While Plato argued that hearing and sight could bring aesthetic pleasure, the experiences of the nose and mouth were fleeting, intellectually bankrupt stimulations. At best, they merely tickled the body. At worst, they turned men into savages. As Plato saw it, our appetite-fueling flavor apparatus—the "part of the soul which desires meats and drinks"—was no better than "a wild animal which was chained up with man." Left to its own devices, this inner beast could provoke such frenzies of gluttony as to make "the whole race an enemy to philosophy and music." Coming from a philosopher, this was an especially heinous crime.

This mind-set was perpetuated by generations of thinkers, who likewise turned up their noses at, well, their noses (and tongues). These were the untrustworthy sensory organs, corrupting gateways to gluttony and vice, all wrapped up with the ugly needs of the flesh. It is "clearly impossible," wrote Thomas Aquinas, "that human happiness consists in pleasures of the body, the chief of which are pleasures of the table and of sex." René Descartes considered sight "the noblest and most comprehensive of the senses." Immanuel Kant, who agreed vision was "noblest," scorned taste and smell as "nothing but senses of organic sensation." (He singled out smell as the "most ungrateful" and "most dispensable" sense, which "it does not pay to cultivate.") This snobbery toward the senses leaked into fields far beyond philosophy. Even scientists declined to research these primitive, obsolete faculties. In a book on odors, Jacques Le Magnen, a groundbreaking twentieth-century researcher focused on taste and olfaction, felt it necessary to justify his interest in what he dubs one of the "minor senses."

I'd heard whispers about a group of aspiring Master Sommeliers who flouted these anti-sense sensibilities at their weekly meetings at the restaurant Eleven Madison Park (EMP, for those in the know).

Theirs was rumored to be the Holy Grail of New York blind tasting groups, the highest-level in the city. One sommelier warned me there was a waiting list to join "because it's so cutthroat." (She'd been shunned.) I'd heard stories of people who were blacklisted for bringing the wrong wine or missing a week without notice. There weren't auditions, applications, or interviews to get in. Instead, like country clubs or Skull and Bones, your best bet was to befriend the right people, work at the right places, and look for occasions, such as competitions, to show you knew your Meursault (a Chardonnay grown in Burgundy's Meursault village) from your Marsannay (a Chardonnay grown about twenty miles over in Burgundy's Marsannay village). I asked Victoria James, a wine prodigy who'd recently earned a spot in the group, whether I might be allowed in. "It's very serious," she said, then repeated that two more times. "It's very serious. It's just *very serious*." She spoke of fights erupting over the typicity of bottles of Chablis. "Like, 'How could you bring this Chablis because 2013 was a warm vintage and obviously it's not showing typically?'"

Blind tasting groups usually segregate along experience level, so I had no business tasting with Master Sommelier candidates. But that's exactly what I intended to do. "Blinding" with strong tasters enhances the feedback you receive, hence groups' pickiness about admitting new members. I met a woman who'd taken a second job, with a two-hour commute, to work for a Master Sommelier—just so she could taste regularly in his presence. Many others fly themselves around the country to do the same. A good coach can tell you if your acid calls are off base, how to distinguish a Sangiovese made in Montalcino from one made in Chianti, and which floral scents are missing from your sense memory.

Although I'd been promised introductions to whoever ran the EMP group, weeks had passed, and despite much nagging, nothing had materialized. Morgan was a member. I emailed him almost immediately after we left Terroir. Could I come?

He was noncommittal at first. I pushed, prodded, and pleaded until, finally, there came a concession. On a frigid day, when most of the group's twelve or so members were swamped with work emergencies, Morgan relented. I'd have to agree to a compromise, however: I could observe and I could taste the wines. But given my level, I couldn't speak.

For the sommeliers in Morgan's blind tasting group, showing up at ten o'clock each Tuesday morning to taste at EMP had all the glamour of a date with the StairMaster. They'd been doing this every week for years. It was their tongue cardio.

But I was not jaded and I was not experienced, and I did not play it cool. I hauled open EMP's large brass doors feeling very impressed, both with the somms with whom I was about to taste, and with myself for having been initiated into this secret wine society, hiding in plain sight in one of the city's most visible restaurants. My grandiose mood was only compounded by the sumptuousness of EMP's formal dining room. It was like getting a hug from someone's extremely rich great-aunt. I parted heavy velvet drapes to reveal an Art Deco masterpiece of a room. Enormous gridded windows looked out over a park, and the double-height ceilings were caked in layers of molding with pink scalloped trim. Morgan waved me over to a linen-covered table in the back, and I sidestepped a florist arranging bouquets of dogwood and amaryllis that would have had trouble fitting into my studio apartment. My boots echoed loudly on the floor, like footsteps in an empty church. And in the food world, there is something approaching holy about EMP. The restaurant has racked up serious accolades, including a spot at number four on the San Pellegrino list of best restaurants in the world. EMP spends ten months training its staff to pour water and employs people with the title of "dreamweaver," whose job it is to enhance the meal through miniature miracles, like delivering a sled to a guest who, over the third course, mentions wanting to play in the snow. Dinner for one begins at $295, takes three and a half hours, and, the theory goes, makes an impression that lasts a lifetime—which is conveniently the amount of time you might need to pay off your credit card bill, if you order some of the top bottles on offer.

Four guys out of the group's twelve or so members had shown up. They'd been tasting together for nearly four years. Dana Gaiser was a sommelier-turned-distributor who'd graduated from Stanford with a degree in mechanical engineering. He was in his midthirties, had frenetic Edward Scissorhands hair, and exuded this-month's-GQ cool in a tight suit and a pink shirt. Jon Ross, who was just a few years younger, had on a rumpled sweatshirt and looked exhausted—no surprise for someone who puts in the punishing seventy-hour workweek that's standard for a sommelier at EMP. "They own you. Like not even vaguely," Morgan told me. Yannick Benjamin was a sommelier at the University Club, a members-only club favored by the city's bankers, lawyers, doctors, and trust funders. A car accident in 2003 had left

Yannick wheelchair-bound, but that didn't stop him from following a long line of Benjamin men into the restaurant business. Morgan was Morgan. All four tasters were prepping for the Master Sommelier Exam. Yannick was attempting it for the ninth time.

Dana, Jon, and Yannick were sullen and sleepy. Morgan chattered like he'd just blown a few lines back in the kitchen. "Has anyone told you the dirty sommelier mnemonic for remembering bottle sizes?" he said, pouring his wines into decanters so that all details about the bottle, including its shape, would be disguised. "'Michael Jackson Really Makes Small Boys Nervous.' So Michael is Magnum; Jackson is Jeroboam; really, Rehobaum; makes, Methuselah; small, Salamanzar; boys, Balthazar; nervous, Nebuchadnezzar." (With slight variations depending on the region, a magnum contains the equivalent of two standard bottles; a Jeroboam holds four; a Rehobaum, six; a Methuselah, eight; and from there the volume increases by four bottles per size up through the Nebuchadnezzar, which holds twenty standard bottles and guarantees a good time.)

I apologized for not having brought wine and offered to bring some next time.

"No, it's okay. If you did, we'd most likely just whine and yell at you about it like little bitches," said Jon.

It wasn't an empty threat. Blind tasting practice works best when sommeliers train with classic examples of wines. The bottles should exemplify the typical style of a Malbec from Mendoza, Argentina, or a Grenache blend from Châteauneuf-du-Pape in France, for instance. "Like, if you bring seven-year-old Chilean Cabernet and an unoaked $16 bottle of Mâcon Chardonnay, you're wasting my fucking time," snapped Morgan. Another no-go was repeatedly showing up with niche grape varietals that were not among the fifty or so believed to be fair game for the Master exam. (Though the Court doesn't reveal what wines are eligible for the test, examinees have spent years trying to reverse engineer what the judges might throw at them, so they have a pretty good idea.)

"Everything still tastes like toothpaste," Jon complained, as we arranged ourselves around a table in the dining room. "Usually brushing my teeth doesn't affect me, but I used a different toothpaste than normal. So I will not be using that one again."

I hoped no one would get close enough to smell the minty freshness of the Listerine I'd gargled before leaving home. Brushing my teeth was also beginning to feel like a bad idea.

We had eight wines to go through. Jon had put out plastic spit buckets, and because service never stops, the choice of sparkling or flat water. Today we'd be "round-tabling": Each person would taste one wine at a time and, per the format of the Master Sommelier Exam, recite their analysis out loud. The others would listen and critique.

"Okay, I'm counting the 'ums'!" Morgan announced. With his theater background, he appreciated the need for polished delivery. Plus, the Master Sommelier blind tasting test allows twenty-five minutes to get through six wines—three white, three red—so with just fourish minutes per glass, each "uhhh" and "hmmm" could eat up valuable time.

Whites were first, and Dana was up.

"He can do a flight on the nose alone," Morgan boasted. Dana didn't correct him.

I picked up my glass and stuck my nose into it. Dana was still inspecting the color, so I took my nose out and examined the liquid. On the spectrum of red or white, this was a white wine. So far, so confident, I thought. Wrong.

"Pale gold, with some rim variation at the meniscus, flecks of gold and green. It's star bright, no signs of gas or sediment, and viscosity is moderate-plus," Dana said in a low monotone, speaking as quickly as he could. So "white" wasn't quite what they were going for.

I sniffed. It smelled, I hated to say it, like wine. *You're a writer, you can do better than that*, I chided myself. I sniffed harder and lifted the glass closer to my face. Wine dribbled into my nostrils, down my chin, and onto my lap. I dabbed at my face with a page from my notebook. I sniffed again—maybe one could say apple. Something sweet? Yes. Apple and sweet, I decided. A flicker of doubt: Could sweetness be smelled?

Dana was already racing ahead. "Ripe peaches and peach candy. Apricot. Meyer lemon. Candied grapefruit. Some very liqueur-like fruits, slightly candied. Tangerine. Candied tangerine and candied orange peel. Getting a slightly Grand Marnier thing going on. Honeysuckle. Um"—Morgan made a check mark—"Lily. Heavy cream. Yogurt. Butter. Butterscotch. Slight hint of tarragon and basil. There's uh"—check—"vanilla and baking spice indicating new oak *barrique.*"

He hadn't even tasted it yet.

I alternated between skepticism and awe. Candied tangerine? Grand Marnier? Really? I rushed to take a sip. I liked the wine, I knew that. The apple flavor was there again . . . right? I mostly tasted Listerine.

Dana took a sip and gargled the wine. He picked up an herb garden and spring bouquet on the palate. Sweet basil, dried lilac, honeysuckle. "There's lilies, Easter lilies, all the types of lilies." He called it dry, with moderate-plus acidity, and moderate-plus alcohol.

Dana paused and took a deep breath, crescendoing to his final conclusion: "I'm going to call this 2010—no, 2011 Viognier. France. Rhône Valley, Northern Rhône, Condrieu."

Morgan pulled out the bottle and read off the label. It was indeed a Viognier, a floral, richly perfumed grape. It was from France, from the Northern Rhône. Within the Northern Rhône, it was from Condrieu, an appellation five hundred acres in size that is about half as big as Central Park. And it was a 2012.

My mouth dropped open. I wanted to applaud. Instead, I adopted the stony façade of the others, who looked unimpressed. Morgan pointed out that Dana had gone ten seconds over his allotted time. Jon quibbled with Dana's acid call.

"I think there's a saltiness in this wine that makes you think the acid is higher," said Jon.

Morgan sniffed at the wine. "It smells like hot dogs."

"Orange Tic Tacs," Jon corrected. "Or rubber chicken."

Dana shook his head. "Rubber chicken is more like . . . Clare Valley. Aussie Riesling."

Morgan, Jon, and Yannick each took a turn blind tasting a white, and after critiquing one another's notes, started in on the reds. Relegated to silence, I listened to their analysis and tried to work out what each wine might be while desperately struggling to detect whiffs of the improbable things they claimed to smell. More than an hour passed in a blur of adjectives spoken into the echoing cavity of a wineglass. "Wet asphalt," "surgical glove," "dried pomegranate," "asparagus pee," "pyrazines," "terpenes," "Dana's taint." A few of these aromas were familiar, some I'd never smelled before, and others referred to chemicals in the wine that I was hearing about for the first time. The guys spent awhile arguing about how to best describe the smell of an oxidized Chenin Blanc. Dana suggested dried cardboard, Jon countered with cereal box or Apple Jacks. Morgan voted Cheerios.

I joined Morgan for lunch afterward at a greasy diner around the corner. We tore into the food, our stomachs frantic after being teased by all the sniffing and tasting with no swallowing. The blind tasting part of Morgan's brain stayed in overdrive. I was getting the sense it never switched off. He described a comparative bacon tasting he'd organized with his roommates the other weekend. He dissected how I could spot Chablis by its "oyster-shell kelp yogurt"–ness. He deconstructed what made my burger delicious. "The whole reason this dish is excellent is the contrast between this sweet-and-sour thing and this salty-fatty thing," he explained through mouthfuls of an egg-salad sandwich. "You can't deny that there's an umami-ness. Why do you put a tomato and some lettuce on it? Tomatoes have a ton of acid. That's why the experience is enjoyable. Because there's the contrast of flavors. The sweetness of the ketchup with the salty-fatty. And yeah, there's a *ton* of vinegar in ketchup."

It wasn't a romantic way to think about a meal. But I appreciated Morgan's deconstruction. It gave me a new way of wallowing around in the pleasure of each bite. Morgan prattled on about what he'd pair with foie gras. I focused on the sugar and acid of the ketchup, and how it played off the fattiness of the fries.

*   *   *

I was allowed to taste with the EMP group the following Tuesday, and every Tuesday after that. My lunches with Morgan became a regular routine and I picked up more about his life story over plates of grilled cheese and pastrami. He'd grown up in Seattle, "solidly middle class," the son of two general internists and the oldest of three kids. His parents drank wine every now and then, usually a half bottle of Kendall-Jackson Chardonnay—the approachable mass-market rom-com of the wine world.

Morgan has always blazed through his passions like a forest fire, consuming everything in his path. "My brain has a tendency to want to organize small differentiating units into systems," he told me. "Part of it is my desire to complete. To know a thing in its entirety, or as close to it as you can." When he was a little kid, he'd sic himself on LEGOs. His mom would buy the most elaborate sets she could find, and he'd assemble them in an afternoon, then never touch them again. He graduated to trading cards. In elementary school, Morgan memorized every Magic: The Gathering card (its mana cost, expansion symbol, supertype, number) in a collection so huge that even now he couldn't lift it if he wanted to. Video games came next. He'd power up a new one and think, "I want to do every single subquest, I want to fight every single monster, I want to solve every single puzzle, because then you've seen it all. You can put it in a box, zip it up, and say, 'Well, that was that world.'" Obviously, when Morgan discovered rock 'n' roll, he was incapable of just enjoying the music. "As soon as I started learning about classic rock, it was like, 'Okay, well, here's Led Zeppelin, now, let's buy every single album, let's listen to every single song and figure out how they all fit together.' Like, 'I'm going to learn everything about these bands. I'm going to learn this fucking music. I'm going to learn everything about all their weird B-sides. I'm going to learn whose girlfriends they fucked.'" And now, wine. At last, Morgan had found a topic with an infinite number of expansion packs.

During his first three years in New York, Morgan balanced acting aspirations with jobs at wine bars around the city, but he soon felt a stronger tug toward wine. He loved talking with people. He even loved being on his feet, a physical aspect of the job that others find exhausting. "I would rather impale myself on a spit than go do temp work," he told me. He abandoned his auditioning after a fall spent working the harvest at a winery in Washington state, where he bunked with a blowtorch-wielding rodeo clown who made sculptures from horseshoes in his spare time. When Morgan returned to the city that winter, in 2011, it was with a singular focus on wine and honing his craft. He got a job managing Corkbuzz, a downtown wine bar for über-oenophiles owned by a Master Sommelier. Then he went to Jean-Georges, then Aureole. Morgan being Morgan, he couldn't be in wine without taking it to its illogical extreme. All the while, he threw himself into books, competitions, classes, and tastings. This wasn't just about selling good bottles. He believed that wine could reshape someone's life. That's why he preferred buying bottles to splurging on sweaters. Sweaters were things. Bottles of wine, said Morgan, "are ways that my humanity will be changed."

Despite his lofty pronouncements, Morgan, as well as many of the other somms I would come to know, was not without a sense of irony. He knew how ridiculous his job could appear to a casual observer—a glorified, overpaid waiter with a drinking problem. Or, even less charitably, a sycophant sponging off the rich and powerful, hawking wines for their price as much as their quality. Morgan was aware that what he was doing was not exactly saving the planet or rescuing orphans. But he had pushed through the self-awareness to the other side. It was *only* wine the same way that a Picasso is *only* paint on canvas and Mozart is *only* vibrations in the air.

Our weekly routine evolved into a semiweekly routine. Morgan finagled me a spot in his other blind tasting group. This one met Saturday mornings at the headquarters of Danny Meyer's Union Square Hospitality Group, the force behind more than a dozen New York restaurants that are each landmarks in their own right. Eventually,

I was even allowed to speak. I was blind tasting, out loud and for all to judge.

Tuesdays we would pair up with partners and take turns going through two different flights of six wines. Saturdays we round-tabled. Whoever was captain that week chose a problem area to drill down on, then bought specific wines around that theme (say, tannic reds or oaked whites from warm climates). The bottles we tasted averaged around $25 each, which was expensive enough to ensure they'd be classic expressions of whatever style they repre-sented, and also cheap enough to keep us from bankruptcy. Still, the costs added up. During his most intense study periods, ahead of big exams, Morgan would drop $250 per week on practice wines. Add that to the cost of flying to be coached by Master Sommeliers, or traveling to the tests themselves, and he was spending about $15,000 each year prepping for the Master Sommelier Exam, a solid chunk of the approximately $72,000 he made annually at Aureole. Morgan shrugged off the expense when I asked about it. "It's still a lot cheaper than a college degree or grad school," he said. Plus it left plenty to splurge on fun wines. Not long after we met, Morgan treated himself to three cases of wine worth $1,200—almost double his monthly rent.

Correctly identifying a wine in a blind tasting feels so impossibly difficult that the first time I did so, only one thought came to mind: I am a genius. I realized, in that moment, that I must be a sensory savant. My taste buds—probably unprecedented in history—were poised to be unleashed on the world. Famous winemakers would beg me to taste their best bottles. I'd field six-figure offers from wine magazines desperate to make me their star critic. Maybe seven-figure.

This fantasy lasted all of thirty-seven seconds, which is exactly the time it took me to start in on the next wine. From the first sip I was lost. Two weeks went by before I correctly called another wine.

Facing down a flight of six wines was like being caught on a booze treadmill set to Usain Bolt mode. The first wine would go okay. By the third I'd be in a full-blown panic. Tannins would be piling up in my mouth. I'd be picking up and putting down glasses, trying to shock my nose into smelling something. *Oak? Pepper? Some pepper somewhere, please?* I'd commit the ultimate blind tasting sin, and try to cheat by grasping for some external logic, beyond the glass, that could provide me with a pattern or clues. *Glass One was Grenache, so would Daniel really bring us a second Grenache?* (Answer: It wasn't, and why not?) Paranoia would set in. *Were all the red wines actually the same thing? Had I lost my sense of smell?* When the timer went off, I didn't stop—I dropped.

Even so, I thought my tasting skills were improving. That was until I received an email from one of the sommeliers I'd partnered with on a recent Tuesday. We'd met that week at Del Frisco's, a Midtown steakhouse that had paintings of naked women hung above its decommissioned cigar lockers. While my partner blinded the wines, I'd done what I saw everyone around me doing: I took notes on what he said, then read them back to him, pointing out the attributes he'd skipped over. Huge. Mistake. Sure, I might have progressed. But I had a long way to go before I was anywhere close to respectable. This was their world, and I'd have to prove myself if I wanted to live in it.

This was made explicitly clear when my partner emailed me a few days later. "I wanted to apologize for being a total dick when we tasted together at Del Frisco's," the guy's email to me began. "Tasting is this sacred thing we do. It is like wings for paratroopers. If you don't have them you're not part of the troop and you'll never understand why. When you began to give me feedback, I thought to myself, 'Who the fuck does this girl think she is?'"

Morgan, who seemed to like having me as his captive audience, volunteered to tutor me in the fundamentals of tasting and suggested I join him at a distributor event. Besides coaching me, he'd be going to rehearse grape varieties he missed during blind tastings and to pick up ideas for winemakers to recommend to guests (or judges, during exams and competitions).

I arrived to find him doing triage on the catalog of wines on offer. There were about ninety-five different producers, each pouring between two and ten bottles each. We had a long day ahead. We would need to be focused and systematic, Morgan warned.

"First, this is a social event unto itself. People are here as much to network as to drink," he said, weaving us through a crowded aisle of tables. "Second, do not swallow or you will be dead."

He paused in front of a row of Champagnes and volunteered our glasses for pours. His eyes bugged out after he took a sip.

"This wine is fascinating!" Morgan yelped. He said this a lot, and it was requiring me to rethink the meaning of the word "fascinating." To Morgan, "fascinating" could apply to: Germany's *Flurbereinigung* land reform in the 1970s owing to the drawbacks of old cadastral maps; something about the nuance of *cru* versus *crû* that may have led to confusion about the actual meaning of Grand Cru; Bolivian *eau de vie*; and the Champagne we were drinking made without *dosage*, a mixture of sugar and wine often added to bottles of sparkling wine, sometimes called the *liqueur d'expédition*. (A quick warning: oenophiles use an unnecessary number of French words in daily life. Towel is *serviette*, bubbles are *pétillance*, and table settings are the *mise-en-place*. Pretentious? *Oui*.)

We stopped by each of the producers that Morgan had staked out in advance. The way he talked about the wines immediately made me curious to smell whatever he'd just tried. "Salami farts," he'd proclaim. We tasted a red from Burgundy he pronounced the "Sophia Loren of wine," a Chablis he called "the crack cocaine of Chardonnay," and a Riesling he christened "the face that launched a thousand ships." An excellent Pinot Noir was a "fuck-you-sideways wine," a big California Cabernet was a "fuck-you wine"—aka a "purple bazooka," aka "solid juice," aka "purple oak juice." He deemed one Sauvignon Blanc "asparagus fart water with extra grapefruit."

Morgan plunged into the five key attributes that make up the "structure" of a wine: sugar, acid, alcohol, tannins, and texture, also referred to as "body." These contribute to our overall impression of a wine, and are in certain ways the Esperanto of wine-speak. Morgan and Jon could spend all day—and probably have—debating whether Viognier smells more like hot dog or rubber chicken. But qualities like the acidity or alcohol in a wine are measurable, objective, and immediately understood.

So how do you distinguish these traits?

Imagine you've got a glass in front of you. Step one: Look at it. Even before involving your nose or tongue, you can pick up clues about structure and flavor. Pinch the stem of the glass with your fingers, then rotate your wrist in a few swift circles, swirling the wine so that it coats the sides of the goblet. Watch the speed and width of the droplets, or "tears," that roll down after you've stilled your hand. Thick, slow tears with clear definition suggest the wine has higher alcohol levels, where thin, quick tears, or wine that falls in sheets, hint at lower alcohol levels.

Next: Smell. Always. And not just in one spot. Hold up the glass so it's nearly parallel to the floor—that way more of the wine's surface area is exposed to the air—and sniff while making the sign of the cross over the liquid with your nostrils, just to be sure you've hit the aromas from every angle. Some people swear by opening their mouths while they sniff, so they pant like a dog. So much for wine being "civilized."

Now you can sip. Swish the wine around your mouth, then purse your lips like you're about to say "oh no" and—*oh no* is right—suck in air over the wine so it feels like it's bubbling on your tongue. "Aerating" the wine, the official term for wine snobs' slurping, helps release its odor molecules, which combine with taste to form flavor. You'll look ridiculous and probably lose friends, but you'll get more from your wine.

Next, spit it out or swallow. Place the tip of your tongue against the roof of your mouth, and pay attention to how much you salivate. A lot or a little? Swimming pool or sprinkler? If you're not sure, tip your head forward so your eyes are facing the floor. If you opened your mouth right now, would you drool? If so, you're tasting a higher-acid wine. If not, it's likely a lower-acid wine. (The former tends to hail from cooler growing regions, and the latter from warmer areas.) To be sure you know what you're looking for, think of a lemon. A sour lemon that you cut in half. A sour, yellow lemon wedge that you squeeze over an empty glass. Now, take that sour lemon juice and raise it to your lips for a drink. Not to get too personal, but how much saliva is in your mouth? You should feel drool pooling on your tongue. That's how our mouths react to sour tastes (or even the thought of sour tastes): We produce saliva, which acts as a buffer to neutralize the harshness of the acid.

Prepare yourself for another sip when you're ready to gauge the alcohol. Table wines generally range from 9 percent to 16 percent alcohol (tequila is around 40 percent, by comparison). A precise sense for alcohol is key: A 1 percent variance could make the difference in whether a blind taster guesses a Riesling is from France or Australia. Alcohol can tip you off to where a bottle's grapes were grown (and much more, like the temperature during a growing season). If you're wondering why, keep in mind that every wine begins its life as a sweet stew of grape juice, called the must, that's all mashed up with grape skins, seeds, stems, and pulp. (Contrary to tasting notes, nothing like honeysuckle, peach, or orange Tic Tacs is added to the wine to flavor it, though some stray spiders, rats, mice, and snakes scooped up from the vineyard can accidentally get mixed in.) Fermentation of the must is kicked off by yeast—whether naturally occurring or added for desired effect—that then converts all or some of the grapes' sugar into alcohol. Warmer climates lead to riper grapes with a higher concentration of sugar, which, by the laws of fermentation, will produce wines with higher alcohol. Grapes from cooler climates generally have lower concentrations of sugar, yielding wines with lower alcohol. So which is it—high or low? Swallow a mouthful of wine and exhale, as if you were trying to check whether your breath stinks. (Spitting will rob you of the full effect.) Take note of how far into your mouth and throat you can feel the burning heat of the alcohol. The back of your tongue? It's probably lower alcohol—around 12 percent for reds. The back of your throat, near your jaw? Medium, closer to 13, edging on 14 percent. Are you warm all the way down by your sternum? Could be 14 plus—high. Alcohol is a feeling more than a taste. Try to remember your last tequila shot, which set fire to your tongue, throat, esophagus, and belly. The more a drink burns, the more alcohol it contains.

Take a sip again. Feeling good yet? On to tannins. These are natural compounds—polyphenols, if you want to get technical—that can come from the skins, stems, or seeds of grapes, as well as the wood barrels in which a wine may have been aged. (The latter is more often responsible for the tannins in white wines, which usually spend less time than reds soaking in skins and seeds.) Tannins are more a texture than a taste, and therefore distinct from whether the wine is "dry," which refers to the absence of sweetness. And yet, confusingly, tannins leave your mouth feeling dried-out and grippy—more like sandpaper for tannic wines (like young Nebbiolo), or like silk for low-tannin wines (say, Pinot Noir). Some tasters swear they can differentiate between tannins that come from grapes, which make their tongues and the roof of their mouths feel rough, and tannins from oak barrels, which dry out the spot between their lips and gums.

The so-called body of a wine, also more touch than taste, derives from its alcohol and sugar content. Think of the difference in viscosity between skim milk, whole milk, and heavy cream. Better yet, hold each in your mouth. That's along the lines of what makes a light-, medium-, or full-bodied wine.

Go ahead and have another sip. Finally, sweetness. Like the other attributes that make up structure, sweetness exists along a spectrum. But instead of "high" on one end and "none" on the other, which would be altogether too reasonable, an early wine-loving sadist decided to label the scale from "sweet" to "dry" with terms like "semi-sweet" and "off-dry" in between. That's right, the erudite wine connoisseur must describe a wet liquid as "dry." Think back to that messy grape sludge, the must: In a "dry" wine, all the sugar was fermented into alcohol. But winemakers will sometimes opt to halt fermentation, so there's sweetness, or "residual sugar," in the final product.

Sweetness should be easy to recognize, since we've all had sugar. Here's where it gets interesting: If the acid in a wine is high enough, we can be fooled into perceiving much less sugar than there really is, or even that there's none at all. Go back to that imaginary lemon juice you squeezed into a glass. Now pretend you've got a second glass with sugar water. Taste the sugar water alone. Ugh, sweet. Try the lemon juice alone. Blech, too sour. Combine equal parts lemon juice and sugar water. Delicious. A touch of acid can transform a saccharine mouthful into a delightful drink, and vice versa. This is Coca-Cola's secret. The ten cubes of sugar contained in a can of Coke would be foul if drunk with tap water. But they become delectable in soda, which pairs the sugar with phosphoric acid in levels that give Coke a pH on par with some animals' stomach acid. A similar logic gives white wines high in acid *and* sugar, like certain Rieslings, the invigorating tension in their tastes that makes them so delightful. An "enlivening energy," Morgan declared when he tasted one such wine, like "balancing a thousand-pound barbell on a tight rope." So how do you tease the two tastes apart? The drool test can alert you to high levels of acid, so you're aware you might be underestimating the sweetness. And since residual sugar can make wines more viscous, you can also sense sweetness by feeling out the weighty thickness or pillowy softness of a wine.

Morgan was taking only two sips of the wines we tasted for every four gulps that I did, and I realized later that professional tasters know to budget their sips and sniffs. "Tasting the same samples many times in succession is useless, such repeated attempts simply result in a total loss of sensitivity," states the famed enologist Émile Peynaud in his handbook, *The Taste of Wine*. Prolonged exposure to a scent makes our noses temporarily "blind" to that odor, a process known as olfactory fatigue. By the third or fourth whiff of a wine, your nose might be saturated with its perfume, so you're no longer sensitive to its smell. This is annoying when you're fighting the clock to guess White Wine Number 3. It's a blessing when you're assigned the middle seat next to a guy who hasn't discovered deodorant. "So long as they have been carefully registered, first impressions are the best," insists Peynaud. (He also frowns on drinking water while tasting wine—it throws off our palates—and I resolved to save hydration for before or after tasting only.)

Morgan and I hadn't even made it halfway around the floor of the distributor tasting. But I'd repeated my analysis of structure— sniff, swish, drool, exhale, spit—so many times, with so many wines, I'd lost count. I was spitting, double-spitting. And yet the alcohol still seeped in through the surface of my mouth. I was feeling ill and a little green.

We bumped into Morgan's friend Jerusha, a young woman our age who worked the floor at a restaurant in Soho. I asked her for any tips on recovering from these marathon tastings, and she suggested detox tea to defend against the alcohol.

Morgan scoffed at us both. He was still going strong. "Being relentless is my defense," he said.

The best tasters train their tongues and noses long before they ever tackle a flight of wines. How I treated my body in the days, hours, and minutes before sitting down to a glass would determine my tasting and smelling success. Put simply: My life needed some drastic rearranging.

Each sommelier has his own routine designed to keep his palate alert and wine-ready. Michael gave up coffee. Kristie insisted on diluting hers with milk. Yannick drank his cold. A different Michael believed ice water was all he needed to jolt his taste buds into action. Paolo Basso, one-time champion and three-time runner-up in the World's Best Sommelier Competition, swore by staying just a bit hungry at all times. Like the mightiest hunters of the animal kingdom, he insisted it made him like "a famished beast who smells his prey."

I surveyed sommeliers for their palate-enhancing techniques. The first step was self-knowledge, they said. I needed to monitor my tongue for its recovery time, which meant how long it took to get rid of the aftertaste of whatever I'd most recently ingested. Through trial and error, I determined my tongue needed around two hours to fully neutralize, which became my cutoff for eating, drinking, or teeth brushing before tasting. This had the added benefit of ensuring I'd always go in hungry, primed to sniff out flavors. Like Morgan, the other wine pros I spoke to had amassed a detailed profile of their noses and tongues' temperaments. "I notice that when I live closer to the water, my palate is better," said Craig Sindelar, a Chicago-based sommelier. Conrad Reddick, Craig's former colleague at the modernist restaurant Alinea, suggested tracking my palate performance against the biodynamic calendar, a chart more often used to guide farmers who harvest their vineyards biodynamically, following principles that meld the nature-conscious values of the organic movement with the good-vibes mysticism of crystal healers. (For example, biodynamic winemakers keen on "helping spirit to penetrate matter" are advised to bury a deer bladder stuffed with yarrow weed in their fields.) Conrad had found bottles' flavor changed depending on whether the biodynamic calendar dubbed it, say, a "fruit day" (better) or "root day" (worse). According to some oenophiles, barometric pressure could also flatter or mute a wine. I started a log of how external factors, like the dry air from my apartment's heater or rainy mornings, seemed to meddle with my sensing.

Next came self-deprivation. There could be no gustatory or olfactory noise to interfere with the signal. Morgan didn't brush his teeth before tastings, believing the mint tainted his taste buds for the morning. Afraid of burning their tongues, the somms Devon Broglie and Craig Collins refused to drink any liquids above a tepid temperature for the entire year and a half before their Master Sommelier Exam. Coffee, soup, tea—they took it all cold. Yannick stuck to iced coffee for the same reason. Cool foods only: check. Others tailored their diets to avoid heavy foods the day before a tasting. I swore off raw onion, garlic, and boozy cocktails, which have a tendency to cling to my tongue like houseguests who've overstayed their welcome. Cigarettes were an obvious liability, but I don't smoke. Andrew Bell, the president of the American Sommelier Association, advised students taking his blind tasting course, in which I'd enrolled, to avoid extreme flavors so they can sensitize their tongues to lower doses of taste stimuli. Having difficulty gauging the alcohol in wines? "Cut out the fucking spirits for a month," he instructed a classmate. Stiff cocktails could make wine, with its lower alcohol level, go down like water. Andrew had even stopped adding extra salt to his food—anything beyond what it was served with—and, at one point, had ditched coffee, calling it "a palate killer." I found this hard to believe, given how many sommeliers enjoyed an espresso-heavy diet. "Everything changes," Andrew insisted. "It obscures your palate." Since I was already trying to make up for lost time, I was willing to try anything that might speed up my improvement. What the hell, I figured: I added coffee to my no-fly list, and figured I'd put down the saltshaker too. As an extra precaution, I gave up superspicy foods after hearing that a friend's father, a renowned French chef, banned his kitchen staff from touching the fiery stuff out of concern that blunted tongues would lead to overseasoned dishes. It *is* possible: Daily exposure to spicy foods can desensitize the tongue's nerve endings to heat, so a dash of Sriracha could escalate to drowning everything in hot sauce. We also seem to adapt to the saltiness of our saliva, which can be affected by the amount of salt we consume. (It's worth noting that spiciness is a temperature sensation that activates pain receptors, not a taste that acts on taste buds.)

And then there was consistency. Sticking to a routine—at tastings and before them—was essential. It ensured you could limit all confounding variables and get down to what was in the wine. Craig Sindelar used a neti pot before tastings to flush out nasal debris. One of the guys in my tasting group traveled with his own granola, so when he tasted on the road, his gustatory baseline wouldn't change. A friend of his, a sommelier in California, knew he performed best when he tasted at ten o'clock in the morning, so when he found out he'd have to take his Advanced Sommelier Exam at eight o'clock Texas time (six in the morning, Pacific time), he reset his internal clock to ensure that come exam day, eight a.m. Texas time would feel like ten a.m. California time, his golden hour. Every day, for three weeks before the test, his wife woke up at four o'clock in the morning to pour him a flight of wines. I was with Morgan at our Saturday blind tasting group when I heard this story. My reaction was "That's insane." Everyone else's was "How far in advance do you know your tasting time?" At several sommeliers' recommendation, I stocked up on my brand of Crest toothpaste to be sure I'd never have to switch. And because consistency means controlling for how

everything around you smells, I went ahead and stockpiled my preferred brands of deodorant, shampoo, conditioner, and body wash,
and switched to scent-free laundry detergent. I'd long ago retired my
perfume, because only an ignoramus wears perfume to a wine tasting.

I began to worry more about issues of technique. I'd been following sommeliers' instructions to build sense memory by smelling plants
and foods at every opportunity. But as I did so, I grew concerned I
might not be smelling in the right way. Should I sniff in short, quick
inhalations or long, deep ones? What should I be thinking about to
make the impression stick? Waving stuff in front of my nose wasn't
enough.

I went to see Jean Claude Delville, a French perfumer who,
coincidentally, had created the fragrance I'd stopped wearing, along
with numerous classics like Clinique's "Happy." He'd memorized more
than 15,000 aromas in his quest to become a "nose"—industry lingo
for perfumer—and offered to help me tackle my smell training more
systematically. I met him at his office, a gleaming Tribeca loft with
high ceilings and white columns, and he whisked me down to his lab,
which was wallpapered in brown glass vials. He dipped two thin pieces
of white paper into a container marked "Pamplewood," and held one
out for me to smell. Apparently, even teaching me to spit had been
premature. "What is important is to learn to breathe," Jean Claude
said, instructing me to follow his lead. He brought the essence to his
nose and drew in a single, long breath, so deep I saw his chest swell. He
held it—*one Mississippi*—then exhaled. "You exhale through your nose
because the molecule gets stuck in your nose otherwise," he coached.
In his student days, he'd take samples of the odors he wanted to master
and lock himself in a dark room, then sniff one at a time while trying
to associate the smell with places, people, moments, or forms. "For
me, patchouli: It's brown, it's red, it's earthy, it's mystic. And the shape
for me is weird. A triangle, because it's aggressive a little bit," he said.
"You have to believe something in order to remember it, good or bad."
Another perfumer, also French, assured me I'd get nowhere unless I
started assigning words to smells. "It is better if you do it aloud," he
said. "Do it in the shower. At breakfast. Lunch. Herbs, spices, meat,

everything. Even in the street. The car, the diesel, the air. When you have time, just a few seconds, you can put words to it. Little by little, you will become better." That night I stood over the kitchen sink flipping open spice jars and inhaling their fragrances one by one. Riding the subway became an exercise in classifying human bodily functions: sweat, urine, faint residual tinge of vomit. I tried to muster the same enthusiasm for these odors as Jean Claude, who delighted in the olfactory tableau of public transportation. He made a point of relishing it each morning. "I inhale and then I hold my breath. And I exhale—wow! It's rich, it's so simple."

The rituals the sommeliers stuck to and the sacrifices they made could often be more superstitious than scientific. But for the people who followed them, they worked. More than that, the stakes were high enough that they were willing to give it a shot.

It surprised me to learn that Morgan did not deny himself much. His approach to tasting was firmly psychological. It started with a mind-set rather than an eating regimen. One of his favorite guides in the matter was *Zen in the Art of Archery*, a German philosopher's account of the six years he spent studying archery with a Zen master in Japan. Morgan emailed me a quote from the book, with the subject line "This Speaks to Me." It read:

> The right shot at the right moment does not come because you do not let go of yourself. You . . . brace yourself for failure. So long as that is so, you have no choice but to call forth something yourself that ought to happen independently of you, and so long as you call it forth your hand will not open in the right way—like the hand of a child.

Morgan provided a gloss to link the passage back to blind tasting. "If you become the action, and execute the process perfectly, you will become the result," he wrote. "Fear and worry are the heart of failure."

As Morgan saw it, blind tasting well depends first and foremost on sharpening your focus and mental control. You have to keep your mind open to the wine's message at the same time that you silence the doubts that inevitably creep into the edges of your brain to whisper *You always miss Moscato.* "It requires consciousness. It requires attention. It requires saying, 'I'm going to be in tune with my senses, and I'm going to listen to this glass of wine,'" Morgan said.

He prescribed a regimen of yoga, which he said helped him practice turning off parts of his brain and staying present in an action—perfect for blind tasting.

"When I get done with those twenty-five minutes, it doesn't feel like any time has gone by," he said of tasting. "It is the absence of the conscious, yammering mind, right? . . . It's about dissolving into the action. It's about unbecoming yourself and becoming this apparatus that does this. You have to surrender yourself to the wine in order to understand it. Like, I can't force this to be California Chardonnay no matter how hard I fucking try. It's teaching yourself how to listen."

Being attentive to taste—learning how to listen—begins by being open to everything around you, Morgan said. He suggested I practice receiving new experiences anywhere. It could start with something as simple as not wearing headphones on the train. "Pull your own narrative out of your ears," Morgan told me. "You're not stepping on a train being like, 'What's going on today? What's out there in the world?' It's just turning inwards, being self-referential."

Whether it was in downward dog or on the floor of a distributor tasting, there seemed to be few moments in Morgan's life—or his fellow somms'—that were not given over to selling, tasting, reviewing, enjoying, or contemplating wine. "It's one of those fields where whenever you're not studying, you feel super guilty and self-loathing," said one sommelier over coffee. Mia, a female sommelier who had gone to Emerson with Morgan, remarked at one of our morning tastings that she reviewed flash cards on her way to work. A fairly routine activity—except Mia biked to work.

In the restaurant hierarchy, sommeliers were the gentle nerds who carried flash cards and chefs were the sexy bad boys with knives who got the girls. Which, whatever—who cares? The somms didn't have time for that stuff anyway. Twelve- to fourteen-hour shifts were routine, so were six-day workweeks. "Five days is a luxury," Victoria scoffed. On their nights off, generally Monday and Tuesday, they hung out with one another at parties that were mostly excuses to try some special wines. Someone might supply a Methuselah of a twenty-year-old California Cabernet, or a bottle of weed wine, made by tossing marijuana buds into the must. Morgan's friend threw a vino-themed bash—"the *Unfair* Game Party"—where everyone had to bring wines too weird for blind tasting. They traveled around the city in packs, usually arriving at bars long after the civilians had cleared out for the night. "Balance" was only in their vocabulary as it applied to the flavor of a wine.

The extended network of the Court became their de facto family. "They're not driven to go start a family right away, because this is very fulfilling," Master Sommelier Laura Williamson told me. A disproportionate number of the sommeliers I met were dating other sommeliers or, at the most exotic, someone else in the wine world. A girlfriend was not part of the equation for Morgan. Part of the problem, he explained one night, was that he couldn't afford tasting menus for himself and a significant other. And he wasn't about to lose the tasting menus.

A Pleasant Stain, but Not a Great One

Benjamin Wallace

Bill Sokolin was making his way across the room to see Rusty Staub when he had the first inkling that something had gone terribly wrong. It was Sunday, April 24, 1989, and Sokolin was at a black-tie, $250-a-head, seven-course, seventeen-wine dinner at the Four Seasons. During the week the restaurant played host to Manhattan's power elite; on Sundays it was often closed to accommodate the great and grand of the wine world at private events such as this. Sokolin, a wine-shop owner, was a controversial figure among his colleagues, known for his roster of well-heeled clients, his loopy newsletter soliloquies, and a Barnumesque promotional style (when a newspaper once termed him "an incorrigible hypemeister," Sokolin wrote to thank the editor). At this moment, the proprietor of D. Sokolin & Co. was navigating the Pool Room, a high-ceilinged, midcentury-modern space bordered with stubby palm trees and surrounding an elevated, square, white marble pool rippling with azure water.

Nearly two hundred people were here, among them every wine retailer of note in the New York area, including Michael Aaron from Sherry-Lehmann and Don Zacharia from Zachys. Former major-league baseball player Staub, now a restaurateur, had brought Mets first baseman Keith Hernandez. But what Sokolin was most excited about, what had goaded him to bring the bottle, were the guests of honor: Châteaux Margaux owners Laura and Corinne Mentzelopoulos and Paul Pontallier, the estate's urbane director.

Sokolin happened to be in possession of a Margaux the likes of which most of these people had never seen. A *1787* Margaux. A Jefferson bottle. The most expensive bottle of wine in the world, as far as Sokolin was concerned. *Guinness* might bestow that honor on Malcolm Forbes, but Sokolin's bottle was insured for $212,000, $56,000 above the price of the Forbes Lafite. Tonight, Sokolin couldn't resist showing the bottle around, and as a former minor-league baseball player, he was especially eager to show it to Staub.

The realization that something was dripping on his leg was not immediate. Sokolin kept walking, but the sensation of moisture didn't go away. He looked down at his tuxedo pants and saw a dark patch.

Had someone spilled coffee on him? He hadn't noticed it. Had he had an accident? He wasn't *that* old. But then—

No.

No.

Sokolin stopped walking.

He turned around and retraced his steps, as if doing so would unwind what he dimly feared was happening.

He got back to the table where he and his wife Gloria were sitting with the heads of Campari and Château & Estate and Southern Wines & Spirits and an executive from American Express.

His leg was still wet. No use putting it off any longer: He opened the bag.

Wine had spilled out. Worse, there were two large holes in the side of the bottle. A pair of irregularly shaped pieces of glass lay at the bottom of the bag.

"I broke the bottle," Sokolin announced, locking eyes with the Campari executive. "I'm going home."

There were gasps. He looked around the table, in shock. The people sitting there looked at him, speechless. And Sokolin walked back across the room, aware of nothing beyond himself and the bottle he clutched upright in its soggy bag. Red drops were falling now, on the blue-and-gray carpet.

Sokolin's Margaux was already dodgy in the eyes of a number of colleagues in the room. It was one of the controversial Jefferson bottles. The level of wine seemed improbably high for something so old. The seal looked new. And in hindsight, his actions at the dinner would strike several guests as suspicious. Sokolin was, after all, a notorious self-promoter who had been touting the bottle aggressively. He had brought a fragile, extremely valuable bottle to a crowded event. He had handled it clumsily. The bottle was insured for a lot of money. And once Sokolin had fully grasped what was going on, he had fled the room.

The bottle's ill-starred journey had begun in late 1987, when Farr Vintners partner Stephen Browett flew from London to Munich. Hardy Rodenstock met him at the airport with the 1787 Margaux, and Browett flew straight to Manchester, where he handed the bottle, tucked inside a tennis bag, to Tim Littler, who had agreed to buy it for £37,000. Littler hailed from an old Cheshire wine-trade family. His grandfather had bought Whitwhams, a Manchester-area merchant, and by the 1980s it was a significant player in the rare-wine market. Browett had lunch with Littler, then boarded a train back to London.

The standard Whitwhams markup was 100 percent, and the bottle was listed in its February 1988 catalog at £75,000. No sooner had the catalog appeared than Littler thought: What's the point of selling the *second*-most expensive bottle of wine in the world? The Forbes bottle had gone for £105,000. In the next Whitwhams catalog, which came out that September, Littler upped the price of his bottle to £125,000.

In the Whitwhams cellar one day, an employee noticed that the bottle was leaking through a bubble in the heavy wax that capped it. One of the firm's directors flew the bottle to Bordeaux to have it recorked at Château Margaux. With Paul Pontallier and Corinne Mentzelopoulos looking on, the cellarmaster added a bit more than an inch of 1959 wine and inserted an unusual, wedge-shaped cork. It fit loosely. Back in Manchester, Littler saw that the bottle continued to ooze.

This time he decided to recork it himself. Recorking was a specialty of Whitwhams, which performed the service on 2,000 bottles of wine a year. Some connoisseurs objected to the practice, and had found wines recorked by Whitwhams, in particular, to be subpar. But Littler defended recorking, which provided a merchant with an opportunity to assess a bottle's contents before reselling it, as a quality-control mechanism that benefited customers.

Normally, recorking a wine was straightforward: take out the old cork, put in a new one. But you had to be careful putting a new cork into the oldest bottles, as the increased air pressure could blow out the base. A 1787 Margaux called for extra caution. Like the Forbes Lafite, this Margaux was in a hand-blown bottle, heavy at the bottom and much thinner near the top. Worried that the glass would shatter, Littler taped the neck and eased the cork out with his hands.

He couldn't let this opportunity pass. He tipped out a few drops of the wine into a glass. It was the color of iodine. Littler tasted it. Later he wouldn't recall the flavor, other than "prunes" and that it was "certainly much more than" merely "interesting" or "alive." He resealed the bottle.

The old-wine market ebbed and flowed. Littler might go half a year without selling a bottle, then move six in a week. All it took was one interested buyer. But after several months he still hadn't found a customer for the Jefferson bottle. Meanwhile, a New York retailer he knew named Bill Sokolin said he had a client who was interested but wanted to see the bottle before committing.

Sokolin had pretty much fallen into the business started by his father. After attending Tufts, where he excelled at baseball, he had played for a string of teams in the Brooklyn Dodgers farm system, then was drafted into the army. Stationed in Virginia, he was spared from combat by his assignment to the service baseball, basketball, and football teams. Sokolin completed his service and, as a stopgap, went to work for his father. At the time, his father sold mainly hard liquor; what little wine he carried was plonk.

This was in the late 1950s, just when well-off Americans were becoming more interested in wine. Bill Sokolin saw an opportunity, and he rebuilt his father's business around Bordeaux. When wine prices started to soar in the 1960s, Sokolin became an evangelist of wine as investment, ultimately writing two books on the topic. William

Buckley Jr. was a longtime client; in his memoir, Buckley wrote of Sokolin's enthusiasm for wine, "It would positively have killed Bill Sokolin if he had been born, say, in Saudi Arabia. I suspect both his hands and both his feet would have been amputated by the time he was sixteen, because Bill Sokolin cannot be kept from wine tasting."

When the ballyhooed 1982 Bordeaux vintage came out, Sokolin sided with a few old-guard critics in arguing that it was overrated, taking out full-page ads in the *New York Times* in which he dismissed the gushing praise for the '82s by up-and-coming wine critic Robert Parker. Sokolin was colossally wrong about the vintage, which proved to be the best investment in wine history and made Parker's name as a critic.

Over the years, through his business, Sokolin met several U.S. presidents. Just after Ronald Reagan was first elected, he called Sokolin and said, "Where's my wine?" Reagan had ordered some from Sokolin on the advice of Bill Buckley. "In front of me," Sokolin replied. He had been unable to deliver the wine to the White House without the approval of the Secret Service. With the approval, Sokolin could get the wine to him in three or four hours. Reagan took care of it right away.

But it was a dead president who tugged at Sokolin's imagination. Having heard of Thomas Jefferson's interest in wine, "I started to read a little, and then I started to read a lot." Sokolin bought more than a hundred books about Jefferson. When Sokolin met Jimmy Carter, he took the opportunity to discuss Jefferson with a sitting president. Sokolin also used the newsletters he sent regularly to his clients as a platform to talk about Jefferson. In one essay, Sokolin argued that it was Jefferson who first introduced wine futures to America. Sokolin had a mystical streak and, in a commentary of which he was especially proud, imagined a three-way conversation among Ernest Hemingway, Jefferson, and Winston Churchill. Another time, he wrote a letter to Ambassador Jefferson as if he were still alive.

Sokolin first heard of the Jefferson bottles when he read an account of the Forbes purchase in *Wine Spectator*. Later, when he visited the Forbes Galleries to view the 1787 Lafite, he was shocked that it was displayed under a spotlight and warned the security guard. Then, when the cork slipped, Sokolin says, Kip Forbes called him and asked what to do. Sokolin told him there were two options: either throw out the wine, or let Sokolin jump on a plane and take it to Lafite for recorking. The Forbeses decided to keep the bottle as it was.

Sokolin learned that he might be able to get his own Jefferson bottle when Littler, with whom he'd done business in the past and who knew of his Jeffersonian proclivities, called and said, "Bill, I think I've got your bottle." Littler said he could arrange for Sokolin to take the bottle on consignment. The two men began to explore their options for complimentary transport. Air France offered to fly Littler and the bottle to America by Concorde, but that would require Littler to get to London. British Airways flew straight from Manchester, and volunteered two first-class tickets—one for Littler, one for the bottle. After making sure Sokolin had obtained insurance, on Friday, October 22, 1988, Littler set out for the Manchester airport.

British Airways issued a press release about the flight and photographed Littler and the bottle checking in and taking their seats on the plane, where a clutch of publicists and flight attendants dressed up the Margaux, peeking out of the same tennis bag in which Littler had received it, with blanket, headphones, and seat belt. Landing at JFK in New York at 6:00 p.m., Littler went through customs, gave the bottle to Sokolin, turned on his heel, and boarded a return flight to England. There, a hand-scrawled fax from his friends at Farr Vintners awaited him. It accompanied one of the pictures of Littler and the bottle that had appeared in a newspaper, and said, "Don't Die of Ignorance: Always wear gloves when you've got your fingers in a punt." In the photo, Littler's thumb was in the "punt," the concavity in the base of a wine bottle.

The following day, Sokolin's interested party had a heart attack while playing golf and died, Sokolin told Littler. Therefore he no longer had a customer. Littler said he was going to be in New York a month later and would collect the bottle at that time. But then Sokolin said he had another client who was interested, and Littler's trip was pushed back a few months. The bottle stayed with Sokolin.

Sokolin displayed it in his shop and encouraged wine journalists to write about it. He also sent a fax to Malcolm Forbes with the latest D. Sokolin price list, touting the arrival of the 1787 Jefferson Margaux:

> *Dear Malcolm,*
>
> *This is an event of some magnitude. And it ain't the price—250,000 for this bottle.*
>
> *Th. Jefferson's spirit is in this bottle.*
>
> *He and G Washington had a COMPANY—called the WINE COMPANY—chartered in 1774.*
>
> *THE PURPOSE—to get the DEMON RUM out of the Colonies—The equivalent of drugs today.*
>
> *And replace it with WINE   WINE*
>
> *It's a good story and better than the ones the candidates have chosen.*
>
> *This little bottle will start drugs out as requested by the SPIRIT OF JEFFERSON . . .*
>
> *Sounds nuts—?*
>
> *I think the bottle would make nice duo at FORBES—and the story is the point . . .*
>
> > *All the best,*
> > *Bill Sokolin*

The story *was* the point, but Forbes wasn't interested. Heeding the salesman's adage that if at first something doesn't sell, you should ask for more, Sokolin kept hiking the price, first to $394,000. Then, after seeing a rickety footstool sell at auction for $290,000, which Sokolin thought absurd, he repriced the bottle at an entirely arbitrary $519,750.

It was during this lull that Sokolin attended the Four Seasons event. The sponsors were Château & Estate and Château Margaux. By the late 1980s, an annual U.S. roadshow was *de rigueur* for the top growths of Bordeaux. While, on a mass scale, America had come late to wine, its high-end collectors had exercised a disproportionate influence on the market since the late 1960s. As of 1990, a quarter of all Pétrus and half of the production of the Domaine de la Romanée-Conti, the most esteemed producer in Burgundy, would be going to the U.S. In the spring of 1989, the Margaux team were in New York to promote the 1986 vintage, considered one of their strongest showings since the Mentzelopoulos family had bought the estate more than a decade earlier.

Corinne Mentzelopoulos began the evening by getting up and talking about the special vintages, 1953 and 1961, that Margaux was providing that night, and about the 1986 wine that would be tasted. Then the meal got under way. A few courses had already been served when Sokolin realized he should have brought the bottle with him. What better occasion to show off this extraordinarily rare bottle of Margaux than at a dinner to honor its makers? He said so to his wife Gloria.

"Don't be ridiculous," she said.

"Nope," he said. "I'm going to get it."

Sokolin took a taxi to the prewar building where he lived on the Upper West Side, across a darkened lawn from the Museum of Natural History. Entering his ninth-floor apartment, Sokolin passed an oversized retro poster ad for Mumm's Champagne and foyer bookcases packed with works about wine and Jefferson. He crossed the blond parquet floor and turned into the dining room, where, instead of wallpaper, the ends of wooden cases that had once contained great wines were arranged in a vinous mosaic. A shelf displayed two reproductions of Jefferson's wineglasses, a gigantic Lafite bottle opened after Gloria's mother's funeral, and an eighteenth-century Madeira decanter Sokolin had opened for the party to launch his book *Liquid Assets*. He retrieved the Jefferson bottle from a freestanding refrigerated wine closet in the corner of the room.

When he arrived back at the Four Seasons, half an hour after he had left, he brought the bottle directly to the Margaux table and said to Madame Mentzelopoulos, "I bet you never saw a bottle this old." She had, of course, seen this very bottle, during its recorking for Whitwhams. Sokolin left it with the table for thirty minutes. "He was showing it to everyone," Julian Niccolini, then the maître d', recalled later. "Everyone was suspicious of this bottle." Before dessert, Sokolin retrieved it from the Margaux table and took it to show to Rusty Staub.

Sokolin was cradling the bottle in a bag, with his left arm, when it happened. Niccolini saw the whole thing. Just inside the Pool Room, to the left of the door, stood a gueridon, a low, metal-topped trolley used as a service station by waiters. When Sokolin was a few steps into the room, headed toward Staub, he brushed past the gueridon. Wine immediately began to spill onto the carpet.

Minutes later, Sokolin was running from the room, trailing splotches of what looked like blood on the pale stone underfoot. He strode down a long, white marble corridor that led to the Grill Room, past the hostess station, and down the stairs to the lobby, which was scattered with black Barcelona chairs. When Sokolin put the bag and bottle down on a counter as he retrieved his coat, more of the wine leaked out, and three people dipped their fingers in it. One, licking his finger, said the wine was "cooked." Niccolini thought it tasted like mud.

Now in his overcoat, Sokolin pushed out through the double doors onto an especially charmless block of midtown Manhattan and flagged down a taxi. Back in the Pool Room, in the spot where he had last been standing, a crowd gathered. In the chaos of his departure, Sokolin had left the two loose bottle shards at the restaurant. Howard Goldberg, from the *New York Times*, took one piece as a souvenir, and Paul Kovi, the co-owner of the restaurant, took the second. Meanwhile, Gloria Sokolin, unaware of what had happened, was wondering where her husband was. Then she saw Goldberg.

"So, the bottle's broken," the *Times* reporter said.

Gloria did a double take. "Excuse me?" she said.

"Bill broke the bottle," Goldberg repeated.

At first Gloria had a hard time believing that her husband could have left without her, but as she continued to look for him without success, it began to sink in. This was a problem. She had no money. She didn't even have the ticket to retrieve her fur coat. Somewhat embarrassed, she had to borrow five dollars from a table-mate for a taxi. Fortunately, her husband had at least had the presence of mind, in his rushed departure, to leave her coat-check ticket with the attendant.

Gloria took a cab home, and on the way, a news report came on the radio about what had happened. She arrived home and, understandably annoyed, allowed herself an I-told-you-so. But she knew how bad it felt to break something. A few years earlier she had been removing her silver chest from its hiding place inside the wine closet when she accidentally broke an 1874 Lafite. She and Bill had literally lapped it up off the floor. He had been understanding then, saying, "Accidents happen."

Now she found her husband "bereft," as she later put it. "Bill was inconsolable." Arriving home, Sokolin had gingerly removed the bottle from its carrier. Only about five ounces of wine, or 20 percent, remained. He went into the kitchen, where the walls were covered in paper, designed by Gloria, featuring a repeating pattern of signatures of great modern French chefs. *Paul Bocuse. Jean Trois-gros. Alain Chapel.* Sokolin poured a small glass for himself, then put the rest of the wine in a small plastic container, which he put in the freezer. He tasted what was in his glass. It was recognizable as wine, but by no means tasted good. He put the empty bottle on a table in the living room.

At midnight, with the arrival of April 25, he turned fifty-eight. Forty minutes into Sokolin's birthday, Howard Goldberg, the *Times* reporter who had made off with a piece of the bottle, telephoned, eager to secure his scoop. He asked if Sokolin had been drunk. Sokolin said he'd only had a single glass of Champagne and hadn't finished any of his glasses of Bordeaux.

"I did something terrible," Sokolin told Goldberg. "I'm very unhappy. I was in shock. I committed murder."

The next morning, Tim Littler was staying with friends in Geneva when his host knocked on his bedroom door and said a reporter was calling from the *New York Times*. Littler didn't think anyone knew where he was, so he wasn't sure how the reporter had tracked him down, but he took the call. Goldberg delivered the bad news. At first, Littler thought it must be an April Fool's joke, but it was already the fourth week of the month, so he quickly gave up on that idea. Several more newspapers called that day.

Littler wasn't worried about the money. His attitude was a shopkeeper's: you break it, you buy it. At first he thought, knowing Sokolin, that it might be a publicity stunt. But once he learned of the precise pattern of breakage, Littler ruled out that theory. If the bottle had fallen on the ground and shattered, that would be one thing, but no one could intentionally and cleanly puncture such an old bottle.

The next several days were a blur of media attention. Sokolin walked to a TV studio, bottle in hand, to appear on Regis Philbin's show. "Murder at Four Seasons" was the headline in *U.S. News & World Report*. *People* went with "Oops!" and dubbed Sokolin's misfortune "the world's most expensive puddle." The *New York Post* blared: "Grapes of Wrath: Clumsy Vintner Breaks a 519G Bottle of Wine." For Fleet Street tabloids, the episode served as a platonic illustration of Yank barbarism. "What a Plonker!" screamed one, while another tossed off a "Thought for Today: There's only one thing worse than an American with no taste: One who buys it, then drops it."

Cartoonists had a field day. "Okay, stand back," a man said to a crowd gathered around a puddle in one cartoon, "and let it breathe." In another, a man opined, of a splotch on the floor, "It's a pleasant stain, I think, but not a great one." Paul Kovi, at the Four Seasons, sent Sokolin a bill for the $360 it had cost the restaurant to have the rug cleaned. Sokolin ignored it. His feeling was that Kovi had gotten about "ten or twenty million dollars" worth of free advertising out of his gaffe. (It would be dwarfed, seventeen years later, when casino developer Steve Wynn put his elbow through a $139-million Picasso.)

When the reporter from *People* came to his home, Sokolin reached for the bottle, which still stood on the table where he had set it down, and almost knocked it over. Sokolin put his hand to his chest as the bottle swayed, but it remained standing. Sokolin retrieved the plastic container from the freezer and let the reporter smell it. It "looked like chocolate-brown goo and emitted an intense aroma not unlike that of stewed prunes," the reporter wrote.

"You think I did it on purpose, don't you?" Sokolin said to the reporter, who concluded that it had been a true accident. Two of the key questions muttered by suspicious colleagues after Sokolin broke the bottle had ready answers: the level of wine was so high, and the seal new, because of the recent recorkings by Margaux and Whitwhams.

Sokolin by now was embracing his fifteen minutes—mugging for the camera, bugging his eyes out, and holding the bottle forth defiantly. He said the bottle had been "worth maybe $10 million or maybe more." He and Gloria, a real-estate broker, found themselves invited to social gatherings that previously would have eluded them. It wasn't clear whether they were guests or entertainment. At one high-powered dinner party, the host introduced Sokolin as "Butterfingers."

The *New York Times* saw a morality tale in what had happened, publishing an editorial that read, in part, "Everyone who has saved a perfume for a worthy occasion and found its lilies have festered by the time she gets around to opening the bottle knows what it is to be a William Sokolin." A William Sokolin! He had become a cautionary archetype. The lesson, the *Times* concluded, was that wine is for drinking rather than saving.

A month after breaking the bottle, Sokolin removed the frozen wine from his freezer and defrosted it. No decanting, no ceremony. He just drank it from a glass. A strange thing had happened in the last month. "It was good, but it wasn't wine," Sokolin recalled. "It was grape juice." The freezing had removed the alcohol, and with it the impurities. At least that was Sokolin's take.

Sokolin says he asked Hardy Rodenstock for a replacement bottle, and Rodenstock replied that it would cost $800,000. "You're crazy," Sokolin told him. The insurance company Frank Crystal & Co. eventually made out a check to "Whitwhams and William Sokolin" in the amount of $197,625 and dated June 7, 1989. The money would go to Tim Littler, who had intended to reclaim the bottle in June, since he had an interested buyer in Japan.

Soon after, Littler and Michael Broadbent were chatting at the Imperial Hotel in Tokyo, when a man approached, ringing a small bell. Littler and Broadbent were old friends, and Whitwhams handled Christie's shipping and customs clearance in Japan. Broadbent was doing an auction there. "Mr. Littler," the bell-ringer said, "you have a fax." It reported that the insurance check had arrived.

"I guess we've lost the record," Broadbent said.

The Wine in the Glass

M.F.K. *Fisher*

Four hundred years before the birth of Christ, a Greek named Theognis wrote, "Wine is wont to show the mind of man."

More than two thousand years later, in 1920, a wise old Englishman named George Saintsbury wrote about wines in his *Notes on a Cellar-Book*: "When they were good they pleased my senses, cheered my spirits, improved my moral and intellectual powers, besides enabling me to confer the same benefits on other people."

Both men, so far apart in time but akin in their broad understanding of their fellows as well as of themselves, agreed with poets and philosophers of every civilization since the first real one that good wine, well drunk, can lend majesty to the human spirit.

How to drink it, once it is poured from its flask or bottle, depends mainly upon the man who does it. It can be a sottish thing, rank with gluttony and brutality, and then its punishment is as sure as hell itself, and as sure an indication of the fool within.

If wine be well drunk, it is as Theognis and Saintsbury said, an indication of a man's spirit as well as of his general attitude toward the rest of his world.

Once in the glass, there are a few simple things which will bring out its character for anyone who looks for more than a liquid to run down his gullet and inspire his soul.

The rules are simple, and if followed will add pleasure to the simplest palate, the simplest meal, and make it grow.

First, each wine should have its own glass, or be rinsed between wines. The glass, preferably stemmed, should be filled only one-third or one-half full.

The rest of it is a natural progression toward the swallowing and then the instinctive wait for the aftertaste, that strange sensory enjoyment which must follow even a sip of decent wine, and which can be like a touch of paradise after a great one.

First, then, the glass should be held against the light of sky or candles or of fire on the hearth, if one is with good friends, or against any light at all—a picnic on a hill, a waterside restaurant, a railroad station between trains.

It will hold in it what Robert Louis Stevenson once called the "blood and the sun in that old flask," and sometimes it will cling tantalizingly to the sides, shifting the light with it, and sometimes it will be as aloof as crystal itself, seeming to disdain what it is held in.

The next step is to savor. What is called the bouquet is the reward for this enjoyable operation, and it can vary from the delicate to the robust. If the wine is cold, the bouquet will be a longer and often more subtle discovery than at room temperature of the smell itself, and the glass can be rotated gently to make the unmistakable odor of this wine or that rise and fume invisibly into the nostrils of its seeker.

Some of the great wines are as much their own bouquet as taste or color or aftertaste, and there are special glasses almost like fat-bottomed chimney pots for the benefit of their sniffers. But for most persons, as well as for most wines, the plainest of glasses—from a tumbler to a simple stemmed glass which will hold any white as well as any red wine—will give ample pleasure to us.

The next step—and by no means the most important, although it is the basic reason for this whole agreeable rigmarole—is to drink the wine.

Sips of it are the best. A great draught is for thirst, and should be left to water, man's ally. A small sip is enough, to begin the full enjoyment of any wine at all. It should be rolled under the tongue and then over it, no matter how unobtrusively, to make all the taste buds spring to their full attention. It can be held for a few seconds in the mouth. Then it rolls down the throat like a blissful messenger of what's to follow, and the promise is good: what is eaten will taste better, and what follows the eating and the drinking will be worthy of them.

There is much written these days about the "ceremonies" of wine tasting and wine drinking, and there is, perhaps of necessity, much balderdash and plain as well as fancy snobbery in it. Perhaps one of the most sensible comments on this pompous attempt to make people take the natural function of wine drinking in snob fashion has been said by the owner of a French château, one of the greatest of the Bordeaux wineries: ". . . Wine is a pleasure, not a puzzling and dreadful duty."

Another good writer about wine enjoyment has said lately in one of the excellent house organs put out by California vintners and growers, "Learn to analyze your sensations and record them in your memory. By so doing, you will recognize the same or similar wine when you meet it again."

This is a most rewarding feeling to any conscious thinking man, whether he wants a bottle of reputable "Red Ink" with his steak or a bottle of champagne to celebrate his daughter's wedding: he knows what he is looking for and what he can spend for it and how much it will give to him. He knows what will please *him*, and will enable him, as Saintsbury said, "to confer the same benefits on other people."

He may have no desire, as do some serious as well as flamboyant "connoisseurs," to be able to recognize a certain year of a certain bottling of a certain section of a certain vineyard, but he will know what he wants: a good red or white or rosé wine from one of California's wine-growing districts, and even, with some practice, the same wine from this or that valley—Santa Clara, San Bernardino, Livermore, Sonoma, Napa. It will be one more door opened to his appreciation of the rare things of life.

He will be able to agree with Shakespeare that "Good wine is a good familiar creature if it be well used."

My Father and the Wine

Irina Dumitrescu

The making of wine binds me to my ancestors who were tough-sinewed peasants and whose feet were rooted in the earth.
—Angelo Pellegrini, The Unprejudiced Palate

Now and then I click a link to find out what the hipsters are up to. The hipsters are raising chickens and slaughtering them at home, I read; the hipsters are distilling hooch. This is trendy and far out and probably how we should all live, despite being smelly and arduous. No doubt they have it right, the hipsters, and if they are fermenting cheese and spritzing meat into sausage casings in Brooklyn, then we will surely soon follow them in the lesser metropolises. But the romance of do-it-yourself is tainted for me. I cannot muster up the enthusiasm to kill my own rabbit and pickle it. There is a droning voice in my head that says, You do this because you never had to. You do it because you do not know the humiliation and occasional physical danger of an immigrant father who held on to his past using food. You do this because the ethics of the undertaking are clear to you, and you don't—yet—understand the exquisite liberation of food that comes from a supermarket.

First, and last, and every time, above all things, was The Wine. It was never just wine, it was always The Wine, that year's massive household production, the gravitational pull of which none of us could escape. This is not because my father came from the country. He was a city boy par excellence, but he could remember days when

Bucharest had dirtier hands, or at least cleaner dirt on its hands. He used to tell me with a grin how when he was a child, chickens were always bought alive. The housewives would go out to the street with a knife and flag down a passing man to kill the bird they wanted to cook for dinner. Businessmen who wanted to display their machismo refused the knife and wrung the chicken's neck barehanded. This was the old Bucharest, when my father's father still had his sausage factory, when salami still hung in their attic to cure and my father was responsible for tending to it. It was when my grandfather still made his own wine.

After we had moved through two new countries and multiple apartments in each, after we had finally settled in a house in the blandest cookie-cutter suburbs we could find, my father started to talk about making wine. Enough moving around and you'll want to reach for a bit of what was good back home. Enough moving around and you'll want to drink, I suppose. The decision to start making wine was helped along by the fact that alcohol sales are controlled by a government monopoly in Ontario, the L.C.B.O., leading to small selection and high prices for a liquid as essential to Romanians as milk is to white-bread North American families. My father saw this as the oppressive fruit of Canadian puritanism, and he set about staging his own private revolution. In this, he had the help of "the Italians," purveyors of everything needed by the suburban vintner with Old World sensibilities: massive bottles, special corks to let the gas out, industrial quantities of grapes, and the facilities for turning them into must. I was in my early teens at this point, still excited by the enterprise and even a little proud. As my father studied the chemistry of winemaking with the assiduousness of the university professor he had once been, I designed wine labels on the computer with the title "Casa Dumitrescu," and struggled to align a sheet of sticky labels in our dot matrix printer so that the graphic would come out right. It was not very good wine, though back then I couldn't tell, but it was ours and it was cheap. My father calculated the cost per liter to two dollars, a magnificent savings to our family over retail wine, and clearly a wise financial move.

A fifty-gallon barrel cut in two will provide two excellent stomping vats. The heftier children and maiden aunts with heavy bottoms will be delighted to do the treading to the accompaniment of a tarantella or lively Irish jig.

Soon enough, our own Casa Dumitrescu became more crowded, as my surviving three grandparents came over from Romania and moved in with us. My grandfather was aged and absent by then, but I still remember him making sausage once, his trembling hands struggling to work the sturdy old meat grinder. My father became more ambitious in his winemaking, deciding that the Italians were good for grapes but that he did not trust their pulping machines not to adulterate his must with traces of other varietals. He went to Price Club, the daddy of Costco and perennial favorite of immigrant families in search of a deal, and bought a giant gray plastic garbage bin. This he carefully washed out, set up in our garage, and filled with muscat grapes. And then, for days on end, my two grandmothers and I stood around this bin and squeezed grapes. With our bare hands. I do not know if you have any experience of making must in this way, but muscats are tough, tight little berries, and you have to strain to crush every last one, and each bunch of grapes made our hands ache even more. My grandmothers and I tried to work out how we might get one of us into the garbage bin to apply feet to our common problem, but it was narrow and had two wheels at the bottom, and hopping in seemed an unsafe, if tempting, proposition. So we squeezed on into the night, tired but not thinking to question my father's imperative. This was, after all, The Wine.

At some point it occurred to my father that the price-gouging, racketeering deviousness of the Ontario government was not limited to wine; a greater injustice was also being perpetrated. A typical Romanian meal begins with plum brandy, *ţuică* in Romanian, or *slivovitz* as it is more widely known in Eastern Europe. Now, while fine wines could be had at extortionate prices, *ţuică* was hard to come by at all in the L.C.B.O. stores, and even when available, it was inevitably industrially produced and tasteless. The situation has improved over the years, but if you wanted a decent țuică in the nineties, you had to smuggle it back from Romania, nonchalantly lying to the customs officer at Pearson Airport and hoping she did not discover the four quarts of hard liquor in plastic bottles and various massive country salamis and cheeses nestled among, and stinking up, your clothing.

But my father, an engineer who had designed a bridge to go over the Danube and paper-light satellites that went into space, and who, even more breathtakingly, had failed two terminally stupid students with parents high up in the Communist Party—failed them not once, not twice, but three times, until the dean took the exams out of his hands to protect him from his own probity—my father was not going to be frustrated in his basic, Romanian male desire for plum brandy at dinner. My father could design a joint for the Canadarm and a wind tunnel for testing airplanes. My father could assemble Ikea furniture efficiently and without error. My father sure as hell could put together his own still.

Now here was more treacherous territory, for while Ontarians were allowed to make wine and beer to their hearts' content, hooch was another matter. You couldn't just have a bunch of grandmas and a teenage girl making it in open daylight. This was closed-garage-door business. The garbage bins multiplied. Now there were some for fermenting plums, some that held a mix of fruit from our own backyard, and just to make any foray into the garage as confusing as possible, a few with enough pickled cabbage and cauliflower to keep a Transylvanian village free of scurvy for a winter. A metal boiler appeared from somewhere, as did a large plastic bucket and some copper tubing. And a spout. My father explained to me the physics of the thing (he was always so good at teaching what he wanted to teach): how the alcohol would be first to vaporize in the boiler due to its lower boiling point, how it would travel up through the copper tubing he had painstakingly coiled and, upon reaching the bucket filled with cold water, would condense and drip out of the spout into a waiting bottle.

The experiment was a success. After his first year of lonely distillation, my father's friends began fermenting plums in their homes, too. Groups of them gathered in our garage in the evening, in the hazy yellow light of the one bulb hanging from the ceiling, and took turns boiling their own ţuică in his still. They smoked and talked for hours, watching the single drops emerge from the spout. It took ages to fill a bottle, and they probably consumed the liquor much faster than they made it. But even then I suspected the true draw was the solitude of the process, the absence of nagging wives, children, and elderly parents, the heavy fumes of hot alcohol, the trancelike peace of drip, drip, drip.

> *In many regions, blackbirds, sparrows, catbirds, robins, and larks are purely destructive and a menace to crops. People now and then complain that their cherries, raspberries, strawberries, or blueberries are entirely eaten by the birds. . . . When this is true, the offending songsters should be captured and eaten.*

Making liquor happened also to be an ecologically responsible hobby, as my father insisted on using the sparse fruit that grew in our yard for experimental blends: a few cherries produced by our insect-decimated trees, some bruised strawberries I had painstakingly planted and tended, the riotous bounty of a raspberry bush that grew beyond our expectations. And then there was the grapevine. Our dining room opened out on to a tiled patio covered by a wooden trellis. My father planted grapevines at the base of the posts that held up the sides of this trellis, and after a while, with a bit of care and nudging and wires to guide them in the right direction, the vines worked their way up the posts and over the wood slats. Their leaves grew large and gave cool shade in the summer. They even grew fruit. But the berries never really ripened; the grapes disappeared or fell to the ground still hard, a source of unending frustration to my father. We found out that the culprit was a raccoon that liked to clamber all over our trellis, disturbing the delicate grapes. Thus began the feud between one, or perhaps more, Upper Canadian raccoons and an East European professor of engineering, and if you have ever had any dealings with raccoons you probably already know who won.

My father began by hanging bells from the trellis, hoping to scare the beast away with noise. Raccoons are not frightened by the tinkling of bells. Then he bought a foul-tasting substance that he painted around the bottoms of the posts, so as to prevent the raccoon from climbing up them. But the trellis was attached to the roof, so the raccoon could reach the vine that way. Clearly it was time for more extreme measures. My father went to Price Club and bought two weapons, a plastic pellet rifle and a pellet pistol. These he placed on the dining-room table, so that if he happened to hear or see a raccoon he could quickly grab a firearm on his way out. When we protested, he insisted he did not want to kill the raccoon, simply to scare it away from the grapes, which had, after all, been destined for greater things. After a few weeks of having two plastic guns lying ready on our table as if we were the Hatfields expecting a visit from the McCoys, my mother put her foot down and made him take them back to the store.

Things were at a standstill when I came back from school one day to find my father covered in blood. Covered in blood, and angry. The story went like this. He had been in the kitchen chopping onions with a large chef's knife when he heard a rustling on the patio. He rushed out of the house, knife still in hand, and there it was: the raccoon. He looked at the animal. It stared right back at him, unfazed. Exactly what happened next is unclear, but there seems to have been a skirmish. My father lunged at the raccoon with his knife, and at the last moment the animal moved out of the way. The knife-tip stuck in the wooden post, the blade broke off from the handle, but my father's hand kept going in its trajectory along the blade. The raccoon escaped unharmed. My father never tried to salvage any of the grapes again.

This was the way things worked in the logic of do-it-yourself. What began as an eminently practical proposition would soon get out of hand. Always, behind the inanities of our everyday existence, there were two unassailable arguments: it was cheaper to do things this way, and it was authentically Romanian, part of our identity. I found it easy to argue against the first. Few normal families buy at retail the amount of wine we produced in a year, so it was hard to be convinced of the great savings involved. We would have simply drunk less, and had fewer authentically Romanian family fights in the middle of dinner, if our wine had cost ten dollars a liter instead of two. But the nod to tradition was harder to counteract because it spoke to something I felt too. True, I longed to eat out in restaurants and use ready-made salad dressings, as native Canadian families did. Still, even then I could tell there were dishes in our cuisine that were better than anything Canada had to offer, and that they were worth extra effort, a bit of sweat, a few burns and cuts. There was an element of community in it too, because you made massive amounts of food and drink partly so you could serve it to other Romanians at parties. Even in a huge city like Toronto, with its thousands of immigrants, there were few Romanian restaurants, and no good ones. If we wanted the food of home we had to make it or have friends who made it. Ideally, everybody prepared his or her own version, and the evenings after a gathering could be spent in fruitful discussion about whose recipe for cabbage rolls was best, whose cooking had too much Hungarian influence, which live-in grandmother was the most gifted baker, whose wine was never going to be as good as my father's.

I think this feeling of diasporic togetherness is part of why my father got involved with the lambs. He had a younger co-worker who ran a farm north of Toronto, an Italian, and therefore automatically a kindred soul. More important, he raised sheep. The succulent memory of a party where a bunch of Romanians set up a spit in their yard and roasted a lamb on it must have gotten to my father because he set about coordinating a mass purchase of lambs for the coming Easter. Fourteen families were in: each would buy half a lamb, and my father would organize it all with his Italian engineer-cum-farmer friend. The deal got messy, for predictable reasons. There were seven lambs ordered for fourteen families, but every family wanted the front part. It was not unusual at that time to hear my father furiously slamming the telephone down and yelling, "I told them at the start, *they* have to decide who gets the ass and who gets the head!"

I was able to maintain a bemused distance from it all until one afternoon when the doorbell rang persistently. I opened the door to see my impatient father, who thrust a large black garbage bag in my arms and said, "Clear some space in the fridge and put this in there." It took me a moment to realize what was happening, but as my arms felt the round contours of a small body through the plastic bag I understood this was one of the lambs, our lamb. Fighting back tears, and as quickly as possible, I shoved bottles and Tupperware aside in the largest part of our fridge, folded in the animal as best I could, and leaned against the door to press it shut. To this day, I can't remember if we got the ass or the head.

Still, after all the drama of his various projects, nobody could have guessed it would be yogurt that would nearly do us all in. Yogurt is a tricky issue: I have inherited some of my father's madness on this point. Since leaving our house in the Toronto suburbs I have moved through five cities in the United States and Germany. In each new home I must spend an enormous amount of energy finding an accept-able yogurt, not too sweet, not bland, not adulterated by bananas or vanilla or cappuccino goji berries, or whatever other abomination is currently being used to sell yogurt to people who actually do not like yogurt. Then I try to find the largest possible container sold of that yogurt, so as never to be without. When I lived in Dallas and was addicted to a Bulgarian-style yogurt made by, appropriately, an aerospace engineer in Austin, I had to fight the urge to buy the gallon-sized jars despite living alone. So I understand my father, understand that once he had found the "Balkan style" yogurt that was closest in taste to what we knew from back home, he didn't want to have to buy a fresh container every day.

The normal thing to do in this circumstance would be to pur-chase a yogurt maker, but making yogurt in miniature cups would not do it for us; it was not really the point of the exercise. Romanians do not serve food in miniature cups. Modest, individual portions are basically inimical to our culture as a whole. Again, my father care-fully explained the process to me: how a cup of starter yogurt would provide enough culture for a gallon of milk, that it was important to keep it warm, but not too hot, over many hours. Instead of a little electric machine, my father used a large pot which he wrapped in towels to keep it cozy overnight after it had been heated on the stove. The resulting yogurt was watery and lacked the firm tartness I loved about our chosen brand, but my father was convinced we would save an enormous amount of money by never having to buy yogurt again. And really, it was the least objectionable of his undertakings: it didn't involve guns or illegal distilling or the transport of dead lambs. Until, that is, I woke up one night to the smell of something burning. The entire house was dark with smoke, and our fire alarm had not sounded. It turned out that my father had forgotten to turn the stove off, and despite the electric element giving off such a small amount of heat, eventually the contents of the pot began to burn, badly. After that, yogurt was something we got at the store, though years later my father did give me a yogurt machine with six little cups that he had found on sale somewhere. I haven't had the courage to use it yet.

When, a year or so later, he managed to burn up the kitchen properly, the ample bounty of Casa Dumitrescu came in handy. It was a simple grease fire that began when he left some onions he was frying to answer the phone, but it destroyed a good deal of our cabinetry before he managed to put it out. My mother was at home to receive the assessor from the insurance company a few weeks later, and since it was lunchtime and his presence in our house made him a kind of guest, she offered him a bowl of soup. He accepted, and, I imagine, warmed and comforted by both soup and the empathetic smiles of my understanding mother, told her his story. He was Polish and was going through a heartbreaking divorce. My mother quite naturally poured him a glass of the house wine, and they continued talking. Afternoon turned into evening, and my father came home from work. Knowing well the therapeutic properties of țuică and assuming that the poor insurance man hadn't had anything so good since leaving his native Poland, my father pulled out a bottle and started filling little glasses. I think the assessment lasted until about 10 p.m. My parents soon had an entirely new kitchen.

Every fall I make wine for the family dinner table and for the good
friends who cross my threshold. These have learned to enjoy it as any
European. They praise its quality and drain their glasses like true sons
of Bacchus. If they do not make it themselves, it is because I dispense
it so freely, frequently bringing it to their table when I dine with them.

The kitchen remodel was a high point, but as the years passed The
Wine became more and more of a burden on our family. Even when
money was tight there was never a question of sitting out a year of
wine production. The economic rationale for it was, after all, unbeat-
able, or, rather, none of us had the emotional energy to challenge
my father on something so clearly central to his life. I grew embarrassed at the gallon-sized jug that was always at the foot of our table,
envied my friends whose parents bought wine in decent, normal-sized
bottles. My father probably knew more about the different varieties
of wine than any of them, but we, his family, didn't. For us there
was no Bordeaux or Côtes du Rhône or Merlot, there was only the
special blend of Casa Dumitrescu, always changing in composition,
always tasting the same. Part of my father's goal in making wine was
to revive our Romanian heritage in Canada, a place that never really
felt like home for him. Unfortunately, what he kept alive for us was
the familiar feeling of life under communism, where you could only
ever have one brand of any product and daren't complain about it
lest the big man who ran things got sour.

　　This is not to say that there were not still occasional moments of
pride, even as my father and I went from being tight accomplices in
my early teens to arguing almost constantly as I approached twenty.
My small residential college at the University of Toronto lived off
stuffy Anglophile pretension and a measure of worldly sophistication, and I discovered to my surprise that I could impress the provost
or an influential alumnus with an exotic bottle of homemade țuică.
As more time passed, I also cared less what other people thought.
Somewhere at the core of my father's obsession was a set of values
that still feel true to me: that wine is just a beverage that goes with
food, neither demon nor fetish; that local stores should not determine

the limits of your culinary pleasure; that there is a warm joy in giving people food you made yourself, even if it is simple. Especially if it is simple. That gardening and cooking and fermenting and decanting can give you, if not a home, then at least a feeling that you belong to yourself even if you're not sure who exactly you are anymore.

As trendy as immigrant foodways and home canning and novels by ethnic women with "spice" in the title are nowadays, the dream of authenticity in food is old romance. When I discovered Angelo Pellegrini's *The Unprejudiced Palate*, originally published in 1948, it seemed I had found my father's script and bible. No wonder my father loved the Italians so! Pellegrini, who left hunger-ravaged Italy and settled in the bountiful Northwest, waxes poetic on the spiritual value of tending a small vegetable garden, the joys of serving guests out of your own cellar, and the sheer deliciousness of fresh ingredients, put together simply but with a measure of peasant cunning. His book is a paean to immigrant wisdom, pungent and coarse though it might seem from the outside. Even in the 1940s, he notes, I read with some guilt, how the second generation grumbles about the unappealing, unhygienic food practices of their Old World parents. And yet Pellegrini is also uncannily like me, a child immigrant who grew into the language of his new home, becoming a professor of English literature. Although his mother did a great deal of the cooking, his father is Pellegrini's model and authority, the one who taught him how to think about food and, naturally, how to make wine. Like Pellegrini, I could write a chapter on "The Things My Fathers Used to Do," but while the émigré Italian paid attention and followed in their footsteps, I strayed.

> There is little else that strengthens the filial bond so much as a father's patient acquiescence in the children's preoccupation with matters a little beyond their years. As they grow older, you will draw more and more upon their assistance at vintage time. At the end of the day's labor you will frequently drink together of the wine produced by your joint efforts. It will be pleasant to observe the children grow conscious of their skill and to see the pride they take in accomplishments realized

under your careful tutelage. In the years ahead, the meaning of these
experiences so intimately related to life will be reflected in the bond
of friendship and understanding between father and son, and in the
family's wholesome attitude toward alcoholic beverage.

I left for graduate school in the wake of one of our family's uglier
moments. That summer my father's get-rich scheme was to buy fixer-
upper houses, renovate them, and resell them at a profit, none of these
activities fitting into what one might call his skill set. My mother
was unwilling to risk their life savings on this business venture, and
he presented her with an ultimatum: compliance or divorce. In the
middle of this, he and I had our worst fight, so furious that when the
power went out all over the eastern seaboard I was sure that my anger
had blown out the lights. We had patched things up into cold civility
by the time my parents drove with me down to New England. At
that point he had also dropped the idea of buying property and with
it, quietly, the threat of divorce. But my mother had not forgotten,
and she had her own thoughts about a marriage that could be traded
in for a rundown house. She made her mind up when, having said
their good-byes to me and set out on the highway, the first thing my
father asked was, "So when are we going to start making The Wine?"

Years later, a family friend confessed to my mother how much he
had dreaded coming over for dinner. You see, when someone makes
their own wine, you can't simply drink it when it's served to you. You
have to comment on it. You have to discuss its qualities, how well
it turned out this year, how successful this particular blend of grapes
was. Basically, you have to act like you're at a wine tasting and it's
the pinnacle of sophistication to detect the fine nuances distinguish-
ing Casa Dumitrescu 1998 from Casa Dumitrescu 1997. A failure of
hospitality of this magnitude is the stuff Greek tragedies are made of,
but its core is innocent, a natural imbalance of interest and passion.
Here is what no one admits in their gleeful reports on the year of
planting their own vegetables, baking their own bread, and brewing
coca-cola with self-harvested cane sugar and home-grown cocaine:

some undertakings require absolute, unyielding dedication, and not every member of the family or community can match it. Oh, it's one thing to go berry picking with the kids on a farm and make a pot of jam at the end of the day. But if you are pickling tomatoes because you miss a taste from your childhood, you have to try to get it right, which means you have to do a lot of pickling. It also means the people around you will have to eat a lot of sour tomatoes while you work out the recipe. Wine is even more demanding, requiring copious equipment, knowledge, and most of all time. It has to be tended, observed, cared for. You have to judge the fermentation, know when to rack it to another bottle, siphoning it away from its sediment. It is intimate, too, in the various demands it makes on the body of its maker: my father labored to lift bottles and bruise grapes, and he always racked wine the old-fashioned, unsanitary way, by sucking on one end of a hose and placing it in the fresh bottle, allowing the pressure to drive the wine into its new receptacle. The liquid that a proud vintner puts on the table is the fruit of months of planning, mixing, crushing, washing, testing, tasting, pouring, and smelling, but all the guest knows is that he is drinking mediocre wine. The wine was my father's second child, one whose faults he couldn't see.

The deep irony of the years that followed the divorce was that my father's liquors improved. His wine was now more than palatable, and his țuică was the real thing, a pleasure to start a meal with. We had all put in time, but he stuck it through. It took a long while for us to be able to talk to each other after our fight and my parents' subsequent split, and even then our encounters were awkward, veins of hurt pulsing under the surface. But it helped that all we ever did, on those tense holiday visits, was eat and drink together. On the worst days, food and alcohol were social lubricants, keeping mouths from talking too much, giving the illusion of celebration and togetherness around a table. On the better days, it was easy to enjoy a good plum brandy, to appreciate it honestly, to see him enjoy the compliment. He would send me off with several bottles to take home with me, some pure țuică, some experiments he had colored with tea, flavored with fruit, or aged in a bourbon wood barrel. I didn't know what to do with that much hard liquor, but inevitably something would come up—an exam passed, a dissertation submitted, another move to yet another new city—and the țuică I found in my stores provided the punctuation.

We do not speak anymore, my father and I. The decision was his. When I went to pack my things for my most recent move, now so far from Toronto that I'm almost back where I started, I found one more plastic bottle of țuică. It was full, and it would clearly be the last I would ever have from his hands. I decided not to put it in the container with all my other belongings, wrapping it instead in a plastic bag and hiding it in my luggage; it was perfectly legal, but it felt illicit. This is also an authentic Romanian gesture, one I performed instinctively. One of my parents' friends escaped from Romania in the 1980s by hiding on a train, leaving his family behind but tightly grasping, under his jacket, two bottles of exquisite wine from the vineyard where he had worked. He opened one bottle with great pomp on his twenty-fifth wedding anniversary, and told his guests he was saving the second for his elder daughter's wedding, which he did not live to see. I did not wait so long. The bottle of țuică was a little crushed by the time it reached my new home, looking as if it might crack the moment I tried to unscrew the cap. But it held, and to celebrate the start of our new life, I poured a generous amount into espresso cups for me and my husband. I expected the fresh, clean punch-in-the-face of all-natural, home-made plum brandy, but that is not what I tasted in the cup. This bottle, it turned out, was one of my father's experiments, an infusion with orange peels that had taken on a powerful bitter note over the years. It was undrinkable.

They will want to suck at the siphon hose and taste whatever you taste. They will laugh and smack their lips and assure you that the wine is very good. When you leave the cellar they will insist on carrying the bottle to the dinner table. As they ascend the stairs with uncertain step, you may be tempted to take the bottle clutched in the infant arms lest it drop with a crash to the pavement. But you will resist the temptation; for it will seem fitting that your children should carry the wine to the dinner table. And as they cling tightly to the bottle, with all the elaborate care of which little ones are capable on such occasions, you may possibly glimpse a comforting symbol—the child drawing closer to the father.

from THE MAKING OF
A GREAT WINE

Edward Steinberg

The north-facing slope of Fasèt is still white with the light snow-fall of yesterday. Vine dressers in Burgundy would have thanked their patron, Saint Vincent, whose day it was. But whoever sent the frosty fluff, this winter's first, the local growers are grateful. As snow melts, the water seeps slowly through the topsoil and into the strata below—emergency moisture deep roots can tap during the desperate days of drought.

The observer's feet may be standing in snow, but his eyes see no trace of it on the slope of San Lorenzo. Patches stand out here and there on contiguous plots. When the cooperative winery of Barbaresco was founded, it classified as prime those vineyards where snow melted first. It knew its Nebbiolo. "The principle that the same variety does better or worse according to where it is planted is admitted and undeniable for all grapes," observes Fantini, "but for Nebbiolo it is really an axiom."

Federico and his crew are at San Lorenzo for the winter pruning. "This is nothing," he responds to a shiverer's lament. "When we did the pruning here four years ago, it was seventeen below." On the Fahrenheit scale, that's about zero.

Working next to Federico is Angelo Lembo. Although he is the fairer of the two, Lembo is from Sicily.

Italian historians still debate whether the process of national unification, which culminated in the proclamation of the Kingdom of Italy in 1861, was a war of liberation led by Piedmont against foreign rulers, as the official version had it at the time, or the covert conquest of the rest of the country by Italy's Prussia. One thing is certain: Vittorio Emanuele II, the second ruler of the Kingdom of Sardinia to bear that name, saw no reason to change the ordinal when he became the first sovereign of the Kingdom of Italy. In his mind, evidently, the new kingdom was merely an extension of the old.

The Piedmontese and other northern leaders knew little or nothing of the South. It was not only geographically that Turin was closer to London than to Lembo's birthplace. Cavour himself admitted that he was much more familiar with England and that he had thought Sicilians spoke Arabic. When southern Italy had been annexed to the new state, one of his close associates, the future prime minister Luigi Carlo Farini, went down to observe the situation. "You call this Italy?" he soon wrote in disbelief. "This is Africa!"

Angelo Lembo left Sicily in the mid-sixties at the age of sixteen, part of a massive wave of emigration to the North. At first he worked at the Fiat automobile plant in Turin. When he started to work at the winery in 1968 the local workers gave him a hard time with their teasing. Luigi Cavallo was especially rough on him. "I can still hear him," says Lembo with a chuckle, "screaming his head off in dialect about southerners not speaking proper Italian!"

Lembo has been pruning these vines for twenty years now. "He knows them so well he calls them by name and talks to them," chortles Federico. "In Piedmontese, of course."

Just as we all still bear signs of our simian past, even the noblest vines are marked by their origins as forest creepers and climbers. Under natural conditions a vine must compete with other plants. Not having a thick trunk to hold it above the ground, it has evolved other means of ensuring itself a place in the sun. It grows rapidly and over a long period of time. Tenacious tendrils enable it to cling to trees and make its way to the top of them.

Nathaniel Hawthorne was fascinated by the vines he saw in Tuscany in 1858. "Nothing can be more picturesque," he wrote in his notebook, "than the spectacle of an old grape-vine . . . clinging round its tree, imprisoning within its strong embrace the friend that supported its tender infancy, converting the tree wholly to its own selfish ends, stretching out its innumerable arms on every bough, and hardly allowing a leaf to sprout except its own."

But the writer also recorded his suspicion that "the vine is a pleasanter object of sight" growing in this way than it is "in countries where it produces a more precious wine, and therefore is trained more artificially."

Hawthorne's suspicion was well-founded. Great wine grapes are the product of strict viti*culture*: of nature highly nurtured. With vines as with us, culture directs the course of nature toward ends of its own.

In the vineyard, where it does not have to compete with trees and can be propped up by a trellis or other support, the vine's vigorous growth has no value. It no longer has to be among the fittest to survive. But the vine has not yet adapted to this civilized mode of existence. It still has the instincts of its forest forebears.

Federico nods his head. The wine lover's view of Nature is too enocentric.

"Nature couldn't care less about wine," he says. "She's interested in seeds."

Like all fruits, grapes are essentially a device of seed dispersal, ensuring the survival of the species. In a sense, the sugar is merely a surplus left over after the seeds have received all the nourishment they need. The more seeds a grape has, the less sugar and more acid it will contain. And since they produce hormones that diffuse into the pulp and stimulate its growth, more seeds mean larger berries and ultimately less concentrated wine.

From nature's point of view, the more grapes the merrier. But a vine produces only a certain amount of the substances that will give the wine color, scent, and flavor. If that amount is spread among many bunches rather than few, the wine will be diluted. Doing what comes naturally, vines are like parents who conceive more children than they have the means to bring up properly.

"If you care about the kids," says Federico, "you have to impose strict discipline." He pauses before making his painful point. "And that includes mutilation."

Perhaps the most striking example of the diversion of natural instincts for epicurean ends used to be seen in the cultivation of tobacco. The tobacco plant's metabolism is geared to nourishing the flower cluster at its top and channels the most nutrients in that direction. In the days when rich-tasting tobacco was in demand among connoisseurs, the inflorescence would be cut as soon as it began to develop, in order to divert the upward-moving savory substances to the highest leaves, which would then be used as wrappers for the finest cigars. Reproduction was sacrificed to enrich the inedible leaves, the prized part of the plant as far as cigars are concerned.

Discipline in the vineyard is imposed through training and pruning. A vine is trained to give a certain form to its permanent and semipermanent parts. It is to this form that pruning returns the vines each year, as a trim periodically does for a haircut. The possible forms are many: close-cropped or expansive; high off the ground or low; freestanding or supported by a vertical or horizontal trellis. The choice depends on the climate, the vigor of the variety, and the kind of wine you want to make.

The vines of San Lorenzo have been trained so that each has a trunk about two feet tall, from which the tangled canes now emerge. Each year's growth and crop of grapes is supported by a trellis over six feet high, which consists of four wires, end posts, and intermediate stakes.

Pruning regulates the vine's annual growth. In strict viticulture, it sacrifices quantity for quality.

It was the Greeks who brought viticultural discipline to Italy. The traveller and geographer Pausanias relates that there was a place where his fellow countrymen venerated the statue of a donkey. The animal had eaten part of a vine, which produced tastier grapes after the mutilation. (Hanging high from an undisciplined, tree-trained vine somewhere else in Greece, the grapes in Aesop's famous fable may not have been sour, as the fox claimed, but they certainly would not have made very good wine.) In Italy, the Etruscans treated grapevines like the cousins of Tarzan's lianas they are, training them on trees and letting them grow freely. Hawthorne's vine was an example of the Etruscan approach, which was still common in central Italy until the 1960s.

The number of buds left on the vine at pruning is the main determinant of the size of the crop. There is no magic number, though. If you leave too many buds, you'll have a large crop of inferior grapes. "But you don't want to prune too short, either," warns Federico. "With too few buds, the vine's energy is channeled into shoot and leaf production. A few years ago, Angelo wanted to reduce his Cabernet Sauvignon crop even further. So we pruned back to just six buds. The vines produced shoots like mad!" What you aim for is an equilibrium between reproduction—that is, grapes—and vegetative growth. Balance is all.

"It all depends" is one of Federico's refrains. The number of buds you leave depends on the variety of the vine, its age, how it has performed in the past, and the soil.

Nebbiolo vines, for instance, rarely produce grapes from the first two buds on a cane, those nearest the trunk. A memory spreads amusement over Federico's face. When he was in California he saw some Nebbiolo vines trained to the widespread cordon spur system, where many short canes, called spurs, are left on the vine, each with only two buds.

"You should have seen them!" he exclaims. "The vines went haywire. They didn't produce a single grape, but what an orgy of leaves!"

The Gaja crew did not do the pruning in the Serralunga vineyard last year because the purchase took place in July. The former owner left an average of 18 buds per vine, but Federico will reduce the number only gradually. "If we started right away pruning there like we do here," he says, "the vine would get fat." It has to get used to producing less. It has to find its balance.

"The best balance is that of old vines," he says. "They have a lot of self-discipline." They're "sagacious" and "restrained"; young ones are "headstrong" and "obstreperous." One of these days, when he has the leisure, Federico will no doubt compose a poem in praise of old vines. But you can be sure they won't be trained Etruscan-style like "the vines that round the thatch-eves run" in Keats's ode "To Autumn."

By nature, Nebbiolo is anything but restrained.

"It's the wildest horse in the rodeo," Federico says. "A real bucking bronco. Reining it is usually a big problem."

But the vines of San Lorenzo are old and the soil is poor. "You don't have to go to great lengths to figure out how to prune here. You could leave these vines twenty buds and they'd still give you very few bunches." He gestures toward some unpruned vines. "You don't see those monstrously long canes here that you do in many Nebbiolo vineyards."

The pruning cuttings of an average vine at San Lorenzo weigh around ten pounds, while those of young Nebbiolo vines in richer soil might weigh thirty or more—the weights of weakness and vigor.

Like a barber about to cut into a shock of shaggy hair, Angelo Lembo sizes up a vine. It is now a tangle of about a dozen wooden canes, all but two of which started out last spring as tender tips of shoots peeking timidly out of bud eyes.

He clips away the "past," the by-now-two-year-old canes that bore last year's shoots and crop. Then he selects one of the two remaining one-year-old canes as the "present," the one that will bear this year's shoots and crop, and trims it so that only eight eyes are left. This cane will be tied along the bottom wire of the trellis and the new shoots will emerge from the dormant buds which formed on the cane during the past growing season. Finally, he cuts back the other cane to a spur with only two buds. This is the "future," from which two shoots will grow. One will be chosen during next winter's pruning as the "present" to bear the grapes for Sorì San Lorenzo 1990 and the other as the new "future."

This is known as cane-and-spur pruning, and the particular version that Federico and his crew are using is called Guyot, after the nineteenth-century French agronomist Jules Guyot, who propagandized it. But the system had already been around for a long time. What could be clearer than the instructions written in 1670 by Sir Thomas Hanmer, who owned a vineyard in, of all places, Wales?:

> Leave . . . one chiefe or master branch . . . let this master branch be left half a yard or a yard long, according to the strength of the vine, and let it be the principal among the branches . . . the lowest of the other branches must be pruned very low or short, leaving only one eye or budd, or two at the most . . . and this short branch . . . is to serve to send forth a master branch for the next year, cutting off the master branch which was left last year. This vine being thus pruned, cut away all the other branches except the two aforesaid.

Federico is working nearby. "We'd like to prune even shorter," he says, "so we could plant more densely. When we replant here, we'd like to bring the density up to over two thousand vines per acre. Like the Merlot over there." He nods in the direction of a plot further along the slope of Masuè. "But to do that we need really weak vines." Greater density increases competition among the roots for nutrients and thus reduces vigor. Sorì San Lorenzo now has just over 1,600 vines per acre.

Federico leaves only seven buds as he trims the "master branch" of a vine. "It's struggling," he explains. "This will help the vine get its energy back."

It turns out that the vines are not all that healthy. "In fact," he says, "a lot of them are sick. They have a virosis." The news sounds terrible, but Federico is nonchalant.

The virosis is called leaf roll because the edges of the leaves curl. As long as the case isn't severe it doesn't affect the quality of the wine, just the vigor and longevity.

"Or rather," says Federico, "by decreasing the vigor it helps produce *better* grapes." He pauses pensively. "Those virus-free vines they've been developing through clonal selection and heat treatment are hard to restrain. Just look at those yields a lot of people are getting nowadays."

Health can be harmful. The paradox is profound.

Federico himself seems tired. Vine after vine, he and his men have been pruning since November.

"Ideally," he says, "it would be better to start later." After the leaves fall, the vine shifts its metabolism and transfers food reserves to the trunk, where they will be stored and thus available to boost the new growth off to a good start in the spring. The transfer takes time. "But there's simply too much work to do. We can't prune all the vines in just a few weeks. So we do the most important vineyards late and rotate the others."

With the new vineyard at Serralunga, the winery now has more than 300,000 vines. "If you put all those cuttings together, you'd have quite a pile of wood!" Federico exclaims.

Some varieties are easier to prune than others. "With Merlot you can prune a vine a minute," says Federico. Its wood is relatively soft and it doesn't present any particular problems. Sauvignon and its Cabernet cousin require the most physical strength. Their tendrils are tenacious and the wood is very tough. Indeed, an old synonym for Cabernet Sauvignon in Bordeaux is Vidure: *vigne dure*, hard vine.

In many vineyards, Nebbiolo is hard to prune, though its wood is tender. "The problem is *how* to prune it," Federico says. "Prune Chardonnay short and it simply produces that much less. If you prune Nebbiolo short, it might produce just a couple of clusters and not even ripen those."

As the snip and snap of the pruners' shears moves steadily down the slope, the line of demarcation is clear. Nature's tangle retreats before the advance of symmetry. Literally on the cutting edge of civilization, the shear-toting sheriffs impose law and order on the wild frontier. Brutal they may be, but even the gentlest lover of wine would hardly think it wrong. In the vineyard, at least, the end justifies the means.

Vigorous pruning is based on two assumptions; if they turn out to be wrong, the grower will grumble. One is that there is a market that will reward his sacrifice of quantity by paying him more for his wine. The other is that nature will do no pruning of her own. A low percentage of fertilization at flowering means an even smaller harvest and hail can reduce it further.

Great wine requires not only the repression of the instincts of the vine, but those of the grower as well. Quantity gratifies immediately; the pleasures of quality are deferred. They are experienced only in the wine and, of course, the price it fetches. No wonder, then, that civilization in a vineyard can create discontent.

Like the vines they tend, vineyard workers can be deeply rooted in history. "Even today," says Federico, "some of them have trouble adjusting when they start to work here. Notions like quality and fine wine are abstractions to them, and they find it hard to understand why abundance should be sacrificed." He smiles wryly. "After all, they don't dash off to comparative tastings after work!"

Until after the Second World War, yields in Barbaresco were tiny by even the highest standards of today. This was not because growers had a commitment to quality as that notion is currently understood, but rather because they lacked the means to produce more. Once they had the means, peasants did not want to miss the historic opportunity to make their dreams of abundance come true.

Aldo Vacca has two uncles who are growers. One of them has a vineyard with six rows of Nebbiolo. "Last year I thinned out the crop in the three bottom rows, the ones that usually produce less ripe grapes," Aldo says, "and got over half a degree more alcohol than in the other rows. You could taste the difference." He scratches his head as he reflects. "My uncles understand the quality issue abstractly, but they have an attachment to quantity that's hereditary. It's in their blood!"

Pietro Rocca's voice is smooth and finely modulated as he talks about Angelo's decision in the mid-sixties to lower yields drastically.

"Angelo's doings were looked upon by most people as anything but angelic," he says with a twinkle in his eye. "In fact, they were considered downright diabolical. In those days, even eighteen buds a vine were thought to be miserably few, and it was common to have two and even three canes with twelve buds each." He chuckles. "You still see vines like that. They're real museum pieces."

Cutting back to twelve buds per vine as Angelo had decided to do meant sacrificing an enormous amount of grapes. Even *one* bud per vine less would have meant a reduction of about 1,600 clusters per acre. The comments of workers at the local tavern expressed doubts about Angelo's sanity. Giovanni Gaja was mayor of Barbaresco at the time and attentive to what people were saying.

"One day he rushed into the house all upset," recalls Angelo. "Everyone in the village is saying we have so few grapes that we're going to go bankrupt!' he exclaimed. 'How on earth are we going to pay the workers?'"

When Angelo Lembo started to work at the winery, the Battle of the Buds was still raging. "Angelo would give us pruning instructions," he says, "but as soon as he had turned his back, Gino and the rest of them would do as they pleased."

Angelo smiles as he sighs. "Ah, Gino! Luigi Cavallo was a pillar of the winery. His dedication was total. He would talk about 'my vines' and 'my grapes.' He would have died rather than miss a day's work because of illness. When it was harvest time, he'd be on the spot before dawn and get furious with the other workers for arriving later." Angelo shakes his head. "But it was quite a battle. He always had an excuse for not pruning shorter. I can still hear the litany. The Kober rootstock is too vigorous; you won't get any grapes. What if flowering is poor? What if it hails?"

The battle didn't end with the buds. There were the root-stocks to be planted in the new vineyards. Angelo wanted the 420A to restrain Nebbiolo's vigor; Cavallo liked vigorous plants and the Kober 5BB gave him what he wanted. There was also the wicker that was traditionally used to tie up canes and shoots to the trellis in the spring.

"Gino would start gathering and stripping reeds in the fall. Months in advance. When spools of wire became available, which enabled you to do the job in a fraction of the time, he wouldn't hear of it. If you gave him a spool, he'd take it and throw it away. You practically had to put it by his bedside and let the idea sink in slowly while he slept! After three years, he started to use wire. Reluctantly."

In those days Angelo was an impetuous young man setting out to conquer the world. Luigi Cavallo was a middle-aged ex-sharecropper who had never been to Turin, but was used to commanding in the vineyard. The conflict was real, but the battle never got bloody.

The young man had come to live in Barbaresco and had learned the dialect he had never spoken at home. Ambitious, but good-natured, he had an intuitive understanding of the people working for him. He took Cavallo out to dinner now and then, talked things over, and tried to get him involved in his plans. If Barbaresco wouldn't bustle, the young man in a hurry would wait.

In the few words that Angelo stood up to say while dessert and coffee were being served during the annual dinner for winery employees just before Christmas, there was, as always, "a warm welcome for Gino Cavallo, who for so many years was a pillar of the winery." Cavallo had a leg amputated a few years ago and doesn't get around much anymore. But he sits almost every day in his courtyard with the beret from which he is never separated on his head. He looks you in the eye and proudly tells the story of how things changed at the winery when Angelo came on the scene.

"I went up to see Angelo at his home when he was starting to take over. He explained to me what he wanted. I'm not interested in having a whole lot of grapes,' he said. The difference between Angelo and his father was like that between night and day."

Cavallo stresses his words with a gesture of his hand, holding his palm down when he says "night" and turning it up when he comes to "day."

"The *geometra* just wanted us to bring in grapes, period. We harvested everything. With Angelo, the music changed completely.

We picked only ripe grapes. We went through the vineyard several times if necessary.

"One Sunday in July Angelo dropped in on me and said that there were too many grapes on the vines down at San Lorenzo. So the next day we started to cut off bunches. People thought he was crazy. The peasants snickered. One of them said, 'I get four times as many grapes in my vineyard!' They didn't understand anything then and they don't understand anything now.

"People came to work here from other places who didn't know anything about this job. I even had to teach a southerner how to do things. Now he really knows his stuff. He's a good man."

Snip! go the shears: the last vine's future has been clipped. San Lorenzo's once dishevelled shocks are now neat and trim. But the crewcut won't last long.

WAR AND THE
WIDOW'S TRIUMPH
Tilar J. Mazzeo

On the eve of the new year in 1813, Barbe-Nicole certainly had plenty of champagne on hand, but this abundance was part of the reason that she had so little to celebrate.

She was glad to see 1813 fade into history. Sales of her wine had been down again that year—down, as she could not help but recognize, a staggering 80 percent since 1805, the year of François's untimely death and her decision to take up running the business. Travel across the continent had become hopelessly unprofitable and increasingly dangerous, and the business was floundering. There was no way to put a positive spin on it. She must have wondered whether the financial risk that she had taken and all the years of hard work were worth the emotional strain. The company was failing, and she knew that the businessmen of Reims—perhaps even her father— would say that this was why women should not run trading houses.

When the bells of the great cathedral of Notre-Dame de Reims rang in the new year, the bitterness in the winter air matched her mood precisely. For Barbe-Nicole could not have been in high spirits when she considered either the year that was passing or the prospects of what was to come. As everyone in Reims understood, the war was edging closer. Napoléon had once said that the countryside of the Champagne would make a perfect battlefield. In this last desperate year, when he still ruled an empire greater than any since Roman times, he would test that hypothesis.

For Barbe-Nicole, his arrival was particularly unwelcome. Already, one could see evidence of the amassing troops in the countryside. If the conflict dragged on, as it had a way of doing, come spring there would be no regular work in the fields or in the vineyards, a grim prospect for anyone whose hopes and fortunes were invested in a harvest. By January, the distant echo of cannon fire resounded faintly through the cobbled streets of Reims, and shopkeepers sweeping the pavement in the bright air would stop to listen solemnly.

No doubt recollecting her own childhood and the frightening escape from the abbey of Saint-Pierre-les-Dames at the height of the Revolution, she hurriedly fetched Clémentine from her convent school in Paris. Clémentine was now fourteen—only a year or two older than Barbe-Nicole had been when the Revolution began—and Barbe-Nicole remembered watching that earlier political upheaval through the cracks of a shuttered window, in hiding. She knew something of what it meant to live in turbulent times and had no intention of trusting her daughter to the care of strangers or even cousins in the midst of a war.

By the end of January, the echoes of cannon fire and horse hooves were no longer faint, and Barbe-Nicole knew it was only a matter of time before there would be troops of one fashion or another in the streets of Reims, looking for food and supplies and shelter and, she had no doubt, as much wine as they could get their hands on.

If her cellars were looted, she would never be able to recover. It would be the end of her business and of the dream that she and François had shared in those first years of their marriage, when life seemed to hold for her such different possibilities. She was sick with worry over the fate of the wine made in that legendary year of the comet, the 1811 vintage, which tasted like dry honey and was slowly turning a light golden hue in the coolness of her cellars. It was a wine destined for greater things than rough soldiers intent on a night's oblivion. It was a wine destined to make her famous, and Barbe-Nicole had some inkling of it. So, in advance of the troops, she ordered her workmen to begin sealing the entrance to her cellars. The wine would wait out the war in uninterrupted darkness.

The arrival of the troops was indeed a certainty. Napoléon was engaged in a bloody contest with the allied coalition in the countryside that stretched just beyond Reims, and it was in the wet, cold landscape of his familiar boyhood Champagne that an empire was to slip from his grasp at last. He would not relinquish it readily. The French routed the Russian and Prussian armies in the village of Montmirail, and the defeated troops retreated to Reims. As evening came, the streets of the city were filled with the ominous sound of metal striking stone and horses and the footfalls of fifteen thousand cold and weary men, dreaming of their homes to the east. The occupation had begun.

Listening from her offices, Barbe-Nicole could hear the chaos in the streets and the loud voices ringing out and the occasional chorus of martial song with words she could not understand. She was waiting for the knock that she knew would come, the knock demanding that she release cases upon cases of wine. Whether they would pay for it was another matter. She surely knew by now that three hundred thousand allied soldiers had taken up residence in occupied Épernay and immediately looted Jean-Remy's cellars. Before the war was over, he would lose more than half a million bottles of champagne.

In despair, she told her cousin in Paris, Mademoiselle Gard—to the family, simply Jennie—that she anticipated the worst. "Everything is going badly," Barbe-Nicole lamented. "I have been occupied for many days with walling up my cellars, but I know full well that this will not prevent them from being robbed and pillaged. If so, I am ruined, so it is best to be resigned and work to survive. I would not regret my losses except for my poor child for whom it would have been better if this Misfortune had come five or six years earlier, because then she would never have known any of the pleasures that she will lose, and which will make her miserable. But I will struggle to do without everything, to sacrifice everything, everything, so that she will be less unhappy." There would be devastating losses for the rest of the family as well. Her brother's textile factory at Saint-Brice was destroyed by the invading troops, and much of the industry of Reims was crippled.

When the Russians arrived at last, it still surprised her, but even more surprising was that they were gentlemen. The leaders of the Prussian and Cossack armies gave their troops free rein to loot and pillage. The Russians were more restrained, and they were determined to keep administrative control of Reims. There was an ugly bureaucratic tussle when the Russian prince leading the armies, Serge Alexandrovich Wolkonsky, insisted that there would be no looting and no retributive requisitions. To the Prussians, the prince sent word that his orders came directly from the czar. There would be no pillaging of Reims. And "as for your insolent threat of sending troops to Rheims," he told the Prussian leaders, "I have forces here to receive them."

For Barbe-Nicole, it was a bittersweet irony. Her cellars would not be looted. They would mostly buy her wine. For years, she had struggled to sell her champagne, and Louis had traveled across half the continent in search of customers in regions as remote as Turkey and Albania. Each time, he had come back disappointed and discouraged. Now, here at her doorstep was an army of men all ready to buy her wine, not the prized 1811 vintage, which she guarded jealously, but the accumulated stock—still fine wines in their own right—that she had been unable to move during the long years of the war. The soldiers, eager to believe the war was almost at an end, drank with enthusiasm. Watching them guzzle her wines, Barbe-Nicole was philosophical. "Today they drink," she said. "Tomorrow they will pay!"

More ironically still, although Barbe-Nicole would not have known it, the arrival of the Russians would also prove a brilliant marketing opportunity for winemakers throughout the Champagne. Although she had already made a name for herself in imperial Russia, had already captured a significant market share in the days before the economic collapse of the war and the closing of the borders, that recognition had surely faded in the years that had followed. These new men would never forget her sparkling wines. Watching the destruction of his cellars, Jean-Rémy also saw the potential. "All these officers who ruin me today," he predicted, "will make my fortune tomorrow. All those who drink my wine are salesmen who, on returning to their own country, will make the product" famous. Barbe-Nicole would benefit from these same ambassadors.

The Russians, however, were not the only ones in the winter of 1814 to enjoy the champagne of the Widow Clicquot. In early March, the French army under the leadership of General Corbineau recaptured Reims. Some joked that Barbe-Nicole and the other wine brokers had done their part for the war effort by supplying the allies with strong local wines. When the French entered Reims, "about a dozen prisoners were made, who had been laid under the table by the first and pacific artillery. At the moment of the attack of the French troops, there remained some drinkers but no soldiers. These, dead drunk, had not heard the sound, 'To horse!'" Of course, the French troops wasted no time in celebrating their victory, either. There is a legend, in fact, that it was during these days that the art of *sabrage*—opening champagne bottles with military sabers—was invented. According to the story, "Madame Clicquot . . . in order to have her land protected, gave Napoléon's officers Champagne and glasses. Being on their horses, they couldn't hold the glass while opening the bottle." So they lopped off the necks of the bottles with their swords, and *sabrage* was born.

These Russian prisoners of war did not suffer long as captives. The French victory was short-lived. A week later, the French were forced to retreat, and the Russians again occupied the town. Finally, in mid-March, a desperate and furious Napoléon vowed that he would sleep that night in Reims, the city that could make kings. In making this vow, Napoléon was confident that he would be graciously welcomed at the Hotel Ponsardin, where he and Josephine had stayed before, the guests of the charming Nicolas, in more promising times.

But Nicolas Ponsardin did not need a comet and the superstitious sensibilities of the peasants, who read in it a chilling portent, to know that Napoléon would not be emperor for long. The coalition was closing in on the French, and defeat seemed inevitable. Still, in the past, Napoléon had succeeded despite insurmountable odds. Who was to say that he might not manage to do so again?

Not for the first time in his eventful life, Nicolas found himself in a delicate and dangerous political position, unwilling to offend Napoléon in the event he was victorious but unprepared to align himself too closely to a man who was not likely to remain in power long. Even worse might be the consequences if the city fell to the emperor's enemies. It was Napoléon who had made Nicolas mayor, as a mark of his special favor. If the political winds shifted in a new direction, it would now make him the target of retribution. So when it was hinted that he should leave town, Nicolas prepared to do the sensible thing. Hedging his bet, he wrote Napoléon a letter, promising that the city of Reims and those who governed it were his stauch allies, and then he hightailed it out of town, leaving the emperor to take his chances. Well in advance of Napoléon's arrival, Nicolas called for his carriage, left word with his children, and went out of town on an extended business trip to the remote city of Le Mans. He did not return to Reims until well after the curtain had closed on the final act.

In the small hours of the morning, long before the dawn, Napoléon passed through the triumphal gates of the city, the same gates that once welcomed kings on their way to their coronation. Despite the darkness and the cold, the city was alive with excitement, and great crowds gathered along the route to welcome the emperor with exuberant cries and banners and speeches and all the pomp and circumstance that could be arranged at such short notice and after years of war. It was Barbe-Nicole who greeted the emperor at the door of the Hôtel Ponsardin, which her father had deserted. She assured Napoléon that the family was waiting to welcome him only a short distance away, at the home of her brother, Jean-Baptiste.

What must Napoléon have thought when he learned that the Hôtel Ponsardin was empty? It is hard to imagine that a man as astute as Napoléon failed to understand the lack of confidence the absence implied. Or perhaps it did not much matter. Nicolas had charged his son with meeting his social and political responsibilities, so Napoléon was welcomed as a personal guest of the family into the elegant mansion on rue de Vesle where Jean-Baptiste lived with his wife, Thérèse.

Napoléon stayed with the Ponsardin family for three nights. For Jean-Baptiste and Thérèse these were thrilling days, filled with important visitors and elegant dinners and the excitement of being at the center of world events. They were also stressful days. Entertaining the emperor in the midst of a war he was in the process of losing was a dicey business.

Thérèse was frantic that her hospitality should be graceful and exacting. As was the custom, she herself filled the emperor's pillows with the softest new down. Jean-Baptiste, meanwhile, must have perceived how politically delicate his father's absence was. And despite Barbe-Nicole's disdain for the emperor and for the commercial ruin he had created, she was far too wise to complicate the family's plight by giving any appearance of disrespect. Only their sister, Clémentine, who was one of Reims's reigning socialites, perhaps welcomed the honor without misgivng.

As the Ponsardin family entertained Napoléon during those fading days of the French Empire, he surely drank some of Barbe-Nicole's champagne. Indeed, he must have tasted that divine vintage of 1811. For a guest as powerful as the emperor of France, for a man known for his love of fine champagnes, Barbe-Nicole would have offered nothing less. She would have done it just to prove to him that Jean-Rémy Moët and Memmie Jacquesson were not the only ones who knew how to craft something marvelous.

She is unlikely to have explained to Napoléon the symbolism of the comet insignia branded on the end of each of her corks in that year's vintage, a comet said by those who worked the vineyards and the fields to prophesy the end of his empire. In the weeks and months that were to come, Napoléon must have remembered those days with the Ponsardins and the champagne of the young Widow Clicquot as the last taste of victory itself, for within three weeks, his meteoric career would be at an end, and Napoléon would find himself stripped of power and sent into a forced exile.

First, however, he would see Jean-Rémy. It must have annoyed Barbe-Nicole to no end. When Napoléon left the Ponsardin family home, he headed directly to Épernay, where he visited one last time with his old friend. Despite the champagne that they undoubtedly shared, it was a somber and serious occasion. Napoléon was too experienced in war not to understand the odds he faced.

The story goes that Jean-Rémy found his friend intently studying a map. Looking up to find Jean-Rémy, Napoléon quietly unpinned his own Legion of Honor, the small but ornate five-starred cross that signified noble rank in imperial France. Napoléon then pinned it on his friend's coat, saying only: "If fate intervenes and dashes my hopes, I want at least to be able to reward you for your loyal service and steadfast courage, but above all for the excellent reputation you have achieved, both here and abroad, for the wines of France." Napoléon was a wine lover to the end. And he was loyal to Jean-Rémy, as always.

Napoléon abdicated the throne of France in early April, and the Russians were briefly in Reims again, celebrating the end of the war in boisterous spirits. Barbe-Nicole had reason to celebrate as well. Russian officers toasting the end of the long campaign toasted with her champagne. Everywhere in the city, "Russian officers . . . lifted the champagne glass to their lips. It was said even that many of them preferred the popping of the bottle of Rheims to the cannon of the Emperor." After long years of war, the British were no less exuberant. Lord Byron wrote to his friend Thomas Moore in the second week of April, "We clareted and champagned till two." Already, champagne was on its way to becoming another word for mass-culture celebration.

Barbe-Nicole was simply glad that the war would soon be over and she would soon be free to gratify the Russian love of fine French wines. "At last the time has come," she said, "when, after the sufferings our town has known, we may breathe freely and hope for a general and permanent peace, and consequently for commercial activity which has stagnated for too long. Thank God I have been spared. My properties and cellars are intact, and I am ready to resume business with all the activity that recent changes will allow."

That the Napoléonic Wars should have ended in the Champagne region is mere happenstance, but it was a pivotal moment in the history of this wine, a moment that forged its cultural identity. Champagne wine was already enjoyed as the drink of festivity. It had been since the earliest days of its history. But a hundred little obstacles had impeded its broad commercial appeal. For centuries, it had been the wine only of the wealthiest and most discerning of connoisseurs, and the total production in France at its prewar height had never been more than four hundred thousand bottles. Within decades of Napoléon's defeat, it would multiply more than tenfold, to over five million.

However much Barbe-Nicole despised Napoléon, his support for the industry and nearly fifteen years of reforms, which had changed everything from the laws of Europe to the condition of roads throughout the empire, made a different future—and her own fame—possible. It was the events that took place that spring in the Champagne, the occasion for half a million soldiers and minor British lords to celebrate the end of an empire with sparkling wine, that transformed champagne into an international cultural phenomenon, rich with universal symbolism and meaning.

Still, when the Russian czar Alexander ordered provisions for a banquet meant to fete three hundred thousand troops at Camp Vertus, the champagne came from the cellars of Jean-Rémy. That even the czar favored her competitor must have been irritating. Perhaps this preference was what focused her energies on getting back to business immediately and recapturing her own share of the Russian market that she and Louis—and François before them—had worked so hard to open.

It would take time to work out the political settlements, but when the end of the war finally came, as she now knew it would, it would be a new beginning for her champagne enterprise. She seized the initiative. By the end of April, even before the peace was yet certain, she had opened her cellars and had returned to work, checking the long rows of casks to see how the vintage had fared, making adjustments and taking notes, and beginning the arduous process of disgorging some of the wines.

If the occupation of Reims had not been a boon, it had not been a disaster, either. "Thanks are due to Heaven," she wrote. "I do not have any losses to regret, and I am too fair to grumble about expenses from which no one will be saved." She sent her workmen back to the vineyards in earnest, all with an eye toward the future, when the trade bans on France would finally be lifted and she could begin shipping her wines again.

Barbe-Nicole was not one to wait passively on fortune, however. She had begun almost instantly planning a daring enterprise, the execution of which would prove to be the greatest gamble of her career. She was at the crossroads of her life, and she knew it. The moment the Bourbon kings of France were restored to the throne, and working in absolute secrecy, with only her trusted salesman, Louis, and their Russian distributor, Monsieur Boissonet, as her conspirators, Barbe-Nicole decided to run the blockades one final time, in advance of the formal restoration of international trade.

As she had discovered that spring, the Russians adored her sweeter, fortified champagnes, and if only she could get her wines there before any of her competitors, there was a nation waiting for its first legal taste of French champagne. It was risky and dangerous, and if she failed, this would be the end.

The stakes could not have been higher. It was a large shipment, and she was sending it without permission or security. She was breaking the law and breaking all the rules of common sense. The plan was to deliver several thousand bottles of champagne by chartered ship, first to the open port of Königsberg (present-day Kalingrad, Russia) and then, the instant the trade ban was lifted, immediately onward the short distance to Russia. If the cargo was discovered traveling without a license, it would be confiscated and destroyed—and much of that amazing vintage of 1811 would be lost forever.

Worse, if her local competitors were to learn of her venture, or if they happened to be plotting one of their own simultaneously, the result would be immediate ruin. Nothing would be more infuriating than Jean-Rémy getting the upper hand in Russia once again. As Barbe-Nicole knew, success depended not just on getting her wines

to Russia but on getting them there first, weeks before other shipments could arrive, when hers would be the only French champagne
available in the ports and markets.

The moment Napoléon abdicated, she began writing letters,
trying to charter a ship in secret. In mid-April came the encouraging news from Louis that Monsieur Rondeaux, a shipping merchant
in Rouen, could help her. There was a ship ready to load her wines
and take them to Russia, if she could get them to Rouen quickly. In
the event Russia was still inaccessible, they had devised elaborate
contingency plans. The wines could surely be sold at Königsberg or
sent on to other ports along the English Channel if needed. She had
learned the lessons from Amsterdam well: Never again would she let
wines go to waste in warehouses.

Louis would travel with the shipment. Her first plan had been
to send six thousand bottles of wine. Then, at the last minute there
were maddening delays. Although the foreign troops had left Reims
and the wines could travel safely, there were few local men able to
help with the cellar work after the long war. "You know," she told
Louis, "our wines must be properly cared for and rebottled before
being shipped and since I have not enough capable workmen to complete this indispensable operation, I must delay deliveries." Finally,
when it came time to load the wines onto the wagon destined for
Paris and then on to Rouen, the final count was 10,550 bottles of
her finest champagne. The news had just arrived that the blockades
on the Baltic ports had been lifted, although bottled French wines
were still banned in Russia.

Still, she was sure that the Russians would welcome her wines.
Soon, other brokers would also be sending shipments. But it might
take them several weeks to arrange a ship, and she had a head start.
It was a race for Russia. Jean-Rémy was already writing to Count
Tolstoy, the grand marshal of the imperial palace in Saint Petersburg, requesting permission to send the czar thirty thousand bottles
of sparkling champagne, and within weeks he would send several
thousand bottles to Russia for the open market, simply on the chance
they would pass customs unimpeded.

On May 20, Louis and the wines left Reims for Paris, on the way to Rouen and the seacoast. The anxiety was at fever pitch. There was no way of knowing if other competitors had come up with the same idea. Perhaps they were already too late. Perhaps the wines would be lost long before they ever reached Russia, victims of uncertain times and a long sea voyage, undertaken far too late in the warm spring season to make any winemaker confident.

Louis would be traveling for weeks with the wines, in harsh conditions, and in Paris he stopped to purchase provisions for the trip, staples like dried ham and biscuits, tea, and apples. He would also need to arrange for his own bed and personal comforts on the ship. Barbe-Nicole was sympathetic. Among the cases of wine, she had also slyly included a present for Louis—some things to feed his "gullet," she told him. It was a hamper filled with small luxuries: one and a half dozen bottles of excellent red wine from nearby Cumières, half a dozen bottles of cognac to warm the chilly evenings, and a small, leather-bound copy of Miguel de Cervantes's *Don Quixote*, the famous Spanish tale of an adventurous knight determined to fight even the most foolhardy battles. Given the risks they were taking and the recklessness of their own adventure, it was a witty present, just Barbe-Nicole's sort of dry humor.

Finally, at eleven o'clock on the night of June 10, Louis and the shipment set sail on the *Zes Gebroeders*, under the command of Captain Cornelius. The crispness of the night air belied what Louis found belowdecks. The ship was infested with lice and vermin, and he was so anxious for the fate of the fragile and pressurized cases of wine rocking in the hold that he determined to sleep on rough nights with the cargo. It could hardly be worse. As Louis knew only too well, the bottles were prone to breakage, and they could shatter with a remarkable force, destroying an entire case at a time.

For the sleepless Louis, it was a long trip. For Barbe-Nicole back home in Reims, the nights and days were even longer. On July 3, nearly a month later, the *Zes Gebroeders* finally crept into the harbor of Königsberg, a Baltic seaport then in Prussian territory. It had been a rough and increasingly warm crossing, and it might already all be over for them. The wines might have burst. Or the changes in the temperature might have caused the wines to go cloudy and ropey. After years of war and terribly depressed sales, there was no margin of error for the company any longer.

The morning when the wines were unloaded dawned stiflingly hot, and Louis opened the first case with a heavy heart. Amazingly, the first bottles that he drew from the packing baskets were absolutely crystalline, and there had been no breakages. It was the same for the second case and the third. Their condition was perfect, "as strong as the wines of Hungary, as yellow as gold, and as sweet as nectar," he wrote. Best of all, "Our ship is the first, in many years, to travel to the North, and from the port of Rouen, filled with the wine of the Champagne."

Their secret ruse had succeeded. None of Barbe-Nicole's competitors had guessed her plan, and the champagne made by the Widow Clicquot created a frenzied competition among purchasers within days of its arrival. Before Louis could have the shipment forwarded to the imperial city of Saint Petersburg—even before the cases were fully unloaded from the *Zes Gebroeders*—clients besieged him at his hotel, begging to be allowed to purchase just a few bottles. On the docks, wine merchants nearly came to blows as the stock apportioned to Königsberg dwindled. With the cunning business acumen that Barbe-Nicole so admired in him, Louis wrote playfully that he was now deliberately playing hard to get and asking prices that she never would have believed possible—an astonishing 5.5 francs a bottle—the equivalent of more than $100 and equal to what she paid her vineyard laborers for an entire week of their backbreaking work.

Learning of their triumph in the dim light of her office, Barbe-Nicole might have brushed a lock of hair back from her cheek and let herself enjoy a slow, broad smile of satisfaction. In that moment, she must have thought about François and about the long summer days when they rode through the fields of the Champagne to inspect the small vineyards at Bouzy or when they simply stopped to look out over the hills in silence. Making this wine had been his dream, and here in front of her was the proof that her faith in that dream had not been wasted. Even Barbe-Nicole could not have dreamed what else was still to come. On this first evening of her success, when she was only just beginning to understand that she was on the verge of something big, something wonderful, she might have indulged her fancy for a moment. Then she put pen to paper, already planning the immediate departure of another shipment of her glorious champagne.

BILLIONAIRE WINOS

Jay McInerney

Their tasting notes would make Robert Parker blush, their thirst would choke a camel, and their pinkies—and noses—are decidedly not in the air. Glass of 1914 Pol Roger, anyone?

Big Boy is standing in the middle of the dining room at Manhattan's three-star Cru restaurant, waving a saber, demanding that everyone shut up and pay attention. It's not easy to shut this crowd up—they've been drinking really expensive wine for four hours, and the adrenaline of big spending is in the air. But Big Boy, aka Rob Rosania, is more than capable of shouting down a roomful of buzzed alpha males. It's his party, and his magnum is bigger than anyone else's magnum. He didn't build a billion-dollar real estate empire by acting like a pussy. Signature sunglasses planted in his curly, dark mane, he's wearing a natty blue Kiton windowpane sports jacket over an open white shirt showing plenty of chest hair, and while he doesn't actually pound his chest, he often gives the impression he's about to. He's in the process of selling off $5 million worth of his wine cellar to the assembled company—plus a few absentee bidders—and even though there are 40 or 50 more lots to go, he wants to celebrate.

After commanding the attention of the room, Rosania hoists a jeroboam of 1945 Bollinger for all to see. Then he lowers the enormous bottle and props it at a 45-degree angle as he prepares to saber it—the most dramatic and traditional method of opening Champagne, certainly no less than a $10,000 bottle deserves, and one that

Rosania has perfected in the several years he's been collecting. For some reason this particular jero (11 more are in the auction) is not cooperating, and it takes Big Boy a few whacks to decapitate it, but no matter. A cheer goes up as the top of the bottle goes flying, and within minutes we're all drinking Bollinger made from grapes that were hanging on their vines when the allies stormed Omaha Beach.

"Shut the fuck up, and let's finish this," says John Kapon, standing a few feet above the crowd, pounding his gavel on the podium like a judge addressing an unruly courtroom. Kapon is the 36-year-old president of Acker Merrall & Condit, which bills itself as America's oldest wine store and has, under his watch, become the world's leading vendor of fine wine at auction. It's not often that you hear an auctioneer address a roomful of well-heeled bidders this way—it's hard to imagine Sotheby's urbane, British-born Jamie Ritchie doing so—but Kapon knows most of the 70 men in the room personally, and the very few women in attendance are accustomed to the high-testosterone world of competitive oenophilia.

The assembled company includes some of the most serious wine collectors on the planet, some of whom have flown in from Europe and the West Coast for this particular auction. None of them remind me of Frasier Crane. Raised pinkies and foppish horticultural analogies have been in short supply all night. Kapon tends to cheerfully mispronounce certain French names; "rock 'n' roll" and "T and A" are among his highest vinous accolades.

The L.A.-based film and television director and philanthropist Jefery Levy is in the process of dropping about $400,000 on vintage Champagne and Burgundy, including a case of '62 Rousseau Chambertin Clos de Bèze for $80,000. Levy has a distinctly Goth look: He's in his customary head-to-toe black, from his shades, formerly owned by Elvis, to his bespoke British crocodile shoes, and when he really wants an auction lot he holds his paddle in the air until Kapon tells him he's bidding against himself. Also in from L.A. is 32-year-old Rudy Kurniawan, who vies with Rosania for the title of MDC (Man with the Deepest Cellar), and is alleged to spend more than a million dollars a month on wine. Kurniawan is from a fabulously wealthy

Chinese family, although his father gave him an Indonesian name to protect his privacy. He is widely believed to have had a major impact on the escalating prices of the fine wine market in the last five years, and the Rosania auction includes some of Rudy's overstock, bottles of Rousseau and Romanée-Conti that would constitute the crown jewels of absolutely anyone else's collection.

While these kinds of multimillion-dollar auctions happen every other week in New York, what made this one—which went down in late April—unusual was the preponderance of old Champagne, a category that was a backwater in the fine wine market until Rosania began collecting it with a vengeance a few years ago after tasting a bottle of 1937 Krug he bought as part of a mixed-case lot. The auction's climax came early on, when two bottles of 1959 Dom Pérignon Rosé—the never commercially released debut vintage—provoked a telephone duel between two European bidders and quickly escalated from the opening price of $6,000. When Kapon slammed his hammer down three minutes and $64,000 later, a new record had been set for Champagne. With the buyer's premium tacked on to the $70,000 hammer price, someone had just paid $85,000 for two 49-year-old bottles of pink bubbly that very few people besides Rosania had ever tasted. The room erupted in cheers and applause. Bear Stearns had collapsed the month before, and the subprime crisis was claiming victims as the dollar continued its precipitous slide, but this and several other spring auctions proved that the market for fine vintage wine remained buoyant.

The celebration lasted till well after two. The exhausted Kapon slipped away. More wine was ordered from Cru's encyclopedic list. Wine director Robert Bohr glided around the room like Jeeves, serenely presiding over the chaos. It had been five hours since we'd finished a three-course meal from chef Shea Gallante, so Big Boy ordered six dozen hot dogs from his favorite East Village stand and six pizzas from Lil' Frankie's, all washed down with an $850 1990 Jaboulet Hermitage La Chapelle.

* * *

A few years ago, I started receiving e-mails detailing bacchanalian gatherings with elaborate tasting notes about wines that most of us could only dream about, sometimes dozens of them: '59 Krugs and '45 Romanée-Contis. It was wine porn spam, which had somehow eluded my filter. The notes were studded with references to Big Boy and King Angry and Hollywood Jef. Who the hell were these guys, I wondered, and why were they drinking so much better than me? The author of the e-mails, I finally learned, was Kapon himself. His fellow Dionysians were members of his tasting group, the Angry Men, which included Rosania, among others. (When I eventually ask why they're called the Angry Men, Kapon shrugs and says "We're New York guys and we don't tolerate bullshit. We're all busting balls and cracking on each other.")

When Kapon joined the business in 1994 after a brief foray into the music business, Acker—established in 1820—was a somewhat sleepy operation doing $4,000,000 a year. (Kapon's father and grandfather had also worked for Acker.) Sotheby's and Christies pretty much had the fine wine auction market to themselves. Like most wine geeks of his generation, Kapon's first love was California Cabernet. The Napa Valley was undergoing a renaissance in the nineties, and the big, ripe, voluptuous, fruit-driven Cabs were easy to love, the vinous equivalent of *Seinfeld*-era Teri Hatcher ("They're real and they're *spectacular*.") So-called cult Cabernets—small production super-extracted wines like Harlan, Colgin, and Bryant Family—were garnering wines 100-point scores from uber-critic Robert Parker and selling for as much as First Growth Bordeaux. (Rosania and Kurniawan also cut their teeth on Napa Cabs—Kurniawan's epiphany wine was a 1995 Opus One Cabernet.) For many serious collectors, these Cabs are the gateway drug that leads them to the hard-core-addictive stuff—first Bordeaux, the motherland of Cabernet Sauvignon, which provided the inspiration for Napa, and then on to the Secret Kingdom that is Burgundy. Like most true geeks, Kapon and his inner circle are Burgundy nuts; at the Rosania auction several people booed when he announced the Bordeaux portion of the sale.

In 1997, Acker sponsored an auction with Phillips de Pury. It and several subsequent auctions, according to Kapon, were a disaster. But he persisted, even as his taste began to shift toward older wines. Sometime in late 2000 or early 2001, Rosania walked into the store on West Seventy-second Street. Neither Kapon nor Rosania can remember the moment exactly, but their meeting would eventually prove to be a milestone in the world of fine wine. Both were around 30. Rosania was a partner in a real estate investment firm, a self-made mogul who was ready to spend some of his growing fortune.

Largely by cultivating young collectors like Rosania and Kurniawan, Kapon has made Acker the leading vendor of fine wines in America, selling more than $60 million a year at auction in the past two years. "John has worked at it," says Peter Meltzer, author of *Keys to the Cellar*, who covers the auction scene for *Wine Spectator*. "I'm very impressed with him. He's really out there. The traditional houses have not been as aggressive. And he really knows what he's doing. He's learned empirically. He will be able to tell you the best vintage of La Tâche tasted in the last five years."

Kapon can talk trash as well as the next Angry Man, but he's a serious taster who, at this point, has probably sampled—and written about—more rare old wines than almost anyone his age on the planet, with the possible exception of Kurniawan and Rosania—wines like the 1870 Mouton or the 1945 Romanée-Conti. And he has the notes to prove it. He knows all the tasting terminology, but he's added some terms of his own, like "whips and chains," which he used recently to describe a young, powerful Champagne, and "vitamins," which seems to refer to the slightly metallic taste of supplement pills. Generally speaking, his notes are livelier than most critics'. Robert Parker may be more influential, while Allen Meadows, author of the newsletter *Burghound*—a friend of Kapon's—is the Pope of Burgundy. But neither of them has tasted some of the rare and old bottles that the Angry Men open at their gatherings, nor do they tend to pronounce upon them so colorfully: "Tighter than a 14-year-old virgin," an Angry Man said of one of Big Boy's Champagnes. "Stinky like the

crack of a 90-year-old nun," another said, nosing a red Burgundy that
was exactly half that age.

Kapon now has his sights set on Asia. This past spring he pre-
sided over an auction at the Island Shangri La ballroom in Hong
Kong that brought in $8.2 million, including $242,000 for a case of
1990 Romanée-Conti, a new record. (One can only hope that the
buyer isn't planning to mix it with Coke or Sprite, as Chinese connoisseurs are alleged to do.) The sale puts Kapon in a good position
to become a leader in the exploding Chinese market.

As for the younger collectors, including Rosania, who are selling, it's hard to say whether they are locking in profits, hedging
against a possible decline, or just editing their collections so they
can buy even more. Probably all of the above. "All I can say is, I've
only seen prices go one way," Kapon says. According to the *Wine
Spectator* Auction Index, worldwide auctions of fine and rare wines
hit a record of $301 million in sales in 2007—a 25 percent increase
over 2006, and 2008 looks as if it may be another record year despite
the deteriorating state of the economy.

Unlike some collectors, this group of Angry Men is drinking as
much as it's hoarding. When I dined with Jef Levy on a recent trip to
Los Angeles, he invited four other friends along to Spago so we could
open more bottles—17 in all, ranging from a 1937 Ausone, which
still had a brooding core of dark fruit, along with a spicy cinnamon
note, to a 1999 La Tâche from Domaine de la Romanée-Conti, with
a flight of Pétrus ('55, '71, and '85) in between. After the first dozen
or so bottles, my writing became hard to read, so I can't tell you much
about the Pétrus. The next night, at Cut, Wolfgang Puck's Beverly
Hills steak house, we limited ourselves to a more modest 12 bottles
going back to the 1929 Haut-Brion.

"Life is short," Rosania says. "You've got to drink it." When
I ask him how many bottles he has in his cellar, he says he has no
idea. When I venture a guess of 50,000, he says, "Hell, I have 50,000
bottles of '96 Champagne." When I tell him that one estimate places
the value of his cellar at $50 million, he shrugs.

Rosania grew up in modest circumstances, and his swaggering mogul manner is tempered by frequent professions of noblesse oblige. "With privilege comes responsibility," he says. (In fact, I've heard him say it four or five times.) After his father died of prostate cancer in 2005, he helped found Mount Sinai Hospital's wine auction. You can't swirl a glass at a Manhattan wine event without hearing testimony to his generosity.

The night before the auction at Cru, I consumed, by my best estimate, some $25,000 to $30,000 worth of Rosania's wine—including the 1945 Mouton and the 1947 Cheval Blanc, two legendary Bordeaux, the former marked by a signature mintiness and the latter so sweet and rich that it reminds people of Port—and I was one of 14 drinkers. And who other than Rosania could tell you that 1914 Pol Roger is one of the greatest Champagnes ever made, much less prove it by pulling it from his cellar and serving it, as he did the night before the auction? For once, the Angry Men seemed stunned nearly to silence.

Considering the age of these wines, it's amazing that most of the ones we tasted were brilliantly preserved, even as they acted their age. Poor storage can result in duds—Champagnes that have turned to sherry and red Burgs that have turned to vinegar.

Then there are the fakes. No one likes to talk about them, any more than swingers like to talk about STDs. But, just as hot art markets breed forgeries, the inexorable rise of the wine market has inevitably created a demand for counterfeit bottles. No one really knows how widespread the problem is, although anyone who has tasted enough will have come up against it. The first time I was aware of the problem was seven or eight years ago when I tasted a suspiciously fruity magnum of 1947 Pétrus, an extremely rare and prized Bordeaux, while dining at the home of Jancis Robinson, one of the world's leading wine critics. After the wealthy friend who'd brought the bottles went home, I asked Jancis if she really thought the wine, which tasted remarkably young and fresh to me, was a '47 Pétrus. "It certainly didn't seem to be," she said diplomatically. I've since heard about a lot of suspicious mags of '47 Pétrus. Given the vineyard's tiny production and the unusual nature of the magnum format, there shouldn't be more than a very few floating around these days.

Needless to say, it's generally the most legendary wines that are being faked, like the '45 Mouton or the '47 Cheval. During the marathon with Levy in Los Angeles, we encountered at least one bottle that was obviously a fake (sent to our table by another collector). One of the reasons that Rosania's Champagne auction attracted such interest was because of its aura of authenticity: Big Boy had purchased most of the stuff from the original buyers in Europe, and the market for vintage Champagne is so undeveloped that nobody has yet bothered to fake the stuff. As for Bordeaux and Burgundy, no one knows how many fraudulent bottles are residing in multimillion-dollar cellars around the world, though sometimes we get a clue.

Recently, billionaire collector William Koch filed a string of lawsuits against dealers and vendors who sold him bottles that were reputedly fakes (see *The Billionaire's Vinegar*, a recent book by Benjamin Wallace), including Eric Greenberg, an Internet consulting ex-billionaire who allegedly sold some 17,000 bottles in an October 2005 Zachys auction. Koch says that before Greenberg went to Zachys, his collection was first rejected by Sotheby's on the grounds that too many bottles were fakes. Acker subsequently held a major auction from Greenberg's so-called Golden Cellar (as opposed to Kurniawan's which is referred to as *The* Cellar).

So far, Kapon has largely managed to stay above the fray, in part, he says, by doing his homework. For the Golden Cellar auction last October, Kapon rejected lots that he found suspect and attached an unprecedented 80 pages of documentation to the catalog. "All the great collections in this country have lemons," he says. "You've got to navigate around them." More recently, he withdrew 22 lots of Kurniawan's Ponsot Burgundy—one of the region's most legendary domains—from the Rosania auction at the last minute after questions were raised about its authenticity.

A few weeks after the Big Boy auction, Kapon agreed to meet me at Veritas, the Flatiron District restaurant that vies with Cru for

the title of Wine Geek Central. Although Cru is his headquarters, Kapon is clearly a regular here and is treated as a visiting dignitary. He arrived with his new girlfriend, Dasha Vlasenko, a statuesque Estonian-born former model several inches taller than him who works in real estate. Kapon, who is in the middle of a divorce from his first wife, met Dasha at a party recently. She took a little while to warm up to him. "He was really persistent," she says.

Kapon, who'd put together five auctions in the space of two months, looked a little ragged, pale, and slightly puffy-faced with a three-day growth. He quickly ordered a $450 1996 Drouhin Marquis de Laguiche Montrachet, a rare white Burgundy, and filled me in on his schedule. Less than three weeks after the Rosania auction, he was busy preparing three more to take place within the month, including the Hong Kong auction. Fans of Kapon's wine porn have bemoaned the fact that he's weeks behind posting his tasting notes, but it doesn't seem like he'll catch up anytime soon. His Hong Kong schedule sounds particularly daunting, at least for his liver, including dinners at which he will be inducted into the Commanderie de Bordeaux, a major Chéteau Pichon-Lalande dinner, and yet another devoted to the wines of the Domaine de la Romanée-Conti.

After we polished off the Montrachet, Kapon ordered a $550 1998 Mugnier Musigny Grand Cru, a rare bottle from another legendary Burgundy vineyard that we both liked a great deal and should have been the wine of the night, except that by the time our second course arrived we'd finished it. So John ordered yet another bottle, a 1971 Roumier Morey-St.-Denis Clos de la Bussière, which as a premier cru, is lower in the hierarchy than the Musigny. But it blew the youngster away. In his newsletter, Kapon later observed of the $425 wine, "autumnal aromas were inviting like football season, and meat dripped from its bones like parking lot cookouts."

Halfway through the '71, Kapon spotted Danny DeVito across the room and asked the sommelier to send him a glass. From our vantage we could see that he was drinking a Colgin Cabernet—very serious juice, if not quite Burgundy. "I don't know if he's a Burgundy man," I said.

"Hey, just open up and say *Ahh*," Kapon said. "You don't have to know it to love it."

And sure enough, a few minutes later, DeVito hoisted the glass aloft and waved Kapon over to his table. I felt like somebody should warn the actor that Burgundy can be extremely addictive and that he was talking to the head pusher man. But it was too late. When Kapon finally returned to our table, 20 minutes later, he had the self-satisfied air of a priest who's made a new convert.

THE 1982 BORDEAUX

Elin McCoy

For many successful people, a singular event catapults them suddenly into a new future. It's as if while they were driving slowly along a highway to their eventual destination something caused them, almost miraculously, to shoot off onto another, faster route, a shortcut to stardom. The watershed event for Parker's career as a wine critic was the 1982 vintage in Bordeaux. Luck had much to do with what happened. Or as Parker would later put it, "Fate smiled on me."

During his flight back to the United States from France on March 21, 1983, Parker worried obsessively that his plane might crash. Though not usually anxious when flying, he was bursting with his first big wine story. He wanted to lean forward in his seat, willing himself closer to the United States and the next issue of *The Wine Advocate*, in the same way he habitually leans forward over the steering wheel when driving from winery to winery in eager anticipation of the next wine. Convinced that the red wines made in Bordeaux in 1982, which he'd tasted during the previous week, were "very great" and the vintage one of the finest of the twentieth century, he was panicky at the thought that if the plane went down he would miss his chance to write about it. He'd crammed his black notebook with notes on dozens of wines. Superlatives studded every page: "stunning," "blockbuster," "prodigious," "incredible," "fantastic," "heavyweight," and more. Parker was champing at the bit to let his readers in on what he considered the greatest wine buys since he'd started tasting wine in 1968.

*   *   *

At the time the world's wine countries still formed a long-accepted hierarchy of quality, like tiers of angels in medieval theology. France resided at the top, of course, and three of its regions—Bordeaux, Burgundy, and Champagne—stood above all others, not just representing wine at its best, but also bestowing status on their buyers, marking them as people blessed with refined taste—and plenty of money. Among this holy triumverate, Bordeaux held primacy of place in the minds (and cellars) of the world's wine collectors. It produced more fine wine than any other region on earth and it was the most aristocratic. Where else could you find so many grey stone châteaux with fairy-tale turrets (and sometimes moats) surrounded by vineyards? The wines of its most important subregion, the Médoc, had been organized and classified into five categories of status (and price)—first through fifth growths—in the mid-nineteenth century. (Only one wine from a commune outside the Médoc couldn't be ignored; the famous Château Haut-Brion in Graves, praised by Thomas Jefferson, had been included as a first growth.) With few exceptions the original rankings of the sixty-one châteaux in that famous 1855 classification had remained intact over 125 years, and a wine's position in it still determined much of its reputation for quality and its price.

Back then, what the harvest was like for Bordeaux was the general bellwether for every new vintage everywhere. Too bad for Italy's Piemont or Spain's Rioja if they had a great vintage when Bordeaux had a poor one. Most of the world assumed their wines from that year were poor, too. History, mystique, and a strong publicity machine combined to elevate Bordeaux to the forefront of everyone's wine consciousness.

The grand properties in the most important communes, or appellations, of the Médoc's boringly flat landscape on the Left Bank (west) of the Gironde estuary—Margaux, St-Julien, Pauillac, and St.-Estèphe—and a few historic ones in Graves, south of the city of Bordeaux, were large and appeared cold and intimidating; they gave "an impression of class, stability, reliability, elegance, permanence, tradition, and unimpeachable status," as American importer Kermit Lynch once put it. But behind the staid serene facades lay the snobbery, rivalries, and intrigue typical of a tightly closed, class-ridden society and a greed-driven merchant mentality. Since Parker, like so many Americans from middle-class backgrounds, was a self-proclaimed egalitarian with few aspirations to move up the social ladder, it was particularly ironic that his initial step to star critic status would result from celebrating a great vintage in this, the most aristocratic of wine regions.

In fact, Parker loved the wines from the great châteaux in the Médoc and Graves and found some of the proprietors he'd met charming, congenial company. But with few exceptions he regarded the scores of smaller, more modest châteaux and properties in the less-celebrated Bordeaux communes of St.-Emilion and tiny Pomerol on the Right Bank of the Gironde as far more friendly, casual, and welcoming. Most of the warm, generously rich wines from Pomerol had barely been known in England and America before the 1960s, though they had found a ready market in Belgium. After Graves had established its own, less elaborate system of ranking in 1953, St.-Emilion followed in 1955; Pomerol had no system at all. Perhaps that was one reason many wine lovers considered the elegant wines of the Médoc the true aristocrats of Bordeaux, even if the top St.-Emilion château, Cheval Blanc, and later Château Ausone and Pomerol's star, Château Pétrus, were often spoken of in the same hushed tones as the top wines of the Left Bank. In the Médoc of the 1970s, each château's ranking put its owner into a social pecking order. Alexis Lichine once observed to me that owners of first growths only dined with owners of other first growths, and so on down the ranks; he, an American, prided himself on being invited to dine with them all. The official first growths— Châteaux Margaux, Lafite-Rothschild, Latour, Haut-Brion, and Mouton-Rothschild, which had been elevated to this elite group in 1973—often behaved like an exclusive club, meeting occasionally in Paris to discuss prices, but the rivalry among them, as among the best second growths, remained intense. (Not, however, as bitter as it had once been, when Baron Philippe de Rothschild of Mouton reportedly stooped to such petty acts as serving bottles of his cousin Baron Elie de Rothschild's Lafite with spicy curried rice at an important lunch to make sure it didn't outshine Mouton.) Each first growth wanted his wine to be recognized as the best, and all took their exalted rank in the world of wine with great seriousness.

In the past, Parker had observed firsthand at Château Mouton-Rothschild what he termed the staff's "inexcusably arrogant and condescending" attitude toward foreigners. Of the illustrious proprietors of the Médoc first growths, only one, Laura Mentzelopoulos of Château Margaux, met personally with Parker in March 1983. He had to make do with the *maîtres de chai*, the cellarmasters. But for the most part, he preferred it that way. On the Right Bank, in Pomerol, on the other hand, Christian Moueix welcomed him at Petrus, and, as he had before, shared his passion for and opinions on wine.

Bordeaux also owed its exalted position to the fact that its wines evolved and developed complexity with bottle age, and could, in great vintages, last for decades. That, plus widespread acceptance of the classification system as a guide to quality and the notion of the "château" as a mark of status, would make the wines blue-chip investments that could be held and traded internationally, creating a virtual stock market of wine. Last but not least, the wines appealed intellectually to wine lovers and connoisseurs. Small differences of soil and climate from appellation to appellation and vineyard to vineyard, the slightly different proportions of related grape varieties in each version of the classic blend, and the effects of ever-changing weather on each vintage translated into subtle and complex variations of flavor and aroma in the wines, creating endless possibilities for fascinating tasting comparisons and discussions—to determine the personality of wines from a particular appellation, like Margaux or St.-Julien, for example, or to understand how the vagaries of weather had marked the different vintages at several châteaux. Bordeaux offered endless scope for quibbling, wrangling, and lively debates among critics, connoisseurs, and collectors; the best wines were not just for drinking but also for thinking and talking about. Bordeaux lovers had their own ideas of which châteaux belonged in which tier of quality, and their choices often related to their own ideas of what the styles of Bordeaux should be. In the past couple of decades the 1855 classification system, perhaps inevitably, had come under attack. Many of the most knowledgeable wine writers in England had weighed in with their own revised classifications, just as Alexis Lichine had, based on their perceptions of contemporary quality, and their demotions and elevations of various châteaux fueled endless debates. But few questioned Bordeaux's stature as the pinnacle of wine quality.

For Parker, Bordeaux had become an ongoing motif, a signature concern that he had raised in his first issue of *The Wine Advocate* as well as in his first interview. Yes, he critiqued wines from all countries and regions, but in the first five years of his newsletter, Parker had returned to criticize Bordeaux again and again and again, as if obsessed with communicating his judgment on which of these grand wines were and were not living up to their reputations. In 1983, it turned out to be the right obsession with the right place at the right time for the American consumer as well as the Bordeaux trade. The way the wines were ranked, made, and sold practically begged for someone like Parker to reassure wine-phobic Americans so the Bordelais could make big inroads into the lucrative growing American market. His rise to power was intimately tied to Bordeaux.

Since 1978, Parker had traveled to Bordeaux twice a year, always spending a week or two there during the annual rite of spring in March when the châteaux welcomed merchants and a handful of journalists into their cellars to taste the wines from the previous fall's harvest in barrel. Basically this was a sales preview for the trade to assess the quality of the vintage and determine demand for the wines, and the first part of the *en primeur*, or futures, campaign. Once the châteaux released their *en primeur* prices, usually starting in April, the merchants would decide what and how much of the new vintage to buy and figure out where they would sell it.

Wandering from château to château tasting great wines sounds glamorous; images of posh hotels, charming old winemakers, and fabulous food and seductive rare wines at long, polished tables in elegant château dining rooms with aristocratic owners in black tie come to mind. But to Parker it was a hectic business trip, and he packed his schedule. His time was all too limited. For convenience he and Pat usually checked into the modern Novotel in Bordeaux Le Lac, a nondescript industrial suburb 9 kilometers north of the city. With its bland but comfortable décor, modern bathrooms, and convenient parking, Novotel (then $38 a night for two) resembled an American-style motel on an interstate highway, surrounded by an anonymous business center and industrial park. From Parker's point of view it offered easy access to the highways circling the city. The exit for the D 2 north to the Médoc was minutes away; Graves was a quick drive south; and conveniently to the east, across the Gironde on the Right Bank, lay St.-Emilion and Pomerol.

That year only a few American journalists besides Parker came to taste the wines in barrel; among them were two major wine critics, Bob Finigan and Terry Robards. A former financial reporter at the *New York Times*, Robards had recently been forced to resign from the *Time's* wine column over a perceived conflict of interest, but now wrote for the *New York Post*; he would soon be named a columnist for *The Wine Spectator*. For most wine writers there was no point in going. The only consumers who cared about detailed notes on individual wines were those fanatics who intended to purchase the wines while they were still aging in French cellars, as wine futures. A few of the largest big-city retailers in America offered them, but since the crisis of the Bordeaux market in the mid-1970s, demand for futures had never rebounded. Besides, analyzing a young Bordeaux in barrel and envisaging accurately what it would become a year and a half later when bottled—much less a decade hence—was thought to require long experience and a professionally trained palate. A *maître de chai*, for example, barrel-tasted his wine hundreds of times, regularly checking its progress from the moment the grape juice fermented into wine until it was finally bottled. A mouthful of raw, unfinished wine typically tasted mouth-scouring; its unpleasant, harsh tannins dominated, but with guidance a professional learned to look beyond that and assess the wine's underlying balance, concentration, and fruit, and its potential quality.

For consumers, wine futures worked a little like financial futures and could be a risky business. You put your money down (a few retailers charged only 50 percent in advance) to reserve a case of wine at a fixed price. If the wine increased in value between then and when you picked it up two years later, after it had been bottled and shipped, you saved money, sometimes a lot of money. As an investment wine could outperform many stocks. The 1975 Château Lafite had sold for $150 to $160 a case as futures; by the time the bottled wine reached New York, it cost triple that, and by 1983 that same case traded for as much as $1,200. But if prices didn't increase, or the exchange rate wasn't in your favor, tying up your capital made no sense. On the other hand, if you didn't purchase top wines produced in tiny quantities when they first hit the market, you might not be able to get your hands on them at all.

The futures market was part of the unique way Bordeaux wines were sold. The châteaux that produced the wine were the highly visible part of Bordeaux, the one that wine-lovers were aware of. The other, more hidden world, was *la place de Bordeaux*, an almost byzantine commercial network of several hundred *négociants*, or merchants, and *courtiers*, or brokers, who sustained the *en primeur* system. The *en primeur* campaign resembled a game, and it worked like this: Each spring the châteaux sold anywhere from 50 to 90 percent of their wines from the previous year's harvest, which was still in barrel, to *négociants*. Acting as diplomatic intermediaries between the châteaux and the *négociants* were the *courtiers*, who put together the deals by acting as brokers to both. The *négociants* kept a (usually) small percentage for stock and sold the rest to importers, who quickly unloaded it to distributors and retailers, who then offered it to consumers. All this was only on paper—nothing more than a sales slip or a contract—as the wines weren't even bottled. The benefits of the system to the châteaux were obvious—immediate cash flow, worldwide distribution two years before the wines were even shipped, and the guarantee that *négociants* would buy even in not-so-good vintages to make sure they would receive allocations of a certain number of cases in the best years. It was left to the *négociants* to build up markets for the wine.

Over the centuries speculation had thrived (as it still does), and during the eighteenth, nineteenth, and much of the twentieth century *négociants* and *courtiers* grew rich and powerful. During that time *négociants* stored the purchased wine in barrel in their own enormous cellars, looking after its development or *élévage*, until it was ready for bottling. Then they bottled, sold, and shipped it. But their power began to diminish around 1970, when all the important châteaux started bottling their own wines, and even further after the market collapse in the mid-1970s, when many went broke. Where once *négociants* held on to huge stocks of wine, only a few now held any, and most functioned essentially as traders or distributors, often specializing in particular markets—Europe, Asia, and United Kingdom supermarket chains.

In this highly complex system, prices and sales were affected and sometimes distorted by many factors, including the quality of the vintage, the size of the crop, strong demand in one country, the state of the world economy, a particular château's reputation, popularity in a specific market, buzz, and gossip. The prices were set by the château owners, who wanted to make as much money as possible—certainly as much as, if not more than, their neighbors. Setting the correct initial price was extremely important, since each player in the chain had to make money. The *négociants'* main concern was to sell all the wines they'd purchased worldwide and make a profit, and they had a much better grasp of the effect of market factors than the châteaux did.

After the 1982 vintage, a new and powerful factor, Robert Parker, entered the mix through an opening in the system.

Since consumers couldn't taste before they bought futures, how did they know whether and what to buy? In England, wine lovers relied on trusted wine merchants who acted as both importers and retailers and had usually tasted the wines. Their lists and descriptions went out to their best customers after they'd decided what to buy from the *négociants*. The situation in the United States was more complicated, a result of liquor license regulations put into place after Repeal. Importers who had tasted the wines had little connection with the general consumer. Instead in most states they had to sell to distributors, who sold to retailers, who sold to consumers. But unlike England, America didn't have a tradition of trusted wine merchants. Added to that was the fact that few retailers—even among those who knew something about wine—had experience with futures. After some of the terrible wines retailers had pushed in the 1970s, few wine lovers had faith in what retailers said. When in doubt they fell back on the best wines in the 1855 classification. A few serious wine lovers happily turned to independent experts like Finigan and Parker.

The *en primeur* market was moribund. Several of the recent vintages had been very good, but everyone was waiting for a truly great vintage that could excite the fickle but rich Americans and once again convince them to buy futures in quantity. To the Bordelais, the 1982 vintage looked like the answer to a prayer.

In wine, timing is everything. Wine begins as grapes, an agricultural product heavily dependent on nature's whims. They need the right weather at exactly the right time to make great wine. From June until October grape growers in Bordeaux scan the skies, tune in the forecast, pray for sun, and worry about rain and hail. A comparison with previous growing conditions is never far from their minds; this is the way they predict what the style and quality of the wines might be. In 1982, the weather was ideal at two critical points, and this made all the difference.

The first was "flowering"—the crucial period when vine blossoms produce grape bunches. Sunny skies and warm temperatures quite early in June provided the perfect conditions for a successful and early flowering, which indicated, if all went well, an early harvest. Since rain would arrive eventually in the fall, the grapes were more likely to have been picked before then. With an early flowering, you were already ahead of the game.

By the end of June, the number of healthy-looking bunches of infant grapes predicted a large crop and therefore an immense amount of wine. Endless rain and gray days over the summer and at harvest would mean thin, light wines, while dry, warm weather would mean ripe grapes with dark skins and very, very good wines. But how good? July was very hot, and wine growers softly voiced the opinion that a little rain to cool the vines down wouldn't be so bad. August was cloudy and warm. Expectations rose. The last part of the growing season, as usual, was a time of suspense. In September, during a three-week burst of intense heat and a number of days when the temperature exceeded 100 degrees, the skins of the grapes darkened and their sugar content soared to record levels. High sugar translates into high alcohol in the wine, and in some of the resulting wines it reached an amazing high of 13.5 percent, a level then more typical of warm California than cool, rainy Bordeaux. The sweltering Mediterranean days were alleviated only by a gusty hot wind that dehydrated the grapes, producing extraordinary concentration. This final burst of warm weather turned an excellent year into an extraordinary one. As consulting oenologist Michel Rolland remembers it, "Everything came at the right moment. They were the best grapes I had ever seen in my life."

All red Bordeaux are blends of two or more grapes in the Cabernet family, which includes Cabernet Sauvignon, Merlot, Cabernet Franc, Petit Verdot, and Malbec. Tannic Cabernet Sauvignon dominates blends on the Left Bank, while plump, plush Merlot is key in Pomerol and St.-Emilion, along with fragrant Cabernet Franc. The Merlot, as always, ripened first, which meant that on the Right Bank châteaux began picking on September thirteenth, one of the earliest harvest dates ever. On the Left Bank, Mouton-Rothschild, anxious to get the grapes in quickly before rain fell and diluted their flavor, hired six hundred pickers, who worked feverishly in torrid heat to bring in the crop in a week instead of the usual three. By the time heavy rain fell on October fifth, the grapes at most properties had already been crushed and the sweet red juice was safely hissing and bubbling wildly in fermentation vats. The weather was so hot that some smaller proprietors had trouble keeping the huge amount of fermenting wine from overheating dangerously; many *maîtres de chai*, even at estates with modern equipment, slept fitfully in the cellar so they could monitor vat temperatures and avoid disaster. Some resorted to setting big blocks of ice on top of the fermenters—even, it was said, throwing them right into the vats (illegal, as it amounted to watering down the wine). The bonanza of grapes coming in all at once put many proprietors in a panic. Some didn't have enough vats to ferment their crushed grapes. The new owner of first-growth Château Margaux, Laura Mentzelopoulos, desperate to find additional fermenters to handle the overflow, phoned her neighbor Alexis Lichine to see if he knew of any that could be had.

Fermentation transforms the sweet grape juice into drier, more complex-flavored wine; the natural yeasts on the grapes convert the sugar to alcohol. The riper the grapes, the more powerful the wine they make, and in 1982 everyone agreed they were absolutely perfectly ripe. As long as they didn't get out of control, the high temperatures during fermentation would ensure that more color, flavor, and tannin would be extracted, giving the wine more of everything. Tasting his raw young wine, the owner of Château Monbousquet waxed lyrical. It was fantastic, he told the *New York Times*, "like jam. . . . like mashed fruit in your mouth."

Soon the wine was transferred into small oak barrels, where it would age for twelve to twenty-four months. By the time Parker arrived in March, many proprietors had already performed the *assemblage*, selecting the individual barrels they planned to combine to make the final *grand vin*. Other barrels would go to make a château's second wine, if they had one, or be sold off in bulk to beef up bottles of shipper wine labeled simply Bordeaux.

The word on the presumed stellar quality of the 1982 vintage had already gone out from the château owners and the trade, as if from on high, and a then little-known French wine writer, Michel Bettane, went so far as to call it the finest since 1929. But did it deserve all the shouting? Parker closely followed the publicity and pondered the question in his office, driving to and from work, and while he and Pat ate dinner at home. The "vintage of a century" claim from the French had been repeated so often in the past fifteen years it was like the story of the boy who cried wolf.

For one thing, Parker knew that often in the greatest vintages of the past, like 1961, the harvest of grapes had been small. It was as if there was only so much lusciousness and richness in any one year and with a small crop, all of it would be concentrated, guaranteeing that the flavor of the wine would be powerful and intense and that the wines would last and last. But the yield per acre in 1982 had been immense, usually a sign that the flavor would be diluted. Still, Professor Émile Peynaud, the famous oenologist and then consultant to forty châteaux, had told Terry Robards of the *New York Times* in December that growers had never before seen "such a level of richness and quantity together." Peynaud compared 1982 to the few canon- ized vintages of the twentieth century 1961, 1959, 1949, and 1947.

Parker admired Peynaud and could hardly wait to taste the wines and decide for himself.

Parker's schedule during his exhausting but exhilarating days in Bordeaux was tight; his first appointments were promptly at 9 A.M. Once worried about his ability to rise early enough to hold a 9-to-5 job, Parker was out of bed at 7:30. He tried to get a solid eight hours' sleep, but sometimes he was bleary-eyed from a restless night in a too-soft hotel bed. He hit the road by 8:30 for eleven- to twelve-hour days of intensive tastings and interviews that rarely ended before 7:30 P.M. On a typical day he visited three châteaux by noon, starting on the hour and allotting forty-five minutes each to taste the 1982, retaste the 1981 and 1980, and ask questions; it was the wine critic's version of the psychoanalyst's fifty-minute hour. Sometimes he lunched at a château where he also tasted, then rushed on to work his way through fifty to one hundred or more samples from a variety of châteaux in a *négociant's* office, as people in the trade did, or went on to more châteaux. Appointments occasionally continued well into the evening. Always in a hurry, Parker bragged that he drove "at a speed that would make macho French actor Jean-Paul Belmondo proud." Frequently he tumbled into bed after midnight and fell asleep looking forward to the same schedule the following day.

It didn't take Parker long to decide he completely agreed with Peynaud. He'd "never tasted so many super-rich, opulent, dramatic wines that had obviously been produced from very ripe, jammy fruit." Cellars in Bordeaux, as everywhere, are damp and cold. In winter months the awful, penetrating cold seeps into your feet and up through your bones until it sets your teeth chattering. March can be one of those times, a raw month with grey skies and rain. But Parker was in heaven standing by the fat barrels stained with wine, happily inhaling the tantalizing strong, sweet smell of aging wine, and he watched with mounting enthusiasm as *maîtres de chai* dipped their pipettes into the barrels and sucked up the amazingly dark, rich-looking red liquid, then dribbled it into his waiting glass. Parker swirled, sniffed, sucked in, and spit the samples onto the cellar floor as beaming *maîtres de chai* looked on. Down in the small black notebook went his notes, with a score range next to them. These were the most thrilling barrel samples he'd ever tasted. Everywhere Parker inquired about the growing season, the harvest, fermentation, and vinification. Pat tasted, too, pulled her coat tighter, and translated.

In Pomerol, at minuscule Château Pétrus, Parker thought their 1982 "was the most perfect and symmetrical wine" he had ever tasted. He was "still staggered" by its sensational quality an hour later. No wonder tall, thoughtful, intense Christian Moueix, the manager and son of one of the château's two owners, told him that the wine "is my legacy . . . the greatest wine" he had ever made. From the first, Parker thought it would probably become *The Wine Advocate's* first 100-point wine, his highest accolade. It reminded him of the glorious 1947, the only wine he'd ever rated 99+.

Many welcomed Parker and Pat with open arms, happy to spread the word to America of the greatness of the vintage. Parker told everyone he wanted to learn, and both château owners and *négociants* were eager to help. At Château Ducru-Beaucaillou, a second-growth St.-Julien that Parker had praised many times in print, the modest owner, Jean-Eugène Borie, poured his 1975, '76, '78, and '81 for

Parker to compare with the 1982 to illustrate just how special and different the vintage was. At first-growth Château Margaux, the grandest and most magnificent château in the Médoc, with its Doric columns and long avenue lined with trees, the final assemblage had not yet been done. Nevertheless the estate manager, Philippe Barré, and Laura Mentzelopoulos, whose late grocery magnate husband had bought the château in 1977, let him taste from several different barrels of Cabernet Sauvignon and Merlot to form his opinion. Parker had been critical of Château Mouton-Rothschild, another first growth, in recent issues of *The Wine Advocate*, so he was pleased when they brought out a sample. He thought it "legendary . . . a wine that will develop into a Mouton of monumental proportions." Raoul Blondin, the venerable cellarmaster dressed in worker's blues and a beret, ranked it with the 1947 and 1961. But at first-growth Château Lafite-Rothschild and Château Latour, Parker was told that only staff were permitted to try the new wine before it was sold. Piqued, he attributed their refusal to "nervousness."

Only a few hours after his plane from France landed at JFK airport, Parker sat in the Pool Room at New York's Four Seasons restaurant at their eighth annual California Barrel Tasting Dinner, surrounded by the crème de la crème of the U.S. wine world: press, winemakers, retailers, and a sprinkling of celebrities. The lavish extravaganza designed to showcase the new vintage of California's state-of-the-art wines, in this case the 1982, had been launched in 1976, and it had become the single most important event on the New York wine calendar. Attending was de rigueur for the city's wine writers and editors; I'd been to most of these events but Parker, rooted in Maryland, never had.

The five-hour dinner required serious gastronomic stamina, never a problem for Parker; six wines, including three barrel samples, accompanied each of the seven courses, and then came dessert. Everyone drank too much; Paul Kovi and Tom Margittai, the owners of the restaurant, frowned on spitting out wine during dinner. Between courses we all circulated to trade wine gossip, which was at least as important as assessing the wines. Word that Parker was just back from tasting the 1982 vintage in Bordeaux rippled around the room, and like many others, John and I were eager to hear his opinion on the wines. How good were they? "Phenomenal! They're great!" Parker enthused, as a few people clustered to hear. I told him we'd just chatted with Robert Finigan, who'd also tasted in Bordeaux and didn't like the wines at all.

Parker had never met Finigan. After we introduced the two of them they chatted politely about the 1982 vintage; Finigan was distinctly cool and aloof. Parker could hardly believe what he was hearing: that Finigan considered the vintage overrated, that he'd tasted dozens of poor wines. The encounter remained vivid in Parker's memory for years. He remembered wondering what Finigan could have tasted, and thinking, "If he really writes that, he's gotta be a fool." The paranoid idea crossed Parker's oversensitive mind that he was the "young guy" and that the more established Finigan was trying to shake his confidence.

Finigan had already committed his thoughts on the 1982s to paper; his March thirtieth newsletter would soon be on its way to subscribers. He doesn't remember meeting Parker that night at all.

The exchange certainly didn't alter Parker's initial view of the 1982s, though he planned to retaste in June just to make sure. Supremely confident of his opinion, he devoted most of his April eleventh issue to a preview report that amounted to a hymn of praise. In the first paragraph he urged his readers to "stock up on some sensational Bordeaux wines." He argued that the buying power of a strong dollar (the exchange rate was a high seven francs to the dollar) and the singular greatness of the vintage—the best since 1961—had created the best opportunity wine consumers had had in the last twenty years. Prices remained reasonable so far because of several good vintages—1978, '79, and '81—still in the pipeline. He put together his analysis of reasons to buy 1982 futures as if he were arguing a major legal case that he knew he couldn't lose.

Compared to average vintages, the 1982s were atypical. But then, most great vintages in Bordeaux were. It was unusual to have

both a huge crop and such concentrated wines. Their high alcohol content, especially in Pomerol, and their ripeness and intensity
of taste reminded many, including Parker, of big, fruity California
Cabernet Sauvignons. Plus they were slightly lower than normal
in acidity. Typical "classically structured" young Bordeaux usually
tasted harsh, tannic, and even unpleasant in barrel, but the tannin
in these wines was covered with so much fruity lushness—Alexis
Lichine called it "puppy fat"—that they were attractive to drink right
from the start. That raised questions about their ageability—one of
the hallmarks of a truly great vintage—as if only Bordeaux mouth-
puckeringly awful in youth could amount to anything later. Even
some in Bordeaux expressed reservations, but Parker confidently
predicted they would age beautifully.

     "Certainly your financial condition will dictate what you decide
to do," he wrote, but "any serious wine enthusiast will want to latch
on to some of these wines now or two years from now." He entertained no doubts.

Parker's opinion of the 1982 Bordeaux jump-started his rise. His
rival Robert Finigan's opinion of the same vintage would trigger his
decline. Finigan first mentioned the potential of the 1982s very briefly
(and positively) in the September 30, 1982 issue of his newsletter,
then again in November, when he reported that producers like Jean-
Pierre Moueix and Alexis Lichine were "rhapsodic about it." Setting
off in early March for a "quick but intensive tasting trip," Finigan
was confident that the wines would be great. The only question in
his mind was how great.

     Although he usually had barrel samples collected and brought
to a couple of central locations so he could taste more efficiently, no
one had yet released their samples to the trade, so Finigan was forced
to slog from château to château, "cajoling" tastes from proprietors
and cellarmasters by promising he would not print notes on certain
wines as prices had not yet been set. After dutifully swirling, sniffing, sipping, and spitting more than fifty wines, "I was startlingly

underwhelmed by most of what I tasted," he wrote in his March 30, 1983 issue. He'd found the wines "disappointing," and even worse, "oafish"; they were too alcoholic, he said, and had little flavor concentration. His assessment: "No—the proverbial thousand times no—it was not the 'vintage of the century.'" While not giving up completely on the wines, he cautioned, "I wouldn't rush out and commit serious dollars in the '82 futures market."

Strong words, and there were more. Finigan called the year "something bizarre," the wines "very odd," and suggested that his readers consider buying instead the "supple and charming" 1980s and "brilliant" 1981s.

When Parker saw a copy of the issue, he thought, "He doesn't know what he's talking about."

Parker arrived in Bordeaux a skeptic and left converted; Finigan came expecting greatness and went away disillusioned. The accounts of the two critics' trips and their reaction to the 1982s revealed their profound differences, as personalities, tasters, and writers.

Parker's prose hummed with energy, excitement, and passion. It was punctuated with exclamation points and grand pronouncements. "I predict 1982 will go down in the annals of Bordeaux wine history," he wrote, adding, "Make no mistake about these 1982s, they are destined to be some of the greatest wines produced in this century," underlining these pronouncements for dramatic emphasis. He described the wines as "profound," "opulent," "fleshy," "chewy," "ripe," "spicy," "rich," "viscous," "big," and "breathtaking," almost tasting them for you, and listed thirty as exceptional or extraordinary. He passed on proprietors' opinions, dropping names. His overwhelming love of these big, rich wines and pleasure in tasting jumped off the page. Never mind that once the wines were in bottle they would taste quite different from these unfinished barrel samples, and that predicting how they would age was chancy at best. Parker threw caution to the winds.

Finigan, on the other hand, came across as a weary judge, intent on impressing his readers with his importance as an insider and his critical powers. Tasting the wines, he wrote, "was no easy task," possible only because of personal contacts "who had come to trust him over the years," as samples were being "carefully guarded." He let his readers know what a tedious chore it was to drive from château to château. Everything was secretive: he gave no names of what he tasted or to whom he talked; some proprietors, he intimated, were "privately less than passionate on behalf of the '82 reds," though he declined to name names. The wines were "diffuse" and "short," hardly what he expected from a great vintage.

Appraising the vintage as a whole and waiting to characterize individual wines much later was the traditional way of writing up the wines of a new vintage, and in this Finigan was following in the footsteps of the British wine critics, who made frequent trips across the Channel to monitor the progress of each new vintage. But in comparison to Parker, he sounded niggling, equivocal, and more than a little pompous.

The debate over the 1982s was on, and would rage for years, with Terry Robards on Finigan's side. Before he'd even tasted the 1982s, Robards had reported that the year was a "heralded vintage" but suggested the 1979s were better buys. On the front page of *The Wine Spectator*, in his very first column in the June first issue on Bordeaux futures as investments, he still advised that "prudent buyers will stay out of the market for now and will focus their buying on . . . '78, '79, and '81."

Such comments did not please the trade. Sam Aaron of Sherry-Lehmann complained that he lost $20,000 in orders for 1982 futures after Robards's report. Aaron was so upset he telephoned Alexis Lichine in Bordeaux, who quickly denounced the American "press campaign" against the '82 vintage. Finigan heard that a group of château proprietors actually discussed banning Robards and him from tasting at their estates in the future, perhaps permanently. "You would have thought I had compared the wines to rat poison," fumed an annoyed Finigan, now claiming that neither he nor Robards was "negative on the wines—we just weren't positive enough." He cynically observed that the Bordeaux trade had a stake in all the positive comments because they wanted all the wines sold before the franc dropped any lower.

Lichine, a consummate and theatrical promoter, wasted no time. On a hot summer day in mid-June he hosted a barrel tasting and lunch in the attractive cellar of his property, Prieuré-Lichine, for the owners of six top châteaux, to prove once and for all how good the 1982s really were. He invited Jon Winroth of the *International Herald Tribune*, *Wine Spectator* publisher Marvin Shanken, and its newly named European correspondent, James Suckling. They were completely seduced.

In fact, the majority of those who'd actually tasted the wines, including British Bordeaux expert David Peppercorn and *New York Times* columnist Frank Prial, also had a favorable view of the 1982s, even if they weren't quite as enthusiastic as Parker. But Parker's detailed over-the-top praise for such a large range of wines virtually ensured he would end up being the vintage's biggest promoter and its most important herald.

If Parker harbored any small doubts about his own judgment, he eliminated them in June, during his regular yearly tasting circuit of France, by comparing hundreds of barrel samples in various *négociant* offices. He had a long discussion with Jean Delmas at Château Haut-Brion, and even perused their archives. There he discovered that people had also had doubts about whether the wines from the famous 1929 vintage would last, and the best were still wonderful more than fifty years later. He spent one of his days on the Right Bank, at a tasting organized by oenologist Michel Rolland, who owned a lab and analyzed wines for over one hundred clients. They'd met the previous summer, and Rolland had offered to arrange a tasting the next time Parker was in Bordeaux. When he told clients an American journalist was coming, all happily contributed samples of their 1982s. Parker tasted all morning and afternoon, and he remained just as excited at the end of the day as he was when he started.

Parker was even more certain of his opinion in his August fourteenth issue. The question is not whether to buy, but when, he wrote, predicting, "I feel absolutely certain that the wines in most demand will be significantly more expensive (perhaps as much as 70 percent more) in two years." For the following year, he would reiterate variations of his basic theme—"buy as much great 1982 as you can afford because there may not be another vintage this great for 50 years." Those who purchased the top wines now would "no doubt have liquid gold sitting in their cellars."

Marvin Shanken didn't like to be wrong. He could see that *The Wine Spectator* had not been on top of the breaking story. In the August 1983 issue, as if to catch up, Suckling wrote two articles on the 1982 vintage. One described the Lichine lunch, and it praised the wines. Robards kept the controversy going by reporting his own view; after tasting sixty wines, he insisted some were "downright flabby." He predicted that "the vintage will be charming to drink at a young age" but he had "reservations about its potential for long aging," reservations shared by producers like Peter Allan Sichel of Château d'Angludet in Margaux.

So far *The Wine Spectator* had been a forum for fairly independent freelance columnists, like Robards, weighing in with their own opinions. There was no collective staff voice taking a stand on the vintage as Parker had back in April. Marvin Shanken was convinced that had to change, and soon.

A testy Finigan was not about to back down, and he vehemently defended his "journalistic dissent" in two fall issues. Wines in the Médoc and Graves were "amiable and sometimes impressive" but hardly vintage-of-the-century quality. While proprietors in St.-Emilion and Pomerol compared the style of their wines to the legendary 1947, to Finigan they excelled "in that alcoholic weight and richness which many consumers, especially the less experienced, will adore." Was that an indirect slap at Parker? There was no reason to buy now, Finigan insisted, all but accusing retailers and the Bordeaux establishment of fooling the customers.

Why was Finigan's view so different? Some theorized that he'd lazily relied too much on the views and vintage report of one respected château owner in Margaux, where most of the 1982s weren't nearly as good as elsewhere. Or perhaps the disagreement was more about the style of the wine. Many in England and France were convinced that the character of the 1982s matched an American taste for ripeness and fruit. Americans usually preferred their own country's wines in those popular and ubiquitous California Cabernet versus Bordeaux blind tastings. The 1982s, too, were "wow" wines, showy and flamboyant, with in-your-face sweet fruit. Would they peak early and fade quickly? In a *New York Times* ad, retailer William Sokolin offered customers who'd already bought 1982 futures the chance to exchange them for 1981 Bordeaux, writing, "It is clear that '81 is a finer, more classically stated vintage."

Meanwhile, back in Bordeaux, the first-growth châteaux, which seemed determined to squeeze as much money as they could from the market, had released the wines as usual in stages, or *tranches*. After the first price, the *prix de sortie*, the cost of the next batch of futures was significantly higher, the next still higher, and so on. Lafite's prices started at 70 percent higher than the year before and quickly escalated. Some of the greedy "super seconds" (the nickname for the top-performing second growths, like Léoville-Las-Cases) waited and waited and waited to see what their neighbors' prices would be, causing havoc. Even lesser châteaux held back a bigger-than-normal percentage of their wine to sell when it had all been bottled. The financial success of this strategy depended heavily on prices rising, which depended on growing demand for the wines, which depended on enthusiasm for the vintage continuing.

And thanks to the promotion of Parker's view in America, it did.

Parker's April issue had an almost immediate impact upon retailers in Washington, D.C., but things really began to heat up in May. Several of the biggest retailers in New York City were already acquainted with his newsletter and since 1981 had occasionally mentioned his recommendations in their newspaper ads, usually alongside those of the more famous Finigan, Robards, and others. But now they jumped on Parker's praise for the 1982 vintage with the speed of a movie publicist capitalizing on a rave review in the

New York Times. As Gerald Asher put it, "Parker came along in the nick of time. The retailers needed a Simon Says, someone whom the public would believe."

In New York, first came Zachy's, a large Westchester County wine shop that had been offering futures since 1978. Their big, splashy ad for 1982 futures trumpeted Parker's prediction that the quality of the wines "will go down in the annals of Bordeaux wine history with such legendary vintages as 1929, 1945, 1959, and 1961" and placed his notes and scores next to wines like Ducru-Beaucaillou, "a staggering wine which should merit a 95 plus score in 2 years." Morrell's championed Parker as "the only wine writer who has comprehensively tasted the '82s on three separate trips to Bordeaux." Sherry-Lehmann quoted him in full-page ads. But few realized just how useful Parker's reviews could be until consumers started buying big. Acker Merrall put fourteen wines and their scores—Parker had rated all but one 90 or above—under the head "Parker's Picks" in an ad, and within five days all the 90+ futures had sold out.

The Wine Advocate had about eight thousand subscribers at that point, but these ads introduced Parker's name to many thousands more. Wine lovers who had never heard of him were soon asking, "Who's this guy Parker?" And when wine shops realized touting this independent expert's view was extremely beneficial to sales, they used his name even more.

The promotion of the 1982 Bordeaux became a national ad campaign for Robert Parker and *The Wine Advocate*, and it didn't cost him a thing.

The buying frenzy nationwide reached almost hysterical levels. In Baltimore, Parker's friend retailer Bob Schindler bought thousands of cases on the basis of his recommendation and sold them all. There were reports of the Los Angeles doctor, purchasing for a group, who placed an order with a San Francisco importer for $100,000 worth of 1982s and the Texas oilman who spent $12,000 on them in an Austin shop. A Long Island importer sold more than two thousand cases of Château Gloria in its first twenty-four hours on the market;

his average customers, who regularly purchased a few cases each from six to eight châteaux, ordered forty to sixty cases. Parker's close friend Dr. Jay Miller rushed off to the State Employee's Credit Union to borrow almost $10,000 to buy sixty cases of wines Parker had recommended. Clearly at least some of the demand was purely speculative, for investment.

"It's like Las Vegas," marveled New York City importer Barry Bassin. "Everyone has to put a quarter in the slot machine." Ab Simon, who by then headed Château & Estates, the largest U.S. importer of fine Bordeaux, admitted "it was almost a stampede." Demand was "way above my expectations, even for an exceptional vintage." The American market gobbled up futures as if it were starving.

All this eventually made an impact in *négociant* offices in Bordeaux; Christopher Cannan of Europvin remembers massive amounts of orders arriving daily from America, and wines made in tiny quantities, such as Pétrus, were soon virtually unobtainable at any price. "It was the heyday of Bordeaux," said *négociant* Dominique Renard. "The Americans were more active than all the other markets and set a precedent for the futures market. It was the strongest sale ever, and the prices soared. Nineteen eighty-two led a whole new group of buyers and speculators to the market."

Americans bought so much that the Bordelais began to call 1982 the American vintage.

In enumerating just why he thought the 1982s were so great, Parker seemed to be setting down his criteria for what constituted a great red wine: First, an incredibly dark color, which he associated with "wines of great concentration." Second, "amazing fruitiness and ripeness" and "fat, fleshy flavors that were viscous and mouthfilling." And third, the high alcohol content that came from "grapes that had achieved perfect maturity." Of the 1982 Petit-Village, Parker said, "If wine were a candy, Petit-Village would be a hypothetical blend of a Milky Way and Reese's Peanut Butter Cup." This type of

wine, opulent, luscious, and tremendously fruity while still in barrel, became a new prototype and set a new standard. In effect, 1982
became the first modern vintage, the harbinger of a particular style
of wine. And it was quite different from what people thought of as
typical Bordeaux—wines that started out austere and undrinkable,
and were slow to develop.

But 1982 was a milestone for other reasons. It came to symbol-
ize a break with Bordeaux's past. It started a new trend of consumers
purchasing fine Bordeaux solely as a financial investment. It ignited
a boom in the American market, and it marked the beginning of a
new, modern way of marketing wine. One négociant observed that
after 1982, the Bordeaux market would never be the same. American retailers and the Bordelais were just beginning to see how useful
Parker could be.

Parker's call on the 1982 vintage was the first big step in building the Parker legend. The debate over the quality of the wines
went on for years, although tastings proved again and again that
he had been right in his extravagant praise—at least for the very
best wines. The speculators who listened to Parker made money.
According to The Wine Spectator's auction correspondent, Peter
Meltzer, between 1983 and 2002 the wines rose 2,012 percent in
value—far outperforming the 770-percent return of the Dow Jones
during the same period.

Within a few years the facts had been simplified, streamlined,
and distorted in small ways to fit neatly within Parker's "Lone Ranger"
image. The idea persisted that he had been the first journalist to proclaim the greatness of 1982, even though that was not true. Parker
himself gave credit to French critic Michel Bettane. But Parker perpetuated the idea that he stood out alone against a "mainstream
American press" who had "unequivocally criticized the vintage and
the style of wines" with "scathing critiques," as well as extending
that criticism to him. In reality, that "mainstream" consisted of three
naysayers—in addition to Robards and Finigan, Dan Berger of the
Los Angeles Times had been lukewarm on the 1982s—and none of

them had written anything negative about him personally. In the first five years of *The Wine Advocate*, Parker had frequently sought to characterize himself as quite different from other wine writers, standing alone for the consumer, and he now used his position on the 1982 vintage to distance himself even more. Later he claimed that at the time the "establishment wine press" had regarded him as "a threat to their . . . influence." But that was hardly the case; in 1983 he was only just beginning to become important.

All during 1983 and the beginning of 1984, Parker knew he was leaving Farm Credit Banks and the law. After tasting the 1982s it seemed harder than ever to go back to an office and attend boring meetings about contracts. He could barely keep up the necessary effort and attention. Fortunately he had the loyalty of several lawyers he'd hired, who covered for him when he stole off to New York for a tasting. He was looking for every possible way out. Early in 1984, Robards, now entrenched at *The Wine Spectator* and *The New York Post*, heard that Parker was trying to set up a meeting with someone at the *New York Times* to discuss taking on the vacant wine critic slot. But nothing came of it; perhaps Parker realized that the *Times* would never allow him to keep publishing *The Wine Advocate*. In any case, Frank Prial returned to New York after his stint in the Paris Bureau office and went back to writing the "Wine Talk" column.

After the April issue reviews of the 1982 Bordeaux and subsequent publicity in wine shop ads, and the continuing controversy with Finigan, many more subscriptions had flowed in to *The Wine Advocate*. The number had jumped to nearly nine thousand. It was close enough. With the 1982 vintage, Parker was now completely convinced of his ability and knew he was outworking his competitors. Finigan, he was sure, was in decline. Parker had put in eleven years at Farm Credit Banks and his ten-year pension benefits were vested. In March 1984, with Pat's blessing, he finally resigned from the practice of law.

He and Pat threw a "retirement" dinner at their home, inviting a few close friends, and they all "got blitzed" on 1980 Chalone Chardonnay and 1961 Jaboulet Hermitage La Chapelle. Parker felt incredibly happy, as though a weight had been lifted from his life. Two weeks later he and Pat left for Bordeaux to taste the 1983 vintage—and to see how those great 1982s were coming along.

REMYSTIFYING WINE

Terry Theise

First of all, everything is unified, everything is linked together, everything is explained by something else and in turn explains another thing. There is nothing separate, that is, nothing that can be named or described separately. In order to describe the first impressions, the first sensations, it is necessary to describe all at once. The new world with which one comes into contact has no sides, so that it is impossible to describe first one side and then the other. All of it is visible at every point.

—P. D. Ouspensky

Either nature has a kind of consciousness, and therefore a purpose, or it does not. In our present state of development, there's no way to know. It's my experience that nature—whether metallic (like my car) or organic (like a plant) or neither (like the wind)—behaves differently if one relates to it as though it is conscious; many have experienced consciousness in rocks, flora, fauna and objects, but our subjective experiences are difficult to demonstrate and impossible to prove. If nature has no consciousness or purpose, I don't see how humanity can, so I choose to believe we all do. That's my sense of things. Again, impossible to prove, especially when the evidence appears to point the other way.

—Michael Ventura

James Hillman and Michael Ventura published a provocative book called *We've Had 100 Years of Psychotherapy and the World's Getting Worse*. Well, we've had what seems like a hundred books purporting to "demystify" wine, and wine is more mysterious than ever. Not that the technocrat-enologist complex hasn't been furiously laboring to remove every pesky variable from wine—damn that nature!—and Lord knows we're ever more inundated with all manner of mass-produced industrial swill, but true wine is *supposed* to be complex, and if you think you know it all, well, pal, you don't know nuthin'.

Ah, but the poor hapless consumer, faced with the groaning shelves of wine bottles with gobbledygook on the labels, or the Talmudic opacity of some eight-pound document called the restaurant wine list—what can we do to help this innocent waif, terrified he'll pick the "wrong" wine? The first thing is to remind him of the nature of the risk. Let's remember, he probably has little to no idea how an automobile actually functions, and if you stuck his head under the hood, he'd think, *Hmm, why yes, that's an engine, all right*, while remaining clueless about how it makes his car move. He's getting ready to spend serious money on a machine whose operation he doesn't understand, yet we're writing books fussing over how difficult wine is? What are you out if you make a "mistake" and buy the "wrong" wine, twenty bucks in a store? This is not a major disappointment.

Underlying the wine-simplification industry is an inferiority complex. Actually, two inferiority complexes. The first belongs to the reader, who thinks he should know more about wine since apparently he can't escape it, and he hates to feel incompetent. The second belongs to wine writers, who feel themselves part of a collective failure to get Americans to drink more wine. Anything we can do, they reason, to make wine *safe* for the novice will cause him to snuggle up to wine, and this is good because we who sell wine for a living want more wine drinkers.

But what if we were talking about literature? Not enough people read, that's for sure. But they like looking at images, this we know, so let's simplify this whole literature business by making graphic books out of all those annoying *wordy* things. Once that's done, let's see if we can eliminate even *more* words, and tell the whole story with drawings. Oh, hell, let's forget about even having an object you have to hold in your hands; let's make a video of it and shove it onto a

screen. I mean, it's the same story, right? Anna still throws herself
in front of the train. Holden's still fussing about the stupid ducks.
What's the difference?

What often underlies the desire to simplify wine, to make it
more "accessible" to everyman, is perilously close to pandering: "If
I kill its essence and make it incredibly simple, then will you start
drinking it?" Why should we enable everyone's childish desire for
things to be predictable? You want predictable, stay clear of wine.
Oh, there's plenty of predictable wine made, and if you find one you
like, then by all means keep drinking and enjoying it. But if you find
yourself curious about wine, you have to accept that uncertainty is
inextricable from the experience. Vintages vary, at least in many of
the Old World's uncertain climates, and the crisp wine you liked this
year could be a voluptuous wine next year. Different growers with
adjacent parcels in the same vineyard will make different-tasting
wine. It isn't total chaos—there are threads of consistency running
through artisanal wines—but to appreciate these wines you need a
tolerance for surprise.

Put it this way: Would you rather watch a ballgame as it's played,
not knowing the outcome? Or would you rather cue up the DVD
player and watch a tape of a game already played, maybe a great game,
but one with no element of surprise?

There's very little that's inherently mystifying about wine;
there's just a huge number of them, from different grapes and different places, and most of them change their taste a little each year. It's
a lot of data, but it isn't integral calculus. There is, though, something that summons the *mystical* in fine wines, and this experience
is available to anyone who's willing to prepare for it. It begins with
being available—in other words, allowing both your attention and
your emotions to respond to sensation, and to feelings of joy in the
face of beauty. This is not a big deal. Say you go for a walk but you're
preoccupied (that damned Blauman contract still isn't signed, and
little Johnny needs braces). You see nothing of your surroundings.
But then your cell phone rings, and it's Jenkins with good news:
"Blauman signed!" And now your mind is liberated, and you don't

just notice things, you notice *everything*. You pick up a leaf and turn it over, and the pattern on the underside is astonishing, my God, look at this, was this always here, do other people know about how amazing this is?

There is nothing esoteric or inaccessible about this state of mind. If you are aware of the world, things will come to your attention. One of them is beauty, and one of the beautiful things is wine. But wine's abilities do not stop at mere sensual beauty. Wine is able to channel multiple currents of beauty, from the pretty to the charming, from the fleeting to the logical, from the passionate to the pensive. And great wine will take you to a question and, wonderfully, deposit you there, without an answer or a map—just looking at the question.

Ambiguous? If you're sitting on a hilltop enjoying a view, you may be able to say, "This is beautiful because I can see a great distance, and the hills fold into one another in an especially comely way, and the river is perfectly situated to give depth to the scene," and that is certainly part of the truth. But beauty has a face that's turned away from the light. Think of music. Can you say *why* a certain piece of music makes you feel so intensely? Probably not. But it has happened to most of us, and we don't think ourselves weird or "new agey" when it does, because this experience, though mystical, is commonplace. It happens with wine too, but it seems outré because wine drinking itself seems the purview of the arugula munchers.

Wine may have a particular hold on this mystical faculty based on the proximity of the parts of the brain that process smells and memories. I've never had my own Proustian moment, but for me wine does something even more astounding than that. I may not suddenly recover my own memories, but a few great wines have seemed to dilate the world so that I seem to experience a *collective* memory. I might smell an old Loire valley Chenin Blanc, and it makes me think of an armoire. That's not too fanciful. But it makes me think of an armoire in a room in a French country house, and I can see the other furniture too, and the view of gardens and fields out the window, and I can almost hear the voices of the people who live in the house, and smell the body scents on the clothes hanging in my make-believe armoire.

So here is silly old me, in my imaginary room with the armoire; I hear the voices and see the fields and smell the smells, but then I sense a kind of rising; I am in the sky somehow, I see the roads link-ing "my" house to the other houses and then to the market village, I see the forests and the horses in the fields, and the kids playing or stealing apples, and the orchard owner running behind them swear-ing, and then I think, *They're not here anymore, where did they go?* And I sense an endless succession of brief lives, of people trying to work, and love, and be safe, and understand what it all means, and I am further away than ever from what it all means but there is within it all a tremendous gravity, tenderness, and sadness for our strange species so heedless and so angelic.

Now, who knows; maybe I'm recovering an embedded memory of some inconsequential scene in Turgenev I read thirty years ago. Or maybe it's a manifestation of wine's strange ability to arouse the imagination. This is the "mystical" facet of wine, and I don't think we should apologize for it or be embarrassed about it or seek to quash it. I think we need not to demystify wine, but to *remystify* it!

I return to the wine in my glass. What I just described took place in a second or two. I haven't figured out how to summon it, but I try to be there when it summons me. It means well by me.

I work with a grower named Martin Nigl, who makes especially ethereal wines, the kinds of wines that pose questions we never thought to ask: How far can refinement be taken? What do we find there? Clarity reveals flavor, as we know, but what is on the far side of clear flavor? I also wonder how wines like Nigl's make me feel, because they don't generate a volume of emotional affect. They are too searching. Perhaps what they generate most is curiosity. If I haven't imagined that wine can offer such pure refinement, what else haven't I imagined?

I think that wines like Nigl's can inculcate an appreciation of detail and design. They're like dew-covered webs you see in the morn-ing, when you pause to appreciate the craft of the weaver, all curled into a tiny nugget, waiting for the sun to strike her. Or hoarfrost on your windows some winter morning, as you study the intricacy of the crystals. When I was a little guy I had a microscope, just a little one but more than a toy, and I loved to look at my slides. And now flavors are under a microscope, showing all the worlds within worlds, all below our vision.

This is not to say that Nigl's wines leave all sensual life behind; far from it. They are feasts for the senses, but theirs is an esoteric cuisine that will feed the hungers you know, and the ones you're unaware of. But you have to be available for this experience, and to listen in a different way. It won't leave you happier, but it does leave you wondering, because there is *more* of you on the other side. And you don't need to contrive some great vast rapture in order to know this moment. It can live, and lives quite easily, in a single sip of wine.

So why not just relax with wine? Don't worry about what you know or don't know. Don't even worry about what you're "supposed" (according to the likes of me) to feel. Just daydream and release your imagination. Believe me, it's more fun than trying to grab a wine, to nail the poor bastard, to dissect it in order to show how cool your palate is. What a pitiable waste! It's like ignoring a rainbow so you can balance your checkbook.

Bear in mind, the cultivation of the mystic isn't only a pursuit of refined experience—in fact, it isn't any sort of *pursuit* at all. The mystic also reveals itself by presenting and encouraging intuition and metaphor. Each of these can come to you if you're relaxed. I recall sitting in a tasting room at the estate of Carl Loewen (from whom we heard in chapter 2) and noticing that I always heard blackbirds when I tasted there. I found a charming connection between the companionship of the songbird and the unassuming but lovely wine. This is probably because Carl's tasting room is just inside his garden, and there's always a blackbird trilling away in the background. Nature does enjoy showcasing her metaphors! But I delight in the juxtaposition of the wine in my glass with the whistling and warbling outside. Here's this little blackbird singing its tiny lungs out, all that energy and melody coming from such a tiny, delicate body, and in the glass there's a wine with 8 percent alcohol, all that energy and melody coming from such a tiny, delicate body. I wonder what the metaphor would be if you were tasting, hmm, in Australia. Some huge malevolent beast bellowing outside in the dust.

If you see the world sacramentally—apart from whatever religious affiliation you may have, or even if you have none at all—you find you have learned to assume that things are connected. Austrian grower Michael Moosbrugger has leased a venerable monastic estate called Schloss Gobelsburg. The land was superb, but the current generation of monks wanted help in modernizing the property and aligning the wines with prevailing standards of quality.

Michael went about upgrading the wines squarely within the context of modern quality-oriented winemaking, and his wines quickly became excellent, even great, as these things are currently understood and evaluated by the critical establishment. Within a few years he had accomplished his goal, only to learn that his true goal lay elsewhere, somewhere both further on and deeper inside.

It started when he tasted through the estate's cellar of old vintages. The wines were different, less modern; the current wines seemed almost sterile in contrast to these mossy old things. And Michael wondered, What guided the old wines? Did those old monks simply lack the know-how of modern cellarmasters? Or was something else at work? The monks kept detailed records. It was easy to see what they did with their wines. But all this did was to ignite a deeper curiosity. What if he went *very* far back, to the period between the end of the Franco-Prussian War and the start of World War I? What did those monks know that we have forgotten?

It is so easy to make this sentimental and trivial. "Return to the wisdom of the monks" is guaranteed to make my eyes glaze over. It is not what I mean. Michael set about to produce a wine—eventually, two wines—as they would have been made almost one hundred years ago. He didn't intend them as an "homage," and certainly not as a pastiche. He couldn't be sure how the wines would be. He only sought to *know*.

"If you consider the span of time between the Romans and the nineteenth century, a Roman who would have been catapulted forward in time would not have been surprised by what he saw," Michael says. "But in the last hundred years, everything has changed, and our own mentalities have changed also. These days we seek to preserve primary fruit as much as possible, and the ways we do it are to ferment at lower temperatures and not to agitate the wine. But until very recently none of this was technologically possible. In those days the guiding idea was that a wine was *schooled*, like a child is schooled—the French call it *élevage*—until it reached a stage in its development when it was ready to drink. And then it was bottled."

How did they know? I asked. "They knew by taste, and also by the extent to which the wine attained the Ideal they had for it." It sounds like a kind of *ripening*, I said. "Yes, exactly; the wine said when it was ready, when it reached the development they'd guided it toward."

Therefore Michael had gone back to a time when oxygen wasn't feared in winemaking. Indeed, it couldn't be avoided, so you adapted to it. You understood wine as a beverage *dependent* on oxygen to create the nongrape flavors by which it was *wine* and not just fermented grape juice. In place of the modern trend for whole-cluster pressing (and the crystalline texture it creates), Michael crushed and pressed his grapes on their skins; he fermented the juice without clarifying it (the old ones used to say he "fermented with all the *schmutz* and bacon"); he eschewed temperature control; he put the wine in old casks and racked it often to *encourage* secondary flavors, the nongrape flavors we call "vinosity," all to replicate this old vinous dialect, which was almost extinct.

What moves me most, apart from the quality of these wines, is what I interpret as Michael's search for *soul*. I imagine we all suspect that soul is, or can be, crowded out by technology, if only because it is so tempting to surrender to the machine's ease, its sterile exactitude, that which we once knew in our fingertips. Each time you flick a switch on a machine you erect a membrane between yourself and your wine. Sometimes this is a necessary evil. I don't want to endorse any kind of feel-good nostalgia. But I like to make meatballs, and while I could easily do the mixture in a food processor, I prefer doing it with my hands because I like that my hands know when it's ready. So I can see how a vintner could be prone to ennui if he merely flicked the switch and the machine did the rest.

I'm not making any sort of Luddite case for pretechnological wines, nor do I suppose they have a nostalgic value. I only share Michael's fascination with how it must have been for the people who made wines as best they could in those times, and created a set of values predicated on what was, and was not, possible. I share Michael's intuition that something of soul, something we may have misplaced, is there to be found. I share that hunger, and I know the rare thing that feeds it. When intuition is all you have, you nurture intuition! And intuition isn't quantifiable, and whatever we can't quantify slips between the threads of what we call understanding. And what we don't understand we call mystic, with mistrust and derision.

There's a lot we can understand about wine, and among those things there's nothing more salient than understanding the *limits* to understanding. Wine is bigger than us, and this is perfect, it is why we spend our lives in love with it; and if this is mystifying, then please, *bring it on*.

CONTRIBUTOR NOTES

Eric Asimov is the chief wine critic of *The New York Times*, where his weekly column appears in the Dining section. He is married to Deborah Hofmann, has two sons, Jack and Peter, and lives in Manhattan.

Bianca Bosker is an award-winning journalist and the author of the *New York Times* bestseller *Cork Dork*. She has written about food, wine, architecture, and technology for *The Atlantic*, *The New Yorker* online, *The New York Times*, *The Wall Street Journal*, and *Food & Wine*, among other publications. The former executive tech editor of *The Huffington Post*, she is a contributing editor at *The Atlantic* and lives in New York City.

Bill Buford is the author of *Among the Thugs* and *Heat: An Amateur's Adventures as Kitchen Slave, Line Cook, Pasta-Maker, and Apprentice to a Dante-Quoting Butcher in Tuscany*. He also wrote "Iconic Dishes," a collection of essays on classic recipes that he prepared with Daniel Boulud, which is included in Boulud's *My French Cuisine*. From 1995, until he left for France, in 2008, Buford was at *The New Yorker*, first as Literary and Fiction Editor and then as a staff writer. He lived in England for eighteen years and founded the literary magazine *Granta*. He was born in Baton Rouge, Louisiana, and now lives in New York City with his wife Jessica Green and their French-speaking sons, George and Frederick. His forthcoming book is *Dirt: My 5 Years in the Ancient City of Lyon, Where My Children Became Frenchies and I Trained to Be a Chef*.

Roald Dahl (1916–1990) was born in Llandaff, South Wales, and went to Repton School in England. As he explains in *Boy*, he turned down the idea of university in favor of a job that would take him to "a wonderful faraway place." In 1933 he joined the Shell Company, which sent him to Mombasa in East Africa. When World War II began in 1939, he became a fighter pilot and in 1942 was made assistant air attaché in Washington, where he started to write short stories. His first major success as a writer for children was in 1964. Thereafter his children's books brought him increasing popularity, and when he died 1990, children mourned the world over.

Stephanie Danler is the author of the critically acclaimed and nationwide best-selling novel, *Sweetbitter*. She lives in Los Angeles.

Michael Dibdin (1947–2007) was born in England and raised in Northern Ireland. He attended Sussex University and the University of Alberta. He spent five years in Perugia, Italy, where he taught English at the local university, and went on to live in Oxford, England and Seattle, Washington. He was the author of eighteen novels, including *Ratking*, which won the Crime Writers' Association Gold Dagger, and *Cabal*, which was awarded the French Grand Prix du Roman Policier. His work has been translated into eighteen languages.

Irina Dumitrescu teaches medieval literature at the University of Bonn. She is the author of *The Experience of Education in Anglo-Saxon Literature* (Cambridge, 2018) and editor of *Rumba Under Fire: The Arts of Survival from West Point to Delhi* (Punctum, 2016). She has written for *The Atlantic, Washington Post, Southwest Review, Yale Review, Aeon, Politico, Serious Eats, Petits Propos Culinaires*, and *LA Review of Books*. Her essays have been nominated for the James Beard Foundation's MFK Fisher Distinguished Writing Award, received the McGinnis-Ritchie Award for nonfiction, and been reprinted in *Best American Essays 2016* and *Best Food Writing 2017*.

M. F. K. Fisher (1908–1992) was one of the great food writers of the twentieth century. Born in 1908 in Albion, Michigan, she grew up in Whittier, California, and was educated at Illinois College, Occidental College, UCLA, and the University of Dijon in France. Fisher travelled to and lived in Europe throughout her adult life. The author of numerous books, magazine articles, novels, and a translation of Brillat-Savarin's *The Physiology of Taste*, she is best remembered for her gastronomical works and the autobiographical nature of her writings about people, places, and food.

Jim Harrison (1937–2016) was the *New York Times*-bestselling author of forty books of fiction, non-fiction, and poetry, including *Legends of the Fall, Dalva*, and *Returning to Earth*. A member of the American Academy of Arts and Letters and winner of a National Endowment for the Arts grant, his work was published in twenty-seven languages.

Don and Petie Kladstrup are former journalists who have written extensively about wine and France for numerous publications. Don, a winner of three Emmys and numerous other awards, was a foreign correspondent for ABC and CBS television news. Petie, an Overseas Press Club winner, was a newspaper journalist and more recently protocol officer for the U.S. ambassador to UNESCO. The Kladstrups divide their time between Paris and Southwestern France.

Matt Kramer is the author of nine critically acclaimed books: *Making Sense of Wine*; *Making Sense of Burgundy*; *Making Sense of California Wine*; *A Passion For Piedmont: Italy's Most Glorious Regional Table*; *Making Sense of Wine—Second Edition*; *Matt Kramer's New California Wine*; and *Matt Kramer's Making Sense of Italian Wine* and *Matt Kramer On Wine*, a collection of his best columns and essays over the years and *True Taste: The Seven Essential Wine Words*. His books have been translated into Korean, Japanese, Portuguese and Swedish.

A.J. Liebling (1904–1963) was born in New York City and joined the staff of *The New Yorker* in 1935, where his "Wayward Press" columns became a model of fine journalistic writing.

Kermit Lynch was born and raised in California. In 1972, he opened a retail wineshop and later began importing and distributing nationally. In 1988, he published *Adventures on the Wine Route*, which won the Veuve Clicquot Wine Book of the Year Award. His second book, *Inspiring Thirst*, was published in 2004. Lynch and his wife, photographer Gail Skoff, divide their time between Berkeley, California and Provence, France—where he says he is "near enough to Domaine Tempier that I can fill up the trunk of my car whenever I need to."

Tilar J. Mazzeo is the Clara C. Piper Associate Professor of English at Colby College, in Waterville, Maine. She is the author of numerous works of narrative nonfiction, and several of her books have been *New York Times*, *San Francisco Chronicle*, and *Los Angeles Times* bestsellers. She divides her time among coastal Maine, New York City, and Saanichton, British Columbia, where she lives with her husband at Parsell Vineyard.

Elin McCoy is an award-winning journalist and author, focusing on the world of wine. She is a wine and spirits columnist for *Bloomberg News*, where she writes for their global news wire, and is a columnist for *Decanter* magazine. McCoy's most recent book, *The Emperor of Wine: The Rise of Robert M. Parker, Jr. and the Reign of American Taste*, garnered international praise and has appeared in five foreign editions. She is also the co-author of *Thinking About Wine* and is currently working on two new wine books.

Jay McInerney is the author of eight novels, two collections of short stories, and three collections of essays on wine. He lives in New York City and Bridgehampton, New York.

Rex Pickett is a director, screenwriter, novelist, and playwright who is best known for his novel *Sideways*, upon which the Alexander Payne film of the same title was adapted. The film garnered over 350 critics and awards organizations accolades. It was nominated for 5 Academy Awards, winning the Oscar for Best Adapted Screenplay; captured 2 Golden Globes; and won a record 6 Indie Spirit Awards. The Writers Guild of America voted *Sideways* as one of the 101 Greatest Screenplays of All Time. Pickett also wrote the screenplay for the Oscar-winning Best Live Action Short *My Mother Dreams the Satan's Disciples in New York*. He has written two sequels to *Sideways*, the second of which won the Gold Medal for Fiction from the prestigious Independent Publisher Book Awards. His new novel *The Archivist* will be issued by Blackstone Publishing in the fall of 2018. He is currently writing *Sideways* the musical. His papers are in Special Collections & Archives at the Geisel Library on the campus of UCSD, Pickett's beloved alma mater. He continues to add to his collection.

Maximillian Potter is the Editor at Large for *Esquire* magazine. He has written two books: "Shadows in the Vineyard: The True Story of the Plot to Poison the World's Greatest Wine," which began with the *Vanity Fair* story, "The Assassin in the Vineyard." *The New York Times* named "Shadows" a Best Wine Book of 2014. Potter co-authored "The Opposite of Woe: My Life in Beer in Politics," the memoir of Colorado Governor John Hickenlooper, for whom Potter served as senior media advisor. Previously, Potter was the executive editor of *5280: Denver's Magazine*; he was a staff writer at *Premiere*, *Philadelphia*, and *GQ* and has been a contributing editor to *Men's Health* and *Details*, and contributor to *Vanity Fair*. A native of Philadelphia with a BA from Allegheny College and MSJ from Northwestern University's Medill School, he lives in Denver.

Jancis Robinson is the author/editor of dozens of wine books, including *Wine Grapes*, *The Oxford Companion to Wine*, and *The World Atlas of Wine*, and regularly contributes to the food & drink section of *The*

Financial Times. She is the recipient of four James Beard Awards, and was the first person outside of the wine trade to pass the rigorous Master of Wine exams. She maintains a website and newsletter focused on fine wine writing at JancisRobinson.com. She lives in London.

Roger Scruton is a graduate of Jesus College, Cambridge, United Kingdom. He has been Professor of Aesthetics at Birkbeck College, London, and University Professor at Boston University. He is currently visiting professor of philosophy at the University of Oxford and Senior Fellow at the Ethics and Public Policy Center, Washington DC. He has published a large number of books, including some works of fiction, and has written and composed two operas. He writes regularly for *The Times*, *The Telegraph*, *The Spectator* and was for many years wine critic for *The New Statesman*.

Julia Flynn Siler is the author of *The House of Mondavi* (Penguin's Gotham Books) and *Lost Kingdom* (Grove Atlantic), both bestsellers. She was a London-based staff writer for the *Wall Street Journal* and *BusinessWeek* magazine and her work has also appeared in *The New York Times*, *The Washington Post*, and the *Oxford Dictionary of Food and Wine*. A 2016–2017 recipient of an NEH Public Scholar Fellowship and the Mayborn Fellowship in Biography, she is at work on her third book, *The White Devil's Daughters*, forthcoming from Alfred A. Knopf. She is a member of the board of the San Francisco-based Litquake Foundation and is a two-term member of the Council of Friends of U.C. Berkeley's Bancroft Library. www.juliaflynnsiler.com

Edward Steinberg studied and taught at Harvard University before moving to Rome, where he has lived for most of his life. He has conducted wine tastings at a leading Roman wine shop, worked as a consultant for the European Community, and written for *Newsweek*.

George M. Taber is the author of the bestselling *Judgment of Paris*, which recounts the story of the famous 1976 event when unknown California wines defeated top French ones. Taber's second book, *To Cork*

or Not to Cork, won the Jane Grigson Award and was a finalist for the James Beard Award. He is also the author of *In Search of Bacchus: Wanderings in the Wonderful World of Wine Tourism* and *Chasing Gold: The Incredible Story of How the Nazis Stole Europe's Bullion*. Before turning to writing books, Taber was a reporter and editor with *TIME* magazine for twenty-one years, based in Bonn, Paris, Houston, and New York.

Terry Theise, winner of the James Beard Foundation's Award for Outstanding Wine and Spirits Professional, is an importer of boutique wines from Germany, Austria, and Champagne. His articles have appeared in *The World of Fine Wine* magazine. He was *Wine & Spirits* Man of the Year in 2001 and *Food and Wine* magazine's Importer of the Year in 2006. His award-winning first book, *Reading Between the Wines*, has been hailed as "the single best book I've ever read on why wine matters" (Karen MacNeil, author of *The Wine Bible*), and he is also the author of *What Makes a Wine Worth Drinking*. He lives in Roslindale, MA.

Benjamin Wallace is a contributing editor at *Vanity Fair* and the author of the *New York Times*-bestselling book *The Billionaire's Vinegar: The Mystery of the World's Most Expensive Bottle of Wine*.

Auberon Waugh (1939–2001) was an English journalist and critic, and the eldest son of Evelyn Waugh. He was the author of five novels and served as a columnist, reviewer, and polemicist on several journals and newspapers including *The Times*, *Private Eye*, the *New Statesman*, the *Evening Standard*, and the *Independent*.

Joseph Wechsberg (1907–1983) was a Jewish Czech writer, journalist, musician, and gourmet. Born in Ostrava, in Moravia, Czechoslovakia, he and his wife requested and received asylum in the United States in 1939 when Germany invaded Czechoslovakia. Over his career he was a prolific writer who wrote over two dozen works of nonfiction, including books on music and musicians, and was a contributing writer at *The New Yorker*.

CREDITS